Preference Data for Environmental Valuation

The monetary valuation of environmental goods and services has evolved from a fringe field of study in the late 1970s and early 1980s to a primary focus of environmental economists over the past decade. Despite its rapid growth, practitioners of valuation techniques often find themselves defending their practices to both users of the results of applied studies and, perhaps more troublingly, to other practitioners.

One of the more heated threads of this internal debate over valuation techniques revolves around the types of data to use in performing a valuation study. In the infant years of the development of valuation techniques, two schools of thought emerged: the revealed preference school and the stated preference school, the latter of which is perhaps most associated with the contingent valuation method. In the midst of this debate an exciting new approach to nonmarket valuation was developed in the 1990s: a combination and joint estimation of revealed preference and stated preference data.

There are two primary objectives for this book. One objective is to fill a gap in the nonmarket valuation "primer" literature. A number of books have appeared over the past decade that develop the theory and methods of nonmarket valuation but each takes an individual nonmarket valuation method approach. This book considers each of these valuation methods in combination with another method. These relationships can be exploited econometrically to obtain more valid and reliable estimates of willingness-to-pay relative to the individual methods. The second objective is to showcase recent and novel applications of data combination and joint estimation via a set of original, state-of-the-art studies that are contributed by leading researchers in the field. This book will be accessible to economists and consultants working in business or government, as well as an invaluable resource for researchers and students alike.

John Whitehead is a Professor in the Department of Economics at Appalachian State University, USA.

Tim Haab is a Professor of Environmental Economics at the Ohio State University, USA.

Ju-Chin Huang is Associate Professor in the Department of Economics at the University of New Hampshire, USA.

Routledge explorations in environmental economics

Edited by Nick Hanley

University of Stirling, UK

Preference Data for Environmental Valuation

Combining revealed and stated approaches

**Edited by John Whitehead, Tim Haab
and Ju-Chin Huang**

Routledge
Taylor & Francis Group

LONDON AND NEW YORK

First published 2011
by Routledge
2 Park Square, Milton Park, Abingdon, Oxon OX14 4RN

Simultaneously published in the USA and Canada
by Routledge
711 Third Avenue, New York, NY 10017

Routledge is an imprint of the Taylor & Francis Group, an informa business

© 2011 selection and editorial matter; John Whitehead, Tim Haab and
Ju-Chin Huang, individual chapters; the contributors

The right of John Whitehead, Tim Haab and Ju-Chin Huang to be
identified as authors of the editorial matter and the authors for their
individual chapters has been asserted by them in accordance with sections
77 and 78 of the Copyright, Designs and Patents Act 1988.

British Library Cataloguing in Publication Data
A catalogue record for this book is available from the British Library

Library of Congress Cataloging in Publication Data
Preference data for environmental valuation : combining revealed and
stated approaches / edited by John Whitehead, Tim Haab and Ju-Chin
Huang.
    p. cm.
    Includes bibliographical references and index.
    1. Environmental economics. 2. Natural resources–Valuation.
    I. Whitehead, John Claiborne, 1963– II. Haab, Timothy C., 1969–
    III. Huang, Ju-chin.
    HC79.E5P6776 2010
    333–dc22
    2010038419

ISBN: 978-0-415-77464-2 (hbk)
ISBN: 978-0-203-82899-1 (ebk)

Typeset in Times
by Wearset Ltd, Boldon, Tyne and Wear

Contents

Figures and tables

Figures

Tables

Contributors

John C. Bergstrom, University of Georgia, Georgia, USA

David T. Butry, Duke University, North Carolina, USA

Brooks Depro, RTI International, North Carolina, USA

Christopher F. Dumas, University of North Carolina at Wilmington, North Carolina, USA

Dietrich Earnhart, Kansas University, Kansas, USA

Kevin J. Egan, University of Toledo, Ohio, USA

Young Sook Eom, Chonbuk National University, Jeonbuk, South Korea

Brett R. Gelso, Johns Hopkins University, Maryland, USA

Juan Marcos Gonzalez-Sepulveda, RTI International, North Carolina, USA

Timothy C. Haab, The Ohio State University, Ohio, USA

Jim Herstine, University of North Carolina at Wilmington, North Carolina, USA

Ju-Chin Huang, University of New Hampshire, New Hampshire, USA

William L. Huth, University of West Florida, Florida, USA

Paul M. Jakus, Utah State University, Utah, USA

Craig E. Landry, East Carolina University, North Carolina, USA

Haiyong Liu, East Carolina University, North Carolina, USA

John B. Loomis, Colorado State University, Colorado, USA

Kenneth E. McConnell, University of Maryland, Maryland, USA

O. Ashton Morgan, Appalachian State University, North Carolina, USA

Kelly Maloney, Kleinschmidt Associates, Maine, USA

George R. Parsons, University of Delaware, Delaware, USA

Sumeet Patil, NEERMAN, Mumbai, India

Subhrendu K. Pattanayak, Duke University, North Carolina, USA

Daniel J. Phaneuf, North Carolina State University, North Carolina, USA

Marty Phillips, Kleinschmidt Associates, Maine, USA

P. Joan Poor, Bemidji State University, Minnesota, USA

Stela Stefanova, University of Delaware, Delaware, USA

V. Kerry Smith, Arizona State University, Arizona, USA

Bin Sun, Fannie Mae, Washington, DC, USA

George Van Houtven, RTI International, North Carolina, USA

John C. Whitehead, Appalachian State University, North Carolina, USA

Min Qiang Zhao, Arizona State University, Arizona, USA and Xiamen University, Fujian, China

Foreword

For those who are relatively new to the field of Environmental and Natural Resources Economics, it is worth reviewing a little history. This two-faceted sub-discipline occupies the territory between mainstream economics and agricultural economics. The combined field has been growing steadily since the 1970s, but the economics departments of a number of leading universities were slow to offer permanent courses in these fields. When I first became interested in the field in the mid 1970s, I was an undergraduate at the University of British Columbia. When I moved east to Princeton University for graduate school, I was somewhat taken aback that natural resource and environmental scholars were not in the thick of things in every economics department among the prestigious universities on the east coast. In fact, I got the distinct impression that this wasn't something that serious economists were supposed to spend their time thinking about. Environmental economics was even viewed as somewhat of a "fringe" field, mostly for liberals.

To embrace environmental economics means to shine a light on the fact that production activities can have side effects that are bad for us. Perhaps environmental economics took a while to gain a foothold in many departments because it nagged at the conscience of mainstream economics. Problems of externalities and public goods pervade the economics of environment and natural resources. Many of the specific topics in Natural Resources Economics are also related to the primary industries populated by farmers, loggers, fishermen and miners, rather than the secondary or services industries populated by indoor factory labor, white-collar office workers, the captains of industry, bankers and stockbrokers. The microeconomic theory of the firm was originally developed in the context of manufacturing as the main stylized example. The "messiness" of negative externalities (pollution), or the inconvenience of bioeconomic constraints or exhaustible resources, could be largely avoided in the traditional fields of mainstream economics.

The first academic generation of environmental economists encountered one excellent reason why the field was not a mainstay of the curriculum in every economics department. There was darned little data. Most of the interesting phenomena are "extra-market" phenomena. The invisible hand of economics could not be relied upon to engineer observable market-clearing prices and quantities. Researchers in many other subfields of economics could simply observe and model the phenomena they were interested in, but environmental and natural resource economists often need to exercise their greatest creativity just to find a way to measure what no markets exist to reveal. Indirect markets (hedonic property values or travel costs) could sometimes be used for partial glimpses of the variables of interest. However, it was recognized early on that sometimes there just isn't—and never will be—any kind of conventional market related to the environmental good or natural resource in question. Hypothetical markets based on survey methods evolved as the only way to learn anything at all about so-called passive use (or non-use) demands for environmental goods.

The trouble with hypothetical markets, however, is that data based on what people merely *say* they would do if they were faced with a particular choice is not "real" data. Economists are still trained, from their academic infancy, to mistrust what people say they will do and to pay attention only to revealed preferences—what people *actually* do when they must put "cash on the barrelhead" (or give up something else) to acquire the good in question. Surveys are associated by economists with the "softer" social sciences, like sociology, rather than the more rigorous "real" sciences like physics (unless, of course, the survey is conducted by a government agency). Economists have for decades sought to pursue their questions more like physicists than sociologists, despite the fact that human behavior is ultimately most of what we study. This long-standing allergy of economists to stated preference survey data was one thing that stunted the growth of environmental and natural resources economics for a long time.

By combining revealed and stated preferences, however, economists gain opportunities to supplement with stated preference data whatever market-related glimpses of revealed preferences for environmental goods might be available. We will always be more skeptical of stated preference data than of revealed preference data, and we will certainly continue to prefer the latter whenever enough of it is available. However, much has been learned over the last few decades about the conditions under which stated preference data can be more (and less) reliable. It seems foolish to foreswear the use of this potentially valuable source of nonmarket information. Stated preference methods can certainly help us learn more about key demands that must be understood better if we are to inform sensible environmental policy choices. This book pulls together, in one place and in common notation, some very valuable guidance on how to lay claim to the "best of both worlds" in exploiting combinations of revealed and stated preference data.

The editors have been kind enough to cite my 1992 paper as one of the first of this genre, although I am not sure whether this makes me feel a little smug or just older than I had realized. That paper was work in progress in 1989, which was the year when I was putting together my tenure file at UCLA. And like the editors, I did not have a paper on the program at the 1996 AERE Workshop that inspired this volume. (When I first read their introduction, I spent much too long wondering whether I should feel slighted. Then I remembered that my second child was born on June 24 of that year.)[1]

The model in my 1992 paper had only a few parameters, but it had to be estimated by maximum likelihood, and I used an old version of GQOPT based on Fortran77 on the UCLA campus mainframe computer. I could set the thing to run and leave the building to get a cup of coffee and it would still be running when I got back. Years later, I had occasion to resurrect the program and run it on a desktop version of GQOPT. It ran in the blink of an eye.... Young folks these days just don't know how easy they have it? We have been saved from plodding maximum likelihood algorithms by spectacular advances in computing. This has allowed us to substitute away from long spells of thumb-twiddling as an input to research.

Computing advances have been important to this literature because researchers who combine revealed and stated preference data must often base their joint models on more than one type of choice. They frequently rely on microeconomic theory as a basis for their confidence that the same "deep" utility parameters underlie these different manifestations of the interaction of preferences with constraints. Each submodel, by itself, might be amenable to estimation using some standard algorithm that is conveniently provided in widely available econometric software packages. However, it is desirable to be able to pool the information.

When combined *without* parameter restrictions, however, the two submodels would tend to produce at least slightly different estimates of what ought to be the same underlying preference parameters. If we have sufficient faith in our theoretical framework, parameters which appear in both submodels should be constrained to be identical. Error variances can also differ, and there may be error covariances across the two submodels, which ought to be accommodated if the revealed- and stated-preference choices are made by the same individuals (where we therefore expect the unobserved determinants to be correlated). The complexity of these pooled models means that researchers who wish to combine stated and revealed preference data often need to develop new estimators.

Modeling and estimation challenges are certainly presented by the task of combining revealed- and stated-preference data. But these types of tasks also offer new research opportunities. This volume will be an excellent addition to the toolkit of both new and experienced researchers. It will allow anyone who is intellectually curious to get up to speed, as efficiently as possible, concerning the strategies that can be employed when using stated preference data to broaden the domain of what we can know, from revealed preferences alone, about demands for environmental goods and natural resources. The editors and authors are to be highly commended for contributing such a valuable new asset for our field.

Trudy Ann Cameron
University of Oregon

Note

1 It should be noted that the lead editor of this book is well-known for his folksy and self-deprecating style. Environmental economists have spent so long being apologetic about the quality of their available data that perhaps the best defense is humor at one's own expense. Many readers will be familiar with the Environmental Economics blog (www.env-econ.net) maintained by Tim Haab and John Whitehead. In fact, while attempting to cut-and-paste the URL, I was again distracted (and entertained) for over an hour by the latest material.

Preface

The monetary valuation of environmental goods and services has evolved from a fringe field of study in the 1970s to a primary focus of environmental economists. Despite its rapid growth, practitioners of valuation techniques often find themselves defending their practices to both users of the results of applied studies and, more troublingly, to other practitioners. One of the more heated threads of this internal debate over valuation techniques revolves around the types of data to use in performing a valuation study.

In the developmental years of valuation techniques, two schools of thought emerged. The first, the revealed preference school, relied on observed behaviors and the relationship between observed behavior and environmental quality to derive values for changes in environmental quality. Techniques such as the travel cost method, averting behaviour, and hedonic pricing methods rely on revealed preference data. The second, the stated preference school, argued that observed behavior is limited to the realm of observable environmental changes (as such is limited in the scope of policy change that can be analyzed) and instead relies on stated responses to hypothetical or constructed environmental scenarios to directly elicit values for such changes. The contingent valuation method is the poster-child for stated preference techniques. Advocates of revealed preference techniques argued that stated preference techniques, and the contingent valuation method particularly, cannot produce accurate estimates of value since they rely exclusively on hypothetical responses to hypothetical scenarios. Stated preference advocates responded that revealed preference techniques are limited in the scope of environmental goods and service that can be valued, ignore passive use values and may result in unreliable estimates due to uncertain recall abilities and measurement error in revealed preference surveys.

In the midst of this debate, Cameron (1992) and Adamowicz *et al.* (1994) introduced an exciting new approach to nonmarket valuation – the combination and joint estimation of revealed preference and stated preference data. The significant contribution was the notion that the advantages of revealed and stated preference data can be exploited while mitigating their disadvantages. In part, these seminal papers led to organization of the 1996 Association of Environmental and Resource Economists (AERE) Workshop held in Lake Tahoe,

California: "Combining Stated Preference Data and Revealed Preference Data to Estimate the Demand for and/or Benefits from Environmental Amenities."

Within this context, all three editors of this book were working in the Department of Economics at East Carolina University when a set of data containing contingent valuation and travel cost variables arrived from the field and our long and rewarding collaboration began. To begin, we wrote an abstract and submitted it for consideration to the organizers of the 1996 AERE Workshop. Not surprisingly, the paper was rejected for the program but, surprisingly, we received a sufficient amount of state travel funds that allowed us to attend. We traveled to the workshop without a paper on the program but sat and listened politely. What we learned at the workshop, combined with the fear of being fired for lack of productivity, led us to revise the paper we proposed and ultimately publish it in a 1997 issue of the *Journal of Environmental Economics and Management*. The point of this boring story is not to convince you that our article was more important than thought by the organizers of the 1996 workshop (ha!), or to get you to cite the article more often (but just in case, see Huang *et al.* 1997), but rather to point out the impact of the 1996 AERE workshop in inspiring this book almost 15 years later.

Data combination and joint estimation has evolved to such a point of maturity in the field of environmental economics that the tenth anniversary of the 1996 AERE Workshop was commemorated by an AERE sponsored session at the 2007 Allied Social Science Association meetings: "Joint Estimation and Environmental Valuation Ten Years Later." The AERE session featured four new papers that covered a broad range of applications that could only have been dreamed about in 1996. Presentation of these papers and the subsequent discussant comments by Trudy Cameron, Vic Adamowicz and Jordan Louviere inspired at least one participant to conclude that data combination and joint estimation will remain an active research area in environmental valuation.

The excitement over the promise of joint estimation methods to "solve" the problems of the contingent valuation method has dimmed. Revealed behavior is required for joint estimation and the current methods for "calibration" of passive use values were largely developed in the experimental economics literature. But a new literature was launched by the AERE workshop that addresses topics such as hypothetical bias of stated preference data, valuation of environmental change beyond the range of historical experience, and development of new econometric and survey methods, among other advances. Joint estimation of revealed and stated preference data has evolved to the point of formal review article maturity (Whitehead *et al.* 2008).

There are two primary objectives for this book. One objective is to fill a gap in the nonmarket valuation "primer" literature. A number of books have appeared over the past decade that develop the theory and methods of nonmarket valuation but each takes an individual nonmarket valuation method approach. In other words, these books consider contingent valuation, hedonic pricing, averting behavior and the travel cost method in isolation and often each topic is treated by a different author (contributed chapter) leading to difficulty with the reader following from one chapter to the next. This book considers each of these valuation methods in combination with another method. For example, contingent valuation method and travel cost method estimates of willingness-to-pay are theoretically related. These relationships can be exploited econometrically to obtain more valid and reliable estimates of willingness-to-pay relative to the individual methods. The second purpose is to showcase recent and novel applications of data combination and joint estimation via a set of original, state-of-the-art studies that are contributed by leading researchers in the field.

The theory and methods chapters of this book are written primarily by the editors of the book allowing the reader to follow chapter to chapter without having to learn new notation and jargon. The frontier studies were solicited from other practitioners and have been edited to remain fairly consistent with the theory and methods section. As such, we hope that the book provides a cohesive treatment from start to finish.

Timothy C. Haab, Ju-Chin Huang and John C. Whitehead

References

Adamowicz, W., J. Louviere and M. Williams (1994) "Combining revealed and stated preference methods for valuing environmental amenities," *Journal of Environmental Economics and Management*, 26: 271–292.

Cameron, T.A. (1992) "Combining contingent valuation and travel cost data for the valuation of nonmarket goods," *Land Economics*, 68: 302–317.

Huang, J.-C., T. Haab and J.C. Whitehead (1997) "Willingness to pay for quality improvements: Should revealed and stated preference data be combined?" *Journal of Environmental Economics and Management*, 34: 240–255.

Whitehead, J.C., S. Pattanayak, G. Van Houtven and B. Gelso (2008) "Combining revealed and stated preference data to estimate the nonmarket value of ecological services: An assessment of the state of the science," *Journal of Economic Surveys*, 22: 872–908.

Acknowledgments

The authors thank Nick Hanley for accepting our proposal for the Routledge Explorations in Environmental Economics series; Rob Langham and Louisa Earls of Routledge for guidance and patience; George Van Houtven, Subhrendu Pattanayak and Brett Gelso for their contributions to an earlier literature review; Kerry Smith for inspiration when presenting an early version of Chapter 12 at ECU in the mid-1990s and while giving us a ride to the airport after the AERE Workshop; and, finally and most importantly, all of the authors for their contributions to this book.

1 Introduction

*John C. Whitehead, Timothy C. Haab and
Ju-Chin Huang*

Stated preference approaches use hypothetical data to estimate the *ex ante*
willingness to pay for various commodities. For example, the contingent valuation method can be used to estimate economic values of environmental
resources, including nonuse values – those environmental values that are enjoyed
by consumers who do not use the environmental resource on-site. Most economists, however, are firmly rooted in the revealed preference paradigm to estimate the use values of environmental resources. Revealed preference approaches
are based on actual choices and actual choices based on real costs and benefits
better reflect environmental values.

During the decade of the 1990s the "contingent valuation debate" dominated
the environmental valuation literature. Economists developed competing damage
estimates associated with the Exxon Valdez oil spill, argued about whether
nonuse values exist and whether the contingent valuation method is able to
accurately measure them. Critics of the contingent valuation method argued that
hypothetical behavior is too inaccurate to use for policy analysis. Proponents
argued that contingent valuation generated value estimates that are no less
accurate than those developed with revealed preference nonmarket valuation
approaches.

Economists tend to consider revealed and stated preference approaches as
substitutes when choosing valuation methods. There are problems with this
attitude. Since the revealed preference approaches rely on historical data,
evaluation of new policies is often limited. Oftentimes, stated preference
methods are the only way to gain policy relevant information. But, stated preference approaches are based on hypothetical survey data and respondents can
be placed in unfamiliar situations. Revealed preference data is firmly planted
in reality.

Since the strengths of the revealed preference approaches are also the weaknesses of the stated preference approaches and vice versa, revealed and stated
preference methods should be considered complements. The combination and
joint estimation of revealed and stated preference data seeks to exploit the contrasting strengths of the revealed and stated approaches while minimizing their
weaknesses (Cameron 1992; Adamowicz *et al.* 1994). Joint estimation has
addressed a wide range of important issues in nonmarket environmental

valuation, including the hypothetical bias of contingent valuation and behavior data, the valuation of quality change that extends beyond the range of historical experience, and the development of new econometric and survey methods that specifically address data combination (Whitehead *et al.* 2008).

Data combination can be used to mitigate a large number of problems. First, some revealed preference data are limited to analyzing a range of behavior in response to a limited range of market or environmental change. Stated preference surveys can be designed to collect data on hypothetical behavior, which allows estimation of behavior beyond the range of historical experience.

Second, general population surveys can be used to survey users and nonusers of an environmental resource and analyze the decision to participate in the market. But these data are limited when trying to understand changes in participation. Combining revealed preference data with stated preference data from surveys of the general population can be used to understand changes in participation and the market size with new products or environmental changes.

Third, there is often high correlation between independent variables in revealed preference data. Multicollinearity among characteristics leads to statistically insignificant coefficient estimates which make it impossible to estimate the value of changes in the variables of interest. A related problem is endogeneity. For example, recreational fishing catch rates are correlated with fishing experience and both variables are related to fishing trip frequency. Analysis of a policy to value an increase in catch rates with revealed preference data can be confounded by fishing experience. An alternative strategy is to combine revealed preference data with stated preference data. Stated preference surveys can be designed to mitigate multicollinearity and endogeneity.

Fourth, revealed preference data collection is relative inefficient. Oftentimes, a revealed preference cross-section survey will collect only one data point. Stated preference surveys can be designed to gather pseudo-panel data, supplementing the single revealed preference data point from a cross-section survey with one, or several, stated preference data points. More information from each respondent can lead to increased econometric efficiency.

Fifth, stated preference data has limitations which can be addressed by combination with revealed preference data. Hypothetical bias results when hypothetical choices do not fully reflect budget and time constraints. Combining stated preference data with revealed preference data grounds hypothetical choices with real choice behavior.

Sixth, combining revealed preference and stated preference data can be used to test the validity of both the revealed and stated preference methods. Convergent validity exists if two methods for measuring an unknown construct (i.e. willingness to pay) yields measures that are not statistically different. Predictive validity of jointly estimated revealed and stated preference data is the ability of the joint models to outperform independently estimated revealed and stated preference data models in predicting actual behavior.

There are a number of types of revealed preference (RP) and stated preference (SP) data combination and joint estimation studies in the literature (see

Whitehead *et al.* 2008 for an extensive review). We consider a data combination study as any research effort that employs both RP and SP data in some way (see Carson *et al.* 1996 for a review of the early data comparison studies). In contrast, a joint estimation study occurs when the relationships between the independent variables and the dependent variables are estimated in a single model. Joint estimation studies are a subset of data combination studies. RP and SP data are combined and analyzed with three major classes of econometric models: frequency data, mixed data, and discrete data models.

Frequency data models

Frequency data econometric models typically involve revealed preference data on recreation trips or some other behavior. These data are combined with stated preference data in which respondents make similar choices under hypothetical conditions. The data from the two sources have the same structure in terms of the continuous form of the dependent variable and similar independent variables, and they can be stacked and jointly estimated. Frequency data models are typically used to combine the travel cost method and the contingent behavior method. The revealed preference component of the survey might ask for the number of recreation trips taken during the past month, season, or year. The stated preference component of these surveys would then ask for the hypothetical number of trips that would be taken (or would have been taken) in the next month, season, or year in an alternative hypothetical situation. Hypothetical scenarios can be constructed for changes in costs and/or benefits of the activity. Frequency data RP-SP studies tend to focus on recreation (e.g. Whitehead *et al.* 2000) but other applications appear in the literature, such as household disposal of solid waste (Nestor 1998), seafood consumption (Huang *et al.* 2004) and agricultural technology (Hubbell *et al.* 2000).

Several RP-SP studies have used pooled data with constrained coefficients to jointly estimate the model (e.g. Layman *et al.* 1996). The problem with this approach is that the correlation in error terms across respondents is ignored. Each observation in the data is assumed to be a separate individual with their own error term instead of each individual having a common error term across observations. Pooling data without taking into account the panel nature of the data can lead to inefficient and inconsistent coefficient estimates. The fixed effects and random effects panel data models have been used to deal with pooling data in the frequency data RP-SP studies (e.g. Englin and Cameron 1996; Whitehead *et al.* 2000).

A major question in all RP-SP models is the consistency of preferences across RP and SP data. Consistency is typically tested with SP demand and slope shifters. Typical results are that the SP quantity intercept is greater than the RP quantity intercept and the SP demand is more elastic than the RP demand (e.g. Azevedo *et al.* 2003). One interpretation of the lack of consistency across RP and SP data is hypothetical bias. Respondents are allowed to report trips that do not fully reflect their actual behavior because they are not faced with the discipline of budget and time constraints. Under this interpretation, a useful result from combining RP and SP data is the "calibration" of SP data by counter-factually eliminating the hypothetical bias.

Another interpretation of the lack of consistency between the RP and SP data is due to differences in errors between RP and SP data (Azevedo *et al.* 2003). Errors in RP data may be due to recall errors, digit bias, and measurement error. Errors in SP data may be due to lack of familiarity with the hypothetical change or uncertainty about future behavior. Because the RP and SP contexts are inherently different, the differences in the data may be expected. The different sources of error can lead to heteroskedasticity between the RP and SP data which can be corrected in standard ways (Azevedo *et al.* 2003).

A lack of consistency between RP and SP data will affect the welfare estimates. Since many studies find that SP demands are more elastic, a common result is that the SP consumer surplus estimates will exceed the RP consumer surplus estimates (Englin and Cameron 1996; Whitehead *et al.* 2000). If the lack of consistency in RP and SP data is due to hypothetical bias, the consumer surplus estimates will converge when the RP model is counterfactually simulated with the SP scenarios.

Mixed data models

Mixed data models involve the combination of two dependent variables that take a different form and resist stacking. These data can be jointly estimated by allowing for error correlation and constraints on model coefficients. Mixed data models have typically been used to combine the contingent valuation method and the travel cost method. These models employ utility-theoretic specifications of the willingness to pay function and specify constraints to be placed on parameters in the jointly estimated model.

In the first empirical application, Cameron (1992) combines the contingent valuation method and the travel cost method in a recreational fishing application. The recreation demand model is based on RP data. The contingent valuation model is a discrete choice of the willingness to continue taking trips when faced with a randomly assigned increased total cost of trips. The combined data allows the demand function to be more fully understood. The RP data allows estimation of only the observable portion of demand. The portion of the demand function at prices between the current price and the choke price is measured with the SP data. Statistical tests for the consistency of the RP and SP data reject consistency. Kling (1997) presents a simulation exercise illustrating the efficiency gains from a version of the Cameron model. Gillig *et al.* (2003) extend Kling's model to allow for truncation of the recreation demand and apply the model with survey data. They find that the precision of willingness-to-pay is improved and that the magnitude of willingness-to-pay is bound from above by the contingent valuation method estimate and from below by the travel cost method estimate.

A number of other studies have estimated mixed models in a variety of ways. Niklitschek and León (1996) develop a model that links SP recreation trips with the willingness to pay for quality improvement. The constrained model is superior to the unconstrained model indicating that preferences are consistent between the RP and SP data. The welfare estimates from the jointly estimated model are between the welfare estimates from the independently estimated willingness to pay and recreation demand models. Huang *et al.* (1997) diverges from the other jointly estimated mixed models by combining discrete choice willingness to pay data and the change in trips that result from a quality improvement. Two models are jointly estimated with and without constraints on parameters that theory suggests should be equal. The first model considers the consistency of RP and SP behavior and the second considers the consistency of SP and SP behavior. The results indicate that the RP and SP behavior is not consistent but the SP and SP behavior is consistent. Cunha-e-Sá *et al.* (2004) re-analyze these data within the Cunha-e-Sá and Ducla-Soares (1999) mixed demand framework and come to similar conclusions. Eom and Larson (2006) improve upon the previous mixed models by estimating nonuse values in a theoretically consistent model.

Discrete data models

Discrete data models are based on random utility theory. With a RP choice, respondents face numerous alternatives with different characteristics. Many of these characteristics are often correlated across alternatives. With a SP choice experiment, respondents are presented with a similar choice among two or more alternatives. Each option has a set of two or more characteristics in an experimental design that breaks the multicollinearity in the revealed preference data. Since both RP and SP data follows from the random utility model, the data can be stacked and jointly estimated. When RP and SP data are stacked and estimated jointly, it is common for the error terms that result from the different data to have unequal variance due to the unfamiliarity of the choice task, a form of hypothetical bias. The difference in the scale parameter will cause the regression coefficients to differ across RP and SP data sets.

It is typical for RP data sets to have some variables that do not change across individuals. In this case, the SP data can be used to identify the effect of the variable on the choices. Also, researchers often encounter RP and SP data sets that exhibit different signs on coefficients for the same variables. In these cases it is possible to jointly estimate the coefficients that have the same signs, estimate the opposite signed coefficients separately, and test the restrictions.

Adamowicz *et al.* (1994) present the first application of RP-SP joint estimation using choice experiments. Their results are typical of the literature. The RP data are limited due to collinearity and the SP data are prone to hypothetical bias. The RP and SP data can be combined once the scale factor is used to adjust the SP coefficients. Adamowicz *et al.* (1997) present an application to moose hunting with a focus on a comparison of RP-SP models with objective or subjective characteristics of the choices. They conclude that the RP-SP model with subjective characteristics outperforms the other models.

Earnhart (2001, 2002) presents an application of the discrete choice RP-SP model to housing choice. The RP component is a discrete choice hedonic model of recent home sales for a sample of recent home buyers. The SP choice set includes randomly drawn houses that were available at the same time as the purchase. The SP choice experiment attempts to simulate the same decision for the households in the recent home sales sample. The focus in Earnhart (2001) is the valuation of water-based (e.g. wetlands) and land-based amenities (e.g. forests). Amenity values are widely divergent for RP and SP models but the joint RP-SP model improves estimation of the amenity values.

More recently, von Haefen and Phaneuf (2008) exploit choice experiment data to deal with unobserved heterogeneity in recreation site choice data. In doing so, they reject the hypothesis of data consistency and illustrate how sensitivity analysis can be used to account for the inconsistency. Axsen *et al.* (2009) jointly estimate discrete data for automobile purchase. Since multiple SP observations are combined with a single RP observation they investigate the effects of alternative weights. They find that joint RP-SP models with more weight on the RP data performs best statistically but, due to multicollinearity, models with more weight on the SP data produce more realistic willingness-to-pay values.

Rest of the book

There are two primary objectives for this book. The first is to provide a systematic, cohesive, and in-depth discussion of the theory and methods of joint estimation. The second purpose of the book is to illustrate the range of joint estimation applications with a number of original studies that are contributed by leading researchers in environmental economics.

In Part I we present chapters covering theory, methods, and applications. In Chapter 2 Ted McConnell provides the theoretical rationale for data combination. The utility-theoretic framework for the combination and joint estimation of revealed and stated preference data is presented. In Chapter 3 Tim Haab presents some of the appropriate statistical techniques and general econometric issues for joint estimation of data. The theoretical examination of data combination will reveal theoretical constraints imposed on estimation and presents econometric hurdles that are difficult to overcome. Many opportunities for joint estimation arise that are not supported by standard statistical packages and the applied researcher is faced with a choice of staying true to theoretical underpinnings or sacrificing theoretical consistency for econometric tractability.

The next three chapters provide technical and practical illustrations for combining different formats of RP and SP data. The type of joint estimation depends on the format of the data: frequency, mixed or discrete choice. The empirical analyses in these chapters are illustrative attempts to estimate a suite of models: RP, SP, and RP-SP models. In Chapter 4 John Whitehead presents some stylized results from frequency data models (and binary discrete data models). In Chapter 5, Ju-Chin Huang illustrates how contingent valuation method data can be combined with recreation trip data in a mixed data framework. In Chapter 6

Whitehead illustrates the joint estimation framework most often employed with choice experiment data but applied here with recreation demand data.

In Part II we present five chapters (Chapters 7–11) that use frequency data. The first four of these are recreation demand applications. Craig Landry and Haiyong Liu compare several econometric models when estimating recreation demand data. Dan Phaneuf and Dietrich Earnhart structurally combine RP recreation trip demand and SP contingent pricing data for parameter estimation and valuation of time. Huang, George Parsons, Joan Poor, and Min Qiang Zhao examine the impact of erosion on beach recreation by estimating recreation demand change models where the demand changes are generated by a conjoint experimental design. Ash Morgan and Bill Huth combine RP diving trips and contingent behavior data to value an artificial reef for recreation diving that is created by sinking a decommissioned missile tracking vessel. Haab, Bin Sun, and Whitehead use variations on applied time series techniques to identify hypothetical bias in repeated question surveys with a seafood consumption application.

In Part III we present four chapters (Chapters 12–15) that use mixed data. Young Sook Eom and Kerry Smith estimate a binary SP demand for organic produce with a continuous RP demand for regular produce in an expected utility framework. David Butry and Subhrendu Pattanayak present a unique study of producer welfare analysis by jointly estimating the profit function of logging and the stated willingness to pay for forest access for the loggers in the Manggarai region of Indonesia. Kevin Egan jointly estimates dichotomous choice contingent valuation and continuous recreation demand data to test weak complementarity. Chris Dumas, Jim Herstine and Whitehead integrate the change in demand from a stated preference model into a willingness-to-pay model to assess the benefits and impacts of dredging in the Atlantic Intracoastal Waterway.

In Part IV we present three chapters (Chapters 16–18) that use multiple choice data. George Parsons and Stela Stefanova present a two-stage linked RP-SP site choice model with an RP trip frequency model to account for substitution over time (delayed consumption) due to short-term closures of recreation sites. Paul Jakus, John Bergstrom, Marty Phillips, and Kelly Maloney estimate a RP repeated nested logit site choice model linked with a SP trip frequency model to evaluate recreation behavioral changes in response to alternative water management scenarios. Finally Brett Gelso estimates RP and SP recreation site choice model with stacked choice experiment data to value green technologies.

In Part V we present two chapters (Chapters 19 and 20) that have implications for benefits transfer. Benefits transfer is used to estimate benefits when time or research budgets are constrained and a primary data study cannot be conducted. Benefit estimates are developed from existing studies for policy analysis. Juan Marcos Gonzalez-Sepulveda and John Loomis jointly estimate binary contingent valuation and continuous recreation demand data and compare benefit transfers to independently estimated models. George Van Houtven, Pattanayak, Sumeet Patil, and Brooks Depro combine RP and SP studies for structural benefit transfer.

In the concluding chapter we discuss gaps in the current literature and new methods and uses of data combination and joint estimation.

References

Adamowicz, W., J. Louviere, and M. Williams (1994) "Combining revealed and stated preference methods for valuing environmental amenities," *Journal of Environmental Economics and Management*, 26: 271–292.

Adamowicz, W., J. Swait, P. Boxall, J. Louviere, and M. Williams (1997) "Perceptions versus objective measures of environmental quality in combined revealed and stated preference models of environmental valuation," *Journal of Environmental Economics and Management*, 32: 65–84.

Axsen, J., D. Mountain, and M. Jaccard (2009) "Combining stated and revealed choice research to simulate preference dynamics: The case of hybrid-electric vehicles," *Resource and Energy Economics*, 31: 221–238.

Azevedo, C.D., J.A. Herriges, and C.L. Kling (2003) "Combining revealed and stated preferences: Consistency tests and their interpretations," *American Journal of Agricultural Economics*, 85: 525–537.

Cameron, T.A. (1992) "Combining contingent valuation and travel cost data for the valuation of nonmarket goods," *Land Economics*, 68: 302–317.

Carson, R.T., N.E. Flores, K.M. Martin, and J.L. Wright (1996) "Contingent valuation and revealed preference methodologies: Comparing the estimates for quasi-public foods," *Land Economics*, 72: 80–99.

Cunha-e-Sá, M.A. and M.M. Ducla-Soares (1999) "Specification tests for mixed demand systems with an emphasis on combining contingent valuation and revealed data," *Journal of Environmental Economics and Management*, 38: 215–233.

Cunha-e-Sá, M., M.M. Ducla-Soares, L.C. Nunes, and P. Polomé (2004) "Consistency in mixed demand systems: Contingent valuation and travel cost data," *American Journal of Agricultural Economics*, 86: 444–454.

Earnhart, D. (2001) "Combining revealed and stated preference methods to value environmental amenities at residential locations," *Land Economics*, 77: 12–29.

Earnhart, D. (2002) "Combining revealed and stated data to examine housing decisions using discrete choice analysis," *Journal of Urban Economics*, 51: 143–169.

Englin, J. and T.A. Cameron (1996) "Augmenting travel cost models with contingent behavior data," *Environmental and Resource Economics*, 7: 133–147.

Eom, Y.-S. and D.M. Larson (2006) "Improving environmental valuation estimates through consistent use of revealed and stated preference information," *Journal of Environmental Economics and Management*, 52: 501–516.

Gillig, D., R.T. Woodward, T. Ozuna Jr., and W.L. Griffin (2003) "Joint estimation of revealed and stated preference data: An application to recreational red snapper valuation," *Agricultural and Resource Economics Review*, 32: 209–221.

Huang, J.-C., T.C. Haab, and J.C. Whitehead (1997) "Willingness to pay for quality Improvements: Should revealed and stated preference data be combined?" *Journal of Environmental Economics and Management*, 34: 240–255.

Huang, J.-C., T.C. Haab, and J.C. Whitehead (2004) "Risk valuation in the presence of risky substitutes: An application to demand for seafood," *Journal of Agricultural and Applied Economics*, 36: 213–228.

Hubbell, B.J., M.C. Marra, and G.A. Carlson (2000) "Estimating the demand for a new technology: Bt cotton and insecticide policies," *American Journal of Agricultural Economics*, 82: 118–132.

Kling, C.L. (1997) "The gains from combining travel cost and contingent valuation data to value nonmarket goods," *Land Economics*, 73: 428–439.

Layman, R.C., J.R. Boyce, and K.R. Criddle (1996) "Economic valuation of chinook salmon sport fishery of the Gulkana River, Alaska, under current and alternate management plans," *Land Economics*, 72: 113–128.

Nestor, D.V. (1998) "Policy evaluation with combined actual and contingent response data," *American Journal of Agricultural Economics*, 80: 264–276.

Niklitschek, M. and J. León (1996) "Combining intended demand and yes/no responses in the estimation of contingent valuation models," *Journal of Environmental Economics and Management*, 31: 387–402.

von Haefen, R.F. and D.J. Phaneuf (2008) "Identifying demand parameters in the presence of unobservables: A combined revealed and stated preference approach," *Journal of Environmental Economics and Management*, 56: 19–32.

Whitehead, J.C., T.C. Haab, and J.-C. Huang (2000) "Measuring recreation benefits of quality improvements with revealed and stated behavior data," *Resource and Energy Economics*, 22: 339–354.

Whitehead, J.C., S. Pattanayek, G. Van Houtven, and B. Gelso (2008) "Combining revealed and stated preference data to estimate the nonmarket value of ecological services: An assessment of the state of the science," *Journal of Economic Surveys*, 22: 872–908.

Part I
Theory and methods

2 Joint estimation of stated and revealed welfare measures

The conceptual basis

Kenneth E. McConnell

Why we combine stated and revealed preferences

The purpose of this chapter is to examine the conceptual foundations for combining models of stated and revealed preferences in empirical applications. Since the advent of stated preference approaches in the 1970s, economists have wondered about the relative virtues of each approach. Comparisons emerged quickly. Bishop and Heberlein (1979) compared contingent valuation measures with real willingness to pay for goose hunting. Brookshire *et al.* (1982) compared contingent valuation measures with hedonic measures for air quality in Los Angeles. These early comparisons were principally concerned with assessing the validity of stated preference approaches. Since then economists have worked steadily to compare and jointly estimate models of revealed preferences and stated preferences.

The motives for jointly estimating revealed and stated preference models have evolved over the years. In the beginning, there was strong objection to the direct questioning approach to valuation, as stated preference approaches were known. Economists tended to believe that only revealed preferences could provide the basis for valuation. The idea that economists could learn anything from direct interviews—so-called survey data—has been debated and discarded several times. Friedman (1953) made the case based on the idea that entrepreneurs don't have to know what they are doing for firms to maximize profits. Mere survival of firms would guarantee profit maximization. Samuelson (1954) argued persuasively that the incentive to free ride would lead respondents to hide their true valuations of public goods.[1] This attitude survived into the 1990s and can be seen in the critique of contingent valuation edited by Hausman (1993). Given this opposition to contingent valuation and other stated preference approaches, much of the early work combining stated and revealed data was motivated by the need to justify the use of stated preferences. The revealed preference approaches would serve as external validity for stated preference results, as Cameron (1992) noted. Carson *et al.* (1996) assessed a large number of studies, and demonstrated that the tendency was for revealed preference values to exceed stated preference values. In these cases, the maintained hypothesis was that revealed preference approaches provided valid measures of welfare, against which stated preferences could be tested.

Much has changed since economists began comparing results of the two approaches to valuation. We have a much clearer idea of the strengths and weaknesses of each approach and most researchers view each approach as advantageous in the appropriate setting. For revealed preferences, there is no apparent incentive problem. It is in the agent's best interest to minimize the costs of obtaining a given level of well-being, which is the behavioral assumption of revealed preferences—all commodities and services are chosen optimally. In practice, recovery of values from observations on behavior runs into two kinds of problems: non-optimizing behavior that provides the basis for behavioral economics[2] and econometric problems. For the most part, the assumption of optimizing behavior for revealed preference activities seems relatively innocuous, with the possible exception of housing purchases. Econometric problems are not so easily dismissed. A variety of econometric issues, from measurement errors in data to unobserved individual heterogeneity, plague the estimation of structural models that lead to valuation. Intensive efforts to eliminate unobserved individual heterogeneity have led to models with practically no focus on behavior, such as the housing study of Chay and Greenstone (2005) (which given its use of subjective assessment of housing values, might as easily be described as stated preferences). Some problems, such as the value of travel time in various travel cost models, have a considerable impact on valuation but remain stubbornly resistant to satisfying solutions. Anyone dissatisfied with a welfare measure from a travel cost model can make a new assumption about the value of travel time to obtain another result. Consequently, while new models such as the generalized corner solution model Phaneuf *et al.* (2000), have improved our ability to handle more realistic patterns of behavior, the growing experience of estimated models has imbued researchers with a healthy skepticism about values derived from revealed preference models.

Stated preference approaches eliminate some of the most severe econometric issues by randomizing the price vector and, occasionally, the attribute vector. Further, they can provide estimates of resource values for goods and services that have not been consumed and hence for which there can be no revealed preference data. However, it is clear that the problem of incentives has not been solved and that the hypothetical nature of stated preferences can be paramount in some settings. The evidence that hypothetical values exceed true values appears strong.[3] Increasingly economists are learning to control this bias with cheap talk and follow-up questions about the degree of certainty.[4] There are in addition other anomalies that separate revealed and stated preferences, the gap between willingness to pay and willingness to accept being the greatest.

Consequently when revealed and stated preferences are jointly estimated, it is no longer reasonable to argue that revealed preferences approaches will be used to "shore up" or demonstrate the validity of stated preference approaches. We have little basis for concluding that either method is more accurate. In fact, researchers should take some care in incorporating what is known about tendencies of revealed and stated preference approaches to yield biased results. Simply doing joint estimation in hopes of improving efficiency, without expecting and exploiting systematic differences in preferences or responses, seems unlikely to increase our knowledge of either approach. Azevedo *et al.* (2003) adopt a skeptical attitude towards both stated and revealed preferences in their joint estimation. They formulate a demand model with hypotheses from some prevalent beliefs about revealed and stated preference outcomes.

Although the playing field is leveled for stated and revealed preferences, there are still good reasons for estimating joint revealed and stated preference models. Models that incorporate both use and nonuse values require stated preference methods but can gain by estimating more complex models with stated and revealed preferences. In the case where there is both use and nonuse (or passive use) value, revealed preference welfare measures will not even be sufficient to estimate use values, as is shown below. And for resources and attributes where there is no history of use, stated preference models are essential. As Azevedo *et al.* (2003) comment, however, when we find that stated and revealed preferences give different results, what do we do? Azevedo and coworkers address this puzzle by pushing more deeply into the potential causes of differences in the approaches, such as the putative ignoring of budget constraints by respondents in stated choice experiments.

This chapter brings together the structures that can be used to jointly estimate revealed and stated preferences. Much of the work in stated and revealed preferences is done in the context of random utility models and choice experiments. The conceptual basis of these models is simple because they typically refer to a choice occasion only. There are important and revealing econometric issues associated with the discrete choice approach. However, the full preference function approach is not needed when the implied discrete choice models are estimated. Rather the more difficult issues arise when various forms of use and nonuse values are estimated. Hence my focus is on the situations where it is necessary to begin with a preference function and derive various models of behavior and value from this function. This approach is occasionally superfluous for valuing price changes only, but when any sort of nonuse (or passive use) values are involved, starting with a prefer-ence function is essential. Much of the work that has been done in this area relates to recreational demand as the use. This chapter follows that literature principally.

The preference functions for valuation responses

We seek money measures of individual welfare as the basis for benefit-cost analysis. The money measures of welfare are units of income and are designed to represent the changes in income that are equivalent to the exogenous change experienced by the individual. These exact welfare measures are the variations in income that equate utility in the states with and without the change and hence start with the preference function. Revealed preference approaches rely on the theoretical constructs of welfare economics to induce these variations in income from observations on behavior. Stated preference approaches are more direct. They attempt to estimate the specific welfare measure that conforms to the variation in income. This difference is not often observed, and for some welfare measurement, for example, income equivalents for price changes, it does not matter a great deal. For more complex cases, such as welfare measures for quality-differentiated goods, the path from behavior to valuation matters a good deal. For hedonic models, the correct welfare measure for a localized change in a public good is the change in the hedonic price, when there is not even a behavioral counterpart based on preferences only.

We begin with a model of an *individual* and not a household. This requires that in fact we are looking only at individuals' decisions or that households have a unified decision process. In the unified model of the household, an individual, presumably the household head, makes an optimal decision for the household. For some types of valuation settings, this is uncontroversial. However, in cases that pertain to critical household issues such as health care, the unified model fails conceptually and is not supported by empirical evidence. These issues involve significant trade-offs among family members.

The individual preference function is denoted $u(z, q)$ where z is a K-dimensional vector of commodities or services chosen and paid for by the individual and q is an M-dimensional vector of commodities or services delivered exogenously (where a single commodity or quality characteristic is the focus, the commodity or quality subscript will be dropped for convenience). These q's have the characteristics of public goods. They are nonrival in consumption and nonexcludable. In most cases it makes no difference to the analysis to assume that q is one-dimensional. We take q to be good, in the sense that increases in q provide a *ceteris paribus* increase in utility. Assume a simple pricing structure in which the individual can purchase goods or services z at fixed prices, p, subject to the budget constraint $p \cdot z \leq y$. Optimal choices lead to the indirect utility function: $v(p, q, y) = max_z \{u(z, q) | p \cdot z \leq y\}$. Note that this assumption precludes hedonic prices, which would arise in response to differences in qualities. Random utility models used in the standard discrete choice contingent valuation format are most often expressed as differences in utility, and in this case the indirect utility function fills the role. But in various cases it may be more useful to employ the expenditure function, given by: $m(p, q, u) = min_z \{p \cdot z | u(z, q) \geq u\}$.

Models of revealed preferences stem from the optimal choices. These choices are given by the income-constant demand functions $z = f(p, q, y)$ while valuation involves the utility-constant demand functions $z = h(p, q, u)$. When q is held constant, the demand curves have well known properties that we will use to recover welfare measures, which is what we hope behavior reveals. The same is true of the indirect utility function and the expenditure function. It is trickier to maintain strong properties in the demand functions or the indirect utility and expenditure function for changes in q. As we shall see, this sometimes leads to difficulties in comparing revealed and stated preferences.

We begin with the definition of welfare measures. The most commonly used measure is compensating variation, defined implicitly as

$$v(p^*, q^*, y - CV) = v(p^0, q^0, y) \tag{2.1}$$

where "0" represents the current or base state of the world and "*" the comparison or "final" state. Writing CV this way will make it positive when final state is an improvement over the initial state and negative when the final state is worse. It is the amount of income given or received that leaves an individual at the base level of well-being following the change. For improvements, it is the maximum willingness to pay. Equivalent variation is the income change that leaves an individual in the final state of welfare at the base conditions.

$$v(p^*, q^*, y) = v(p^0, q^0, y + EV) \tag{2.2}$$

The convention is that EV is positive when the final state is preferred to the initial state. For improvements it is the minimum amount of income that would be accepted to forego the improvement.

We typically find willingness to accept, *wta*, and willingness to pay, *wtp*, more frequently employed in stated preferences studies. This is because questions are framed in terms of *wta* or *wtp*, explicitly or implicitly. In stylized form, we ask respondents what is the maximum amount they would be willing to pay for a given scenario. Hence willingness to pay is asked when there is an improvement. We define it as

$$v(p - \Delta p, q + \Delta q, y - wtp) = v(p^0, q^0, y) \tag{2.3}$$

for $\Delta p \geq 0$, $\Delta q \geq 0$ so that $v(p - \Delta p, q + \Delta q, y) \geq v(p^0, q^0, y)$. By virtue of the wording of a question, the willingness to accept question is asked when the proposed state is worse than the initial state:

$$v(p - \Delta p, q + \Delta q, y) = v(p^0, q^0, y + wta) \tag{2.4}$$

In the revealed preference case, the base or status quo case is fixed, but the baseline case can be manipulated in stated preferences designs. Stated preference models normally assume that the current or base state of the world is the status quo, which defines the "0" state in the models here. In an experimental context, researchers can manipulate the status quo states with different designs. Randomizing on the state, one group would start with the "*" state and another with "0" state. In his seminal paper on the endowment effect, Knetsch (1989) randomizes on whether a student receives a mug or a candy bar, which becomes the status quo.

The welfare measures show no surprises. However, the fact that it is easy to relate the variation concepts, CV and EV, to willingness to accept and willingness to pay brings us to a more substantive issue. In all of the empirical work on revealed preferences, there is practically no evidence that EV and CV are significantly different.[5] In the myriad stated choice studies, there is ample evidence that *wta* can be substantially greater than *wtp*. In a study based on experimental and stated preference data through 2001, Horowitz and McConnell (2002) find that *wta* is on average about five times the value of *wtp*. These differences cannot be made consistent with any reasonable form of neoclassical preferences. It thus stands as one of the anomalies that separate revealed versus stated preferences.

The range of potential welfare measures

The indirect utility function for an individual contains three kinds of arguments—prices for a vector of purchased goods, income and services and a vector of goods and services that are not purchased but provided exogenously to the individual. These are public goods or quasi-public goods. All welfare measures relate to changes in the exogenous arguments. Since changes in income are themselves welfare measures, we have only two kinds of welfare measures—one for prices and one for public goods. In practice the conceptual measures can be adapted to many different circumstances. To estimate jointly revealed and stated preferences for the full range of measures, we need the revealed preference measures wherever they are available.

Beginning with a change in the price vector, we write the welfare effect of this price change as

$$CV = m(p^0, q, u^0) - m(p^*, q, u^0) = y - m(p^*, q, u^0) \tag{2.5}$$

This expresses compensating variation when u^0 is the initial utility level. The impact of a price change is the most familiar, given by the areas under the appropriate demand curves. Consider a single price change so that we can dispense with commodity subscripts. Then CV can be expressed equivalently as

$$CV = -\int_{p^0}^{p^*} h(p, q, u^0)dp = -\int_{p^0}^{p^*} m_p(p, q, u^0)dp, \tag{2.6}$$

where the minus sign meets the conventional that changes for the worse are negative. In this case the price is increasing making $CV < 0$ (unchanging prices have been suppressed). It is common knowledge that the CV for a price change is the area under the utility-constant demand curve between the old and the new price. But this is a happy coincidence of welfare and behavior brought about by the envelope theorem: the utility-constant demand curve is the derivative of the expenditure function with respect to price. The neatness of the result in equation (2.6) is not duplicated for any other welfare measure, even though in many cases marginal values for exogenous variables are easy to write down. Implementation requires that we be able to recover the expenditure function by integrating back from the income-constant demand curve to the expenditure function.

Stated preference methods have also been called direct approaches because they do not feed through behavioral models. Respondents to stated choice questions need only assess their valuation for the price change and then respond by giving their true value. For the revealed preference valuation, we may observe the behavior, but we must then extract the valuation by estimating the demand curve and then computing the *CV*. In principle, there are two options for revealed preferences, each beginning with estimating the income-constant demand curve. If this demand curve comes from a preference function, then the parameters of the preference function will have been estimated, so that the welfare measure can be calculated directly. Along these lines, Englin and Cameron (1996) combine data from contingent behavior responses and revealed preference data to create a panel of income constant demands.[6] The second approach is to integrate the income-constant demand curve back to the expenditure function to get the welfare measure, as described in Hanemann (1980) and Hausman (1981). Hence the steps between observing behavior and calculating welfare for revealed preferences are more in number and complexity even for price changes, the simplest measure of welfare.

In estimating the welfare effects of a price change, no restrictions on the preference function are needed. This will not necessarily be true when we examine the welfare effects of changes in the public good. This can be a relatively pure public good, such as clean air, or it can be a publically provided characteristic of a private good, such as the water quality of a lake used for recreational purposes. For simplicity we change one element of the vector q. As expressed through the expenditure function, the variation equals

$$CV=m(p, q, u)-m(p, q^*, u)=y-m(p, q^*, u) \qquad (2.7)$$

In principle, this welfare measure can be summoned up by a thoughtful individual in response to a question about the maximum willingness to pay for the change in q. However, there is no revealed preference counterpart to the price change. In the case of pure public goods, welfare effects cannot be recovered from observations on behavior.

There is an intermediate case between a pure public good, in which there is no plausible way of recovering welfare measures from revealed preferences, and the pure private case where no restrictions on preference functions are needed. This calls for the weak complementarity restrictions on preferences that lets the value of the public good be measured in the market for a private good. The welfare measure is precisely what's given in equation (2.2). However, we add a restriction that connects the public good with a private *nonmarket* commodity: without the commodity, the public good brings no utility. The well-known weak complementarity restriction is

$$\partial v(p^*, q, y)/\partial q=0 \text{ or } \partial m(p^*, q, u)/\partial q=0 \qquad (2.8)$$

where p^* is the choke price for the commodity that is complementary to the public good. The simplest way to think about weak complementarity is the recreation-lake nexus. Suppose q represents the water quality level of the lake—say clarity—and z represents visits to the lake. Then weak complementarity holds when there is no nonuse value that is derived from the lake. The utility from improved water quality in the lake is zero when the lake is not used. Weak complementarity exists when the public good is simply a characteristic of the nonmarket commodity. Because the commodity in not marketed, the "price" will not be a function of the public good. Under this restriction on preferences we have grounds for using stated or revealed preferences for recovering the welfare measure. With the restriction in (2.8) we know that the change in the area under the utility-constant demand curve is given by

$$CV = \int_p^{p^*} h(t, q^*, u)dt - \int_p^{p^*} h(t, q^0, u)dt \qquad (2.9)$$

where q^0 is the initial quality and q^* the final quality. This expression will be positive if $q^* > q^0$. This is not quite what we get from revealed preference, because it is the change in the area under the utility-constant demand curve. If we have the income-constant demand curve, we can integrate back to the expenditure function and then from the expenditure get the change in the area under the utility constant demand curve, which under weak complementarity is the difference in the expenditure function at the initial and new level of the public good. As Larson (1991) shows, it is necessary to impose the weak complementarity assumption as an initial condition on the constant of integration in this calculation.

The assumption that the commodity is not marketed is critical. If the commodity were priced according to the q embodied in it, then we would be in the world of hedonic prices. Recreational demand is an appropriate application for the weak complementary application because there is no entry price set by the market. It would also fit the demand for residential water, where the water quality is publically determined and rates are only distantly related to water quality characteristics. When there is an active market for the commodity, we would expect commodities with higher quality to be sold for higher prices, leading to a hedonic market, discussed below.

The final measure that one might seek is the value of a change in a pure public good. The direct utility function for this case can be written $u(z, q) = G(u^*(z), q)$, where G is increasing in q and u^* and $u^*(z)$ is a satisfactory utility function for private commodities on its own. In this case, first order conditions for the private goods are of the form $\dfrac{\partial G(.,.)}{\partial u^*} \dfrac{\partial u^*}{\partial z_j} \div \dfrac{\partial G(.,.)}{\partial u^*} \dfrac{\partial u^*}{\partial z_i} = \dfrac{\dfrac{\partial u^*(z)}{\partial z_j}}{\dfrac{\partial u^*(z)}{\partial z_i}} = \dfrac{p_j}{p_i}$ so that the income constant demand curves are independent of the public good. In this case we are interested in a pure public good, such as regional visibility, which by assumption at least would not affect the income-constant demand for goods. The corresponding indirect utility function for this case is $v(p, q, y) = G(v^*(p, y), q)$ where v^* corresponds to u^*. Given this kind of structure, there is no behavior that can be utilized for welfare estimation. The relevant welfare measure in this case is simple the value of the change in the public good:

$$v(p, q+\Delta q, y-CV)=v(p, q, y) \tag{2.10}$$

or $G(v^*(p, y-CV), q+\Delta q)=G(v^*(p, y), q)$. Income constant demand functions are independent of the public good q, so no information on the public good can be gained from these demands.

Note that the utility-constant demands do depend on the public good. The expenditure function from this utility function is $m(p, G^{-1}(u, g))$, so the utility constant demand is of the form $z=h(p, G^{-1}(u, q))$. The integrating back procedure will not work because the income-constant demand does not have information about the public good. Even estimating demand functions derived from a specified direct or indirect utility function cannot be expected to give information on the public good when the utility function is of the form $G^{-1}(v^*(p, y), q)$. Consequently, in the extreme case of a pure public good, where there is only nonuse value, there is limited gain in combining revealed and stated preferences. Estimating the revealed preferences portions of the utility function can improve the efficiency of the stated preference estimates. But the only evidence about public goods would come from stated preference empirics. On the other hand, however, the access value or welfare effect of price changes for private goods is impacted through changes in public goods, at least in principle. This effect comes through the income effect inherent in the relation

$$z=h(p, G^{-1}(u, q))=f[p, m(p, G^{-1}(u, q))].$$

Note however that this holds for all goods consumed by the individual, not just a good that might be related to the resource.

Implementation

Given the three potential welfare measures—a price change, a change in the public good weakly complementary to a private good, and a change in a pure public good, we now look at how we would combine models of stated and revealed preferences. We leave the goals of combining these measures open. It can be to gain efficiency or merely to see how various measures compare. One clear finding worth joint estimation is that when weak complementarity does not hold, even use value won't be measured exactly with revealed preference models without information on nonuse values.

Case 1: Price changes

With price changes, the welfare measure is the willingness to pay or willingness to accept for a price change. In the typical application for environmental and resource economics, the price change is one that is sufficiently high to reduce the demand to zero. Hence what we are really valuing is access but we do it through price changes. For revealed preferences, the welfare measure comes from demand functions. When we value price changes, we work with the demand function for revealed preferences. For stated preferences, there are two alternatives: willingness to pay questions about price changes or contingent behavior questions.

In the case of price changes, we can eschew preference functions, sticking to the analysis of demand functions. The essence of joint estimation of stated and revealed preferences with a demand function is the construction of econometric models of demand that can incorporate contingent behavior and revealed preferences. In one of the first investigations of stated and revealed preferences, Adamowicz et al. (1994) used a discrete choice analysis to compare models. Englin and Cameron (1996) combine contingent behavior and revealed preference data to estimate a panel of recreational demand functions. Azevedo et al. (2003) also estimate a series of demand functions combining observations on observed demand and contingent behavior for the same site. There is little need of theory in these cases of comparing observed behavior with contingent choice, where the principal issues are econometric. Hence this section will focus on combining revealed behavior and stated willingness to pay based on preference function parameters.

Joint estimation would proceed with basic information about the income-constant demand curve and the portion of the preference function that is necessary to estimate the appropriate income variation welfare measure. That is, we will have $z=f(p, y)$. If this is sufficiently tractable to integrate back, we can obtain $z=h(p, u)$ (the number of tractable cases is quite small). If we think about this parametrically, suppose that we recover a vector of parameters β from the revealed preference model. These parameters belong to the preference function. This same vector can be estimated from the stated preference methods, though the parameters may be transformed in some way. A simple example illustrates this. Consider the well-known example of income-constant demand curve of the form: $z=\exp(\alpha+\beta p+\delta y)$. The parameters α, β, δ can be estimated with observations on z, p, y. Along a given indifference curve, $v(p, y)=u^0$ letting $y=m(p, u^0)$ gives the identity $v(p, m(p, u^0))=u^0$, which leads to the differential equation

$$\frac{dm}{dp} \bigg/ \frac{dm}{dp} = z = f(p, m(p, u^0)).$$ Substituting m for y in the demand function

and gives $\dfrac{dm}{dp}=\exp(\alpha+\beta p+\delta m)$, which integrates to the expenditure function

$m(p, u)=-\delta^{-1}\ln(-\delta(\exp((\alpha+\beta p)-\delta c(u)))$ where $c(u)$ is an increasing transformation of utility, u, and the indirect utility function $v(p, q)=-\delta^{-1}e^{-\delta y}+\beta^{-1}e^{\alpha+\beta p}$.

Consider an illustrative discrete choice contingent valuation question: "The management is considering a price increase of Δp for this site. Would you buy an annual pass for a payment of B to avoid paying this price increase?" Then we would have a set of responses to this question, and the probability of a yes response in terms of the parameters of the utility function would be

$$\Pr(yes) = \Pr(v(p, y-B) + \varepsilon_0 > v(p + \Delta p, y)) + \varepsilon_1)$$
$$= \Pr(-\delta^{-1} e^{-\delta(y-B)} + -\beta^{-1} e^{\alpha + \beta p} + \varepsilon_0 > -\delta^{-1} e^{-\delta y} + \beta^{-1} e^{\alpha + \beta(p + \Delta p)} + \varepsilon_1) \qquad (2.11)$$

where the ε_i are additive random errors. This is an example of recovering the same set of parameters using observations on revealed preferences or a stated preference approach. It works in this case because both approaches attempt to estimate the same preference parameters. In the absence of concerns about bias from either approach, the advantage of joint estimation here would be greater efficiency. There is room for more refined hypotheses such as Azevedo *et al.* (2003) incorporated in estimating income-constant demand functions from both types of data. We would combine observations on behavior with stated preference experiments to estimate the parameters jointly with the density for demand given by $z = \exp(\alpha + \beta p + \delta y)$ where the appropriate error term is included in the demand function.

Note that the stated preference questions could also be asked by using the demand function to formulate consumer surplus in almost precisely the same way. When we use consumer surplus, we would ask the same question: "Would you be willing to pay B to avoid the price increase?" But the probability statement would compare the consumer surplus lost from a higher price with the payment B. It would be written

$$\Pr(yes) = Prob[B + \varepsilon_0 < \beta^{-1} \exp(\alpha + \beta p + \delta y) \times \exp(\beta \Delta p - 1) + \varepsilon_1].$$

The term on the right hand side is the area under the demand curve from p to $p + \Delta p$. Because this is an income-constant demand curve, the expression will not be quite the same if we write the expression for the area under the utility-constant demand curve, the more exact value (given the empirical evidence on the size of the income effect, this is not likely to matter). Note that the random terms here are different from the randomness in equation (2.11).

Cameron (1992) executed one of the earliest jointly estimated models for stated and revealed preferences in a similar way. The revealed preference part was the annual demand for recreational fishing. The stated preference part was a dichotomous choice model of the question "If your annual expenditure were E, would you still go fishing?" Primitive preferences were formed with a quadratic utility function of the form, $u(z_1, z_2) = \beta_1 z_1 + \beta_2 z_2 + \beta_{12} z_1 z_{12} + 0.5 \beta_{11} z_1^2 + 0.5 \beta_{22} z_2^2$ where z_1 is the composite commodity and z_2 is the demand for trips. The composite good price is unitary and the trip demand price is p. This function gives an estimable demand function. Cameron used the conditional indirect utility function for the discrete response to the contingent choice question. The probability that an individual responds yes to the stated preference question is the probability that $u(y, 0) < max_{z2} u(y - E - pz_2, z_2)$. The likelihood function would be formed with a randomized version of the stated preference response and the density function of trips beginning with the demand curve derived from the quadratic utility function. Cameron (1992) used both parts to estimate the parameters rather than test whether the stated preference parameters are equal to the revealed preferences parameters.

Case 2: Changes in quasi-public goods

Next we look at joint estimation of stated and revealed preferences when the goal is to estimate the value of a change in a weakly complementary public good, what is sometimes called a quasi-public good. Compared with straight-forward welfare measures of price changes, this task is more difficult. Essentially we are interested in determining the welfare measure for a change in a public good given in equation (2.7), but we are willing to maintain the assumption of weak complementarity, as in equation (2.8). Then this value can be obtained with the demand for a private good. See Larson (1991) for an early application. In this case, the change in the area under the utility-constant demand curve induced by the change in the public good equals the welfare effect of the change in the public good. In principle this case of joint estimation requires care with the distinction between the utility-constant and income-constant demand curve. The response of the income-constant demand for the private good to changes in the public good may not always be amenable to welfare measurement. We can write the connection between the income-constant and utility-constant demand curves as $h(p, q, u) = f(p, q, m(p, q, u))$, so that the effect of a change in q is given by

$$\frac{\partial h(p,q,u)}{\partial q} = \frac{\partial f(p,q,m(p,q,u))}{\partial q} + \frac{\partial f(p,q,m)}{\partial m} \cdot \frac{\partial m}{\partial q} \qquad (2.12)$$

The utility constant demand curve will shift out when the quality characteristic is desirable—i.e. it increases utility. The income-constant demand curve shift equals the utility-constant shift less the term $\dfrac{\partial f(p,q,m)}{\partial m} \cdot \dfrac{\partial m}{\partial q}$, which will be negative when the good has a positive income effect. Hence the income-constant demand curve can shift in or out with changes in the quality characteristic.[7] In the extreme case, the welfare estimate obtained from the income-constant demand curve would give the wrong sign, leaving the approximation of the true welfare measure obtained from using the income-constant demand curve a poor one.

When we begin with a parametric preference function and derive the demand function we have a direct way of combining preferences. Examples tend to be sparse with parameters but useful in illustrating various points. Consider the linear expenditure system used in this context by Larson (1991) and later adapted for the more general case by Phanuef et al. (2000). The utility function is given by $u(z, q) = \ln(z_2) + b(q)\ln(z_2 + 1)$, where z_1 is a composite commodity and z_2 is the commodity of interest. Here $b(q)$ is a known paramet-ric function, increasing in the public good (for example $b=\exp(\gamma q+\theta W)$ where W is a vector of household characteristics influencing utility). The budget con-straint is $y=z_1+pz_2$ where price of the composite commodity is one. Error terms can be introduced as measurement error in z_1. The income-constant demand function is given by:

$$z_2 = -1 + \frac{b(q)}{(1+b(q))} \frac{(y+p)}{p} \tag{2.13}$$

which would have the error term added for estimation. The parameters in this equation can be estimated with data on prices, quality and revealed behavior on commodity levels. To derive the stated preference model, we use the indirect utility function:

$$v(p, q, y) = b\ln\left(\frac{b}{p}\right) + (1+b)\ln\left(\frac{y+p}{1+b}\right) \text{ where } b \equiv b(q). \tag{2.14}$$

An exact statement of the willingness to pay for an improvement in quality can be derived from this. Let $b'=b(q')$, $t=0$, ,. A discrete choice contingent valuation question of the form "Would you pay \$T for an improvement in quality?" would then be written:

$$\Pr(yes) = \Pr\left(b^*\ln\left(\frac{b^*}{p}\right) + (1+b^*)\ln\left(\frac{y-T+p}{1+b^*}\right) > b^0\ln\left(\frac{b^0}{p}\right) + (1+b^0)\ln\left(\frac{y+p}{1+b^0}\right)\right). \tag{2.15}$$

An error term would have to be added to both sides in the standard way for a discrete choice. From this probability we can construct the likelihood function that would facilitate the estimation of the function b, which depends on q as well as other demand shifters. The probability is highly nonlinear in the parameters but it leads to the estimation of the same parameters as the demand function, and responses from the stated and revealed questions can be combined in one likeli-hood function. The part contributed by revealed preferences would be the density for observed trips, which would be derived from the demand function in equa-tion (2.13). Equation (2.14) would provide the likelihood function from the stated preference respondents.

Still another approach for recovering information about preferences was employed by Whitehead (1995) in an extension of McConnell (1990). In analyz-ing a discrete choice contingent valuation question, he employs the standard ref-erendum model. Instead of specifying the primal preference function, he derives the comparative static properties of the difference in expenditure functions. This approach then lets him develop a prediction of quantity demanded that can be used to compare with revealed preference data.

To illustrate this approach, suppose that the question is framed in the equivalent variation mode: the reference state is $u^* = v(p, q^*, y)$ and the respondent is asked "Would you pay T to prevent the decline to q?" The respondent will compare T with the change in the expenditure function, given by $EV = m(p, q, u^*) - m(p, q^*, u^*) = m(p, q, v(p, q^*, y)) - m(p, q^*, v(p, q^*, y))$. The indirect utility function is substituted for u^* to capture differences in p, q, y across respondents. Differentiating the last two terms on the right hand side and substituting in for the marginal utility of income and the commodity demand gives

$$\frac{\partial EV}{\partial p} = z(p, q, y) - z(p, q^*, y) \times \frac{m_u(p, q^*, u^*)}{m_u(p, q, u^*)}.$$ The derivative will be positive, zero

or negative depending on whether $\dfrac{m_u(p, q^*, u^*)}{m_u(p, q, u^*)}$ is greater than or less than one.

The relative sizes depend on how the marginal utility of income changes with quality (Whitehead 1995). In his empirical analysis, Whitehead sets up a structure that lets this parameter be determined empirically. The change in the commodity demand can then be recovered, at which point it can be compared with revealed preference results.

To summarize, when the goal is to value the change in a quasi-public good, there are several approaches to combining empirical preference studies. In the comparison approach one would simply calculate and compare welfare estimates from the two approaches. A method that can lead to greater insight would start the stated and revealed preference approaches with the same model. As long as there is no nonuse value, it would be feasible to employ an income-constant demand curve that could be integrated back to an expenditure function for welfare measurement. A second option would be to start with the same preference function as illustrated with the linear expenditure system in equations (2.13)–(2.15). A third approach would start with the properties of the difference in expenditure function as in Whitehead (1995).

Case 3: Changes in pure public goods

The third case for combining stated and revealed preferences occurs when individuals have some nonuse values for the resources. In this case the welfare measure is given by equation (2.7) (or the equivalent statement with indirect utility). With potential nonuse value, we reject weak complementarity for at least some of the beneficiaries. This choice must be made on practical considerations. Weak complementarity is not a testable assumption with revealed preference data. Researchers must have a sufficient understanding of the resource to determine whether it is salient enough to warrant the estimation of nonuse values. It will always be possible to argue for the presence of nonuse values. Almost every resource has its advocates, people who would give up income to preserve it. But the tools of valuation are not sufficiently precise to undertake cost-effective estimation of nonuse values in every study.

When nonuse and use values are both present, the model of preferences must accommodate the full range of preferences. The general case for nonuse involves three arrangements of preferences for three kinds of values for the public good: (1) nonuse only, (2) both use and nonuse and (3) use. only. For nonuse value only, weak complementarity is not an issue. When beneficiaries receive use and nonuse, weak complementarity is not present. But for the third type of value, we assume the presence of individuals who have use value but not nonuse value.

Combining stated and revealed preferences in the presence of nonuse values would be warranted when the utility function of a typical individual could be represented as $u(z, q) = G(u^*(z, q), q)$. In this case the public good is valued for two sorts of reasons—it is complementary to an activity that takes place on site, and for its own sake. Salient biological resources as the public good fit the application here. Whale-watching trips are complementary to the stock of blue whales but individuals could value the preservation and presence of blue whales even if they do not go whale watching. When stated and revealed preferences are combined with this preference function, the revealed preference part is straightforward. Income-constant demand functions will be consistent with the $u^*(z, q)$ portion of the preference function. Stated preferences can be applied to capture total value, in which case there will be overlap with revealed preference results. Stated preference practitioners may also wish to estimate only the nonuse portion of preferences or values.

A careful look at how the different values emerge reveals an unexpected role for stated preference models. We write the expenditure function associated with $G(u^*(z, q), q)$ as $m(p, q, G^{-1}(q, u))$ where u is minimum utility to be achieved. We can decompose values as follows. The total value from a change in q is

$$TV = m(p, q^0, G^{-1}(q^0, u)) - m(p, q^*, G^{-1}(q^*, u)) \tag{2.16}$$

Here the change in q generates both use and nonuse values. Nonuse value is the value associated with a change in q when there is no use, represented here by the choke price:

$$NUV = m(p^*, q^0, G^{-1}(q^0, u)) - m(p^*, q^*, G^{-1}(q^*, u)) \tag{2.17}$$

By subtracting nonuse from total value and rearranging terms, we get use value:

$$UV = m(p, q^*, G^{-1}(q^*, u)) - m(p^*, q^*, G^{-1}(q^*, u)) -$$
$$[m(p, q^*, G^{-1}(q^0, u)) - m(p^*, q^0, G^{-1}(q^0, u))] \tag{2.18}$$

The first two terms are the area under the utility-constant demand curve at q^* and the second two terms the same area at q^0. The key issue here is that the utility constant demand shifters include $G^{-1}(q, u)$ and q. The term $G^{-1}(q, u)$ relates to nonuse value and cannot be recovered from an income constant demand function. Since the income-constant demand curve has no trace of the nonuse term, integrating back will not recover nonuse values. Hence we have a setting where estimating nonuse value contributes to our ability to estimate use values.

Given the links among the different values, it is essential to begin with a common preference function. In its parametric form, such a utility function will have some overlap in the parameters of non-use value and use value. Eom and Larson (2006) provide an insightful illustration of combining stated and revealed preferences when there is non-use value. For analytical tractability, they assume an income-constant function that is parsimonious in parameters and can be integrated back from the demand function. The parsimony is quite useful, however, because the parameters relate to specific values. They begin with a demand curve of the form $z=\exp(\alpha+\beta p+\delta y+\gamma q)$. This integrates to the expenditure

function $m(p, q, G^{-1}(u, q))=-\delta^{-1}\ln\left(-\dfrac{\delta}{\beta}\exp(\alpha+\beta p+\gamma q)-\delta G^{-1}(u,q)\right)$ where the

constant of integration, $G^{-1}(u, q)$, is an increasing function of u and a decreasing function of the public good q. In this case, the constant of integration depends upon the public good because of the assumption that there is non-use value. Eom and Larson assume that $G^{-1}(u, q)=\exp(\sigma\delta q)u$. Here it is easier to revert to indirect utility functions to recover all the values in equations (2.16)–(2.18). This all leads to the indirect utility function $v(p, q, y)=\exp(-\sigma\delta q)[-\delta^{-1}\exp(-\delta y)-\beta^{-1}\exp(\alpha+\beta p+\gamma q)]$. The general expressions for CV when there is total value, nonuse only and use can be written implicitly with this indirect utility function.

We write out the expressions that give the desired values. First we write the nonuse value, which would be estimated for respondents who were screened to assure that they would not use the resource. Nonuse value is present when there is no use of the resource, that is, at the choke price of z. In the current case, the choke price goes to infinity, giving

$$\exp(\sigma\delta q^*)[-\delta^{-1}\exp(-\delta(y-CV_{NU}))]=\exp(\sigma\delta q^0)[-\delta^{-1}\exp(-\delta y)]. \tag{2.19}$$

We can solve for nonuse value and observe that it is independent of income: $CV_{NU}=\sigma\delta(q^0-q^*)$. This independence is a result of the specification $G^{-1}(u, q)=\exp(\sigma\delta q)u$, a natural and parsimonious choice. A slightly more complex specification, for example, $G^{-1}(u, q)=\exp(\sigma\delta q)u+bq$, would give an income effect but be difficult to estimate. Setting up equation (2.19) as a discrete version of stated choice would permit the identification of the parameter $\sigma\delta$ but cannot identify these parameters separately.

The implicit CV for total value comes from setting up a discrete choice question for total value. The pool of respondents would be any user and would assume that these users would also have nonuse value.

$$\exp(-\sigma\delta q^*)[-\delta^{-1}\exp(-\delta(y-CV_{TV})-\beta^{-1}\exp(\alpha+\beta p+\gamma q^*)] =$$
$$\exp(-\sigma\delta q^0)[-\delta^{-1}\exp(-\delta y)-\beta^{-1}\exp(\alpha+\beta p+\gamma q^0)]. \qquad (2.20)$$

The measure CV_{TV} is on average what would be recovered from a respondent who used the resource and also had nonuse value. Maximization of the appropriate likelihood function would lead to the recovery of all of the parameters if there is variation in price and quality. This measure depends on income.

We would recover total value and use value from stated preferences, or from the stated preference portion of the likelihood function. The revealed preference contribution to our understanding of preferences comes from the demand curve. This would involve observations on trips, so that the likelihood contribution would be the probability density function of trips. The demand curve is $z = \exp(\alpha+\beta p+\delta y+\gamma q)$ which would also include a random element.[8] With variation in price across respondents all parameters can be estimated from the stated preference question.

The stylized likelihood function looks like this:

$$L(\alpha, \beta, \gamma, \sigma\delta) = \Pi_{users\ only}\ f(z|\alpha, \beta, \gamma, \delta)$$

$$\times\ \Pi_{users\ \&\ nonusers}\ [\Pr(yes|\alpha, \beta, \gamma, \delta)^{I_{yes}} \cdot \Pr(no|\alpha, \beta, \gamma, \delta)^{I_{no}}]$$

$$\times\ \Pi_{nonusers\ only}\ [\Pr(yes|\sigma\delta)^{I_{yes}} \cdot \Pr(no|\sigma\delta)^{I_{no}}] \qquad (2.21)$$

where the products of contributions to the likelihood function are over the subsamples of those with use value only (*users only*), those with both use and nonuse value (*users and nonusers*) and those with nonuse value only (*nonusers only*). The user only sample contributions to the likelihood function are derived from revealed preferences over z with density function $f(z|\alpha, \beta, \gamma, \delta)$. The contributions for the two subsamples with some nonuse value are derived from stated preferences—in this stylized case a simple yes/no decision over a set of attributes and prices with respective probabilities Pr(yes) and Pr(no). The dummy indicator variables $I_{yes} \in \{0, 1\}$ and $I_{no} \in \{0, 1\}$ serve to partition the subsample into those accepting the relevant offer and those rejecting.

Writing the likelihood function like this shows the advantages of combining revealed and stated preferences in the use and nonuse case. From the revealed preference data we can recover parameters related to use. From the subjects with use and nonuse values (to be determined by survey results) we recover estimates of $\alpha, \beta, \gamma, \delta$ as well as $\sigma\delta$ and from the nonuse only we recover $\sigma\delta$. Hence we get additional efficiency by having each type of beneficiary contribute to the likelihood function. Further, because we can recover the parameter σ, we can test whether weak complementarity holds. This then represents the full advantage of combining revealed and stated preferences. In the event that demand is estimated in the absence of changes in quality, stated preference results make it feasible to recover all preference parameters anyway.

Hedonic models

Stated preference and revealed preference studies have rarely been estimated jointly in hedonic models, with good reason. The difficulty is that hedonic outcomes are equilibrium outcomes, and the hedonic market can only reveal evidence of the marginal values of attributes without strong additional assumptions. Two revealed preference models are employed to uncover household preferences: hedonic price equations and equilibrium discrete choice models. The typical hedonic price function depends on housing and neighborhood characteristics and environmental attributes: $P = h(q_1, q_2, q_2, q_a, \ldots, q_j)$ where the q's are the attributes and P is the hedonic price. In the case of housing, the hedonic price equation is determined by the stock of housing and the level of neighborhood and environmental attributes as well as the distribution of buyers and their preferences in the housing market. So the structure of hedonic models is not relevant for stated preferences. One possibility is to elicit marginal values of environmental attributes in a stated preference study and compare them with the hedonic marginal values, given by $\frac{\partial h}{\partial q_i}$.

A more promising revealed preference approach treats the choice of a house as a choice among alternatives as one would model with random utility models, with the attributes q_1, q_2, etc. This approach, taken by Earnhart (2002), then can be combined with choice experiments that mimic the market in the sense of depending on the housing attributes. The difficulty of this approach lies with the equilibrium nature of hedonic markets. To estimate discrete choice models effectively, it is necessary to impose the supply equals demand condition for the housing market. This involves estimating an equilibrium model along the lines of the Berry *et al.* (1995) models. These models are considerable undertakings to estimate. Although the models of Berry and coworkers entail several steps in the estimation, it is quite feasible that parameter values for stated preference models—specifically choice experiments—could ease the burden of estimating these models. One of the significant advantages of choice experiments is the ability to reduce collinearity among attributes that plagues attempts to discriminate among models. A stated choice model that could provide estimates of certain housing attributes could prove an integral part of the Berry *et al.* model.

Summing up

This chapter has addressed the construction of models for combining data from stated and revealed preference surveys. Models that begin with preferences are essential when the perceived values include nonuse as well as use motives. In the cases where the research begins with a preference function, all types of values—from use to pure nonuse—can be included separately in a likelihood function. The advantage of starting with a preference function is that it can relate to the various motives for valuing goods and services.

A remaining puzzle in combining stated and revealed preference models concerns the role of the income effect. When nonuse value is present, the impact of the public good will be felt through the income effect. However, available evidence offers considerable support to the idea that the income effect is much larger in stated preference results. Hence beginning with a model that parameterizes the income effect but imposes different income effects along the lines of Azevedo *et al.* is a potential avenue for investigating this issue when combining stated and revealed preferences.

Notes

1 He later took a more optimistic attitude however (Samuelson, 1958), offering a proposal for valuing public goods.
2 We are less accustomed to seeing behavioral anomalies in valuation via revealed preferences but part of this is due to the lack of searching. For example, Simonson and Loewenstein (2006) show that framing caused by previous experience in the housing market has an impact on housing prices.
3 See Horowitz *et al.* (forthcoming) and Blumenschein *et al.* (2008).
4 Blumenschein *et al.* (2008) compare these two approaches, concluding that questions about the degree of certainty attached to responses works better.
5 One exception to this is Tra (2010).
6 One of the significant advantages of this approach is to allow a fixed effect, thereby eliminating unobserved individual heterogeneity.
7 This can illustrated with repackaging. Suppose $u(z, q)=u^*(q \cdot z_1, z_{-1})$ where the vector $z = z_1, z_{-1}$. For any range of prices and income where demand for z_1 is inelastic, we will find $\frac{\partial z_1}{\partial q} \leq 0$. See Chapter 4 in Bockstael and McConnell (2006).
8 Eom and Larson's (page 507) specification includes a random term in the exponential function on the right hand side.

References

Adamowicz, W., J. Louviere, and M. Williams (1994) "Combining revealed and stated preference methods for valuing environmental amenities," *Journal of Environmental Economics and Management*, 26: 271–292.

Azevedo, C.D., J.A. Herriges, and C.L. Kling (2003) "Combining revealed and stated preferences: consistency tests and their interpretations," *American Journal of Agricultural Economics*, 85: 525–537.

Berry, S., J. Levinsohn, and A. Pakes (1995) "Automobile prices in market equilibrium," *Econometrica*, 63: 841–890.

Bishop, R.C. and T.A. Heberlein (1979) "Measuring values of extramarket goods: Are indirect measures biased?" *American Journal of Agricultural Economics*, 61: 926–930.

Blumenschein, K., G.C. Blomquist, M. Johannesson, N. Horn, and P.R. Freeman (2008)

"Eliciting willingness to pay without bias: Evidence from a field experiment," *Economic Journal*, 118: 114–137.

Bockstael, N.E. and K.E. McConnell (2006) *Environmental and Resource Valuation with Revealed Preferences*, New York: Springer.

Brookshire, D.S., M.A. Thayer, W.D. Schulze, and R.C. d'Arge (1982) "Valuing public goods: a comparison of survey and hedonic approaches," *American Economic Review*, 72: 165–177.

Cameron, T.A. (1992) "Combining contingent valuation and travel cost data for the valuation of nonmarket goods," *Land Economics*, 68: 302–317.

Carson, R., N. Flores, K. Martin, and J. Wright (1996) "Contingent valuation and revealed preference methodologies: comparing the estimates for quasi-public goods," *Land Economics*, 72: 113–128.

Chay, K.Y., and M. Greenstone (2005) "Does air quality matter? Evidence from the housing market," *Journal of Political Economy*, 113: 376–424.

Earnhart, D. (2002) "Combining revealed and stated data to examine housing decisions using discrete choice," *Journal of Urban Economics*, 51: 143–169.

Englin, J. and T. Cameron (1996) "Augmenting travel cost models with contingent behavior data," *Environmental and Resource Economics*, 7: 133–147.

Eom, Y.-S. and D.M Larson (2006) "Improving environmental valuation estimates through consistent use of multiple information," *Journal of Environmental Economics and Management*, 52: 501–516.

Friedman, M. (1953) *Essays in Positive Economics*, Chicago, IL: University of Chicago Press.

Hanemann, W.M. (1980) "Measuring the worth of natural resource facilities: Comment," *Land Economics*, 56: 482–486.

Hausman, J.A. (1981) "Exact consumer's surplus and deadweight loss," *American Economic Review*, 71: 662–676.

Hausman, J. (ed.) (1993) *Contingent Valuation: A Critical Assessment*, Amsterdam: North-Holland.

Horowitz, J. and K.E. McConnell (2002) "A review of WTA/WTP studies," *Journal of Environmental Economics and Management*, 44: 426–447.

Horowitz, J., K.E. McConnell, and J. Murphy (forthcoming) "Behavioral foundations of environmental economics and valuation," in J. List and M. Price (eds.), *Handbook of Experimental Economics and the Environment*.

Knetsch, J. (1989) "The endowment effect and evidence of irreversible indifference curves," *American Economic Review*, 79: 1277–1284.

Larson, D. (1991) "Recovering weakly complementary preferences," *Journal of Environmental Economics and Management*, 21: 97–109.

McConnell, K.E. (1990) "Models for referendum data," *Journal of Environmental Economics and Management*, 18: 19–34.

Phaneuf, D.J., J.A. Herriges, and C.L. Kling (2000) "Estimation and welfare calculations in a generalized corner solution model with an application to recreation demand," *Review of Economics and Statistics*, 82: 83–92.

Samuelson, P.A. (1954) "The pure theory of public expenditure" *Review of Economics and Statistics*, 36: 387–389.

Samuelson, P.A. 1958. "Aspects of public expenditure theories," *Review of Economics and Statistics*, 40: 332–338.

Simonson, U. and G. Loewenstein (2006) "Mistake #37: The effect of previously encountered prices on current housing demand," *Economic Journal*, 116: 175–199.

Tra, C.I. (2010) "A discrete choice equilibrium approach to valuing large environmental changes," *Journal of Public Economics*, 94: 183–196.

Whitehead, J.C. (1995) "Willingness to pay for quality improvements: Comparative statics and interpretation of contingent valuation results," *Land Economics*, 71: 207–215.

3 The basics of estimating preference functions for combining stated and revealed preferences

Timothy C. Haab

Introduction

In Chapter 2, Ted McConnell lays out the theory behind combining behavioral data from various sources. In simplest form, the practical task of drawing inferences from joint stated and revealed preference models boils down to estimating appropriate models for the data collection efforts at hand while imposing consistency in the underlying preference structure. In this chapter, we explore some of the practical speed bumps that arise when different types of preference data are combined in a single estimation attempt. Herein, we assume a basic familiarity with standard models for non-market valuation and maximum likelihood estimation, at least to the extent of estimating preprogrammed models from econometric packages such as SAS and LIMDEP.[1]

Specifying consistent preference functions

As McConnell points out in Chapter 2, estimating joint revealed and stated preference models ultimately boils down to estimating models with a consistent preference structure. The theory bifurcates the potentially estimable functions nicely into Marshallian (Indirect Utility, Ordinary Demand, Consumer Surplus) and Hicksian (Expenditures, Compensated Demand, Compensating/Equivalent Variation) designations. It would be useful if practical models allowed for a similar dual designation. To an extent they do. Stated preferences often rely on Hicksian measures/preference functions, e.g. contingent valuation responses, and revealed preferences often rely on observations in a Marshallian world, e.g. trip data for travel cost models. But, unfortunately, the distinction is not always clear: e.g. contingent behavior can be stated preferences in a Marshallian world. While potentially useful, such a strict codification is unnecessary for practical purposes. What is important, however, is an understanding of the role econometric errors play in joint estimation.

To illustrate some of the issues, consider the estimation of a semi-log Marshallian demand curve as laid out by Eom and Larson (2006):

$$x(p, q, m) = e^{\alpha + \beta p + \gamma q + \delta m} \tag{3.1}$$

where x denotes the ordinary demand for recreation trips, p is the price associated with x, q is an exogenous quality attribute of the destination site and m is income. Solving the differential equation implied by Shephard's Lemma and the identity defining the relationship between Hicksian and Marshallian demands yields a quasi-expenditure function of the form:

$$E(p, q, U) = -\frac{1}{\delta} \ln\left(-\frac{\beta}{\delta} e^{(\alpha+\beta p+\gamma q)} - \delta\theta(q,U)\right) \qquad (3.2)$$

where U is the baseline utility level, and $\theta(q, U)$ is a constant of integration which Eom and Larson parameterize as $\theta(q, U) = e^{\delta\phi}U$ and interpret this function as non-use value.

To combine the data from the recreation demand study (revealed preferences) with data from a contingent valuation study to estimate the value of a change in q from q^0 and q^1, the willingness to pay function consistent with (3.1) is the difference in quasi-expenditure functions (3.2) holding prices and utility constant:

$$WTP(q^0, q^1) = -\frac{1}{\delta} \ln\left(-\frac{\delta}{\beta} e^{\alpha+\beta p+\gamma q^1+\delta m} + \left(1+\frac{\delta}{\beta} e^{\alpha+\beta p+\gamma q^0+\delta m}\right) e^{\delta\phi(q^1-q^0)}\right) \qquad (3.3)$$

Equations (3.1) and (3.3) form a system of preference consistent functions to be estimated simultaneously. To facilitate joint estimation, Eom and Larson introduce additive error components into each equation recognizing possible correlation between the errors:

$$\tilde{x}(p, q, m) = e^{\alpha+\beta p+\gamma q+\delta m+\eta} \qquad (3.4a)$$

$$\widetilde{WTP}(q^0, q^1) = WTP(q^0, q^1) + \varepsilon \qquad (3.4b)$$

$$\varepsilon, \eta \sim BVN(0, 0, \sigma_\varepsilon, \sigma_\eta, \rho) \qquad (3.4c)$$

Unfortunately, the logic underlying the jump from equation (3.1) and (3.3) to the joint system (3.4) becomes fuzzy when error terms are introduced for estimation.

To see this, consider again equation (3.3) which upon substitution from (3.1) can be written:

$$WTP(q^0, q^1) = -\frac{1}{\delta} \ln\left(-\frac{\delta}{\beta} x(p,q^1,m) + \left(1+\frac{\delta}{\beta} x(p,q^0,m)\right) e^{\delta\phi(q^1-q^0)}\right) \qquad (3.5)$$

It now becomes clear that the willingness to pay function to be estimated from the stated preference data is a function of the Marshallian demands. One can imagine two possible estimation strategies:

Strategy 1: Estimate the system (3.4) by substituting (3.3) into (3.4b) and jointly estimating (3.4a) and (3.4b) by restricting the parameters of the substituted Marshallian demand to be the same across the two equations.

Strategy 2: Estimate the system (3.4) by substituting (3.5) into (3.4b) and jointly estimating (3.4a) and (3.4b) by substituting the observed Marshallian quantities into (3.4b).

In estimation strategy 1, the parameteric specification for the Marshallian demand is substituted into the WTP function to obtain a system of two equations with overlapping parameters to be estimated. In contrast, strategy 2 relies on the actual observed values rather than the parametric functions for *x*. In a world without uncertainty or error, this distinction is irrelevant: The observed quantity exactly equals the functional prediction. But, tautologically, in a world without uncertainty, estimation is irrelevant. Because we know that we cannot exactly specify preference functions for every individual, we are forced to introduce error to estimate these relationships. It is the assumed source of this error that becomes critical for estimating the joint system.

Sources of error and joint estimation

Continuing the example from the previous section, consider two common sources of error frequent in applied econometrics: specification error and recall bias.[2] As applied to the current example, specification error results when the researcher misspecifies the functional relationship between the independent variables and the observed quantities. In other words, the observed quantities (*x*'s) are correct, but the researcher either assumes the wrong functional form to be estimated, or incompletely specifies the set of independent variables to be included. Whatever the cause, specification error is not an error made by the individual in reporting the value of *x*, but instead an error on the part of the researcher in failing to correctly specify the relationship. Recognizing that the reported value for the quantity demanded is the true value, estimation should proceed consistent with strategy 2: Specify the system to be estimated in terms of observed quantities.

Recall the system to be estimated from (3.4):

$$\tilde{x}(p, q, m) = e^{\alpha + \beta p + \gamma q + \delta m + \eta} \tag{3.4a}$$

$$\widetilde{WTP}(q^0, q^1) = WTP(q^0, q^1) + \varepsilon \tag{3.4b}$$

$$\varepsilon, \eta \sim BVN(0, 0, \sigma_\varepsilon, \sigma_\eta, \rho) \tag{3.4c}$$

As noted in (3.5), the WTP function in (3.4b) is a function of the Marshallian demands. If the error in the Marshallian demand (3.4a) is from specification error, then the observed *x*'s are correct and these are the quantities to be substituted into (3.4b) for estimation and the system becomes:

$$\tilde{x}(p, q, m) = e^{\alpha + \beta p + \gamma q + \delta m + \eta} \tag{3.6a}$$

$$WTP(q^0, q^1) = -\frac{1}{\delta} \ln \left[-\frac{\delta}{\beta} x(p, q^1, m) + \left(1 + \frac{\delta}{\beta} x(p, q^0, m)\right) e^{\delta\phi(q^1 - q^0)} \right] + \varepsilon \tag{3.6b}$$

$$\varepsilon, \eta \sim BVN(0, 0, \sigma_\varepsilon, \sigma_\eta, \rho) \tag{3.6c}$$

where *x*(*p*, *q*, *m*) is the observed *x*.

Contrast specification error with recall bias. Recall bias results from the inability of survey respondents to correctly recall the exact value of x, typical of survey responses. In the case of recreation demand, respondents are often asked the number of trips made over a previous season (month, summer, year...). This is a difficult task and recall is imperfect. It is assumed that respondents can, on average get their responses correct, but the reported quantity demanded is not necessarily the true quantity demanded.

Consistent with estimation strategy 1, in the case of recall bias, the correct demand to substitute into (3.4b) is the demand after resolution of the error. In most cases this will be the expected Marshallian demand found by integrating (3.4a) over the support of η.[3]

$$\tilde{x}(p, q, m) = e^{\alpha + \beta p + \gamma q + \delta m + \eta} \tag{3.7a}$$

$$WTP(q^0, q^1) = -\frac{1}{\delta} \ln \left(-\frac{\delta}{\beta} E_\eta(x(p,q^1,m)) + \left(1 + \frac{\delta}{\beta} E_\eta(x(p,q^0,m)) \right) e^{\delta \phi(q^1 - q^0)} \right) + \varepsilon \tag{3.7b}$$

$$\varepsilon, \eta \sim BVN(0, 0, \sigma_\varepsilon, \sigma_\eta, \rho) \tag{3.7c}$$

Consequences of using the wrong error

In estimation of a single equation (e.g. the Marshallian demand only), the source of the error can be inconsequential as long as the error has a zero mean and constant variance. However, as closer examination of the example from the previous section reveals, the source of the error becomes critical in joint estimation. Estimation of the wrong system will result in bad statistical properties of the resulting estimates.

To begin to investigate the potential problems with failing to recognize the source of the error, we will continue the specific example from the previous section. In practice, the estimation of the system described by equations (3.6) is relatively simpler than the system in equations (3.7). Because exact quantities are substituted rather than complicated parametric functions, estimation proceeds by specifying the joint distribution for ε and η, deriving the resulting likelihood function and using standard (but potentially complicated) techniques for estimating the parameters of the two equations of interest. The resulting parameter estimates represent estimates of the parameters of the underlying preference structure, and because both equations are consistent with a common preference function, the parameter estimates can be used for a number of purposes, perhaps most importantly value calculation.

Such use of the parameter estimates relies on the accurate estimation of the parameters. But, accurate estimation relies on the correct attribution for the source of the error. If a researcher ignores the source or mistakenly attributes the error to the wrong source, the resulting parameter estimates are minimally inefficient and likely inconsistent. Consider a case where the researcher estimates the system (3.6), but in reality the error is due at least partially to recall bias. Upon substitution of the observed quantities into equation (3.6b), equation (3.6b) is misspecified. Ultimately this is a case of measurement error[4] and the resulting parameter estimates are inconsistent. Inconsistent parameter estimates are wrong and any subsequent calculations derived from such estimates will be wrong as well.

Similar arguments can be made for estimating a model that assumes recall bias as the source of the error when in fact the error is due to the wrong specification. Failure to properly account for the source of the econometric error introduced into preference consistent systems of equations will result in inconsistent parameter estimates. However, consistent estimation typically relies on complicated estimation techniques that are not readily available with standard econometric packages.

Functional forms and econometric tractability

In addition to the issues surrounding the introduction of the error, perhaps a more difficult problem to solve arises in estimating the non-linear functional forms that often accompany preference consistent systems of joint equations. Applied economists often search for models that can be estimated within the framework of existing econometric packages. Highly complex functional forms and error distributions, while academically glamorous, often introduce levels of complication beyond those necessary to draw practical conclusions. Considering the case of a typical linear Marshallian demand:

$$x(p, m) = \alpha + \beta p + \gamma m \tag{3.8}$$

The preference-consistent compensating variation of a price change from p^0 to p^1 is:

$$CV = \left(\frac{x(p^1, m)}{\gamma} + \frac{\beta}{\gamma^2} \right) [-e^{\gamma(p^1 - p^0)}] \left(\frac{x(p^0, m)}{\gamma} + \frac{\beta}{\gamma^2} \right) \tag{3.9}$$

Estimation of the demand function alone is straightforward, and the techniques applied in the next section are readily adaptable to estimation of the linear demand function.

Likewise, it would be straightforward to specify a willingness to pay function (linear, semi-log) that is readily estimable using accessible techniques, but the preference-consistency Marshallian demand will be a highly non-linear function of the preference parameters and not readily estimable. In general, joint estimation of preference consistent revealed and stated preference systems requires specialized likelihood functions and often leads to tenuous estimation results subject to sensitivity to the assumed functional forms. The complexity of the system leaves the applied researcher with the unfortunate but perhaps necessary decision to sacrifice theoretical consistency for econometric tractability.

Basic econometric models for stated and revealed preferences

In the current chapter, there will be no attempt to maintain preference-consistency throughout. Instead, we will look at some of the basic techniques that can be used to estimate models and then talk about some of the adjustments that can be made to at least give a nod toward preference consistency. Starting in Part II of this book, numerous examples of combining revealed and stated preference are offered. Some of the authors have chosen to estimate fully preference-consistent models, while others have chosen to sacrifice preference-consistency for econometric tractability. Although it would be desirable to present a comprehensive framework for the econometric analysis of joint data, as the following chapters demonstrate, each data collection effort and modeling exercise provides unique combinations that cannot be comprehensively treated in a single chapter.

The remainder of this chapter introduces econometric models that are readily adaptable to joint estimation with revealed and stated preference data. This is not an attempt to provide a comprehensive introduction to the econometrics of nonmarket valuation (see Haab and McConnell 2000 for that), but rather to give the flavor of the econometric modeling decisions that must be made when combining different types of data and some of the issues that arise when combining data sources, within the context of these basic models. The subsequent chapters provide more details and some excellent examples of the richness that combining data sources affords.

Modeling discrete choices in the random utility framework

Consider the case of an individual faced with the decision between discrete alternatives. This decision could be in the form of stated preference between purchasing a change in environmental quality for an offered price (dichotomous choice contingent valuation), the stated choice from among a set of products that vary by attribute level (conjoint/choice experiments) or the revealed choice of recreation destination from among a set of possible alternatives (recreation site choice model). In each of these cases, stated or revealed choice can be modeled as the revelation of the utility maximizing alternative. Suppose the indirect utility of alternative j is denoted v_j. Then the decision to choose alternative j over all other alternatives available occurs if the indirect utility of alternative j, conditioned on all of the attributes of j, outweighs the indirect utility of any other alternative (k) within the set of all available alternatives (S), conditional on their attributes. The discrete choice decision rule becomes:

$$i \text{ chooses } j \text{ if } v_j > v_k \text{ for all } k \neq j \text{ and } k, j \in S \qquad (3.10)$$

In the case of dichotomous choice contingent valuation where an individual is asked whether he would be willing to pay a prespecified price for a given improvement in environmental quality, k is the status quo situation, and j is the state of the world after paying the price, but receiving improved quality in return. The individual chooses j (to pay) if the utility of paying and receiving improved quality outweighs the utility of not paying and keeping quality at current levels. For a recreation site choice model in which an individual is faced with a potentially large number of possible destination on each choice occasion, the individual chooses to take a trip to site j if the utility of visiting site j outweighs the utility of visiting any other destination chosen from among all of the possible destinations (each utility conditioned on the specific attributes of that alternative).

To account for preference uncertainty or misspecification on the part of the researcher, we cavalierly, given our discussion of the importance of the source of error in the first half of this chapter, introduce an additive random error component to the indirect utility of each alternative:

$$v_j = \tilde{v}_j + \varepsilon_j \tag{3.11}$$

where $\tilde{v}_j$ is a deterministic utility component, conditional on the attributes of the individual and alternative and ε_j is a mean zero random variable following an assumed distribution. It is the form of this assumed distribution that will ultimately determine the type of model to be estimated.

Given this random utility treatment, the decision rule for the stated or revealed choice of each respondent then becomes a probabilistic decision rule:

$$Prob(i\ chooses\ j) = Prob(v_j > v_k)\ for\ all\ k \neq j\ and\ k, j \in S \tag{3.12}$$

Substituting the additive form for the indirect utility, and rearranging, the probabilistic decision rule becomes:

$$Prob(i\ chooses\ j) = Prob(\varepsilon_j > \varepsilon_k = \tilde{v}_j - \tilde{v}_k)\ for\ all\ k \neq j\ and\ k, j \in S \tag{3.13}$$

The standard estimation of discrete decisions, whether stated or revealed, comes down to a version of (3.13). Typically, linear forms are assumed for the indirect utility function. Because the decision rule relies on differences in indirect utility between alternatives, the specification of the indirect utility function requires something to vary between alternatives; otherwise the desired effect will cancel when differences are taken. This causes concern when individual specific characteristics are to be included in the decision rule. Since individual characteristics, such as age, education, and income do not vary by alternative, but obviously affect decisions, it becomes necessary to specify an indirect utility function that varies structurally across alternatives for these individual specific attributes:

$$\tilde{v}_j = z_i \beta_j + z_{ij} \theta \tag{3.14}$$

where β_j is a vector of alternative specific parameters corresponding to the vector of individual specific attributes (z_i), and θ is a vector of non-alternative specific parameters corresponding to the vector of alternative specific attributes (z_{ij}) which can also include attributes that vary by individual and alternative (such as travel cost from i's home to destination j) but must at least vary by alternative.

The utility difference to be compared across alternatives is then:

$$\widetilde{v}_j - \widetilde{v}_k = z_i(\beta_j - \beta_k) + (z_{ij} - z_{ik})\theta \tag{3.15}$$

Of importance here is the interpretation of the parameters. When individual specific attributes are involved, the decision to choose an alternative is determined by the magnitude of the associated parameter relative to that same parameter for all other attributes. But, when an attribute varies by alternative, relative differences in the magnitude of the attribute across alternatives matters.

To estimate the parameters, we must now assume a distribution for the error difference in order to find a closed form for the probabilistic decision rule in (3.13). Typical models assume one of two distributions for ε_j: Normal or extreme-value. If we assume a normal distribution for the error term, then the error difference $\varepsilon_j - \varepsilon_k$ is also normally distributed, and the choice probability defined in (3.13) is 1 minus the cumulative distribution function from a normal distribution evaluated at the utility difference in (3.15). The resulting model from normal error differences is a Probit model (a binary probit for a dichotomous choice, or a multinomial Probit for a choice from among more than two alternatives). If instead, we assume an extreme-value distribution for the error then the error differences are logistically distributed and the resulting models are Logits (binary Logit for a dichotomous choice and multinomial/conditional Logit for a choice among more than two alternatives). While students often fret over the distinction between the two distributions, the practical choice between the distributions is ultimately one of researcher preference and typically has little impact on the final estimation results.

Modeling continuous quantities

The modeling of continuous choice quantities turns out to be relatively straightforward compared to discrete choices. Whether the responses are revealed (e.g. trip demand) or stated (e.g. contingent behavior) the modeling of responses comes down to identifying the form of the quantity to be modeled and then choosing the appropriate distribution to model responses. Consider a continuous quantity demanded x as a function of prices (p), income (m) and a quality attribute (q): $x(p, m, q)$. For most cases, the quantity measured fits into one of three categories: continuous, limited or count.

Continuous dependent variable

A continuous dependent variable occurs if x can take on any real value over the infinite range. While continuity is useful for estimation, it is unlikely that many observable quantities used in combined stated and revealed are truly continuous and assuming continuity can be questionable. Nevertheless, standard techniques for the estimation of continuous quantity models boil down to two decisions on the part of the researcher:

1   the specification of the relationship between the independent variables, model parameters and an unobservable random disturbance, and
2   the distribution of the unobservable random component.

The simplest of the continuous models specifies the each observation (indexed i) of an observable, continuous dependent variable (x_i) as a linear function of the independent variables (z_i) with a mean zero, constant variance random disturbance $\varepsilon_i \sim (0, \sigma^2)$ added:

$$x_i = z_i\beta + \varepsilon_i, \; \varepsilon_i \sim (0, \sigma^2) \tag{3.16}$$

where β is a vector of parameters conformable to z_i. Given these simplistic assumptions, the Ordinary Least Squares estimator serves to provide unbiased parameter estimates.

While the simplicity of estimation may overwhelm the desire for preference consistency, often some desire for consistency with reality prevails and the researcher desires to, at the very least, estimate a model that disallows predictions of negative quantities for the observed quantity. The most common functional transformation used to ensure non-negativity is the exponential transformation such that:

$$x_i = e^{z_i\beta + \varepsilon_i}, \; \varepsilon_i \sim (0, \sigma^2) \tag{3.17}$$

Taking the natural logarithm of both sides yields a model estimable within the OLS framework:

$$\ln(x_i) = z_i\beta + \varepsilon_i, \; \varepsilon_i \sim (0, \sigma^2) \tag{3.18}$$

Dealing with Zeros

While equations (3.16) and (3.18) afford the luxury of simplicity in estimation, researchers are sometimes faced with data inconsistent with the assumed structure for estimation. One particularly troublesome reality is the zeros that sometimes accompany stated and revealed preference data. It is not uncommon in recreation demand or contingent behavior surveys to find that more than half of the population takes no trips to the site of interest in the specified time period. While nothing in the continuous specification of a demand function, like that in (3.16), forbids a zero observation for the dependent variable, the likelihood of observing any particular observation exactly equal to zero is negligible: The likelihood of observing a particular sample with half of the observations massed at zero is even smaller.

The problem of zeros is complicated further if the researcher wants to rule out negative values. Because the natural logarithm of zero is undefined by computers (try plugging it in to your calculator), estimating an exponential model of the form of (3.17) is impossible if any zeros are present. A number of ad hoc fixes have been proposed, all of which leave a funny taste: Simply dropping the zeros results in sample selection problems, while adding a small positive number to every observation creates an entirely new functional form with unknown properties.

To deal with larger than expected number of zeros, we can turn to distributions that allow for a mass of observations. Often called point mass distributions, the most commonly applied form for the distribution is:

$$f(x_i) = \begin{cases} G(-z_i\beta) \ if \ x_i = 0 \\ g(z_i\beta) \ if \ x_i > 0 \end{cases} \tag{3.19}$$

where $g(x)$ and $G(x)$ are the probability density and cumulative distribution functions associated with a latent continuous demand function: $x_i^* = z_i\beta + \varepsilon_i$.

The intuition behind equation (3.19) goes like this: Somewhere out there in the universe, there exists a continuous quantity x_i^* that our worldly eyes won't allow us to see. If the universe decides to reveal itself to us, then the worldly manifestations of $x_i^* > 0$ take the form of observed quantities x_i which occur with probability $g(x^*)$. Otherwise, the universe only reveals a worldly indicator $(x = 0)$ of the universal quantity $(x_i^* = z_i\beta + \varepsilon_i \leq 0)$ with probability $G(-z_i\beta)$.

The decision rule (3.19) is to be recognized as a variation of the oft-applied Tobit regression model. Because it solves the distributional problems of a mass of zeros frequently observed in "continuous" data, the silliness of the underlying story of a mysterious fully-continuous quantity is often overlooked for the sake of some consistency with observation. However, a more careful treatment of the observed quantities can result in readily estimable models that don't require mythical stories to hold together.

Count data models

The quantities of interest in revealed preference models and to a lesser extent stated preferences can come in the form of non-negative integers, or counts. For example, how many trips did you take to the shore last year, or how many donuts did you eat last month. In such cases, it seems somewhat questionable, and possibly silly, to model the response as if it were a continuous variable that can take on any real value. Readily available count data routines provide a means of estimating models with count valued dependent variables. The two most common count valued regression models are the Poisson and the Negative Binomial. We will first consider the Negative Binomial since it is the more general of the two and then talk briefly about the special case Poisson.

Consider a count valued random variable, x_i, drawn from the set of non-negative integers: $x_i \in \{0, 1, 2, 3, \ldots\}$. Assuming x_i is drawn from a Negative

Binomial distribution, the probability density function for x_i is the messy looking:

$$Pr(x_i=x)=\frac{\Gamma\left(x+\frac{1}{\alpha}\right)}{\Gamma(x+1)\Gamma\left(\frac{1}{\alpha}\right)}\left(\frac{\frac{1}{\alpha}}{\frac{1}{\alpha}+\lambda_i}\right)^{\frac{1}{\alpha}}\left(\frac{\lambda_i}{\frac{1}{\alpha}+\lambda_i}\right)^x \tag{3.20}$$

where α and λ are distributional parameters to be estimated and $\Gamma(z)$ is the incomplete gamma function.[5] While the distribution itself looks complicated, estimation is relatively straightforward. Most standard econometric packages have built-in Negative Binomial regression routines that will provide maximum likelihood estimates for α and λ. A full exposition of the estimation of such models is available in Haab and McConnell (2002), but for our purposes here, we will focus on the incorporation of covariates and interpretation of model estimates for standard models.

The parameter λ_i is the non-negative expected value of the Negative Binomial distribution $(E(x_i)=\lambda_i)$. Covariates are typically incorporated into the Negative Binomial regression model through an exponential parametric mean specification: $\lambda_i=e^{z_i\beta}$.

The estimates of β from the Negative Binomial are thus interpreted the same as in any exponential regression function: as the semi-elasticity effects of the associated covariate on the expected value of the dependent variable. That is, the estimated β's are the estimated percentage changes in the expected value of the dependent variable due to a unit change in the corresponding covariate.

In addition to estimates of the β's, Negative Binomial regression routines will also provide maximum likelihood estimates of the additional distributional parameter, α. Referred to as the dispersion parameter, α can be interpreted loosely as the count data equivalent of a variance parameter. For the Negative Binomial distribution in equation (3.20), the variance of the dependent variable, x_i, is: $V(x_i)=\lambda_i(1+\alpha\lambda_i)$. For $\alpha>0$, the variance of the dependent variable exceeds the expected value, $V(x_i)>\lambda_i$. In such a case, the dependent variable is said to exhibit overdispersion. For $\alpha<0$, $V(x_i)<\lambda_i$ and the dependent variable is said to exhibit underdispersion. If $\alpha=0$, then the variance and expectation are identical and the dependent variable is equi-dispersed.

The special case where the dependent variable is equi-dispersed (equal mean and variance) is important because it highlights a common mistake in estimating count data models. While not obvious, if $\alpha=0$, the Negative Binomial distribution collapses to the much simpler Poisson distribution:[6]

$$Pr(x_i=x)=\frac{e^{-\lambda}\lambda_i^x}{x!}.$$

The Poisson model is oft-applied to count data for its presumed simplicity, but in practice, it is rare to find cases where the presumption of equidispersion,

$\alpha = 0$, is valid. Much more often, at least in our experience, revealed and stated preference count data is overdispersed and the Poisson is misspecified—resulting in inconsistent estimates of the parameters of interest. A tell-tale sign of overdispersion in a Poisson regression model is unbelievably small p-values (large z-statistics) for most estimated parameters. While tempting to attribute large z-statistics to brilliance in data collection and model selection, the reality is quite the opposite: extraordinary fit of a Poisson regression model is more likely a signal of ignorance of overdispersion by the practitioner.[7] The knowing researcher will always estimate the more general Negative Binomial model.

Basic econometrics and combining data types

The early sections of this chapter focus on the consistent modeling of preferences across data types. The previous section describes the simplest models that are commonly used for applied estimation in revealed and stated preference settings. The gulf between these sections is obvious and highlights the reality that combining different types of data often requires the researcher to make difficult modeling decisions in order to combine data types to readily estimable models. While estimating the "correct" model is desirable, reality often intercedes and the practitioner must sacrifice correctness for tractability. In the following chapters, you will see examples of both strategies: correctness and tractability. You will see strategies for using basic econometric models to combine revealed and stated preference data with similarities (e.g. revealed and contingent behavior data on a similar quantity), and strategies for estimating complex econometric models that attempt to maintain preference consistency throughout. Our goal here is not to recommend one particular strategy for estimating combined models, but rather to highlight a few of the strategies available and stress the importance of validity and reliability in the modeling choices.

Notes

1 For an overview of such models, see Haab and McConnell (2002).
2 Although not the only two sources of error, specification error and recall bias serve as specific representations of two broader categories of error: errors made by the researcher and errors made by the respondent.
3 For the semi-log case described here, the mean and median of equation (3.7a) differ (see Haab and McConnell 2002 for details). The correct measure of central tendency to use in estimation is left as an open question.
4 For a textbook discussion of measurement error, see Chapter 12 of Greene (2008).
5 $\Gamma(z) = \int_0^\infty y^{z-1} e^{-y} dy$.
6 See Haab and McConnell (2002) Appendix B for a demonstration.
7 As I tell my applied econometrics students, "If you get frustrated by your inability to get significant parameter estimates in your models, run a Poisson. It might not be correct, but you'll at least feel better about yourself for a little bit while you look at z-statistics in the double or triple digits."

References

Eom, Y. and D. Larson (2006) Improving environmental valuation estimates through consistent use of revealed and stated preference information, *Journal of Environmental Economics and Management*, 52: 501–516.

Greene, W. (2008) *Econometric Analysis*, sixth edition, Upper Saddle River, NJ: Pearson Education, Inc.

Haab, T.C. and K.E. McConnell (2002) *Valuing Environmental and Natural Resources: The Econometrics of Nonmarket Valuation*, Cheltenham: Edward Elgar Publishing.

4 Dichotomous and frequency data joint estimation

John C. Whitehead

Introduction

Discrete choice revealed and stated preference data can be used to elicit information about participation in an activity or market. Revealed and stated preference
frequency data can be used to elicit information about the intensity of consumption
of environmental-related goods and services such as recreation trips and seafood
meals, among a number of other possibilities. One limitation of the revealed preference data arises over measurement of environmental values when environmental
conditions change. For example, improvements in environmental quality might
lead to a shift of the recreation demand curve. Stated preference data can be used
to better estimate the demand shifts and resulting changes in environmental values.
In these situations stated preference data is typically layered into (i.e. stacked with)
revealed preference data and standard econometric models can be used.

Discrete choice data is elicited with closed-ended questions. For example,
respondents could be asked a question that requires a yes or no answer such as:
"Do you drink filtered water from the tap?" Frequency data can be elicited in
surveys with open or closed-ended questions. For example, respondents could be
asked open ended questions: "How many recreation trips did you take last year
to...?" Similar closed-ended questions could be asked where the answer categories are given as categories and the resulting data could be treated as continuous. However, researchers should pay attention to the form and distribution of
the dependent variable as there are several econometric models that can be
applied to frequency data such as ordinary least squares, Tobit, Poisson, negative
binomial and interval data regression models.

Combining dichotomous and frequency data involves stacking observations.
For example, consider a choice situation where Y is the dependent (i.e. choice)
variable and X is the independent variable:

$$Y_j = \alpha_j + \beta_j X_j + \varepsilon_j \tag{4.1}$$

where α and β are coefficients to be estimated, ε is the error term and $j=r$, s to
indicate revealed and stated preference data. In other words, separate revealed
and stated preference models would involve two equations

$$Y_r = \alpha_r + \beta_r X_r + \varepsilon_r$$
$$Y_s = \alpha_s + \beta_s X_s + \varepsilon_s$$

(4.2)

Data with two values with various categorical labels attached are dichotomous (i.e. binary) choice data

$$Y_j = \begin{cases} 1 & yes \\ 0 & no \end{cases}$$

(4.3)

Respondents may reveal their behavior or state their intentions to participate in recreation activity, averting or some other type of behavior. Data with a large number of potential values without categorical labels attached are frequency data. For example, count data consists of non-negative integers

$$Y_j = 0, 1, 2, 3 \ldots$$

(4.4)

With both dichotomous and frequency data, analysis proceeds after stacking rows of data in the same columns. In Figure 4.1 we provide an illustration with continuous variables. The sample data includes three respondents with identification (ID) numbers 1001, 1002, and 1003. The SP variable is a dummy variable that indicates whether the data source is revealed preference (SP=0) or stated preference (SP=1). Each respondent has one revealed preference observation and two stated preference observations. The dependent variable, Y, consists of integers. There are three independent variables. X1 is observed for both revealed and stated preference scenarios, say the travel cost associated with recreation trips. X2 might be a hypothetical scenario treatment variable that is only collected in the stated preference survey. The revealed preference scenario is associated with a constant value, X2=1, while the stated preference scenario values range up to 5. The SPX1 variable is the SP variable interacted with X1.

ID	SP	Y	X1	X2	SPX1
1001	0	8	15	1	0
1001	1	5	27	2	27
1001	1	8	21	3	21
1002	0	7	21	1	0
1002	1	7	31	3	31
1002	1	5	19	4	19
1003	0	3	12	1	0
1003	1	5	14	5	14
1003	1	2	19	1	19

Figure 4.1 Revealed and stated preference data.

When jointly estimating the dichotomous or continuous revealed and stated data it is combined into a single equation. If the revealed and stated preference data coefficients are constrained to be equal, r=s, then the data is stacked as above (indicated by notation r, s) and the basic model is estimated

$$Y_{r,s} = \alpha_{r=s} + \beta_{r=s} X_{r,s} + \varepsilon_{r=s}$$ (4.5)

However, this framework is typically naïve in that revealed and stated preference data often diverge for various reasons. The first-order test for divergence is to allow the coefficients to vary

$$Y_{r,s} = \alpha + \gamma SP + \beta X_{r,s} + \delta(SP \times X_{r,s}) + \varepsilon_{r=s}$$ (4.6)

The γ and δ regression coefficients allow tests for compatibility between the data formats. If γ and δ are both statistically insignificant then the model collapses to the basic model (4.5) and the revealed and stated preference data are compatible. If γ and/or δ are statistically significant then the intercept and/or slope differs between the revealed and stated preference data. If the coefficient on the SP dummy variable, γ, is statistically significant then the revealed and stated preference intercepts are $\alpha_r = \alpha$ and $\alpha_s = \alpha + \gamma$, respectively. If the coefficient on the SP slope interaction variable, δ, is statistically significant then the revealed and stated preference slopes are $\beta_r = \beta$ and $\beta_s = \beta + \delta$, respectively.

Additionally, the error terms between the two sources of data may differ. It is not surprising if the variance of the error for stated preference data is greater than the variance of the error for the revealed preference data. The nonconstant error term results in the classic heteroskedasticity problem. Heteroskedasticity leads to increased variance of the regression coefficients but it does not lead to biased coefficient estimates.

In the rest of this chapter we implement this basic framework with application to joint estimation of dichotomous and frequency revealed and stated preference data. We provide an empirical example for each type of data. The case studies concern hurricane evacuation and seafood demand. In the following chapter we focus on combining dichotomous and frequency data in the same model (i.e. mixed data).

Dichotomous data

In order to examine issues related to dichotomous data we use revealed and stated preference hurricane evacuation data (Whitehead 2008). Hurricane evacuation is a form of averting behavior in which individuals and households must respond to a risky situation. The household chooses to evacuate (Y = 1) or not (Y = 0). One limitation of revealed preference related to risky situations is that of limitations in the variation of risk. Stated preference data can be used to assess behavior over the full range of risk, even catastrophic risk, which might be faced.

The sample of respondents consists of Brunswick, New Hanover, and Pender County residents in southeastern North Carolina. A total of 411 households participated in a telephone survey during March 2001, a period after a number of hurricane landings in the Carolinas. Twenty-five percent of the households evacuated their homes for Hurricane Bonnie (a category 3 storm on the Saffir-Simpson hurricane scale) in 1996, 17 percent evacuated for Hurricane Dennis (category 1) in 1999, and 42 percent evacuated for Hurricane Floyd (category 4) in 1999. Fifty percent evacuated their homes for at least one storm. For the purposes of this illustration, we include only those respondents who did not receive a voluntary or mandatory evacuation order during Hurricane Floyd (n=275). Twenty-eight percent of these respondents evacuated for Hurricane Floyd.

In the survey we asked questions about perceived safety and evacuations during a hypothetical hurricane. The purpose of this analysis is to understand the role that hurricane intensity plays during hurricane evacuations. This is an advantage of stated preference questions since most of the respondents have not experienced catastrophic storms. If researchers rely on revealed preference data then evacuation behavior for relatively low intensity storms can be better understood, but forecasts beyond the range of historical experience may be in error.

To understand how people think that they will respond in various situations, each respondent was asked to respond to one hypothetical hurricane scenario. The scenarios were the same except the category of the hurricane varied with about 20 percent of the respondents being assigned a storm from each of the five Saffir-Simpson categories. To be certain that the respondents have the same understanding of the categories, the section of the survey began with an overview of the hurricane rating system and described the hypothetical storm:

> Next I'd like to know what you would do in case of a hurricane during the next hurricane season. The Atlantic hurricane season runs from June 1–November 30. Please consider the following information ... hurricanes are rated on a scale of 1 to 5. Category 1 is a minimal hurricane, 2 is moderate, 3 is extensive, 4 is extreme and 5 is catastrophic. Floyd was a category 4 hurricane, Bonnie was a category 3 and Dennis was a category 1. Suppose a category 5 hurricane is approaching NC. The hurricane has winds greater than 155 miles per hour and an expected storm surge greater than 18 feet above normal.

After hearing the scenario, the respondents were asked how safe they would feel and whether or not they would evacuate if they were faced with a hurricane watch, a voluntary evacuation, a mandatory evacuation, and a hurricane warning. Each of these terms was defined as part of the question. For example, the first question asked about a hurricane watch:

> A "hurricane watch" means that a hurricane poses a possible threat. If a hurricane watch is announced for this hurricane, how safe would you feel in your home? Would you feel very safe, somewhat safe, or not safe at all?

Fifty-five percent, 30 percent and 15 percent of respondents felt very safe, somewhat safe and not safe at all under a hurricane watch. There are statistically
significant differences in these frequencies across risk levels (i.e. storm
intensity). We then asked: "Would you evacuate your home to go someplace
safer?" Overall, 24 percent of respondents state that they would evacuate for the
hypothetical hurricane. Seven percent stated that they would evacuate for the
category 1 storm under a hurricane watch. Fifteen, 20, 29 and 51 percent state
that they would evacuate for category 2, 3, 4 and 5 storms under a hurricane
watch.

Respondents who evacuated for previous storms were asked to estimate the
amount of money they spent for lodging, food and beverages, travel, entertain-
ment, and other items during their period of evacuation. Of the 78 respondents
who evacuated the mean total evacuation cost is $436. The minimum is 0 and
the maximum is $2056. One type of empirical averting behavior study estimates
the determinants of averting behavior. A problem is the missing expenditure data
for those who do not exhibit averting behavior. While stated preference data can
be used to fill in the missing data at the averting behavior decision stage of the
analysis, this study was not designed as such. In order to present a model that
illustrates the issues in dichotomous choice models we topcode the cost data at
the seventy-fifth percentile of the distribution ($593) and replace the zero values
with the topcoded value. We use the same cost variable for the stated preference
evacuation.

The dichotomous choice of hurricane evacuation can be framed as a comparison of utility functions

$$v(h', m - c) \overset{>}{\underset{<}{=}} v(h^o, m) \tag{4.7}$$

where v is indirect utility, h is health status, m is income and c is cost. Households must compare a risky, low-cost state of the world, $h^o < h'$, with a low risk,
high-cost state of the world and choose whether to evacuate or not. The
probability of an evacuation is the probability that the difference in utility is
positive (or equal to zero)

$$\pi\Big(v(h', m - c) - v(h^o, m)\Big) \geq 0 \tag{4.8}$$

Haab and McConnell (2003) show how (4.8) can be estimated as a utility
difference.

The potential gains from data combination and joint estimation are illustrated
in Table 4.1 where we estimate the effects of risk, measured as storm intensity,
and cost on averting behavior (i.e., evacuation). We use the probit model
assuming a normal distribution for the difference in utility error term. In the first
model we focus on the revealed preference data. Since the revealed behavior is
associated with a single storm we are not able to assess the effects of risk on
behavior. The effect of cost is negative as predicted by economic theory. The
positive constant measures the utility difference between evacuation and staying

Table 4.1 Probit models of hurricane evacuation

Variable	RP		SP		RP-SP		RP-SP		RP-SP	
	Coeff.	t-stat.	Coeff.	t-stat.	Coeff.	t-stat.	Coeff.	t-stat.	Coeff.	t-stat.
Constant	3.233	6.82	−0.664	−1.91	0.146	0.45	0.156	0.44	2.814	4.26
Cost	−0.007	−8.65	−0.002	−3.46	−0.004	−9.66	−0.005	−7.55	−0.010	−7.36
SSHS2	–	–	0.566	1.67	0.775	2.11	0.923	2.49	0.725	1.57
SSHS3	–	–	0.772	2.35	0.985	2.77	1.107	3.17	0.884	1.97
SSHS4	–	–	1.083	3.28	1.262	4.11	1.508	4.54	1.441	2.99
SSHS5	–	–	1.637	5.20	1.907	5.54	2.293	5.71	2.170	4.48
SP	–	–	–	–	–	–	–	–	−3.638	−5.08
SP × Cost	–	–	–	–	–	–	–	–	0.007	5.47
ρ	–	–	–	–	–	–	0.279	2.32	0.438	3.62
LLF	−97.97		−127.45		−243.45		−240.98		−219.94	
Cases	275		275		275		275		275	
Periods	1		1		2		2		2	
	WTP	t-stat	WTP	t-stat	WTP	t-stat	WTP	t-stat	WTP	t-stat
SSHS1	–		−357.59	−1.34	37.30	0.46	33.74	0.46	287.83	5.87
SSHS2	–		−52.76	−0.27	235.09	3.80	232.85	4.28	362.02	8.87
SSHS3	–		58.38	0.35	288.86	5.24	272.62	5.51	378.21	9.44
SSHS4	437.11	24.15	226.13	1.66	359.56	13.57	359.03	12.37	435.26	30.19
SSHS5	–		524.84	5.77	524.19	11.89	528.53	13.09	509.85	13.87

home when faced with the risk of a hurricane. Since the coefficient on cost is a measure of the marginal utility of income, the ratio between the utility difference and marginal utility of income measures the willingness-to-pay. The willingness-to-pay to avoid the risk associated with a category 4 storm is $437.

The second model considers only the stated preference data. The obvious gain from the SP model is the ability to measure the effect of risk on the averting behavior decision. We include dummy variables to control for risk (SSHS = Saffir-Simpson Hurricane Scale). We find that increasing risk leads to increasing probability of evacuation. The effect of cost is negative but the coefficient is significantly lower in absolute value than the cost coefficient in the revealed preference model. This result suggests that respondents pay less attention to cost when making the hypothetical decision.

When estimating willingness-to-pay to avoid the change in health status from the storm event, the utility difference is the combination of the constant and the coefficients on the risk variables. Willingness-to-pay is not significantly different from zero for storms rated below category 4. The stated preference willingness-to-pay associated with a category 4 storm is only 48 percent of the revealed preference willingness-to-pay. This indicates bias in either the stated preference or the revealed preference data. Typically, analysts give the benefit of doubt to the revealed preference willingness-to-pay. However, since it is not possible for the willingness-to-pay associated with a category 5 storm to be estimated with the revealed preference data, $535 is the best available estimate.

In the third model of Table 4.1 we combine the data and jointly estimate the factors affecting both revealed and stated preference evacuation in a pooled model (i.e. assuming the decisions are independent across respondents). We find similar results to the separately estimated revealed preference model and stated preference model. The jointly estimated coefficient on the cost variable falls in between the separately estimated coefficients. The willingness-to-pay estimates for avoiding the four lowest storm categories are higher compared to the stated preference model. The major gain from the jointly estimated model is the increased econometric efficiency from a larger sample. Another gain may be decreased bias in the coefficient and willingness-to-pay estimates.

In the fourth model we estimate a random effects probit model. Coefficient and willingness-to-pay results are very similar to the pooled model suggesting the pooled model is sufficient. However, the coefficient on the ρ coefficient is positive and statistically significant indicating that a portion of the error term is constant across respondents. Accounting for this portion of the error term leads to lower standard errors on the risk coefficients.

In the fifth model of Table 4.1 we estimate the determinants of evacuation behavior while controlling for the hypothetical nature of the stated preference data with the SP dummy variable and the SP dummy variable interacted with the cost variable. Overall, the results are similar to the previous three models but important differences arise. First, the constant term is statistically significant when controlling for hypothetical data with the stated preference dummy variable. This indicates that respondents are less likely to state that they would evacuate relative to the actual situation which is consistent with the raw data where 29 percent evacuated for hurricane Floyd while 24 percent state they would evacuate for a category 4 storm. Second, the coefficient on the cost variable is statistically different for the revealed and stated preference data, as suggested by the estimates in the separately estimated models. Setting the stated preference dummy and interaction variables equal to zero, simulating revealed preference data, leads to statistically significant willingness-to-pay estimates for all of the risk levels. The category 4 willingness-to-pay estimate is not statistically different from the estimate in the revealed preference model, suggesting that the bias in all of the willingness-to-pay estimates that arose from the stated preference data has been resolved.

Frequency data

A limitation of revealed preference data for market demands is the lack of price variation and simultaneous equations. If one wished to estimate the effects of a government policy in a market, the analysis would be limited to changes in expenditures as prices of many goods and services exhibit little variation. When prices change it is necessary to deal with simultaneous equations models since the price change could be due to demand or supply changes. Environmental valuation with market goods arises with the averting behavior method, where consumers and households purchase goods that act as a line of defense with dealing with environmental problems. For example, purchases of a water filter or bottled water are substitutes for tap water contamination.

As an example of the price variation advantages of stated preferences we use data on seafood consumption with effects of fish kills and government programs from a phone-mail-phone survey of mid-Atlantic residents (Whitehead *et al.* 2003). The purpose of the survey was to estimate the costs of fish kills and benefits of government programs that might mitigate those costs. The theoretical benefits are the changes in consumer surplus that would be realized in different situations.

We conducted a phone-mail-phone survey of seafood eaters in the eastern parts of Maryland, North Carolina, and Virginia and all of Delaware during 1999. During the first phone telephone interview, conducted from June through November, we collected information on revealed and stated seafood demand under a variety of pricing scenarios. Respondents were first asked how many seafood meals they ate the previous month (revealed preference) and how many they would eat the next month (stated preference). They were asked how many seafood meals they would eat next month if seafood meal prices went up by one of four different prices ($1, $3, $5, $7) while all other food prices remain the same. Also they were asked how many seafood meals they would eat next month if price went down by one of four different prices ($1, $2, $3, $4) while all other food prices remain the same. Price changes were randomly assigned to respondents.

An information brochure was mailed to respondents who agreed to participate in the second telephone survey. The major part of the information is the brochure titled "What you should know about Pfiesteria." Each mail packet also included a combination of brochure inserts. In the hypothetical fish kill insert, respondents in North Carolina were asked to consider a hypothetical press release about a fish kill in the Neuse River near New Bern, NC. The wording for the hypothetical press release followed closely the wording of actual government press releases describing fish kill events. Another insert provided further information about fish kills and a proposed mandatory seafood inspection program. The final insert, "counter information" is intended to enforce the notion of the safety of seafood. About 80 percent of the sample received the Pfiesteria brochure and 40 percent received the counter information. About 20 percent received neither source of information. All respondents received either the major or minor fish kill scenario.

About three weeks after the information was mailed, interviewers contacted the respondents to the first survey. The main purpose of these questions is to determine if seafood demand and other variables change after receiving the informational inserts. Respondents were asked five additional seafood consumption questions: how much seafood they ate during the past month (revealed preference), how much they would eat next month, how much they would eat next month after the fish kill, how much they would eat next month after the fish kill and with the seafood inspection program and, finally, how much they would eat next month after the fish kill, with the seafood inspection program and a higher price for seafood meals ($1, $3, $5, or $7).

In this section we focus on North Carolinians who responded to both surveys (n=459). From the first survey the average number of seafood meals that respondents ate during the most recent month is 4.22. Respondents state that they will eat 4.30 meals during the next month. With a price increase respondents state they will eat 3.37 meals. With a price decrease respondents state they will eat 5.27 meals. In the second survey the number of seafood meals eaten during the past month is 3.59 (revealed) and the next month is 3.59 (stated). With a fish kill the number of meals falls to 2.76. With a mandatory seafood inspection program and a fish kill the number of meals is 3.46. With a mandatory seafood inspection program, a fish kill and higher seafood prices the number of meals is 2.76.

We use fixed effects and random effects Poisson panel data models

Fixed effects: $y_{it} = \alpha_i + \beta' x_t + \varepsilon_{it}$ $\hspace{4cm}$ (4.9)

Random effects: $y_{it} = \alpha + \beta' x_t + \gamma' z_i + \mu_i + \varepsilon_{it}$ $\hspace{2.5cm}$ (4.10)

The fixed effects model employs an implicit individual-specific constant term, α_i. The independent variables are those that change across time for each individual, x_t. The random effects model includes a common constant term, α, and allows estimation of the individual specific variables, z_i. If individual specific variables are correlated with the price and other terms then the coefficients on the random effects model coefficients may be inconsistent. An advantage of the fixed effects model is that it avoids this inconsistency. An advantage of the random effects model it that it allows estimation in the effects of individual specific variables. Random effects models can also be more efficient.

We present fixed and random effects model estimates in Table 4.2 for the first and second surveys separately and then combined. The first survey data has four observations for each respondent while the second survey data has five observations for each respondent. The average, or typical, prices of seafood at restaurants and at home were obtained from respondents during the survey. The seafood meal price for each individual is measured as the weighted average of the restaurant and home-cooked seafood meals. The average price of all meals is about $10. The randomly assigned seafood meal price changes are added to this price in the appropriate scenarios. In the random effects models we include income as the only individual specific variable. The mean of income is $51.39 (in thousands).

The first survey fixed effects model includes only the price and stated preference variables. The effect of price on quantity is negative, as expected. The coefficient on the stated preference variable is not statistically different from zero, which is consistent with the univariate summary of means across scenario. Consumer surplus and price elasticity estimates are calculated and presented at the bottom of Table 4.2. The consumer surplus per seafood meal is $14 and the price elasticity of demand is -0.28. The random effects model finds similar results. The consumer surplus and elasticity estimates are not significantly different from the fixed effects estimates. In addition to the price and stated preference coefficients we are able to estimate the effect of income on seafood meals. The income elasticity is 0.37.

The second survey models include dummy variables for minor and major fish kills, the seafood inspection program (SIP), the brochure, and counter information. There are five observations for each respondent. A limitation of the second survey is that there is only one price change question relative to two price change questions in the first survey. Plus the price change question is asked in conjunction with the seafood inspection program. Nevertheless, the fixed effects demand models are similar between the first and second surveys. The consumer surplus and elasticity estimates are no different. Since the fish kill and seafood inspection scenarios are introduced after the first two seafood consumption questions we are able to obtain estimates of their effects. The fish kill has a negative affect on consumption and the seafood inspection program has a positive effect. The fish kill decreases consumer surplus per meal by about $4 and the seafood inspection program increases it by about the same amount. The price elasticity of demand from the random effects model is about half the size, in absolute value, as that from the fixed effects model.

In the second survey random effects model we find some differences with the fixed effects model. The coefficient on the price variable is lower and this results in a consumer surplus per meal estimate which is almost 100 percent larger and the difference is statistically significant at the 0.05 level. Income, fish kill, brochure, and counter information results are similar. Since the brochure and

Table 4.2 Poisson seafood demand models

Variable	First survey				Second survey				First and second surveys			
	Fixed effects		Random effects		Fixed effects		Random effects		Fixed effects		Random effects	
	Coeff.	t-stat.	Coeff.	t-stat.	Coeff.	t-stat.	Coeff.	t-stat.	Coeff.	t-stat.	Coeff.	t-stat.
Constant	—	—	1.602	17.29	—	—	1.213	8.64	—	—	1.607	18.29
Price	-0.071	-14.73	-0.053	-13.51	-0.069	-8.46	-0.038	-6.64	-0.068	-16.68	-0.053	-14.70
Income	—	—	0.007	5.68	—	—	0.007	5.64	—	—	0.007	6.31
SP	0.037	1.41	0.037	0.57	0.001	0.02	0.001	0.00	0.024	1.13	0.024	0.41
Minor	—	—	—	—	-0.282	-6.38	-0.279	-3.30	-0.273	-6.93	-0.273	-5.50
Major	—	—	—	—	-0.244	-5.57	-0.248	-2.84	-0.276	-7.09	-0.276	-5.51
SIP	—	—	—	—	0.245	6.76	0.191	3.62	0.241	7.00	0.216	4.18
Brochure	—	—	—	—	—	—	0.098	0.35	0.083	1.96	0.084	4.11
Counter	—	—	—	—	—	—	-0.010	-0.14	-0.011	-0.30	-0.010	-0.60
Second survey	—	—	—	—	—	—	—	—	-0.241	-6.79	-0.242	-7.46
Alpha	—	—	0.419	13.22	—	—	0.562	14.49	—	—	0.432	12.98
LLF	-2060.00		-3776.97		-2462.96		-4186.54		-6038.48		-8053.85	
Cases	459		459		459		459		459		459	
Periods	4		4		5		5		9		9	
Consumer surplus per meal	14.17	14.73	18.92	13.51	14.40	8.46	26.32	6.64	14.72	16.68	18.91	14.70
Price elasticity	-0.28	-14.73	-0.21	-13.51	-0.28	-8.46	-0.15	-6.64	-0.27	-16.68	-0.21	-14.70

counter information treatments do not vary across the five seafood consumption questions in the second survey, the fixed effects model does not estimate coefficients for their effect. The random effects model finds that there are no differences in seafood consumption between respondents who received the information and those who did not. The stated preference coefficient in both models indicates no hypothetical bias is present in these data.

In the combined survey models we find results most similar to the first survey for consumer surplus and price elasticity. The additional observations lead to more precise estimates of several coefficients. In the fixed effects models we are now able to estimate coefficients for the information brochure and additional counter information. In both models we find that the brochure increases seafood consumption. A dummy variable for the second survey indicates that seafood consumption falls. Again, the stated preference coefficient in both models indicates no hypothetical bias is present in these data.

Conclusions

In this chapter we have illustrated some basic ways to combine and jointly estimate revealed and stated preference data with dichotomous and continuous dependent variables. These empirical examples illustrate some common problems with revealed and stated preference data: (1) revealed preference data does not allow estimation of parameters beyond historical experience and (2) stated preference behavior may be subject to hypothetical bias, although, hypothetical bias is not a foregone conclusion. The gains from data combination and joint estimation are the additional parameters introduced in the hypothetical scenarios and the ability to construct policy relevant willingness-to-pay estimates from those scenarios. Basic econometric modeling can be used to mitigate the hypothetical bias, allowing a model that enjoys the benefits of stated preference data without the costs. Our applications in this chapter illustrate joint estimation with the averting behavior method. However, the approach is not limited to this method. In fact, most applications with this type of joint estimation employ the travel cost method with recreation demand data. In Part III of this book we present a number of additional applications of stacked data.

References

Haab, T.C. and K.E. McConnell (2003) *Valuing Environmental and Natural Resources: The Econometrics of Non-market Valuation*, Cheltenham: Edward Elgar.
Whitehead, J.C. (2008) "Willingness to pay for hurricane evacuation cost insurance," *Southern Business and Economic Journal*, 31(3–4): 73–86.
Whitehead, J.C., T.C. Haab, and G. Parsons (2003) "Economic effects of Pfiesteria," *Ocean and Coastal Management*, 46(9): 845–858.

5   Combining dichotomous choice willingness to pay response and recreation demand data

Ju-Chin Huang

Introduction

Dichotomous choice willingness to pay (WTP) response and recreation trips are the two types of data most commonly collected for non-market valuation. In order to serve different purposes and conserve survey time, most surveys collect one or the other type of data but infrequently collect both. As discussed in Chapter 1, there are advantages of having both. They can be compared to ensure validity of data and they can be used in joint estimation to improve estimation efficiency. A distinct advantage of combining the two types of data, recognized by researchers in recent years, is that together they can be used to recover all parameters in the utility function and help subdivide the estimated total economic value into use and non-use values (e.g. Huang *et al.* 1997; Eom and Larson 2006). In this chapter, two applications are presented to illustrate a theoretically consistent joint estimation procedure, following Huang *et al.* (1997), and issues that may arise in combining the two types of data. A study that employs the joint estimation procedure in Eom and Larson (2006) is presented in Chapter 14.

Conceptual framework and empirical model

As seen in Chapter 2, an individual's response to dichotomous choice WTP questions and recreation trip decisions can be described in a unified utility theoretic framework. To be specific for the applications in this chapter, a utility theoretic framework, following Whitehead (1995), is outlined as follows. Suppose the interest is to estimate the economic value of some environmental quality change that can affect recreation trip decisions. Let $x(p, q, y, z)$ be the utility maximized, optimal demand for recreation trips that is a function of p (travel costs), q (environmental quality relevant to the trips), y (income), and z (individual and/or recreation site characteristics other than q). Let q_0 be the initial quality and q_1 be the degraded, new quality level. The scenario here is that there is an anticipated decrease in q in the future that the new $q=q_1<q_0$ unless certain action is taken. Define the expenditure function $m(p, q, z, u)$ as a function of p, q, z, and u (utility index). Let u_0 be the reference utility level at q_0. Then, the

WTP for maintaining the quality level at q_0 can be expressed as $m(p, q_1, z, u_0) - m(p, q_0, z, u_0)$. Substituting the reference level of utility $u_0 = v(p, q_0, y, z)$ into the expression, we have the Hicksian variation function:

$$s = m(p, q_1, z, v(p, q_0, y, z)) - y. \tag{5.1}$$

Comparative static analysis of the variation function helps analytically connect the WTP for quality change and the change in demand for recreation trips in response to the quality change. Differentiating the variation function with respect to income,

$$\partial s / \partial y = m_v v_y^0 - 1 = \gamma - 1, \tag{5.2}$$

Where $\gamma = m_v v_y^0$, m_v is the marginal cost of utility and v_y^0 is the marginal utility of income evaluated at q_0. If marginal cost of utility is equal to the inverse of the marginal utility of income or $\gamma = 1$, then there is no income effect on WTP. Differentiating the variation function with respect to p, it gives $\partial s / \partial p = m_p + m_v v_p^0$. Utilizing $\gamma = m_v v_y^0$ and applying Roy's identity and Shephard's lemma, it is seen that $\partial s / \partial p = x^h(\cdot, u_0) - \gamma x^m(p, q_0, y, z)$, where $x^h(\cdot)$ and $x^m(\cdot)$ are Hicksian and Marshallian demands, respectively. Replacing $x^h(\cdot)$ by $x^m(\cdot)$ at the optimum, we have

$$\partial s / \partial p = x^m(p, q_1, y, z) - \gamma x^m(p, q_0, y, z) = x_1 - \gamma x_0. \tag{5.3}$$

Hence, the marginal effect of price on willingness to pay for the quality change is associated with the trips taken at the different quality levels. If γ is close to 1, the (negative) price effect is equal to the change in number of trips taken due to the quality change. Rearranging the terms in (5.3), we have $x^m(p, q_1, y, z) = \partial s / \partial p + \gamma x^m(p, q_0, y, z)$. Empirically if we regress x_1 on x_0, the estimated coefficients are linked to the marginal effects of p and y on WTP.

The above analytical results serve as the basis to construct a likelihood function that combines the information of WTP response and recreation trips to estimate the parameters in the underlying utility function for welfare analysis. Assuming a linear approximation of the variation function and incorporating the analytical connections between s and x, an empirical model consisting of two equations is presented as follows. For simplicity, other variables such as individual and site characteristics are omitted from the presentation.

$$s = \alpha + \beta p + (\gamma - 1) y + \varepsilon_1, \tag{5.4}$$

$$x_1 = \beta + \gamma(x_0 + \varepsilon_2). \tag{5.5}$$

As seen, analytically the two equations share common parameters. The equality of parameters in the two equations, hence the theoretical consistency between the WTP response and the trip information, can be tested in the empirical analysis.

A joint distribution of s and x is assumed.

$$\begin{bmatrix} s \\ x_1 \end{bmatrix} \sim N\left(\begin{bmatrix} \alpha + \beta p + (\gamma - 1)y \\ \beta + \gamma x_0 \end{bmatrix}, \begin{bmatrix} \sigma_1^2 & \gamma\sigma_{12} \\ \gamma\sigma_{12} & \gamma^2\sigma_2^2 \end{bmatrix} \right), \tag{5.6}$$

where $\sigma_{12} = \rho/(\sigma_1\sigma_2)$. A twist in the derivation of the empirical model based on the joint distribution in (5.6) is that typically s is not observed. Rather, dichotomous responses (of yes or no) to a bid amount for a proposed quality change are elicited in surveys that we only know whether the WTP is greater than or less than the bid, often referred to as the single-bound WTP. It is also common to elicit a second yes-no response to a higher or lower bid following the response of yes or no to the first bid. If the underlying true WTP is assumed fixed and uninfluenced by the follow-up bid question, the two proposed bids serve as bounds of the true underlying WTP, the double-bound WTP, and an interval-data probit model can be used to analyze the data (Alberini 1995). It is also possible that survey respondents form two different WTP values when confronted with each of the two bid questions. Under this assumption, a bivariate probit model can be used to analyze the two discrete WTP responses from the same respondent (Cameron and Quiggin 1994). In a simulation study, Alberini (1995) shows that the simpler interval-data probit model approximates the bivariate probit model well and is often superior to the bivariate model. In this chapter, we utilize the interval-data probit model to analyze the double-bound WTP data.

To combine a single-bound or double-bound WTP response with the trip demand estimation in a likelihood function, an important additional step is to rewrite the joint distribution as the product of the distribution of s_i conditional on x_i and the distribution of x_i: $f(s_i, x_i) = f(s_i|x_i)f(x_i)$. The conditional distribution of s_i can be shown as follows:

$$s \mid x_1 \sim N\left(\alpha + \beta p + (\gamma - 1)y + \rho\sigma_1\left(\frac{x_1 - \beta - \gamma x_0}{\gamma\sigma_2} \right), (1 - \rho^2)\sigma_1^2 \right). \tag{5.7}$$

Given the conditional mean of s, a single-bound WTP response can be analyzed alone by a simple probit model and a double-bound WTP can be analyzed with an interval-data probit model. Define two indicator variables that $I_1 = 1$ if yes to the first bid and $I_1 = 0$ otherwise; $I_2 = 1$ if yes to the second bid and $I_2 = 0$ otherwise. Let t_1 and t_2 be the first and second bid values, respectively. The joint distribution of the discrete double-bound WTP responses and the trips can be written as follows:

$$P\left(yes, yes \mid x_1\right)^{I_1 I_2} P\left(yes, no \mid x_1\right)^{I_1(1-I_2)} P\left(no, yes \mid x_1\right)^{(1-I_1)I_2}$$

$$P\left(no, no \mid x_1\right)^{(1-I_1)(1-I_2)} f\left(x_1\right)$$

$$\tag{5.8}$$

$$= f\left(x_1\right) P\left(s \geq t_2 \mid x_1\right)^{I_1 I_2} P\left(t_1 \leq s < t_2 \mid x_1\right)^{I_1(1-I_2)} P\left(t_2 \leq s < t_1 \mid x_1\right)^{(1-I_1)I_2}$$

$$P\left(s < t_2 \mid x_1\right)^{(1-I_1)(1-I_2)}$$

where $f(x_1)$ is the density function of x_1. We are now ready to write out the log-likelihood function to jointly estimate the recreation trips and the double-bound WTP responses. A subscript i is added in the log-likelihood function to indicate multiple observations.

$$\log L = -\frac{n}{2}\log\left(2\pi\sigma_2^2\right) - \frac{1}{2}\sum_{i=1}^{n}\left(\frac{\frac{1}{\gamma}x_{1i} - \frac{\beta}{\gamma} - x_{0i}}{\sigma_2}\right)^2$$

$$+ \sum_{i=1}^{n}I_{1i}I_{2i}\log\left[\Phi(k_{2i})\right] + \sum_{i=1}^{n}I_{1i}\left(1 - I_{i2}\right)\log\left[\Phi(k_{2i}) - \Phi(k_{1i})\right]$$

$$+ \sum_{i=1}^{n}(1 - I_{1i})I_{2i}\log\left[\Phi(k_{1i}) - \Phi(k_{2i})\right] + \sum_{i=1}^{n}(1 - I_{1i})(1 - I_{2i})\log\left[\Phi(k_{2i})\right], \quad (5.9)$$

where $\Phi(\cdot)$ is the standard normal cumulative distribution function;

$$k_{1i} = \frac{\dfrac{-t_{1i} + \alpha + \beta p_i + (\gamma - 1)y_i}{\sigma_1} + \rho\dfrac{\frac{1}{\gamma}x_{1i} - \frac{\beta}{\gamma} - x_{0i}}{\sigma_2}}{\left(1 - \rho^2\right)^{\frac{1}{2}}}; \quad (5.10)$$

$$k_{2i} = \frac{\dfrac{-t_{2i} + \alpha + \beta p_i + (\gamma - 1)y_i}{\sigma_1} + \rho\dfrac{\frac{1}{\gamma}x_{1i} - \frac{\beta}{\gamma} - x_{0i}}{\sigma_2}}{\left(1 - \rho^2\right)^{\frac{1}{2}}}. \quad (5.11)$$

The above log-likelihood function can be easily simplified to analyze the single-bound WTP data by taking out all references to I_2 and k_2 (see Huang *et al.* 1997). It incorporates the analytical connections between the WTP response and trip information; i.e. the parameters in the s and x functions are constrained according to the underlying utility function. To test the consistency of data, the likelihood function can be estimated without the parameter constraints between s and x. Note that the above likelihood function can be difficult to estimate. It is recommended to estimate separately the s and x function first, then use the parameter estimates as the starting values for the joint estimation. The standard travel cost models can be estimated to derive the use value of quality change associated with recreation trips. Along with the estimated s function, we can divide the estimated total value into use and non-use values.

Application 1: willingness to pay for restoring water quality

The first illustrative application is based on a telephone survey conducted in 1995, regarding recreation trips to the Pamlico and Albemarle Sounds in Eastern

North Carolina (Huang *et al.* 1997). The telephone interviews were computer-assisted and conducted by trained interviewers. There were two versions of the survey that differed by the definition of the included studied area. In this application, the data from the version that collected trip information to Pamlico Sound are used. Survey respondents were asked the number of trips taken and anticipated number of trips to be taken in the following year. The valuation scenario was to restore the deteriorated water quality to the 1981 level. Both the anticipated number of trips under restored level of water quality and the WTP to restore the water quality were elicited. Four initial bid values ($100, $200, $300, $400) were chosen based on pretests. Each survey respondent was randomly assigned one of the bid values in the first discrete response WTP question. Depending on their response of yes or no to the first WTP question, a second discrete response WTP question, with a new bid value that was either twice or half of the first bid value, was asked. The final sample size for analysis is 279. Table 5.1 provides summary statistics of the relevant variables. There are three trip variables: the *ex post* number of trips taken in 1995, the *ex ante* anticipated number of trips in the following year, and the *ex ante* anticipated number of trips in the following year with restored water quality. The travel cost variable measures the own-price of a recreation trip, including time and travel costs of a round trip to the Pamlico Sound. Approximately 40 percent of respondents responded yes to the first bid and 27 percent responded yes to the second bid.

One important issue is how to measure the change in number of trips in response to the proposed quality change. One may compute the difference between the *ex post* trips taken in the surveyed year and the *ex ante* stated trips under improved quality. Alternatively, we may compute the difference between the *ex ante* planned trips in the following year and the stated trips under improved quality. The former utilizes both the revealed and stated data, while the latter uses solely the stated data. As seen in the analytical model presented above, assuming a unified underlying utility function, the change in trips is analytically linked to the WTP for the quality change. Empirically it can be

Table 5.1 Water quality study: summary statistics[1]

Variable	Mean	Standard deviation	Minimum	Maximum
Travel cost (p)	86.675	56.274	6.946	356.058
Travel cost–substitute site (pSub)				
Ex post trips (q)	1.294	4.061	0	1
Ex ante trips (q)	1.735	4.478	0	1
Ex ante trips (q^*)	2.470	5.416	0	1
Income (y)	31.479	21.518	5	85
Bid 1 (t_1)	222.939	115.260	100	400
Bid 2 (t_2)	229.212	194.755	50	800
YES1 (I_1)	0.394	0.490	0	1
YES2 (I_2)	0.269	0.444	0	1

Note
1 Sample size = 279.

tested in the joint estimation to determine which of the two trip change measures (or both) will be theoretically consistent with the WTP response to the proposed quality change. In other words, the consistency of combining the revealed and stated trip data is a testable hypothesis in the joint estimation.

We first estimate three travel cost models to examine respectively the *ex post* trips, *ex ante* trips, and *ex ante* trips under improved water quality. The results are given in Table 5.2. The travel cost variable is negative and significant in all three trip equations. There is also a significant, positive, income effect in the demand for recreation trips. The average consumer surplus per trip ranges from $45 to $79 across the three models. Combined with the predicted number of trips per person, the average per person annual consumer surplus of recreation trips to the Pamlico Sound are computed and given at the bottom of Table 5.2. Depending on which measure of trip change is used, the increased recreation value from the improved water quality is about $81 (=$165–$84) or $125 (=$165–$40).

Next we combine the trip change and discrete WTP responses and estimate the log-likelihood function in (5.9). A few variations of the model are estimated. First, to compute the trip changes in response to the proposed water quality change, we use two alternative measures of trips as the baseline to be compared to the stated number of trips under restored water quality: one baseline trip measure is the *ex post* number of trips taken in the current year and the other is the *ex ante* stated number trips to be taken in the following year. Second, to test for compatibility between the trip change and WTP responses, we estimate both the unconstrained model that allows all parameters in the likelihood function to be estimated freely and the constrained model that imposes the parameter equalities between s and x as indicated in (5.9). Four joint models are estimated and results are presented in Table 5.3.

The first two estimated models in Table 5.3 incorporate the *ex post* number of trips taken in the survey year as the baseline (x_0) for comparison with the stated number of trips under restored water quality. In both the unconstrained and constrained models, all parameter estimates are significant with expected signs. The correlation between s and x (i.e. ρ) is significant. The average WTP estimates based on the two models are around $108 and $103, respectively. To examine the legitimacy of parameter constraints, a likelihood ratio test is constructed based on the log-likelihood values of these two models. The parameter constraints are rejected at $\alpha=0.01$ ($\chi^2=14.33$, d.f.$=2$), which implies potential incompatibility between the trip change and the WTP responses.

The last two columns of Table 5.3 report both the unconstrained and constrained models using the *ex ante* stated number of trips for the following year as the baseline (x_0) to compute the trip change in response to the proposed water quality change. All estimates are significant with expected signs. The estimated average WTP from the two models are around $108 and $107, respectively. The likelihood ratio test for parameter constraints are rejected at $\alpha=0.05$ but cannot be rejected at $\alpha=0.01$ ($\chi^2=8.76$, d.f.$=2$). In a relative sense, the trip change computed based on the stated future trips seems more compatible to the WTP responses than the trip change computed based on the *ex post* trips taken in the

Table 5.2 Water quality study: travel cost models (negative binomial regression)[1,2]

Variable	Ex post trips (q_0)	Ex ante trips (q_0)	Ex ante trips (q_1)
Constant	0.479 (0.621)	0.880* (0.454)	1.189*** (0.303)
Travel cost	−0.022** (0.009)	−0.016*** (0.006)	−0.013*** (0.003)
Income	0.041** (0.021)	0.027* (0.014)	0.021** (0.010)
Travel cost–sub site			
α (dispersion parameter)	11.786*** (2.234)	7.193*** (1.152)	4.057*** (0.518)
LLF	−273.625	−367.944	−487.183
χ^2	956.222	1024.898	1103.423
Consumer surplus per trip	45.566*** (19.130)	60.956*** (21.317)	78.697*** (19.806)
Predicted trips	0.880*** (0.209)	1.380*** (0.263)	2.098*** (0.272)
Annual consumer surplus	40.077*** (17.893)	84.099*** (30.432)	165.140*** (43.472)

Notes
1 Standard error are reported in parentheses.
2 *, **, *** indicate significance at the 0.10, 0.05, and 0.01 levels, respectively.

survey year. The findings are consistent with the results in Huang *et al.* (1997) that utilized both versions of the same survey. As seen in Table 5.2, the estimated use value based on the *ex ante* stated trips in the following year is $81. Comparing it to the estimated total WTP from the joint model in column 4 of Table 5.3, the non-use value can be estimated to be around $26.

In this application, we utilize the revealed recreation trip information, the contingent trip behavior, and the information of dichotomous choice WTP with a follow up. In addition to improved estimation efficiency, collecting both revealed and stated preference data from the same survey respondents enable us to test the compatibility of the revealed and stated data, and to decompose the total WTP into use and non-use values. Note that the compatibility of revealed and stated data is directly influenced by the design of the valuation scenario. In the next application, we show an example where combining revealed and stated preference data may not be appropriate.

Application 2: economic values of beach nourishment

The second application is based on a telephone survey conducted in 2004 to investigate how beach nourishment affects visits to the ocean front beaches in five counties along the southeastern North Carolina (NC) coast (from the Beaufort/Morehead City area in Carteret County to the South Carolina border) (Herstine *et al.* 2005). There are in total 17 beaches in the studied coastal area. The sampling population was the residents within 120 miles of the studied area. A beach nourishment project to widen the beaches through periodic sand replenishments was presented to survey respondents. The change in beach visits due to the beach nourishment project was elicited. An annual parking permit at all beaches along the southeastern NC coast was introduced as the payment vehicle to derive the WTP for the nourishment project. The dichotomous choice WTP with a follow-up questioning format was used in the contingent valuation questions. Similar to the Pamlico Sound study, this survey collected data on the number of beach trips taken in the previous year (*ex post* trips), as well as stated (*ex ante*) future beach trips with and without the proposed beach nourishment project in the survey year. Travel costs were computed the same way as those in the Pamlico Sound study. Socio-economic information of survey respondents was also elicited. In addition, information on alternative beaches visited by the survey respondents was elicited in the survey to enable the construction of travel costs of substitute sites.

Table 5.4 gives the data summary. The average number of beach trips in the previous year is 6.9 trips, while the average anticipated number of trips in the survey year is 9.5 trips. Although it is not statistically significant, the difference between the *ex post* trips taken in the previous year and stated future trips seems large (2.6 trips) and has no obvious explanation. The average stated number of trips with beach nourishment is 10.5 trips. The average one trip increase in response to the proposed beach nourishment project in future visits to the studied area seems plausible. Introducing an annual parking permit as the payment

Table 5.3 Water quality study: Joint estimation of trip demand and double-bound willingness to pay[1,2]

Model	Ex post (q_0) and ex ante (q_1) trips		Ex ante (q_0, q_1) trips	
	Unconstrained	Constrained	Unconstrained	Constrained
$\hat{\alpha}$ (CVM)	110.304*** (30.971)	193.937*** (20.745)	113.322*** (30.928)	172.373*** (18.723)
$\hat{\beta}$ (CVM)	−0.523 (0.327)	−0.686*** (0.140)	−0.539* (0.328)	−0.404*** (0.101)
$\hat{\beta}$ (Trips)	−0.887*** (0.166)	–	−0.451*** (0.109)	–
$\hat{\gamma}$ (CVM)	3.918*** (0.865)	0.870*** (0.030)	3.160*** (0.869)	0.883*** (0.019)
$\hat{\gamma}$ (Trips)	0.883*** (0.032)	–	0.885*** (0.020)	–
$\hat{\sigma}_1$	229.959*** (16.433)	239.15*** (17.192)	229.267*** (16.371)	234.000*** (16.724)
$\hat{\sigma}_2$	2.770*** (0.117)	2.776*** (0.118)	1.846*** (0.078)	1.846*** (0.078)
$\hat{\rho}$	−0.138*** (0.062)	−0.124*** (0.062)	−0.101 (0.064)	−0.103 (0.063)
LLF	−1,049.286	−1,056.452	−937.212	−941.592
Likelihood ratio		14.332		8.760
WTP	107.680*** (16.073)	102.810*** (16.692)	108.146*** (16.022)	106.869*** (16.264)
Predicted trips (q^*)	2.47	2.28	2.47	2.42

Notes
1 Standard errors are reported in parentheses.
2 *, **, *** indicate significance at the 0.10, 0.05, and 0.01 levels, respectively.

vehicle to derive the WTP for the proposed beach nourishment project can be problematic. Since parking is related to access to beaches, there is a possibility of protest bids against imposing a fee to beach access. Further, it might not be plausible to assume one parking permit to be used in all beaches in five counties. Without WTP responses to various inclusions of beaches, it is not possible to examine scope effects. The issues surrounding the use of an annual parking permit as the payment vehicle can result in incompatibility of trip change in response to beach nourishment and the discrete choice WTP responses in joint estimation.

Similar to the Pamlico Sound study, we estimate three travel cost models for the *ex post* trips in the previous year, stated future trips, and stated future trips with beach nourishment. The travel cost of a substitute area is included in all models. The estimation results and corresponding consumer surplus measures are presented in Table 5.5. All coefficient estimates are significant with expected signs. The trip demand equations are downward sloping with positive income effects; the higher the travel cost of the substitute area, the higher is the demand for trips at the studied area. The estimated per trip consumer surplus is between $140 to $160; the estimated annual consumer surpluses from the three models are $1039, $1274, and $1379, respectively. As discussed in the previous application, the change in consumer surplus of beach trips can be computed by subtracting either one of the first two estimated consumer surplus measures from the last one; hence the estimated change in consumer surplus is either $105 or $341, depending on the choice of the base model for comparison.

We again show four models that jointly estimate s and x. The first two models employ the ex post trips as x_0 in the x equation. Also, the theoretically consistent parameter restrictions between s and x are imposed in one of the two models. The other two models, one with parameter constraints, use the stated future trips as x_0. The results of joint estimation are presented in Table 5.6.

The first two columns of Table 5.6 present the two models that incorporate the *ex post* number of trips taken in the previous year as the baseline (x_0) for

Table 5.4 Beach nourishment study: summary statistics[1]

Variable	Mean	Standard deviation	Minimum	Maximum
Travel cost (p)	92.361	60.701	2.814	218.239
Travel cost−substitute site (pSub)	201.912	55.983	64.944	401.025
Ex post trips (q)	6.937	10.663	0	70
Ex ante trips (q)	9.537	12.231	0	75
Ex ante trips (q^*)	10.547	13.102	1	75
Income (y)	59.117	26.523	10	100
Bid 1 (t_1)	25.288	12.443	10	40
Bid 2 (t_2)	26.939	22.515	5	50
YES1 (I_1)	0.488	0.500	0	1
YES2 (I_2)	0.516	0.500	0	1

Note
1 Sample size = 521.

Table 5.5 Beach nourishment study: travel cost models (negative binomial regression)[1,2]

Variable	Ex post trips (q_0)	Ex ante trips (q_0)	Ex ante trips (q_1)
Constant	1.504*** (0.154)[a]	2.097*** (0.127)	2.201*** (0.123)
Travel cost	−0.006*** (0.001)	−0.007*** (0.001)	−0.007*** (0.001)
Income	0.008*** (0.002)	0.006*** (0.002)	0.005*** (0.002)
Travel cost–sub site	0.002** (0.001)	0.002** (0.001)	0.002** (0.001)
α (dispersion parameter)	1.355*** (0.105)	0.908*** (0.079)	0.848*** (0.076)
χ^2	3742.54	3638.05	3810.96
Consumer surplus per trip	$158.02*** (24.78)	$142.67*** (17.09)	$140.08*** (15.86)
Predicted trips	6.57*** (0.32)	8.93*** (0.39)	9.85*** (0.42)
Annual consumer surplus	$1,038.82*** (167.48)	$1,274.08*** (160.30)	$1,379.39*** (165.69)

Notes
1 Standard errors are reported in parentheses.
2 *, **, *** indicate significance at the 0.10, 0.05, and 0.01 levels, respectively.

Table 5.6 Beach nourishment study: joint estimation of trip demand and double-bound willingness to pay[1,2]

Model	Ex post (q_0) and ex ante (q_1) trips		Ex ante (q_0, q_1) trips	
	Unconstrained	Constrained	Unconstrained	Constrained
$\hat{\alpha}$	23.290*** (4.523)	23.596*** (4.658)	24.025*** (4.514)	24.070*** (4.522)
$\hat{\beta}$(CVM)	−0.003 (0.024)	−0.007 (0.023)	−0.011 (0.023)	−0.015 (0.023)
$\hat{\beta}$(Trips)	−3.308*** (0.416)	–	−0.711*** (0.196)	–
$\hat{\gamma}$(CVM)	1.028*** (0.057)	0.869*** (0.019)	1.029*** (0.058)	0.947*** (0.009)
$\hat{\gamma}$(Trips)	0.971*** (0.027)	–	0.972*** (0.012)	–
$\hat{\delta}_1$(pSub)	0.014 (0.027)	0.058*** (0.025)	0.014 (0.027)	0.038 (0.024)
$\hat{\sigma}_1$	25.975*** (1.079)	26.266*** (1.093)	25.959*** (1.078)	26.028*** (1.080)
$\hat{\sigma}_2$	7.040*** (0.218)	7.588*** (0.236)	3.519*** (0.109)	3.561*** (0.110)
$\hat{\rho}$	−0.100** (0.051)	−0.059 (0.054)	−0.087* (0.051)	−0.065 (0.051)
LLF	−2,615.365	−2,659.263	−2,254.508	−2,262.222
Likelihood ratio		87.796		15.428
WTP	27.545*** (1.206)	26.944*** (1.301)	27.513*** (1.205)	27.256*** (1.218)
Predicted trips (q^*)	10.55	7.99	10.55	10.08

Notes
1 Standard errors are reported in parentheses.
2 *, **, *** indicate significance at the 0.10, 0.05, and 0.01 levels, respectively.

comparison with the stated number of trips under beach nourishment. The correlation between s and x (i.e. ρ) is significant in the unconstrained model. The average WTP estimates based on the two models are around $27. The likelihood ratio test is performed to examine the parameter restrictions between s and x. The parameter constraints are rejected at $\alpha = 0.01$ ($\chi^2 = 87.80$, d.f. $= 2$) that the data in the trip change and the WTP responses are not compatible.

The last two columns of Table 5.6 report the unconstrained and constrained models using the *ex ante* stated number of trips for the upcoming year as the baseline (x_0) to compute the trip change in response to the proposed beach nourishment project. The estimated average WTP from the two models are around $10. The likelihood ratio test for parameter constraints are again rejected ($\chi^2 = 15.43$, d.f. $= 2$), indicating incompatibility between the trip change data and the WTP responses. The incompatibility is also evidenced as the estimated change in the annual consumer surplus (the use value) is more than ten-fold of the estimated total WTP for beach nourishment. In this application, the trip change data and the WTP responses cannot be analyzed jointly. The imposition of parking permits can have implications on beach access that is not the ideal payment vehicle to value beach nourishment. Further, aggregating trips from all beaches in southeastern NC to estimate one travel cost model might have reduced the precision of estimation. Unfortunately there is no sufficient information in the survey to estimate travel cost models at different levels of aggregation to test for scope effects.

Conclusion

In this chapter we detail the analytical and econometric models behind the joint estimation of the travel cost model and the discrete choice WTP responses. As discussed, one advantage of joint estimation is enabling decomposition of total WTP into use and non-use values. Two applications are presented to demonstrate the joint estimation and computation of welfare measures. As seen, the compatibility of the two types of data is essential to the success of joint estimation. When collecting data to be used for joint estimation, special care must be taken to design the survey with joint estimation as a goal and to pretest the survey design to ensure data compatibility.

References

Alberini, Anna (1995) "Efficiency vs bias of willingness to pay estimates: Bivariate and interval data models," *Journal of Environmental Economics and Management*, 29(2): 169–180.

Cameron, Trudy A. and John Quiggin (1994) "Estimation using contingent valuation Data from a 'dichotomous choice with follow-up' questionnaire," *Journal of Environmental Economics and Management*, 27(3): 218–234.

Eom, Young-Sook and Douglas M. Larson (2006) "Improving environmental valuation estimates through consistent use of multiple information," *Journal of Environmental Economics and Management*, 52(1): 501–516.

Herstine, Jim, Jeffery Hill, Bob Buerger, John Whitehead, and Carla Isom (2005) "Determination of recreation demand for federal shore protection study area: Overview and
methodology," final report prepared for The U.S. Army Corps of Engineers, Wilmington District, online, available at: www.appstate.edu/ ~whiteheadjc/research/usace.pdf.

Huang, Ju-Chin, Timothy C. Haab, and John C. Whitehead (1997) "Willingness to pay
for quality improvements: Can revealed and stated preference data be combined?"
Journal of Environmental Economics and Management, 34(3): 240–255, 1997.

Whitehead, John C. (1995) "Willingness to pay for quality improvements: Comparative
statics and interpretation of contingent valuation results," *Land Economics*, 71(2):
207–215.

6 Multiple choice discrete data joint estimation

John C. Whitehead

Introduction

For many researchers in other fields (i.e. transportation and marketing), the use of "attribute-based methods" (Holmes and Adamowicz 2003) is synonymous (although inaccurate) with data combination and joint estimation in environmental economics. Choice experiments have become a popular approach to estimating the value of environmental amenities, especially in the context of recreation choices. There are other sources available for description on choice experiment survey design and analysis (Louviere *et al.* 2000). In this book, we recognize that the empirical methods developed in the transportation, marketing and (later) environmental economics literatures can also be used to jointly estimate data other than that elicited in choice experiments. In this chapter we provide two illustrations. First, revealed preference recreation site selection choices are often elicited during the recreation season with on-site surveys. Revealed preference data can be gathered on the total number of trips taken to that point. In order to estimate seasonal trips, stated preference trip data can be elicited for the rest of the season. In another application we illustrate how dichotomous choice contingent valuation for site access can be combined with recreation site selection data in order to increase the range of costs considered by respondents and generate gains from joint estimation.

Econometric model

Random utility theory is the basis for models involving joint estimation of revealed preference (RP) and stated preference (SP) discrete choices:

$$U_{ij} = v_{ij} + \varepsilon_{ij}$$
$$= \beta' x_{ij} + \varepsilon_{ij} \tag{6.1}$$

where U_{ij} is the utility individual i receives from alternative j, $i = 1, \ldots, I, j = 1, \ldots, J$, $v_{ij} = \beta' x_{ij}$ is the systematic portion of utility, β is a vector of parameters and x_{ij} is a vector of variables specific to the choice, and ε is the random error. The probability of individual i choosing alternative j is

$$\pi_{ij} = \Pr\left(v_{ij} + \varepsilon_{ij} > v_{ik} + \varepsilon_{ik}; \forall k \in J\right) \tag{6.2}$$

When the random errors are independent and identically distributed (IID) Gumbel errors, the multinomial logit (MNL) model results

$$\pi_{ij} = \frac{\exp(\mu\beta'x_{ij})}{\displaystyle\sum_{j=1}^{J}\exp(\mu\beta'x_{ij})} \tag{6.3}$$

where π_{ij} is the probability that individual i chooses site j and μ is the scale factor which is inversely related to the variance of the error term (Swait and Louiviere 1993).

Since both revealed and stated preference data follow the theoretical choice framework above, the MNL model can be used to combine and jointly estimate revealed and stated preference data. Suppose the MNL is used to estimate the probability of the RP choice of alternative j, π_{Rij},

$$\pi_{Rij} = \frac{\exp(\mu_R\beta'_R x_{ij})}{\displaystyle\sum_{j=1}^{J}\exp(\mu_R\beta'_R x_{ij})} \tag{6.4}$$

where β_R is the vector of RP parameters and μ_R is the RP scale parameter. With identical elements in the x_{ij} vector, a similar model results when the MNL is used to estimate the SP choice probabilities

$$\pi_{Sij} = \frac{\exp(\mu_S\beta'_S x_{ij})}{\displaystyle\sum_{j=1}^{J}\exp(\mu_S\beta'_S x_{ij})} \tag{6.5}$$

When RP or SP data are estimated separately the scale parameter is arbitrarily set equal to one. When RP and SP data are stacked and estimated jointly, it is common for the error terms that result from the different data to have unequal variance leading to unequal scale parameters. When $\mu_R = 1$ it is typical for the SP data to have a higher variance due to the unfamiliarity of the choice task, $0 < \mu_S < 1$. The difference in the scale parameter will cause the MNL coefficients to differ.

In these applications we estimate the relative scale factor using the joint estimation procedure described in Hensher *et al.* (2005) and implemented with NLOGIT 4.0 (Greene 2007). The procedure involves construction of an artificial nested logit model with twice as many choice alternatives as actually observed. In other words, each respondent's RP (SP) observation is also allowed to choose from the SP (RP) alternatives. The variance of the RP nest is constrained equal to one while the variance of the SP alternatives is allowed to diverge from one. The nested logit model scales the SP coefficients so that the RP and SP data can be combined and jointly estimated.

Each variance of the error term is an inverse function of the individual scale factor

$$\sigma^2 = \frac{\pi^2}{6\mu^2} \tag{6.6}$$

When the scale parameter for the RP data is set equal to one, $1 = 1/\mu_R$, the nested logit model will estimate the relative scale factor for the SP data as the inclusive value for the SP data.

$$\theta_S = \frac{\sigma_S^2}{\sigma_R^2} = \frac{1/\mu_S^2}{1/\mu_R^2} \tag{6.7}$$

Random utility models can be used to estimate a variety of willingness-to-pay values. Haab and McConnell (2003) show that the willingness to pay for the elimination of an alternative from the choice set is

$$WTP(j) = \frac{\ln\left(1 - prob(j)\right)}{\beta_C} \tag{6.8}$$

where $prob(j)$ is the unconditional probability of choosing alternative j and β_C is the coefficient on the cost variable which measures the marginal utility of income. The willingness-to-pay for a change in a characteristic across all alternatives is

$$WTP(\Delta q) = \frac{\Delta q \beta_q}{\beta_C} \tag{6.9}$$

where Δq is the change in the alternative characteristic and β_q is the coefficient on the characteristic variable (Haab and McConnell 2003).

Augmenting in-season site selection data

One limitation of revealed preference data is the relative inefficiency of data collection. Oftentimes, a revealed preference cross-section survey will collect only one data point. Cross-section, time series (i.e. panel) surveys collect more data from each respondent under possibly different conditions when allowing time for changes in behavior. However, this significantly increases the costs of data collection and panel data are prone to a significant loss of respondents potentially leading to sample selection problems. Supplementing the single data point from a cross-section survey with one, or several, stated preference questions can significantly increase the sample size. These additional stated preference choice occasions can be combined with revealed preference data to provide more information about the preferences of each individual in the sample. More information from each respondent can lead to increased econometric efficiency.

Many recreation data sets are gathered on-site within the recreation season. In order to aggregate economic value, estimates of seasonal or annual trips are needed. Seasonal trip estimates can be obtained by combining revealed preference trips during the pre-interview portion of the season and stated preference questions about the remainder of the season. In this section we combine these types of data in a random utility model of recreational fishing choice and investigate the effects of data combination on willingness-to-pay per trip for site access and catch.

We use data from an intercept survey of for-hire recreational anglers that was collected as part of an economic study of the Atlantic Intracoastal Waterway in North Carolina (Herstine 2007). Funding to complete the intercept survey never materialized and this component of the study is incomplete and has not been reported previously. Nevertheless, the data is suitable to illustrate the gains from joint estimation with data collection during an in-season survey. Two-hundred fifty-three surveys were conducted from June to November in 2006. Two hundred and thirteen completed surveys are used in this analysis. The average annual household income of the interviewed angler is $68000 and the average number of years schooling is 15. The typical angler is married with a household size of three. Eighty-seven percent of the anglers are male and the average age is 39.

We asked a number of questions about the trip on which the angler was interviewed. Fifty-seven percent of the trips were part of an overnight visit to the North Carolina coast. Fishing was the primary reason for 73 percent of the trips. Eighty-eight percent of the trips are charter trips with the rest being party (i.e. head) boat trips. The average number of passengers on each trip was almost nine. On average, anglers caught two mackerel (i.e. king and Spanish mackerel), three coastal migratory pelagic fish (i.e. dolphin, tuna and wahoo) and less than one bottom fish (i.e. grouper and snapper). Anglers caught almost two uncategorized species of fish per trip.

We consider four different fishing launch sites in three regions of the North Carolina coast. Almost half of all interviewed trips originate from the Outer Banks. In the northern, more populated, portion of the Outer Banks, trips originating from Manteo and Oregon Inlet represent 36 percent of all trips. In the southern part of the Outer Banks, 12 percent of all trips originate from Hatteras Village. Eleven percent of all trips originate from Atlantic Beach and Morehead City on the central North Carolina coast. Forty-two percent of all trips originate from Carolina Beach on the southern portion of the North Carolina coast.

Forty-six percent of all angler trips are between three and 40 miles offshore, 27 percent of all trips involved fishing no more than three miles offshore (i.e. inshore), and 27 percent of all trips fished more than 40 miles from shore. We define the choice set dependent on three characteristics of the trip: launch location, offshore distance and charter or party boat trip. Twenty-eight percent of all trips are inshore charter trips that originate from Carolina Beach. Twenty-one percent of all trips are charter trips that originate from the northern

Outer Banks and fish between three and 40 miles from shore. Fifteen percent of all trips are charter trips that originate from the northern Outer Banks and fish more than 40 miles from shore. The rest of the trip combinations represent less than 10 percent of the sample.

The unit of analysis in the demand model is the number of trips in each county location. The RP trip question is: "Including this trip, how many saltwater recreational fishing trips have you taken in this county since Memorial Day?" Respondents are asked to separate these trips into charter trips and party boat trips with the next two questions: "How many of these saltwater trips are charter boat trips? How many of these saltwater trips are party boat trips?" Respondents are then asked for the number of trips that they plan to take during the rest of the season in the intercept county: "How many more saltwater recreational fishing trips do you plan to take in this county from now until Thanksgiving?"

In total, respondents take almost two fishing trips in the intercepted county with averages of 1.17 RP charter trips and 0.62 SP charter trips. Respondents take averages of 0.17 RP party boat trips and 0.02 SP party boat trips in the intercepted county. The total number of trips used in the empirical analysis is 418. Note that the data are incomplete in that it would be useful to have all of the anglers' fishing trips in the sample. Notably, we are missing charter and party boat trips taken outside of the county of intercept.

We estimate RP, SP and joint RP-SP logit models. The RP model is estimated with 212 anglers who took 282 trips from the intercepted county from the beginning of the fishing season to the date of the intercept survey. The SP model is estimated with 96 anglers who plan to take 136 trips from the intercepted county over the rest of the fishing season. One hundred eighty-six anglers report zero planned trips. The jointly estimated model combines the RP and SP data and is estimated with 212 anglers who took or plan to take 418 trips.

Each model includes cost and quality characteristics for all of the trips in the choice set. The travel cost variable is measured as $f + cd + \gamma w(d/mph)$, where f is the charter or party boat fee, c is the cost per mile driven (\$0.37/mile), d is round-trip distance, γ is the opportunity cost of time (0.33), w is the hourly wage rate estimated as household income divided by 2000 hours worked and mph is miles per hour (50). Distance is measured using the ZIPFIP correction (i.e. a 10 percent increase in North Carolina) for "great circle" (i.e. straight line) distances from the home zip code to the launch site (Hellerstein *et al.* 1993). The mean of the travel cost component of the trip cost variable across all alternatives and trips ($n = 4664$) is \$269 with a range of \$1 to \$979. The conditional mean of charter/party boat fee at each site/mode/distance alternative is included as an additional cost variable, f. The mean fee across all alternatives and trips is \$199 with a range of \$81 to \$297. The travel cost variable varies across anglers due to the individual variation in distance and household income. The remaining potential independent variables do not vary across individuals. We consider a very simple model with only site-mode specific mean mackerel catch and coastal migratory pelagic fish (tuna, dolphin, wahoo) catch as independent trip quality variables. The estimation results are reported in Table 6.1.

Table 6.1 Conditional logit site choice models

	RP		SP		RP-SP	
	Coeff.	*t-ratio*	*Coeff.*	*t-ratio*	*Coeff.*	*t-ratio*
Travel cost	−0.007	−7.65	−0.006	−4.50	−0.006	−8.75
King and Spanish mackerel catch	0.141	5.60	0.230	6.23	0.149	7.80
Tuna, dolphin, wahoo catch	0.278	9.81	0.327	7.74	0.266	11.18
θ_S	–	–	–	–	1.269	19.86
Log-likelihood	−622.53		−288.41		−1188.82	
R^2	0.08		0.12		0.31	
Cases	212		96		212	
Choices	11		11		11	
Trips	282		136		418	

Examining all three models, the RP, SP and jointly estimated RP-SP logit models, the sign on each coefficient is as expected in each model. Anglers are more likely to choose alternatives as the cost falls and as the quality (i.e. catch) rises. Each coefficient estimate is statistically significant at $\alpha=0.01$. The scale parameter is significantly greater than one which indicates that the variance in the stated preference data is greater than the variance in the revealed preference data.

The coefficient estimates in the SP model are greater than in the RP model. This indicates that anglers pay less attention to trip cost and more attention to catch when making forecasts about their trip behavior over the remainder of the fishing season. The joint estimation catch coefficients are closer in magnitude to the RP model. The joint estimation trip cost coefficient is in between the RP and SP model coefficients and slightly closer to the SP model coefficient.

The willingness-to-pay for site access ranges from a low of $19 per trip for Hatteras Village to $83 per trip for Carolina Beach in the RP-SP model (Table 6.2). There are large differences in the point estimates of willingness-to-pay between the RP and SP models. The SP willingness-to-pay is 47 percent greater, 10 percent less, 63 percent less and 47 percent greater than the RP model estimates for the four sites. The 95 percent confidence intervals for the RP willingness-to-pay do not include the SP willingness-to-pay point estimate except in the case of Hatteras Village. The relatively wide 95 percent confidence interval on the SP willingness-to-pay estimates allows the confidence intervals to overlap for all willingness-to-pay estimates leading to a conclusion of no statistical difference. However, economically significant differences, especially in the context of benefit-cost analysis, are apparent. The in-season survey is likely to underestimate the access value of Manteo/Oregon Inlet and Carolina Beach and overestimate the Atlantic Beach/Morehead City access value.

Willingness-to-pay per trip for an additional mackerel (caught and kept) is $24 and $42 for an additional coastal migratory pelagic fish according to the RP-SP model. Again, we find evidence of significant economic differences

Table 6.2 Willingness to pay per trip

Site access	RP		SP		RP-SP	
	WTP	stand. error	WTP	stand. error	WTP	stand. error
Manteo/Oregon Inlet	58.10	7.60	85.59	19.03	69.06	7.89
Hatteras Village	18.99	2.48	17.00	3.78	19.28	2.20
Atlantic Beach/Morehead City	24.30	3.18	8.93	1.99	20.56	2.35
Carolina Beach	70.01	9.16	102.97	22.90	83.13	9.50
Additional catch						
King and Spanish mackerel	20.20	3.79	38.85	9.51	23.56	3.12
Tuna, dolphin, wahoo	39.80	3.63	55.26	9.06	41.95	2.91

between the RP and SP data but fail to find significant statistical differences. The SP willingness-to-pay estimates are 92 percent and 39 percent greater than the RP willingness-to-pay estimates for mackerel and coastal migratory pelagic fish. The 95 percent confidence intervals for the RP willingness-to-pay estimates do not include the SP willingness-to-pay point estimates. But, due to relatively large SP standard errors, the RP and SP confidence intervals overlap. The willingness-to-pay estimates from the RP-SP model are closer to the RP model values. We conclude that the SP model would overstate the economic value of catch. Joint estimation of the RP-SP data avoids upward biased willingness-to-pay.

Augmenting site selection data with contingent valuation data

In this section we illustrate how one can jointly estimate site selection decisions and dichotomous choice willingness-to-pay in a RUM framework. A limitation of on-site data collection is that variation in behavior is constrained by the current alternatives and the choke price is not known. In this example we augment site selection data with a contingent valuation scenario that presents a higher cost of access and asks respondents if they would still take the trip. We are able to introduce the "no trip" option that has been found to be important in choice experiments with our contingent valuation question.

We use data from an on-site beach recreation survey conducted during 2003 at Bogue Banks, Topsail Island and Brunswick County in North Carolina (Herstine *et al.* 2004). The 67 miles of oceanfront beach encompasses ten beaches: (1) Atlantic Beach, Salter Path/Indian Beach, Pine Knoll Shores and Emerald Isle on Bogue Banks, (2) North Topsail Beach, Surf City and Topsail Beach in Topsail Island and (3) Caswell Beach, Oak Island and Holden Beach in Brunswick County. We use data from 387 beach goers who were taking day trips during the interview. The average household income is almost $52 thousand. Forty-five percent of respondents are male. The average amount of time spent on the beach is four hours and the average party size is almost four people.

The survey contains a contingent valuation method (CVM) question and enough information necessary to conduct a site selection RUM analysis. Both approaches are designed to estimate the economic benefits of a day trip at a particular site. The CVM question asks beach goers if they would be willing to pay higher travel costs and still visit the particular beach of the interview. The question is in the dichotomous choice (i.e. yes/no) format with randomly assigned values for higher travel costs as the payment vehicle. Survey respondents were asked:

> Some beach trips cost more than others. For example, on an overnight beach trip you may spend money for food, travel expenses, and lodging. On a day trip you may only spend money for gas. What do you expect will be your total expenses as an individual for this beach trip?

and

> Beach trip costs change over time. For example, gas prices fell during the 1990s and rose during the first part of 2003. Would you have come to this island for your beach trip if your total trip costs were $A more than the amount you just reported?

Answer categories included "yes", "no" and "don't know". "Don't know" responses are recoded as "no" responses. Each survey receives a randomly assigned value for $A. The enumerator chose from $5, $10, $25, $50 or $75. The percentage of respondents who answer "yes" declines from about 90 percent at the $5 and $10 bids to 30 percent at the $75 bid. The nonparametric Turnbull willingness-to-pay estimate of the value of beach access is $34 (standard error=4.04).

The RP site selection data indicates that Emerald Isle, North Topsail Beach, Atlantic Beach and Surf City are the most popular beaches in the sample. These four beaches are also those with the greatest number of parking spaces and length. Other site characteristic variables are beach width and population. The mean of the travel cost variable across all RP and SP alternatives and trips ($n=3870$) is $84 and $85 with a range of $1 to $301 and $1 to $311, respectively.

The SP site selection variable is constructed from the dichotomous choice willingness-to-pay data and the RP data. The respondents who stated that they would not visit the island with the higher access cost are coded as taking no trip. Our assumption is that if the respondent stated they would not visit the island then they would not take the trip. A number of respondents at each beach state that they would not take the trip when faced with the higher cost. In total, 34 percent of respondents would not take the trip.

In Table 6.3 we present the independently estimated RP and SP models and the jointly estimated RP-SP model. In addition to the beach characteristics variables we include travel cost, an alternative specific constant for the no trip option and income interacted with alternative specific constants. The travel cost variable is constructed in the same way as that described in the previous section with two differences. First, the cost per mile is $0.35 instead of $0.37 reflecting the earlier date for data collection. Second, the contingent valuation bid amount is included instead of the party/charter fee.

Our results are as expected. The scale parameter is significantly greater than one which indicates that the variance in the stated preference data is greater than the variance in the revealed preference data. Beach recreation site choice is negatively affected by the travel cost and resident population and positively affected by the number of parking spaces, beach length and beach width. Demonstrating a gain from joint estimation is the parking spaces coefficient, which becomes statistically significant only in the jointly estimated model. In the SP and RP-SP models, the no trip option generates positive utility considering respondents avoid higher trip cost. In the RP model, when the income variables are estimated relative to the omitted beach, all but two coefficients are statistically significant. In the SP model the income variables are estimated relative to the no trip alternative specific constant and only the Surf City coefficient is positive and statistically significant suggesting that respondents failed to fully consider their income constraints when considering the contingent valuation question. In the RP-SP model, the income effects pattern is similar to the RP data model.

The travel cost coefficients vary across RP, SP and RP-SP models. The variation is reflected in the willingness-to-pay estimates (Table 6.4). Willingness-to-pay for site access and site characteristics is significantly greater in the SP model

Table 6.3 Random utility site selection models

	RP		SP		RP-SP	
	Coeff.	*t-stat.*	*Coeff.*	*t-stat.*	*Coeff.*	*t-stat.*
Travel cost	-0.088	-12.07	-0.004	-1.93	-0.018	-10.97
Parking spaces	0.001	1.43	0.001	1.24	0.001	2.07
Beach length	0.127	2.71	0.189	3.51	0.156	4.50
Beach width	0.030	3.56	0.019	2.21	0.017	3.09
Population	-0.369	-2.70	-0.367	-2.44	-0.313	-3.24
No trip	–	–	4.583	4.84	3.600	5.78
Beach 1 * income	0.026	2.84	0.008	1.24	0.018	3.43
Beach 2 * income	0.028	3.26	0.003	0.43	0.011	1.93
Beach 3 * income	0.028	3.34	0.008	1.00	0.015	2.57
Beach 4 * income	0.023	2.87	0.008	1.41	0.017	3.52
Beach 5 * income	0.022	2.88	0.010	1.70	0.017	3.44
Beach 6 * income	0.023	3.41	0.019	3.50	0.025	5.51
Beach 7 * income	-0.004	-0.42	-0.014	-1.46	-0.005	-0.80
Beach 8 * income	0.015	2.03	0.010	1.32	0.020	3.25
Beach 9 * income	0.011	0.84	0.006	0.47	0.012	1.34
Beach 10 * income	–	–	-0.005	-0.66	0.006	0.98
Scale	–	–	–	–	1.130	20.47
Log-likelihood	-608.39		-765.17		-2034.55	
Cases	387		387		774	
Alternatives	10		11		21	

Table 6.4 Willingness-to-pay per beach trip

Site Access	RP		SP		RP-SP	
	WTP	stand. error	WTP	stand. error	WTP	stand. error
Bogue Banks	5.49	12.07	126.16	1.93	27.34	10.97
Topsail Island	4.41	12.07	101.34	1.93	21.96	10.97
Brunswick County	1.40	12.07	32.20	1.93	6.98	10.97
Site characteristics (change in)						
Parking spaces (100)	0.92	1.41	22.27	1.03	5.30	2.03
Width (100 ft)	3.37	3.62	495.64	1.48	9.77	2.88
Population (1000)	−4.16	−2.67	−95.41	−1.50	−17.59	−3.01

relative to the RP model, perhaps reflecting hypothetical bias in the contingent valuation data. None of the willingness-to-pay values for site characteristics are statistically significant from the SP model. The willingness-to-pay estimates from the jointly estimated model are between the RP and SP estimates but closer in value to the RP model estimates. Note that willingness-to-pay for site access to Bogue Banks and Topsail Island is not different from the Turnbull estimate. These results suggest that by including the no trip option, increasing the range of costs considered by survey respondents, reveals a higher value for beach site access and characteristics than that revealed by variation in travel costs across beaches. When faced with even greater travel costs at their chosen beaches, respondents may be willing to pay even more to visit. With this inter-pretation, the independently estimated RP model estimates are downwardly biased.

Conclusions

In this chapter we combine and jointly estimate revealed preference data col-lected with on-site surveys and stated preference data eliciting (1) recreation trips during the remainder of the recreation season and (2) the trip participation decision. The models are implemented using the scaling technique designed for choice experiments. We find that there are potential gains from joint estimation. In Part IV of this book we present three additional applications of multiple choice discrete data combination and joint estimation.

References

Greene, W.H. (2007) *NLOGIT Version 4.0*, Econometric Software, Bellport, NY.
Haab, T.C. and K.E. McConnell (2003) *Valuing Environmental and Natural Resources: The Econometrics of Non-market Valuation*, Cheltenham: Edward Elgar.
Hellerstein, D., D. Woo, D. McCollum, and D. Donnelly (1993) *ZIPFIP: A Zip and FIPS Database*, Washington DC: US Department of Agriculture.

Hensher, D.A., J.M. Rose, and W.H. Greene (2005) *Applied Choice Analysis: A Primer*, Cambridge/New York: Cambridge University Press.

Herstine, J., C. Dumas, and J. Whitehead (2007) *Economic Impacts and Economic Benefits of Recreational Boating Along the Atlantic Intracoastal Waterway (AIWW) in North Carolina*, final report prepared for North Carolina Sea Grant *et al.* Wilmington, NC, online, available at: www.ncbiwa.org/AIWWbenefits.pdf.

Herstine, J., J. Hill, B. Buerger, and C. Isom (2004) *Determination of Recreation Demand for Federal Shore Protection Study Area*, final report prepared for the US Army Corps of Engineers, Wilmington District, online, available at: www.appstate. edu/~whiteheadjc/research/usace.pdf.

Holmes, T.P. and W.L. Adamowicz (2003) "Attribute-based methods," in P.A. Champ, K.J. Boyle, and T.C. Brown (eds.), *A Primer on Nonmarket Valuation*, Dordrecht: Kluwer.

Louviere, J.J., D.A. Hensher, and J.D. Swait (2000) *Stated Choice Methods: Analysis and Application*, Cambridge/New York: Cambridge University Press.

Swait, J. and J. Louviere (1993) "The role of the scale parameter in the estimation and comparison of multinomial logit models," *Journal of Marketing Research*, 30: 305–314.

Part II
Frequency data

7 Econometric models for joint estimation of revealed and stated preference site-frequency recreation demand models

Craig E. Landry and Haiyong Liu

Introduction

Whitehead, Pattanayak *et al.* (2008) review the strengths and weaknesses of joint estimation with revealed preference (RP) and stated preference (SP) data. In this chapter we explore stacked RP-SP econometric models for site-frequency demand estimation (as opposed to site choice models, valuation functions, or mixed models). Our focus is on SP data that reflect changes in exogenous contextual factors (such as environmental quality). We identify relative merits and demerits of each model, and illustrate each approach with a sample of North Carolina beach recreation data.

Stacking revealed and stated preference site-frequency demand data

Site-frequency demand models are composed of equations that seek to quantify the relationship between the number of trips taken to a site and exogenous factors, such as travel cost to the site, travel cost to substitute sites, the prices of complementary goods, income, and experience. Quasi-panels of site-frequency data can be created by collecting information on the number of trips in the current period (RP) and the number of trips that would be taken under different or similar conditions in future periods (SP).[1] Frequency demand equations may be stacked into a system of equations for multiple sites (e.g. von Haefen *et al.* 2004), which may also include a quasi-panel dimension.

Count data models are often used to estimate site-frequency recreation demand equations. These models are appropriate because they treat the dependent variable as a non-negative integer. The most basic count data model is Poisson regression:

$$f\left(y_i \mid x_i\right) = \frac{\exp(-\mu_i)\mu_i^{y_i}}{y_i!}, \, y_i = 0, 1, 2, \ldots \tag{7.1}$$

where i indexes individuals, y_i is revealed or stated frequency of site visitation, $\mu_i = \exp(x_i\beta)$ is the conditional expected value of y_i, x_i is a $k \times 1$ vector of covariates (including a constant term in most cases), and β is a $k \times 1$ vector of parameters to be estimated. Note there is no stochastic error term in (7.1). The basic Poisson specification does not allow for random variation in recreation demand; all variation in the conditional expectation of recreation demand is captured by the included independent variables and estimated parameters.

Poisson regression models impose equality of conditional mean and conditional variance of recreation demand: $Var(y_i|x_i)=\mu_i$. Data, however, often do not support this equidispersion restriction. Overdispersion implies that $Var(y_i|x_i)>\mu_i$, and this is commonly found in recreation demand data (Cameron and Trivedi 1998; Egan and Herriges 2006; Landry and Liu 2009). Overdispersion and unexplained randomness in recreation demand can arise from a mixed Poisson distribution, where an unobserved error term is appended to the conditional mean function, $E[y_i|x_i]=\exp(x_i\beta+\varepsilon_i)$. If $\exp(\varepsilon_i)$ is distributed Gamma(α^{-1}, $\alpha\mu_i$), the resulting mixed model is Negative Binomial. A generalized version of the Negative Binomial (GNB) model is:

$$f(y_i \mid x_i)=\frac{\Gamma(y_i+\alpha^{-1}\mu_i^{2-p})\alpha^{y_i}\mu_i^{(py_i-2y_i)}(1+\alpha\mu_i^{p-1})^{-(y_i+\alpha^{-1}\mu_i^{2-p})}}{\Gamma(y_i+1)\Gamma(\alpha^{-1}\mu_i^{2-p})},$$
$$y_i=0, 1, 2,\ldots \tag{7.2}$$

where α and p are additional parameters that allow for flexibility in dispersion. For GNB, $Var[y_i|x_i]=\mu_i+\alpha\mu_i^p$, and this specification nests models NB1 ($p=1$) and NB2 ($p=2$) (Cameron and Trivedi 1998). For NB1, the conditional variance is a linear transformation of the mean, $Var[y_i|x_i]=\mu_i(1+\alpha)$, while for NB2 conditional variance is a quadratic transformation of the mean, $Var[y_i|x_i]=\mu_i(1+\alpha\mu_i)$. For GNB, dispersion (variance divided by the mean)^2 is $1+\alpha\mu_i^{p-1}$, while dispersion is a constant for NB1 ($1+\alpha$) and an affine transformation of the mean for NB2 ($1+\alpha\mu_i$). Likelihood ratio tests (LRT) of null hypothesis $\alpha=0$ can provide evidence of overdispersion,[3] while tests of restrictions on p can provide evidence on NB1 and NB2 specifications.

To build a quasi-panel of site-frequency data, consider a J-vector of recreation demand counts, $y_i=[y_{ij}]$. Let there be one observation per individual on RP ($j=1$), with remaining observations pertaining to SP ($j=2,\ldots, J$). Further, let $j=2$ correspond with planned demand under current conditions (q_i), while $j=3,\ldots, J$ correspond with planned demand under different conditions ($q_3,\ldots, q_J$). We can expect that these counts will exhibit correlation. We may not, however, be able to sign some correlations a priori, due to differences in the way SP scenarios can impact demand. We consider a number of specifications for introducing correlation, focusing exclusively on models with SP data on demand under either identical conditions or changes in environmental quality, access conditions, management regime, or other exogenous factors. For these types of models, there is no variation in most covariates across equations, save for treatment dummy variables. Under these conditions, fixed effects specifications are not very robust because they require variation within the j-dimension for parameter identification (e.g. Englin and Cameron 1996).[4] As such, we focus on different ways to employ or approximate random effects. Besides the distributional restrictions implied by different specifications, other important issues in estimation include the ability to incorporate unrestricted correlation structures, allow for general representations of dispersion, and incorporate differences in scale across RP and SP demand. The latter is especially important, as empirical evidence suggests that the scale of RP and SP demand are often different, and these differences must be incorporated in order to test for differences in demand parameters (Whitehead, Pattanayek *et al.* 2008).

Multivariate Poisson mixtures

Egan and Herriges (2006) employ a Multivariate Poisson Lognormal (MPLN) model (Aitchison and Ho 1989) to introduce cross-equation correlations in quasi-panel data. Employing the Poisson specification in (7.1), with $E[y_i|x_i] = \exp(x_{ij}\beta + \varepsilon_i)$ and assuming $\varepsilon_i = [\varepsilon_{ij}]$ follows a multivariate normal distribution ($\varepsilon_i \sim N(0, \Omega)$), the likelihood function is:

$$L_i = f(y_i \mid x_i) = \int \cdots \int \prod_{j=1}^{J} \frac{\exp(\mu_{ij})\mu_{ij}^{y_{ij}}}{y_{ij}!} \frac{\exp(-\frac{1}{2}\varepsilon_i'\Omega^{-1}\varepsilon_i)}{(2\pi)^{J/2}|\Omega|^{1/2}} d\varepsilon_i, \, y_i = 0, 1, 2, \ldots \quad (7.3)$$

for $y_i = [y_{ij}]$. Equation (7.3) is a mixture of Poisson and lognormal distributions, which obviates equidispersion in Poisson. The conditional mean and variance are $E(y_{ij}|x_{ij}) = \exp(x_{ij}\beta_j + \frac{1}{2}\sigma_j^2) \equiv \delta_{ij}$ and $Var(y_{ij}|x_{ij}) = \delta_{ij} + [\exp(\sigma_j^2) - 1]\delta_{ij}^2$, respectively. This specification is very flexible in allowing for differences in scale across RP and SP scenarios. As shown by Egan and Herriges, cross-equation correlations are unrestricted and given by $Cov[y_{ij}, y_{ik}] = \delta_{ij}[\exp(\sigma_{jk}) - 1]\delta_{ik}, j \neq k$. Dispersion for individual i under conditions j is $1 + [\exp(\sigma_j^2) - 1]\delta_{ij}$.

The MPLN likelihood function in (7.3) is a J-dimensional integral. The model can be estimated using the maximum simulated likelihood method proposed by Munkin and Trivedi (1999). Following Train (1999), Halton sequences are used to numerically compute a multidimensional integral in estimation of the MPLN model. In particular, 1000 Halton draws are employed to approximate integration over the J-dimensional integral. Estimation involves programming in statistical software packages that can solve optimization problems associated with maximum likelihood methods (e.g. GAUSS, Matlab).[5]

To facilitate estimation, Egan and Herriges impose restrictions on the structure of the covariance matrix. Assume that the unobserved error components for stated trips have the same correlations with each other (though different variances) and the same correlations with observed trips. Under this specification, the covariance matrix takes the following form:

$$\Omega = \begin{vmatrix} \sigma_1^2 & \rho_{rp}\sigma_1\sigma_2 & \cdots & \rho_{rp}\sigma_1\sigma_J \\ \rho_{rp}\sigma_2\sigma_1 & \sigma_2^2 & \cdots & \vdots \\ \vdots & \vdots & \ddots & \rho_{sp}\sigma_{J-1}\sigma_J \\ \rho_{rp}\sigma_J\sigma_1 & \cdots & \rho_{sp}\sigma_J\sigma_{J-1} & \sigma_J^2 \end{vmatrix}.$$

In our application, these restrictions prove critical to obtaining convergence of parameter estimates.

An alternative to the MPLN model is the Multivariate Poisson Gamma (MPG) specification, which was first introduced by Arbous and Kerrich (1951) in a bivariate application and subsequently extended by Bates and Neyman (1952) and Nelson (1985). The MPG is commonly known as Random Effects Poisson. In particular, let $\varepsilon_{ij}=\varepsilon_i$ and assume $\exp(\varepsilon_i)$ follows a Gamma(α^{-1}, α) distribution with a mean of 1 and a variance of α. Thus, the probability density function in (7.1) is:

$$
f(y_i \mid x_i) = \frac{\Gamma\left(\sum_{j=1}^{J} y_{ij} + \alpha\right)\alpha^{\alpha}\left(\sum_{j=1}^{J} \mu_{ij} + \alpha\right)^{-\left(\sum_{j=1}^{J} y_{ij} + \alpha\right)}}{\Gamma(\alpha)} \prod_{j=1}^{J} \frac{\mu_{ij}^{y_{ij}}}{y_{ij}!},
\tag{7.4}
$$

with the likelihood function given as the sum of (7.4) over all individuals. The corresponding conditional means and variance are given by $E(y_{ij}|x_{ij})=\mu_{ij}$ and $Var(y_{ij}|x_{ij})=\mu_{ij}+\alpha^{-1}(\mu_{ij})^2$. The covariance between trips for individual i is given by $Cov[y_{ij}, y_{ik}]=\alpha^{-1}(\mu_{ij}\mu_{ik})$, $j\neq k$, which imposes positive correlation among demand equations, the magnitude of which is largely determined by a single parameter α. Moreover, this model does not allow for differences in scale across RP and SP.[6] This model is NB2 with analogous dispersion as indicated above. Given the closed-form nature of the likelihood function, the estimation procedure is rather straightforward and can be executed in many statistical software programs (e.g. *xtpoisson* command in Stata).

Random effects negative binomial

Random effects count models where the underlying distribution is Negative Binomial (NB1) were introduced by Hausman *et al.* (1984).[7] In the standard Random Effects Negative Binomial (RENB) model, dispersion, $(1+\alpha)$, is allowed to vary randomly across individuals, rather than being constant; specifically, $1/(1+ \alpha_i)$ is assumed to follow a parametric form. For example, $1/(1+\alpha_i) \sim$ Beta(r, s) is one of the most commonly used distributions (Hausman *et al.* 1984; Liang and Zeger 1986; Stata 2005). An important attraction of the Beta form is that the joint probability of observing a set of trips for individual i is now given by a closed form expression:

$$
L_i = \frac{\Gamma(r+s)\Gamma\left(r+\sum_{j=1}^{J}\mu_{ij}\right)\Gamma\left(s+\sum_{j=1}^{J}y_{ij}\right)}{\Gamma(r)\Gamma(s)\Gamma\left(r+s+\sum_{j=1}^{J}\mu_{ij}+\sum_{j=1}^{J}y_{ij}\right)} \prod_{j=1}^{J} \frac{\Gamma(\mu_{ij}+y_{ij})}{\Gamma(\mu_{ij})\Gamma(y_{ij}+1)}.
\tag{7.5}
$$

In this model, conditional mean and variance are given by $E(y_{ij}|\alpha_i,x_{ij})=\mu_{ij}\alpha_i$ and $\text{Var}(y_{ij}|\alpha_i,x_{ij})=\mu_{ij}(\alpha_i+\alpha_i^2)$, respectively, with $E(\alpha_i)=s/(r-1)$. The dispersion for this model is $1+\alpha_i$, which can vary across individuals but remains constant across trips. For individual i, different trip demand equations have the same alpha so RENB does introduce correlation in dispersion for the same individual. The y_{ij}, however, are independent across trips j, and therefore the covariance across trips is zero.

Unlike MPLN and other random effects models, this RENB formulation does not specify the heterogeneity term as an additive common effect in the conditional mean of trips. Greene (2007) points out that the relationship between heterogeneity and μ_{ij} is unclear. Moreover, there is no economic interpretation of r and s. Nonetheless, this estimator is adopted by several statistical packages (e.g. *xtnbreg* command in Stata).

Discrete factors method

Discrete Factors Method (DFM) was introduced by Heckman and Singer (1984) as an approach for modeling unobserved heterogeneity in panel data. DFM is a non-parametric approximation of random effects. Let the conditional mean of trips be $E(y_{ij}|x_{ij})=\exp(x_{ij}\beta_j+\mu_{ij})=\mu_{ij}\exp(\varepsilon_{ij})$, and let the random effect be decomposed as follows: $\varepsilon_{ij}=\gamma_j\lambda_i$, where λ_i represents a point of support for the distribution of μ_{ij} that is common to all demand equations for the same individual, and γ_j is a factor loading that is common to a specific demand treatment across all individuals. DFM approximates λ_i with a step function that takes K discrete values. The loading factors (γ_j) rescale unobserved heterogeneity into a recreation demand effect that can vary across demand types (RP, SP, and treatment conditions q_j). A priori we do not know to which class of heterogeneity each individual belongs. The likelihood function for individual i is thus:

$$
\begin{aligned}
L_i &= \sum_{k=1}^{K}\left\{\pi(\lambda_k)\Pr\left[y_{i1},...,y_{iJ}\mid x_{ij},\lambda_k\right]\right\} \\
&= \sum_{k=1}^{K}\left\{\pi(\lambda_k)\prod_{j}\Pr(y_{ij}\mid x_{ij},\lambda_k)\right\},
\end{aligned}
\tag{7.6}
$$

where $\pi(\lambda_k)$ is the probability of individual i having heterogeneity level k.[8] DFM imposes a restriction that all unobserved heterogeneity and correlation among the individual demand equations enters the full model through the factor loadings γ_j and the factor λ_k, with $\pi(\lambda_k)>0$, $\forall k-1,...,K$. Since cross-equation correlation is captured by the random effect term $\mu_{kj}=\gamma_j\lambda_k$, the joint probability of vector y_i conditional on λ_k and observables x_{ij} is equal to the product of their univariate densities conditional on λ_k and x_{ij}, as indicated in equation (7.6).

This non-parametric specification for unobserved heterogeneity can be combined with any of the parametric specifications for count demand to produce a semi-parametric estimator. Employing the GNB specification, individual i's contribution to the likelihood function, L_i, can be rewritten as:

$$\sum_{k=1}^{K}\left\{\pi(\lambda_k)\prod_{j}\frac{\Gamma(y_{ij}+\alpha_j^{-1}\mu_{ijk}^{2-P})\alpha_j^{y_{ij}}\mu_{ijk}^{(py_{ij}-2y_{ij})}(1+\alpha_j\mu_{ijk}^{p-1})^{-(y_{ij}+\alpha_i^{-1}\mu_{ijk}^{2-P})}}{\Gamma(y_{ij}+1)\Gamma(\alpha_j^{-1}\mu_{ijk}^{2-P})}\right\}. \quad (7.7)$$

Note the conditional mean $E(y_{ijk}|x_{ij},\lambda_k)=\mu_{ij}\exp(\gamma_j\lambda_k)$ reflects individual-level observables, demand treatment, and heterogeneity type. Assuming that x and λ are independent, we can thus express the conditional mean as a product of expectations. Substituting our discrete representation for unobserved heterogeneity and integrating, we have:

$$E(v_{ij}\mid x_{ij})=\sum_{k=1}^{K}[\pi(\lambda_k)\exp(\gamma_j\lambda_k)]\mu_{ij}, \quad (7.8)$$

where the first term represents the expected value of $\gamma_j\lambda$ and $\mu_{ij}=\exp(x'_{ij}\beta_j)$. The conditional variance for DFM-GNB is $\mu_{ijk}=\alpha_j\mu_{ijk}^P$. The common heterogeneity term allows for unrestricted cross-equation correlation: $\text{cov}[\mu_{ij},\mu_{ik}]=\gamma_j\gamma_k\neq 0$ for any two demand equations $j\neq k$.[9] The sample likelihood function is derived as the product of (7.7) over all N individuals.

Without loss of generality, λ is confined to the unit interval:

$$\lambda_1=0$$

$$\lambda_j=\frac{1}{1+\exp(\overline{\lambda_j})},j=2,...,K-1 \quad (7.9)$$

$$\lambda_K=1.$$

The transformed probability weights are given as follows:

$$\pi(\lambda_k)=\frac{\exp\overline{\theta_k}}{1+\sum_{k'=1}^{K-1}\exp\overline{\theta_{k'}}},k=1,...,K-1$$

$$\pi(\lambda_k)=\frac{1}{1+\sum_{k'=1}^{K-1}\exp\overline{\theta_{k'}}},k=K. \quad (7.10)$$

The logit kernals in (7.9) and (7.10) are strictly concave, facilitating optimization procedures. Note that the $K-2$ vector $\overline{\lambda}$ and the $K-1$ vector $\overline{\theta}$ are parameters to be estimated, along with J vectors α and γ, the standard vector of demand parameters β, and the NB exponent p. The support points, λ_k, and the transformed probabilities, $\pi(\lambda_k)$, can be calculated from the parameter estimates via equations (7.9) and (7.10).

The number of classes K in DFM is not part of the optimization process from which the parameter estimates are derived. Conventional specification tests used for maximum likelihood estimates are not valid in this context because likelihood function values under the null are at the boundary of the parameter space. Empirically, researchers can use various information criteria, such as Akaike Information Criteria (AIC) and Bayesian Information Criteria (BIC) to help determine the number of classes.[10]

Empirical analysis

The telephone survey data utilized herein, originally analyzed in Whitehead, Dumas *et al.* (2008), contain information on recreation demand for coastal North Carolina residents. In addition to revealed preference visitation behavior, the data include stated preference responses, describing intended visitation in the subsequent year assuming that conditions remain the same, as well as how beach goers would change their visitation behavior in the subsequent year in response to hypothetical improvement in beach access and beach width.[11] The raw data indicate that the average person took 11 trips last year and plans to take 13 trips in the future if conditions don't change. Average demand under the improved access (beach width) scenario is 17 (14).

Whitehead *et al.* (2000) propose gathering data on SP demand under current conditions. Evidence of changes in SP demand under current conditions may indicate hypothetical bias — plans for future behavior (often optimistic) that apportion less gravity to economic constraints or reflect lack of sufficient cognitive effort. On the other hand, such changes may indicate evolving expectations of complement or substitute prices, income, or changes in information or conditions that are beyond control of the analyst. Regardless of the nature of the changes, we would like to be able to control for them in the model, effectively netting them out in the estimation process. We follow this method, allowing for shift in demand via $j-1$ SP dummy variables. In this specification, dummy variable $sp = 1$ for $j = 2$, 3, or 4; dummy variable $access = 1$ for $j = 3$; and dummy variable $width = 1$ for $j = 4$.[12]

Employing each of the four econometric models outlined above, we explore estimation and welfare analysis for stacked site-frequency recreation demand. We make no claims that our econometric models are exhaustive; we hope simply to point out practical differences and potential problems in estimation and application with common models. Our baseline empirical specification is:

$$y_{ij} = \exp(\beta_0 + \beta_{op}op_i + \beta_{cp}cp_i + \beta_m m_i + X'_{ij}\beta_X + \varepsilon_{ij}) \tag{7.11}$$

where op_i is the own price travel cost for individual i, cp_i represents cross price travel cost for individual i, m_i is income, X_{ij} is a vector of individual characteristics and treatment dummy variables, and ε_{ij} is an error term. For the MPG specification, $\varepsilon_{ij} = \varepsilon_i$, where ε_i follows a Gamma distribution, and for RENB specification, $\varepsilon_{ij} = 0$, with random variation arising through the α_i parameter (which does not affect $E(y_{ij})$). The MPLN and DFM models each make an assumption about the multivariate distribution of $\varepsilon_i = [\varepsilon_{ij}]$. For MPLN, $\varepsilon_i \sim N(0, \Omega)$, while for DFM-GNB ε_i is Gamma distributed and additional variation is introduced by μ_{ij} decomposed into individual i and panel j specific components, $\varepsilon_{ij} = \gamma_j \lambda_i$, where λ_i is approximated by a step function that takes K discrete values.

Annual consumer surplus for beach access under conditions j is the integral of equation (7.11) over travel cost (own-price — op) from the average price to infinity:

$$CS_j = \int_{op^0}^{\infty} \exp(z_j' \tilde{\beta} + \beta_{op} C) dC \qquad (7.12)$$

$$= -\frac{E(y_{ij} \mid x_{ij})}{\beta_{op}}$$

where z_{ij} is a vector of other variables and parameters that influence the conditional mean (depending upon the model). Equation (7.12) can be evaluated at the mean of x, or at the individual level and averaged over the entire sample. For DFM:

$$CS_j = \sum_{k=1}^{K} [\Pr(\lambda_k) \exp(\gamma_j \lambda_k)] \int_{op^0}^{\infty} \exp(z_j' \tilde{\beta} + \beta_{op} C) dC \qquad (7.13)$$

$$= \sum_{k=1}^{K} [\Pr(\lambda_k) \exp(\gamma_j \lambda_k)] \frac{\mu_j}{-\beta_{op}}$$

The summation term in equation (7.13) is the expected demand effect associated with unobserved heterogeneity.

Results and discussion

Regression results are presented in Table 7.1. For all specifications, most parameter estimates are statistically significant with expected signs, and LRTs indicate joint significance of all models at conventional levels. Each specification treats unobserved heterogeneity differently, and thus parameter estimates differ (significantly at conventional levels). The MPLN model suggests recreation demand is price elastic ($\varepsilon_{op}^{MPLN} = -1.24$); MPG results suggest approximately unitary elasticity ($\varepsilon_{op}^{MPG} = -0.979$), while RENB and DFM each indicate inelastic demand ($\varepsilon_{op}^{RENB} = 0.272$ and $\varepsilon_{op}^{DFM} = -0.531$). Cross-price ($\varepsilon_{cp}^{MPLN} = 1.030$, ($\varepsilon_{cp}^{MPG} = 0.947$, $\varepsilon_{cp}^{RENB} = -0.119$, $\varepsilon_{cp}^{DFM} = 0.376$) and income elasticities ($\varepsilon_{m}^{MPLN} = 1.046$, $\varepsilon_{m}^{MPG} = 0.554$, $\varepsilon_{m}^{RENB} = 0.474$, $\varepsilon_{m}^{DFM} = 0.149$) show a similar pattern of differences across specifications. The cross-price parameter for RENB has a counter-intuitive sign, but is statistically insignificant. All models indicate that beach recreation is a normal good. The MPLN specification consistently produces the most elastic estimates in our application.

The MPG model does not allow for differences in scale across RP and SP data. The RENB model allows for differences in scale at the individual level, but not across the panel dimension. Only the mean is recovered, which we estimate

Table 7.1 Econometric results for stacked revealed and stated preference frequency demand models[1]

	MPLN Parameter estimate	MPLN Standard error	MPG Parameter estimate	MPG Standard error	RENB Parameter estimate	RENB Standard error	DFM Parameter estimate	DFM Standard error
Own-price	−0.0139	0.0002	−0.0109	0.0008	−0.0030	0.0007	−0.0059	0.0002
Cross-price	0.0051	0.0002	0.0047	0.0009	−0.0006[2]	0.0008	0.0019	0.0002
Income	0.0178	0.0006	0.0094	0.0021	0.0081	0.0018	0.0025	0.0005
Married	−1.0539	0.0291	−0.4959	0.1031	−0.3002	0.0891	−0.2091	0.0234
Age	0.0027	0.0009	−0.0023[2]	0.0029	−0.0073	0.0025	−0.0029	0.0006
Intercept	1.5781	0.0591	2.1107	0.1685	2.3109	0.1749	1.0118	0.0544
sp	0.3195	0.0359	0.1634	0.0159	0.2451	0.0300	0.0954[2]	0.1016
Access	0.3090	0.0258	0.2703	0.0143	0.2760	0.0262	0.3106	0.0912
Width	0.1016	0.0334	0.0826	0.0149	0.0947	0.0271	0.1127[2]	0.1157
Other parameters	$\sigma_1=1.5430$	0.0292	$\alpha=1.0685$	0.0529	$r=2.3112$	0.1436	$\alpha_1=0.0230$	0.0039
	$\sigma_2=1.4582$	0.0263			$s=1.7783$	0.1202	$\alpha_2=0.0035$	0.0010
	$\sigma_3=1.4168$	0.0205					$\alpha_3=0.0026$	0.0007
	$\sigma_4=1.4405$	0.0312					$\alpha_4=0.0027$	0.0008
	$prp=0.8606$	0.0031					$p=3.1232$	0.0555
	$prp=0.9862$	0.0009					$\gamma_1=2.9055$	0.1279
							$\gamma_2=3.2118$	0.1510
							$\gamma_3=3.1447$	0.0968
							$\gamma_4=3.1688$	0.1203
							$\bar{\mu}_2=0.7346$	0.0282
							$\mu_2=-0.466$	0.0325
							$\bar{\theta}_1=1.4701$	0.1332
							$\bar{\theta}_2=1.1110$	0.1413
							$\bar{\theta}_3=0.5290^2$	1.6665
lnL	−7652.12		−8519.601		−7676.814		−7547.403	
AIC	−11.5468		−12.8457		−11.5780		−11.4012	
BIC	−11.5976		−12.8796		−11.6152		−11.4791	

Notes
1 N=664.
2 Not statistically significant at 5% level.

at $E(\alpha)=s/(r-1)=1.356$. Both DFM and MPLN allow for differences in scale across RP and SP. DFM estimates suggest that RP scale is statistically different from SP scale, but SP scale factors are not statistically different from one another. The MPLN specification differs from the other models in the way over-dispersion is introduced–Log-normal error distribution rather than Gamma. For MPLN, most of the sigma terms are not statistically different from one another (except for σ_3 in comparison with σ_1). MPG imposes positive correlations among trips, while RENB assumes independence of trip demand equations for a given individual. Both DFM and MPLN allow for unrestricted cross-correlations. Nonetheless, all estimated covariance terms are positive.

For the MPLN specification we find evidence of demand shifts under SP scenarios and additional shift for the *access* and *width* scenarios. Consistent with the raw data, results suggest that SP demand increases relative to RP. Likewise, MPG and RENB indicate increasing demand for SP overall and under improvement scenarios. Results for the DFM model, however, find no effect of SP and only an increase for improved *access*.

Thus, under the DFM specification, conventional parameters of RP and SP demand equations under equivalent conditions are not significantly different. We note, however, that the unique factor loadings (γ_j) for all scenarios are statistically significant and positive. Since the factor loadings rescale unobserved heterogeneity, the γ_j coefficients can be interpreted as interaction terms for SP and scenario indicators with unobserved heterogeneity. As the estimated loading factors are positive, conditional demand will shift relative to RP.

Additional parameter estimates for the DFM model include the generalized negative binomial term ($p=3.123$) and parameters of the distribution of unobserved heterogeneity. We reject NB1 and NB2 specifications using LRTs. The distribution of unobserved heterogeneity parameters are recovered from the econometric estimates via (7.8) and (7.9). The lowest heterogeneity type ($\lambda_1=0$) has the highest probability (43 percent), and larger values of $\lambda-\lambda_2=0.324$, $\lambda_3=0.614$, $\lambda_4=1.00$ exhibit monotonically decreasing probabilities of 30 percent, 17 percent, and 10 percent, respectively.

Table 7.2 presents conditional expectations of demand and consumer surplus estimates evaluated at the means of the data. MPG, RENB, and DFM produce within sample underpredictions for the number of trips in all scenarios, while MPLN overpredicts the number of trips. The average trips for the raw data are included in the last column for comparison. While the underpredictions are modest, the overpredictions of MPLN are rather large–approximately double the raw data. We find that the MPLN specification is sensitive to outliers in our application. Removing extreme observations on recreation demand partially addresses this problem.

The fifth and sixth rows of Table 7.2 contain conditional demand with *sp* set equal to zero in order to excise any SP bias (be it hypothetical or some other influence not related to the quality change). For the access scenario, number of trips increases between 13 (MPLN) and 60 (DFM) percent over the RP baseline. For the beach width scenario, MPLN predicts the number of trips go down

Table 7.2 Conditional demand and consumer surplus estimates

	MPLN	MPG	RENB	DFM	Raw data
$E(y_1|\bar{x})$	20.10	8.98	8.80	8.41	11.08
$E(y_2|\bar{x})$	24.36	10.58	11.25	11.41	13.05
$E(y_3|\bar{x})$	31.27	13.86	14.82	14.85	17.10
$E(y_4|\bar{x})$	26.29	11.49	12.37	12.39	14.17
$E(y_3|\bar{x})^1$	22.72	11.77	11.60	13.50	–
$E(y_4|\bar{x})^1$	19.10	9.75	9.68	11.26	–
CS_1	\$1446.50	\$820.71	\$2892.80	\$1416.80	–
CS_2	\$1753.12	\$966.37	\$3696.30	\$1922.20	–
CS_3	\$2249.89	\$1266.26	\$4871.32	\$2502.31	–
CS_4	\$1891.45	\$1049.57	\$4063.49	\$2087.87	–
CS_3^1	\$1634.57	\$1075.41	\$3812.39	\$2274.68	–
CS_4^1	\$1374.16	\$891.37	\$3180.16	\$1897.93	–

Note
1 Corrected for SP bias (hypothetical or otherwise) by setting $sp=0$ in expression for conditional mean.

relative to RP. The rest of the models predict an increase, ranging from 9 (MPG) and 34 (DFM) percent.

Each of the conditional trip demand estimates can be used to produce a measure of annual consumer surplus via equations (7.12) or (7.13). For revealed preference demand, consumer surplus ranges from \$820 (MPG) to \$2900 (RENB), with MPLN and DFM intermediate at around \$1400 per year. Increases in consumer surplus are proportional to the change in conditional demand, producing bias corrected estimates ranging from \$1075 (MPG) to \$3812 (RENB) per year (CS=\$1635 for MPLN and CS=\$2274 for DFM) for the access scenario. These are considerable increases over baseline welfare. For the beach width scenario, only MPG, RENB, and DFM produce estimates indicating an increase in consumer surplus (bias-corrected estimates of \$891, \$3180, and \$1898, respectively).

Conclusions

In this chapter we have explored specification, estimation, and welfare analysis for random effects models used to estimate stacked site-frequency recreation demand models. Two common models offered by many statistical packages are Multivariate Poisson-Gamma (MPG) and Random Effects Negative Binomial (RENB). The MPG model restricts cross-equation correlations to be positive, is somewhat limiting in terms of model dispersion, and does not allow for scale differences across RP and SP counts. RENB, on the other hand, allows dispersion to vary randomly across individuals, but not across demand equations for a given individual. Moreover, RENB does not allow for cross-equation correlations for a given individual; this limitation could be very serious in some cases

(e.g. correction for onsite sampling (Egan and Herriges 2006)). Another important feature of RENB is that unlike other random effects count data models it
introduces a common factor to the conditional dispersion, instead of an additive
common factor to the conditional mean trips. The Multivariate Poisson-
Lognormal (MPLN) and Discrete Factors Method (DFM) models appear to be
more flexible than MPG and RENB specifications in terms of a lack of restrictions on cross-model covariance, flexibility of count dispersion, and allowance
for differences in scale across RP and SP. Unfortunately, both MPLN and DFM
have yet to be incorporated into statistical packages so programming with
scientific computing software is required.

All models appear to fit our beach recreation data reasonably well. Information criteria support the DFM specification, with the MPLN specification a close
second. While in our application the MPLN model produces the most responsive
elasticity estimates, it remains to be seen whether this is an artifact of the model
or specific to our dataset. MPLN produces the largest estimates of conditional
recreation demand, almost twice the size of the raw data. Other models slightly
underpredict the conditional mean. In terms of consumer surplus estimation,
MPG and RENB tend to produce estimates at the extreme, with MPLN and
DFM producing more moderate estimates. If unable to program an estimator,
MPG would likely be preferred over RENB since it allows for cross-equation
correlation. MPLN and DFM offer much more flexibility in correlation,
dispersion, and scale. DFM is robust to misspecification of the distribution of
unobserved heterogeneity.

Notes

1 We refer to such data as quasi-panel data, because multiple observations are available
   on each individual, but the data in this dimension are not conventional time-series. RP
   and SP data are also referred to as observed and contingent behavior, respectively.
2 This is also known as the "variance-mean ratio" (Mullahy 1997; Winkelmann 1995).
3 In addition, it is common to inspect moments of the raw data. The score tests derived
   by Dean (1992) are commonly used in diagnosing overdispersion.
4 The Gamma functional form actually makes identification possible in the case of a
   fixed effects negative binomial model even without cross-trip variations. Identification, however, is derived from functional form and is sensitive to misspecification
   (Hausman et al. 1984).
5 Thanks are due to Kevin Egan and Joe Herriges for providing the GAUSS code for
   this estimation procedure.
6 Hausman et al. (1984) build this model by assuming the Poisson parameter in a standard Poisson distribution to follow a gamma distribution with shape parameters (μ_{ij}, 1/
   α_i). The likelihood function cannot be easily modified to allow for differences in scale
   because there is only one free parameter in the Gamma distribution, which is necessary for a closed-form solution.
7 Cameron and Trivedi (1998) offer further detailed technical discussion on specification issues.
8 As indicated by Greene (2003: 440), if the class probabilities are fixed and only a
   constant term is included as a covariate in the mean of the distribution of the random
   component, then DFM is equivalent to the Latent Class Model (Boxall and Adamowicz 2002; Provencher et al. 2002) in modeling the distribution of unobserved

heterogeneity. Unlike DFM, LCM produces separate covariate parameter estimates for each latent segment.

9 See the online appendix of Landry and Liu (2009) for an illustration that one can readily use discrete factors to approximate a multivariate random distribution.

10 Wedel and Kamakura (2000) provide an alternative approach, called the entropy index, to test the significance of classifications.

11 The interested reader is referred to Whitehead, Dumas *et al.* (2008) for more information on the survey and data.

12 One could argue that dummy variables are a somewhat crude way to parameterize SP demand changes. If we were curious about possible changes in price, income, or substitute price elasticity, then we should undoubtedly interact these covariates with the SP dummy variables. If, however, welfare estimation is our primary goal, the use of demand shifters is most suitable, as allowing for changes in own-price coefficient may lead to theoretically inconsistent results.

References

Arbous, A.G. and J.E. Kerrich (1951) "Accident statistics and the concept of accident proneness," *Biometrika*, 37: 340–41.

Atchison, J. and C.H. Ho (1989) "The multivariate Poisson-log normal distribution," *Biometrika*, 76: 643–53.

Bates, G.E. and J. Neyman (1952) "Contributions to the theory of accident proneness I: An optimistic model of the correlation between light and severe accidents," *University of California Publications in Statistics*, 1: 212–53.

Boxall, P.C. and W.L. Adamowicz (2002) "Understanding heterogeneous preferences in random utility models: A latent class approach," *Environmental and Resource Economics*, 23: 421–46.

Cameron, A.C. and P.K. Trivedi (1998) *Regression Analysis of Count Data*, Cambridge: Cambridge University Press.

Dean, C.B. (1992) "Testing for overdispersion in Poisson and binomial regression models," *Journal of the American Statistical Association*, 87: 451–57.

Egan, K. and J. Herriges (2006) "Multivariate count data regression models with individual panel data from an on-site sample," *Journal of Environmental Economics and Management*, 52: 567–81.

Englin, J. and T.A. Cameron (1996) "Augmenting Travel Cost Models with Contingent Behavior Data," *Environmental and Resource Econonomics*, 7: 133–47.

Greene, W. (2003) *Econometric Analysis*, fifth edition, Upper Saddle River, NJ: Prentice Hall.

Greene, W. (2007) *Fixed and Random Effects Models for Count Data*, Leonard N. Stern School of Business Papers, Department of Economics Working Paper No. 07–16.

Hausman, J., B.H. Hall, and Z. Griliches (1984) "Econometric models for count data with an application to the patents-R&D relationship," *Econometrica*, 52: 909–38.

Heckman, J.J. and B. Singer (1984) "A method for minimizing the impact of distributional assumptions in econometric models for duration data," *Econometrica*, 52: 271–320.

Landry, C.E. and H. Liu (2009) "A semi-parametric estimator for revealed and stated preference data: An application to recreational beach visitation," *Journal of Environmental Econonomics and Management*, 57: 205–18.

Liang, K.Y. and S.L. Zeger (1986) "Longitudinal data analysis using generalized linear models," *Biometrika*, 73: 13–22.

Mullahy, J. (1997) "Heterogeneity, excess zeros, and the structure of count data models," *Journal of Applied Econometrics*, 12: 337–50.

Munkin, M.K. and P.K. Trivedi (1999) "Simulated maximum likelihood estimation of multivariate mixed-Poisson regression models, with application," *Econometrics Journal*, 2: 29–48.

Nelson, J.F. (1985) "Multivariate Gamma-Poisson models," *Journal of the American Statistical Association*, 80: 254–83.

Provencher, B., K.A. Baerenklau, and R.C. Bishop (2002) "A finite mixture logit model of recreational angling with serially correlated random utility," *American Journal of Agricultural Economics*, 84: 1066–75.

Stata (2005) *Longitudinal/Panel Data Reference Manual*, College Station, TX: Stata Press.

Train, K. (1999) "Halton sequences for mixed logit," Econometrics Working Paper No. 0012002, Berkeley, CA: University of California.

von Haefen, R.H., D.J. Phaneuf, and G.R. Parsons (2004) "Estimation and welfare analysis with large demand systems," *Journal of Business and Economic Statistics*, 22: 194–205.

Wedel, M. and W.A. Kamakura (2000) *Market Segmentation: Conceptual Methodological Foundations*, Boston, MA: Kluwer Academic.

Whitehead, J.C., T.C. Haab, and J.C. Huang (2000) "Measuring recreation benefits of quality improvements with revealed and stated behavior data," *Resource and Energy Economics*, 22: 339–54.

Whitehead, J.C., C.F. Dumas, J. Herstine, J. Hill, and B. Buerger (2008) "Valuing beach access and width with revealed and stated preference data," *Marine Resource Economics*, 23: 119–35.

Whitehead, J.C., S. Pattanayek, G. Van Houtven and B. Gelso (2008) "Combining revealed and stated preference data to estimate nonmarket value of ecological services: an assessment of the state of the science," *Journal of Economic Surveys*, 22: 872–908.

Winkelmann, R. (1995) "Duration dependence and dispersion in count-data models," *Journal of Business and Economic Statistics*, 13: 467–74.

8 Combining multiple revealed and stated preference data sources

A recreation demand application

Daniel J. Phaneuf and Dietrich Earnhart

Introduction

In this chapter we provide an example of structurally combining revealed preference (RP) and stated preference (SP) data to address parameter estimation and the valuation of time in a recreation demand context. In particular, we combine observations on actual recreation site visitation with three forms of SP data that include future behavior at baseline conditions, contingent behavior at changed conditions, and contingent pricing (i.e. reporting a choke price). By integrating these data sources into a structural, two-constraint model of recreation demand we demonstrate the payoff to collecting RP and SP data that provide related, but distinctly different, vehicles for quantifying individuals' preferences.

Our application examines recreation visits to Clinton Lake near Lawrence, Kansas, during the summer of 1998. An on-site survey of individual visitors provided information on the number of (actual) trips made to the lake, expected future trips, and changes in future trips resulting from hypothetical changes in the money and time costs of access. The latter are examples of contingent behavior data. The survey also solicited information on how much money and time costs of access would need to increase before the person would stop visiting the lake; the responses constitute our contingent pricing data. The different SP questions provide information on how time and money costs determine different elements of peoples' overall behavior. Said another way, the contingent behavior data and contingent pricing data serve as natural counterparts. While the contingent behavior data reflects the intensive margin relationship between price (travel cost) and visits along the interior of the demand curve, the contingent pricing data measures the reservation (or choke) price that determines the person's extensive margin decision to visit the lake or not. Our first contribution in this chapter, therefore, is to provide an empirical framework for exploiting the different theoretical aspects that are relevant for the data-generating process.

Our second contribution centers on the opportunity cost of time aspect of our application. While several recent studies combine RP and SP data in recreation studies (e.g. Adamowicz *et al.* 1994; Cameron, 1992; Layman *et al.* 1996; Herriges *et al.* 1999; Huang *et al.* 1997; Cameron *et al.* 1996; Adamowicz *et al.*

1997), surprisingly few (Earnhart, 2004, is one example) use combined data methods to address time valuation directly. In this chapter, we extend Earnhart's (2004) earlier analysis by incorporating money and time contingent pricing data–along with the money and time contingent behavior data–to measure the implicit time-money tradeoffs that identify lake visitors' opportunity cost of time. In the process, we evaluate the extent to which our contingent pricing approach helps to better value time costs, while assessing whether the additional cognitive challenge for respondents is justified by the additional information.

The remainder of this chapter is organized as follows. The next section provides a conceptual basis for our combined data empirical models. We focus on demonstrating both the role of the dual-constraint model and how our contingent behavior and contingent pricing data trace out different elements of visitors' preferences. In the third section we describe our application. In the fourth we lay out our econometric model and describe our estimation results. Section 5 concludes.

Conceptual framework

To motivate our econometric model, consider the following conceptual model of lake visitors' behavior. Suppose an individual derives utility from visits to a single recreation site and a composite good that consists of spending on all other commodities. The price of a visit to the recreation site consists of two components: (a) the money costs of travel and entry, and (b) the opportunity cost of travel time. Denote trips to the recreation site by X and the full price of a trip by p, which depends on the money cost of accessing the site (i.e. travel cost and site entry fees), c, the time expenditures needed to access the site (i.e. travel time), t, and the opportunity cost of time, ϕ, which may be endogenously or exogenously determined, according to this relationship: $p = c + (\phi \times t)$. Furthermore, denote annual income by y, where it is understood that income is 'full' income in the sense that it includes earned income plus the monetary value of residual, non-work time. Under these definitions, our model is consistent with the two-constraint duality requirements and results described by Larson and Shaikh (2001).

Denoting the indirect utility function by $V(p, y)$, it follows from Roy's identity that the ordinary demand curve $X(\cdot)$ links to the preference function by the following relationship:

$$X(p,y) = \frac{-\partial V/\partial p}{\partial V/\partial y}. \tag{8.1}$$

Furthermore, the choke price, $\hat{p}$, which represents the price at which the person chooses to consume exactly zero trips, is implicitly defined by:

$$\frac{-\partial V(\hat{p}, y)/\partial p}{\partial V(\hat{p}, y)/\partial y} = 0. \tag{8.2}$$

While the choke price can be determined by an infinite number of combinations of c and t, we focus on two particular expressions of the choke price. These two expressions take as given one of the two cost components: either baseline money costs, denoted by c_0, or baseline time expenditures, denoted by t_0. Then we derive the increase in the other cost component that results in zero consumption. In our notation, these two expressions are defined by: (a) $\hat{p} = c_0 + (\phi \times \hat{t})$; and (b) $\hat{p} = \hat{c} + (\phi \times t_0)$, where $\hat{t}$ and $\hat{c}$ are the time and money cost choke price determinants, respectively.

Equations (8.1) and (8.2) help illustrate the payoff to our combined RP and SP data gathering exercise. If we denote p_0 as the baseline access price, consisting of the baseline money and time components c_0 and t_0, then observed trips at baseline conditions, X_0, provide one point on the demand curve and correspondingly one point on the indifference map. Likewise, responses to hypothetical changes in c or t that are gathered via the survey provide additional points on the demand curve and in preference space via the pivoting of the budget constraint. These points provide data on the *intensive* margin relationship between price and visits along the interior of the demand curve. In contrast, information on time and money choke prices ($\hat{t}$ and $\hat{c}$) help identify points on the demand curve and in preference space that are generally not revealed by observations on trip-taking behavior alone. These points provide data on a person's *extensive* margin decision to visit the lake or not.

These general ideas are further illustrated by Figure 8.1, which depicts two indifference maps, each of which has recreation trips X on the horizontal axis and spending on all other commodities on the vertical axis. Since trips to the recreation site are not an essential good the indifference curves intersect the vertical axis. On the top panel the baseline budget constraint (reflecting baseline travel costs) is labeled as p^0. A tangency with the indifference curve U^0 gives rise to the observed baseline number of trips, denoted by X^0. This tangency represents the RP data point. By manipulating the price experimentally – via

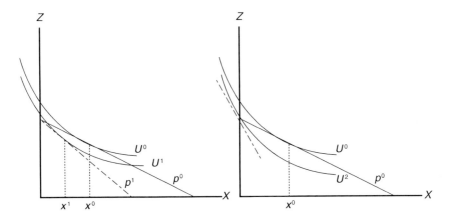

Figure 8.1 Indifference maps.

hypothetically given increases in money costs or time costs of access to the site–we observe SP data points like X^1. This point is determined by the tangency of the hypothetical budget line p^1 with a different point in the indifference map on U^1. Additional contingent behavior questions would provide additional SP data points, which would aid in further tracing out the shape of the preference function.

The bottom panel in Figure 8.1 extends this concept to contingent pricing. Once again the RP outcome is given by p^0 and X^0. The dashed line shows the person's endogenous reservation price $\hat{p}$–the price at which she is indifferent between consuming zero recreation trips and some positive quantity. To the extent that people are able cognitively to answer questions related to money and time choke prices, responses from this type of SP question can provide information on a portion of the preference function that is important for non-market valuation, but difficult to measure with RP data alone.

Each of the budget lines in Figure 8.1 can be manipulated or solicited in SP surveys using the time or money components of the price of recreation trips. This is useful because it allows us to generate orthogonal variability in the two components of the overall recreation price, and then compare changes in trip-taking behavior prompted by the manipulations in one or both components. This type of experimental design provides indirect observations on people making time-money tradeoffs within the context of the behavior in which we are directly interested. Therefore, experimentally altering time and money prices in the context of a structural model as described above provides the additional benefit of allowing estimation of factors that determine the opportunity cost of time.

This conceptual framework identifies the following critical dimensions that link recreation demand, prices, and preferences: travel cost and behavior under baseline conditions, changes in expected behavior resulting from changes in time costs or money costs, and choke prices as reflected by increases in either the money component or time component of travel cost. Our empirical analysis exploits data on all of these critical dimensions, as well as data on expected future behavior under baseline conditions.

Application to water recreation demand in Kansas

To examine preferences for recreation demand and the proper measurement of time, this study relies on survey data on actual and hypothetical recreation at Clinton Lake, a reservoir located near Lawrence, Kansas.[1] The survey was implemented on site in the late summer of 1998. Unlike some previous studies, the sampling framework did not limit contact to only one adult from each recreation group (e.g. Loomis and Gonzalez-Caban 1997) since each recreator has her own time costs and pays an individual entrance fee. Three hundred ten surveys were started and at least partially completed.

The economic section of the survey instrument elicited information on the respondents' one-way travel distance and time to Clinton Lake and information on respondents' recreation behavior. It then asked behavioral questions. First,

the survey solicited information from respondents on their RP behavior as measured by actual (*ex post*) visits over the preceding 12-month period. Second, the
survey gathered information on baseline SP behavior as measured by intended
(*ex ante*) demand under actual/normal/current conditions over the coming
12-month period. Third, the survey elicited responses to alternative price conditions and alternative demand conditions that help to examine the valuation of
time costs.

The demographic section of the survey gathered information on employment status, capacity to work at a paid job on the day of visit, and hourly wage
or annual salary.[2] Using wage/salary data and one-way travel distance and
time, we calculate respondents' travel costs associated with recreating at
Clinton Lake. Transport costs equal the product of two-way travel distance and
$0.31 per mile, the IRS official rate of auto travel reimbursement for 1998.
Time costs are computed as the round trip travel time from the person's home.
In our analysis we consider two different specifications for the opportunity
cost of time: an exogenous fraction of the wage rate and an endogenous fraction. For each of these, we compute the average hourly wage using the midpoint of the respondent's identified wage, salary, or income bracket (except the
top bracket, where the bottom point is used) after dividing salary by 2,000
hours per year. For our exogenous fraction we assume that one-third of the
wage rate is the opportunity cost of time.[3] Access fees equal $1 per person for
Clinton Lake.

Based on RP data and baseline SP data it is difficult to assess separately the
individual money and time components of travel costs, since time and transport
costs are highly collinear. This lack of orthogonal variability makes it difficult to
infer time-money tradeoffs from recreation behavior alone and usually necessi-
tates using an exogenous fraction of the wage rate as the opportunity cost of
time. With these difficulties in mind, the survey presented additional hypothetical
scenarios. Consider first the contingent behavior questions. The survey generated
additional variation in money and time costs by asking respondents the following
questions:

a   "How many fewer recreational trips would you take if the access fee
    increased by $A?"
b   "How many fewer recreational trips would you take if your one-way travel
    time increased by B minutes?"

For this research project, A = 3 and B = 30. These questions ask the respondent to
re-examine intended visitation rather than reconsider in hindsight its previously
chosen visitation. This approach seems more appropriate for a contingent framework since respondents may be more willing to modify their perceptions of
future, as opposed to past, recreation conditions.[4]

Contingent pricing data serves as the natural counterpart to contingent behavior
data. While contingent behavior data reflect behavioral responses to various price
contingencies, contingent pricing data reflect pricing responses to various

behavioral contingencies. In this particular application, our analysis focuses on the behavioral contingency of zero demand. Specifically, the survey asks respondents to state the travel cost increase–in either time expenditures or money costs–needed to drive visits to zero. Given baseline costs, these responses identify each respondent's choke price. Each contingent pricing question relates to its contingent behavior counterpart and was presented as follows:

c   "How much would the access fee need to increase before you would stop visiting?"

d   "How much would the travel time need to increase before you would stop visiting?"[5]

Answers to these four additional survey questions provide complementary sources of information–along with the RP and SP baseline information–for identifying the parameters of the preference function in general and the opportunity cost of time in particular. Together the six endogenous responses can be thought of as providing six related points on the preference function, as shown conceptually in Figure 8.1. Questions (a) and (b), in particular, allow us to assess marginal responses to price changes, while questions (c) and (d) allow us to assess the component of demand related to the participation decision.

Of the 310 surveys started and at least partially completed, 259 provided complete information on travel time, travel distance, and wages or salary, and responded to all the contingent behavior and contingent pricing questions. We restrict our analysis to only these 259 observations.[6] Table 8.1 summarizes the responses to the key survey questions for these 259 recreators.

Table 8.1 Summary statistics

Variable	Mean	Standard deviation	Median
Baseline data			
Observed visits	5.57	6.52	3.00
Expected (ex ante) visits	6.64	6.81	4.50
Travel cost (dollars)	18.49	10.12	15.75
Time expenditure (minutes)	72.06	35.13	60.00
Contingent behavior data			
Reduced vists–access fee	2.64	4.51	1.00
Reduced visits–extra time	2.69	3.50	2.00
Contingent pricing data			
Money choke price (dollars)[1]	24.60	14.64	22.60
Time choke price (minutes)[1]	120.14	56.43	110.00
Respondent characteristics			
Annual income	29,534	25,797	15,000
Average hourly wage	14.77	12.90	7.50

Note
1 Computed using baseline money or time plus the response to the SP question.

Empirical modeling

Specification .

Our objective is to specify an econometric model that allows us to combine the different data sources described above in a single, structurally-consistent manner. To this end, we consider a linear demand equation given by the following:

$$X_i = \alpha + \beta \left(c_i + \left(\phi_i \times t_i \right) \right) + \gamma y_i, \qquad (8.3)$$

where X_i represents visits to Clinton Lake by person i, and c_i, t_i, y_i, and ϕ_i represent, respectively, baseline money costs, baseline time expenditures, income, and the opportunity cost of time. Our analysis estimates the demand parameters $\{\alpha, \beta, \gamma\}$. Conditional on assumptions regarding the opportunity cost of time, which we discuss below, we use the expression in (8.3) to derive a six-dimension system of estimating equations, each corresponding to one of the six response variables described above. Consider first the demand levels based on the RP trip observations, and responses to the SP expected future use under baseline conditions questions:

$$
\begin{aligned}
x_i^{RP} &= \alpha + \beta(c_i + \phi_i t_i) + \gamma y_i + \varepsilon_i^1, \\
x_i^{SP} &= \alpha + \beta(c_i + \phi_i t_i) + \gamma y_i + \varepsilon_i^2,
\end{aligned} \qquad (8.4)
$$

where money costs, c_i, and time expenditures, t_i, take their baseline (observed) values. The error terms, ε_i^j, for $j=1$ and 2, represent measurement error and/or unobserved heterogeneity. Consider next equations that reflect *changes* in demand that were recorded in response to the hypothetical increases in time costs and money costs. Starting from the demand level equation, we can express the (positively recorded) changes in demand as the following:

$$
\begin{aligned}
\Delta X_i^c &= \beta(c_i^1 - c_i) + \varepsilon_i^3, \\
\Delta X_i^t &= \beta \phi_i (t_i^1 - t_i) + \varepsilon_i^4,
\end{aligned} \qquad (8.5)
$$

where c_i^1 and t_i^1 are the experimentally-designed higher money and time costs, respectively. Recall that in our application the difference of $c_1 - c_0$ is \$3 and the difference of $t_1 - t_0$ equals 60 minutes. Similar to above, the error terms ε_i^j, for $j=3$ and 4, represent determinants of the change in demand not captured by the parametric specification. Finally, consider equations that reflect answers to the time and money contingent pricing questions described above. To derive these equations, we set equation (8.3) equal to zero and solve for the relevant time choke price or money choke price, which leads to the following relationships:

$$
\begin{aligned}
\hat{c}_i &= -\left(\alpha + \beta \phi_i t_i + \gamma y_i\right)/\beta + \varepsilon_i^5, \\
\hat{t}_i &= -\left(\alpha + \beta c_i + \gamma y_i\right)/\beta \phi_i + \varepsilon_i^6,
\end{aligned} \qquad (8.6)
$$

where the error terms once again reflect unobserved heterogeneity and/or measurement error.

To form an estimable model, we assume a parametric distribution for the error terms, $\varepsilon_i = (\varepsilon_i^1, \ldots, \varepsilon_i^6)$. Then we estimate the demand parameters jointly based on the six equations using maximum likelihood. Treatment of the assumed error distribution presents several challenges. First, the variable X_i^{RP} in equation (8.4) is truncated, in that the on-site sampling framework implies that all recorded visit totals are greater than or equal to one. Note, however, that this concern does not extend to the variable X_i^{SP}, in that the SP responses can in principle be zero. Second, both ΔX_i^c and ΔX_i^t are censored variables in that the upper limit of the change is constrained by X_i^{SP}, and the lower limit by zero. Finally, the equations in (8.6) are non-linear in parameters. For these reasons we make the simplifying assumption that the elements of ε_i are independent normal random variables such that $\varepsilon_i^j \sim N(0, \sigma_j^2)$, for $j = 1, \ldots, 6$. Note that this assumption ignores any correlation across the errors in the six equations – an assumption that is unlikely to hold in practice. Nonetheless, the independence assumption allows us to address the censoring and truncation challenges equation by equation in standard ways when constructing the likelihood function, while imposing the cross-equation parameter restrictions implied by our structural model. We discuss possibilities for relaxing this independence assumption below.

Our final specification topic concerns the opportunity cost of time. We consider models that include both an exogenously given fraction of the wage rate, and models that endogenously estimate this fraction. For the former, we assume that $\phi_i = 0.33 \times wage_i$; that is, we assume that the opportunity cost of time is one-third the wage rate. For the latter, we assume that $\phi_i = \theta \times wage_i$, where $\theta > 0$ is a parameter that we estimate along with the other demand equation parameters.

Lastly, to fit the data associated with the six-equation models, we include two separate intercepts. First, we include a level intercept, labeled by α, in the estimating equations that correspond to equation (8.4) above. And we include a choke price intercept, labeled α-*choke*, in the estimating equations that correspond to equation (8.6). Use of a single intercept in our initial model runs caused convergence problems in our maximum likelihood routines. The need for this deviation from our pure structural model may reflect the cognitive difficulty respondents faced when answering the contingent pricing questions. Similarly, it may reflect a general tendency among level SP responses (as opposed to changes-in SP responses) to differ from their RP counterparts. Whitehead *et al.* (2010) provide a further example of this in the context of contingent behavior questions.

Results

To evaluate our data-combining strategy, we present results for four- and six-equation models, in which the former models do not include the two equations for the time and money choke prices. For each we examine exogenous and endogenous specifications for the opportunity cost of time. Tables 8.2 and 8.3 show the estimation results.

Table 8.2 Four equation models

Parameter	Exogenous opp. cost		Endogenous opp. cost	
	Estimate	t-statistic	Estimate	t-statistic
Intercept	5.932	8.341	5.073	5.848
Own price	–0.148	–5.307	–0.098	–2.447
Income	0.044	2.779	0.065	3.353
Variance 1[1]	7.412	21.112	7.426	21.081
Variance 2[1]	6.751	21.008	6.735	21.114
Variance 3[1]	10.385	11.573	10.449	11.597
Variance 4[1]	7.102	13.442	6.913	13.370
Opp. cost. time (ϕ)	0.330	N/A	0.876	1.796

Note
1 Variance estimates refer to the distributions for the additive error terms in the four behavioral equations.

Consider first the four-equation models. For both specifications of the opportunity cost of time, all parameters are significant and of the expected sign. In particular, the own price effect is negative and the income effect (measured in thousands of dollars) is positive. We find demand to be more price elastic (i.e. the own price effect is larger in magnitude) in the model that sets the opportunity cost of time to be one-third the wage rate. For the endogenous opportunity cost of time model, we estimate 0.87 to be the appropriate fraction of the wage rate to use as the opportunity cost of time. In other words, the value $\phi = 0.87$ maximizes the likelihood function once we treat ϕ as an unknown parameter within the system. Thus, based on this point estimate, our data suggest that the opportunity cost of time is more than double what is often assumed. We note, however, that we cannot reject the null hypothesis that $\phi = 0.33$ for the endogenous time value model using conventional statistical cutoff levels. Specifically, a one-sided 95 percent confidence interval indicates a proportion between 0.076 and 1.67 of the wage, in which the literature consensus lies. Based on the results of the four-equation models, we tentatively conclude that little information is gained regarding the opportunity cost of time from the data-combining exercise, since the associated estimate lacks sufficient precision. Of course, our exercise certainly provides extra observations on price and quantity, which should contribute to more precise estimates of the other demand parameters.

Conclusions are somewhat different based on the results of the six-equation models, which are shown in Table 8.3. Across both the exogenous and endogenous time cost specifications, we find intuitively-signed and significant estimates for the demand parameters. Unlike the four-equation models, we find roughly comparable magnitudes for the own-price effect. The income effect is notably smaller in the endogenous time cost specification. The major difference concerns the opportunity cost of time. Here the addition of the time and money choke price equations reduces our estimate of the opportunity cost of time to just over 3 percent of the wage. This estimate is statistically and clearly economically

Table 8.3 Six equation models

Parameter	Exogenous opp. cost		Endogenous opp. cost	
	Estimate	t-statistic	Estimate	t-statistic
Intercept	5.604	8.934	5.890	7.500
Choke price intercept	2.825	4.053	3.310	3.308
Own price	−0.127	−4.088	−0.135	−3.303
Income	0.035	3.614	0.009	1.864
Variance 1[1]	7.552	20.620	7.491	20.861
Variance 2[1]	6.721	21.117	6.698	21.273
Variance 3[1]	10.331	11.715	10.385	11.598
Variance 4[1]	6.861	14.218	7.657	13.357
Variance 5[1]	13.355	22.416	11.338	22.124
Variance 6[1]	131.109	22.643	131.003	20.810
Opp. cost. time (ϕ)	0.330	N/A	0.034	5.914

Note
1 Variance estimates refer to the distributions for the additive error terms in the six behavioral equations.

different from the exogenous assumption of one-third the wage rate. This large difference between the four- and six-equation models suggests something important is at play in the choke price information, a point to which we return below.

To further compare the four sets of estimates, we compute the welfare effects based on the results of each model associated with the $3 increase in access costs and the 60-minute increase in round-trip travel time. Following the results of Hausman (1981), as explained in Freeman (2003: 70), the expenditure function associated with the linear demand equation given in (8.3) is the following:

$$E(p,U) = \left(U \times e^{\gamma p}\right) - \gamma^{-1}\left[\alpha + \beta p + \beta/\gamma\right], \tag{8.7}$$

where U is the reference utility level. At baseline conditions, expenditures are equal to observed income; we use this identity to compute the level of utility at baseline conditions, U^0, via equation (8.7). With the value for baseline utility U^0 in hand, the WTP for a given person for a change in price from p to p^1 is computed using the following formula:

$$WTP = y - \left\{U^0 \times e^{\gamma p^1} - \gamma^{-1}\left[\alpha + \beta p^1 + \beta/\gamma\right]\right\}, \tag{8.8}$$

where y is observed income and the demand parameters are obtained from the econometric models. Note that *WTP* is negative for price increases, since more money is needed to obtain the baseline utility when prices are higher.

Table 8.4 displays the results of our welfare analysis. The mean estimates are based on averages for the sample, and standard errors are calculated using 100 Krinsky and Robb (1986) draws of the parameter vectors. We find few

Table 8.4 Welfare estimates[1]

Model	$3 additional fee	1 hour extra travel
4 equation, exogenous time cost	−$9.99 (1.71)	−$14.46 (2.44)
4 equation, endogenous time cost	−$11.44 (1.93)	−$40.84 (36.65)
6 equation, exogenous time cost	−$10.03 (1.31)	−$14.27 (2.31)
6 equation, endogenous time cost	−$9.91 (1.06)	−$1.71 (0.30)

Note
1 Estimates are per person, per season. Standard errors given in parenthesis.

differences across the four models for the scenario involving an additional $3 fee, with the models suggesting an average welfare loss of $10 to $12 per season. The results are much more variable for the extra time cost scenario. Here the exogenous time value models (which assume an opportunity cost of time of one-third the wage rate) suggest welfare estimates of over $14 per person from the added round-trip travel time of 60 minutes, while the endogenous time value models suggest welfare estimates between $1.70 per person and $41 per person, though we note that there is substantial uncertainty surrounding the latter estimate. The variation in these welfare measures is consistent with the substantially different estimates of the time value magnitude.

Discussion

Our goal in this chapter has been to describe an approach for combining different data sources gathered using both RP and SP solicitation. Our maintained assumptions are that different margins of behavior can be observed through different experimental scenarios, and that information gleaned from the scenarios should be viewed as coming from the same underlying preference function. Given these assumptions, we suggest a conceptual framework that pulls together the different behavioral margins relevant for the data generating process, and present a structural econometric model that combines all the information in a single estimation routine.

Our findings confirm much of the accumulated wisdom in the literature on RP and SP. Combining actual and stated behavior data in our case is analytically and statistically simple, and seems appropriate for the given application, even though we do not present formal tests of parameter equality. Thus, the advertised ability of combined RP and SP data models (at least when behavior is the dependent variable) to provide additional variability for identification seems valid in our case. Abstracting from the opportunity cost of time, the similarity of the welfare measures for the access fee scenario across all four models also suggests some robustness in this dimension of our combined RP and SP specifications.

Matters are less clear when we consider the role of the contingent pricing information and the opportunity cost of time. We argue that the ability to implicitly observe people making time-money tradeoffs is a genuine strength of the SP solicitation strategy used in the Clinton Lake survey. For the four-equation models, we find a point estimate of the opportunity cost of time that is more than double the typical assumption in the literature. Though this estimate is not statistically different from one-third the wage rate, the estimate is illustrative of the potential difference we might uncover using this technique. It is an open question whether our sample is underpowered to detect a difference, or the literature consensus is indeed correct for this application and specification.

A dramatic deviation from the typical one-third the wage rate assumption is found when using the contingent pricing equations. Here, answers to the time and money choke solicitations suggest people were much more constrained by money than by time. This difference in constraints manifests itself in the small estimated opportunity cost of time. This observation leads to two discussion points. First, the cognitive difficulty in answering the continent behavior questions is undoubtedly high. It may be that the information content in these answers is comparatively low, in which case we may want to discount the finding of the low opportunity cost of time. Alternatively, the finding may be genuine: for this class of visitors engaged in a very local recreation experience, travel time may be something close to a non-binding constraint. Judging which explanation is correct will require additional research on SP survey design and validity.

We conclude by noting that our analysis is exploratory and could be generalized in many dimensions. First, a natural generalization of the econometric model would be to allow correlated errors across the six equations. This generalization may improve the efficiency of our estimates but will involve substantial computational challenges since the effects of individual-equation censoring and truncation will spill into the system as a whole. Second, another worthy generalization would pursue alternative functional specifications for the opportunity cost of time that allow time values to shift with an individual recreator's circumstances, such as the flexibility of the person's work schedule (i.e. ability to work on the day of recreation), and socio-economic characteristics, such as age.

Acknowledgements

We wish to thank several people for their guidance and assistance. First, we thank V. Kerry Smith, Michael Hanemann, Cathy Kling, Ju-Chin Huang, and Nathan Knust for expanding our understanding and encouraging our exploration. Dietrich Earnhart thanks Todd Abplanalp and Maria Martinez for their excellent research assistance. Finally, we thank the US Army Corp of Engineers and Clinton State Park for their support and assistance

Notes

1 The survey instrument was developed according to the responses of two focus groups – one including water recreators and one including fishermen – and a pretest of ten respondents. A copy of the survey instrument is available from the authors upon request.

2 The demographic section of the survey also gathered information on gender, age, marital status, number of children, and zip code. The economic section of the survey also gathered details on duration of visit (day versus overnight), fishing activity (yes or no), catch rate of anglers, entrance into the lake water (yes or no), and the perception of water quality (scale of one to five from very low to very high). Using wage/salary data, we calculate annual income. For salaried workers, it equals their salary. For wage earners, it equals full-time earnings based on the respondent's identified wage bracket midpoint. A summary of these data are available upon request.

3 Most of the previous studies examining the proper valuation of time use the full wage rate and one-third the wage rate as the two relevant benchmark rates (Feather and Shaw 1999; Englin and Shonkwiler 1995; Smith *et al.* 1983; McConnell and Strand 1981). The treatment of non-employed recreators remains an open question. Some studies explicitly place zero value on their time (e.g. Adamowicz *et al.* 1997). Other studies implicitly place zero value on their time by using the respondents' reported hourly wage rate (e.g. Englin and Cameron 1996; Cameron *et al.* 1996). Haab and McConnell (1996) implicitly place a zero value on the time of retired respondents by using the respondents' reported occupational category to determine the hourly wage rate. Some other studies implicitly place positive value on non-employed respondents' time by using hedonic wage estimates (e.g. Smith *et al.* 1983) or generating proxy wage rates based on respondents' reported annual income (Englin and Shonkwiler 1995; McConnell and Strand 1981; Herriges *et al.* 1999).

4 Huang *et al.* (1997) also use contingent behavior questions that ask the respondent to re-examine intended visitation. In their application, the questions pose a hypothetical increase in water quality.

5 Given the symmetry of the contingent behavior and contingent pricing questions, the survey instrument poses them in an interwoven fashion as shown below:

- How many times do you intend to visit the lake in the next 12 months?
- Suppose that, for each visit to Clinton Lake, you and other visitors were charged an additional fee of $3, and the collected fees were pooled with general federal revenues. How many fewer times in the next 12 months would you visit?
- How much would this additional fee need to be in order for you to stop visiting the lake altogether?
- If your travel time to the lake increased by 30 minutes (due to construction, for example), how many fewer times would you visit the lake in the next 12 months?
- How much longer (in minutes) would your travel time need to be in order for you to stop visiting the lake altogether?

6 Full documentation on the database is available upon request from the authors.

References

Adamowicz, Wiktor, J. Louviere, and M. Williams (1994) "Combining revealed and stated preference methods for valuing environmental amenities," *Journal of Environmental Economics and Management*, 26: 271–292.

Adamowicz, Wiktor, Joffre Swait, Peter Boxall, Jordan Louviere, and Michael Williams (1997) "Perceptions versus objective measures of environmental quality in combined revealed and stated preference models of environmental valuation," *Journal of Environmental Economics and Management*, 32: 65–84.

Cameron, Trudy Ann (1992) "Combining contingent valuation and travel cost data for the valuation of nonmarket goods," *Land Economics*, 68: 302–317.

Cameron, Trudy Ann, W. Douglas Shaw, Shannon E. Ragland, J. Mac Callaway, and Sally Keefe (1996) "Using actual and contingent behavior data with differing levels of time aggregation to model recreation demand," *Journal of Agricultural and Resource Economics*, 21: 130–149.

Earnhart, Dietrich (2004) "Time is money: Improved valuation of time and transportation costs," *Environmental and Resource Economics*, 29: 159–190.

Englin, Jeffery and Trudy Ann Cameron (1996) "Augmenting travel cost models with contingent behavior data," *Environmental and Resource Economics*, 7: 133–147.

Englin, Jeffrey and J.S. Shonkwiler (1995) "Modeling recreation demand in the presence of unobservable travel costs: Toward a travel price model," *Journal of Environmental Economics and Management*, 29: 368–377.

Feather, Peter and W. Douglas Shaw (1999) "Estimating the cost of leisure time for recreation demand models," *Journal of Environmental Economics and Management*, 38: 49–65.

Freeman III, A. Myrick (2003) *The Measurement of Environmental and Resource Values: Theory and Measurement*, second edition, Washington, DC: Resources for the Future.

Haab, Timothy C. and Kenneth E. McConnell (1996) "Count data models and the problem of zeros in recreation demand analysis," *American Journal of Agricultural Economics*, 78: 89–102.

Hausman, Jerry A. (1981) "Exact consumer's surplus and deadweight loss," *American Economic Review*, American Economic Association, 71: 662–676.

Herriges, Joseph, Catherine Kling, and Christopher Azevedo (1999) "Linking revealed and stated preferences to test external validity," Working Paper 99-WP 222, Iowa State University, online, available at: www.card.iastate.edu/publications/DBS/ PDFFiles/99wp222. pdf.

Huang, Ju-Chin, Timothy Haab, and John Whitehead (1997) "Willingness to pay for quality improvements: Should revealed and stated preference data be combined?" *Journal of Environmental Economics and Management*, 34: 240–255.

Krinsky, I. and A. Robb (1986) "On approximating the statistical properties of elasticities," *Review of Economics and Statistics*, 68: 715–19.

Larson, Douglas (1993) "Joint recreation choices and implied values of time," *Land Economics*, 69: 270–86.

Larson, Douglas and Sabina Shaikh (2001) "Empirical specifications requirements for two-constraint modle of recreation choice," *American Journal of Agricultural Economics*, 83: 428–440.

Layman, R.C., J. Boyce, and K. Criddle (1996) "Economic valuation of the Chinook salmon sport fishery of the Gulkana River, Alaska under current and alternative management plans," *Land Economics*, 72: 113–128.

Loomis, John B. and Armando Gonzalez-Caban (1997) "How certain are visitors of their economic values of river recreation: An evaluation using repeated questioning and revealed preference," *Water Resources Research*, 33: 1187–1193.

McConnell, K.E. and Ivar Strand (1981) "Measuring the cost of time in recreational demand analysis: An application to sport fishing," *American Journal of Agricultural Economics*, 63: 153–156.

Smith, V. Kerry, William Desvousges, and Matthew McGivney (1983) "The opportunity cost of travel time in recreation demand models," *Land Economics*, 59: 259–278.

Whitehead, John C., Daniel J. Phaneuf, Christopher F. Dumas, Jim Herstine, Jeffrey Hill, and Bob Buerger (2010) "Convergent validity of revealed and stated recreation behavior with quality change: A comparison of multiple and single site demands," *Environmental and Resource Economics*, 45: 91–112.

9 Combined conjoint-travel cost demand model for measuring the impact of erosion and erosion control programs on beach recreation

Ju-Chin Huang, George R. Parsons, P. Joan Poor, and Min Qiang Zhao

Introduction

Ocean beaches are important natural resources. Beach-related recreational activities in coastal areas also contribute significantly to local economies. According to the U.S. Army Corps of Engineers, close to half of the United States beaches are experiencing significant erosion problems. Beach erosion can be caused by a combination of human-induced development, global rising of the sea level, occasional violent weather systems, and chronic sediment transport by waves. Beach erosion results in losses of recreational beaches, tourist-related business, ocean front properties, land for aquaculture, and wildlife habitat.

Various erosion control programs/plans have been implemented in U.S. coastal areas. Most of the available erosion control methods have multiple effects, both positive and negative, on the beach and its surrounding environment. For example, some erosion control programs require installation of visible structures that can affect both the aesthetics of beaches and the overall experience of the beach trip itself. It is also possible for certain erosion control methods to initiate or accelerate erosion on neighboring beaches or affect coastal wildlife habitat. Some programs that require maintenance and adjustments may result in restricted use of beaches over a period of time.[1] If these effects are not considered when developing erosion control programs, non-optimal choices can result.

There are many studies examining the effectiveness and economic values of beach protection/preservation (e.g. Curtis and Shows 1984; Bishop and Boyle 1985; Lindsay *et al.* 1992; U.S. Army Corps of Engineers 1994; Stronge 1995; Dobkowski 1998). However, none of these studies emphasizes the potential multiple effects of erosion control methods on the coastal environment and the associated tradeoffs. In his review of the empirical literature on the economic value of marine recreation, Freeman (1995) points out that very few economic valuation studies have been done with a focus on the role of qualitative attributes of beaches.

The purpose of this study is to examine the impact of erosion and erosion control on beach recreation. A typical erosion control program is designed for the purpose of alleviating the effects of erosion. However, as discussed, it can also change the beach features and environment, visible structure on a beach, degraded conditions for wildlife viewing and so forth, thus directly affecting individuals' trip decisions. Further, beach visitors may react to various negative impacts differently, and the reaction to the impacts may be influenced by the type of activities that the visitors are engaged in. The variation in recreation activity across users is an important issue, yet less frequently addressed in empirical studies of recreation demand. A single trip demand model for all trips to a particular site assumes that all trips share common activities (or a single activity). Smith (1991) emphasizes that individuals are expected to have different demands for site services when they undertake different activities. Parsons (2003) argues that the more dissimilar the uses are, the greater the need is to disaggregate the model by type of use. Beach users clearly participate in different activities and the effects of erosion and erosion control programs are likely to vary across individuals given their different uses of the beach. Failure to recognize the differential effects of erosion control on beach activities may result in biased welfare measures.

In this study, the multiple effects of a beach erosion control program on the beach environment are viewed as the "attributes" of the program, and their impacts on demand for beach trips are examined. Trip frequency and contingent behavior data regarding program preferences are collected by randomly interviewing visitors at eight beaches in New Hampshire and Maine. In the survey, individuals are presented with hypothetical erosion control programs that have varying effects on the beach environment. The conjoint questioning format enables us to value the potential negative effects of an erosion control program on recreational beach use. We also elicit detailed information on types of recreation activity and compile the beach characteristics database. These data are incorporated into our trip demand analysis. We estimate a pooled single site travel cost model ("pooled" across eight beaches) and a set of trip change equations to capture effects of erosion and control methods. Recreation values associated with erosion and erosion control are computed for various beaches that are characterized by their popular activities and services. We find that erosion control is not necessarily beneficial when the erosion is relatively small. Further, the same erosion control program can generate different recreation values at different beaches because of the heterogeneity across beaches.

Conjoint design of contingent behavior beach recreation survey

We conducted three focus group meetings. These included seacoast residents, inland residents, and ocean front property owners in New Hampshire and southern Maine. The purpose of these meetings was to investigate individuals' perceptions of beach erosion, erosion control devices, and the impact of both on beach recreation. We found that most of the focus group participants were familiar with erosion control techniques. Most were supportive of the preservation of existing beaches through erosion control methods but were also concerned about the potential side effects of erosion control devices such as dangers to swimmers, impact on wildlife, impact on aesthetics, and water quality decline. The cost of implementing erosion control devices was of little concern to participants. They also felt that it would be difficult to evaluate the impact of erosion and erosion control if particular beach uses were not clearly described.

Based on the results of the focus groups, we developed an in-person trip frequency survey using a conjoint design to depict possible combinations of the side effects (impact attributes) of erosion control. In the conjoint questions, we asked people if erosion and the "multi-attribute" erosion control programs would affect the number of trips taken to the beach. Posters with information on erosion and erosion control were shown while the survey was administered to ensure a basic understanding of the issues.

The in-person interviews were conducted at eight beaches in New Hampshire and southern Maine in August, 2002. Three of the eight beaches are in New Hampshire. Individual trip information including size of party, length of stay, beach activities, and demographics was collected. Beach activities were grouped in advance according to the factor analysis results in an unpublished study by Leeworthy *et al.* (1987) and reproduced in Smith (1991). Respondents were asked to check all activity groups that applied to their trips. They were presented with a hypothetical scenario regarding erosion at the beach where they were interviewed and asked if they would consequently change their trip behavior in the following year. Respondents were then presented with two hypothetical erosion control programs (one at a time) that would prevent the stated erosion, but these erosion control programs could potentially alter the beach environment. Under the premise that all proposed erosion control programs could prevent erosion, each program was described according to a set of five potential effects on the beach environment. Respondents were asked how their beach trips would change with these erosion control programs. The five beach attributes affected by the programs include: visible structure (beach aesthetics), danger to swimmers, wildlife viewing, salt water quality, and sand quality.

The level of beach erosion and erosion control impact attributes were varied randomly across survey respondent according to an orthogonal main effects experimental design (Lorenzen and Anderson 1993).[2] The design of erosion control programs is summarized in Table 9.1. In our trip frequency analysis we

Table 9.1 Assigned levels of erosion and erosion control effects in the conjoint design

Attributes of an erosion control program (variable name)	Levels
Erosion	1, 4, 7, 10, 15, 25 (Feet/Year)
Visible structure on beach (ATT1)	Yes, No
1/1000 chance of minor injury to swimmers (ATT2)	Yes, No
Wildlife viewing reduced by 50% (ATT3)	Yes, No
Deterioration (10%) of salt water quality near beach (ATT4)	Yes, No
Sand quality: coarser sand with small rocks (ATT5)	Yes, No

use the following trip information from respondents: number of trips taken this year, reported change in number of trips given a hypothetical level of beach erosion, reported change in number of trips if an erosion control program (with certain impacts on beach environment) is put in place to prevent the beach erosion, reported change in number of trips for an alternative erosion control program.

An example of our contingent behavior questions to elicit responses of reported changes in trips listed above is given in the Appendix to this chapter. We consider day trips only in this analysis. Travel cost is assumed to be $0.35 per mile and the opportunity cost of travel time is assumed to be one third of the hourly wage rate (wage=income/2,080).[3] Table 9.2 summarizes the survey data and includes definitions of variables used in the regression analysis for the demand for day trips.

Approximately two-thirds of the survey respondents are New Hampshire or Maine residents. On average, each survey respondent took 16.37 trips during the year. The median is six trips, so that the distribution is right skewed, and close to 90 percent of respondents took 40 trips or less. One of the six levels of erosion (1, 4, 7, 10, 15, 25 feet/year) was randomly presented to respondents with an average of 10 feet. On average, erosion lead to 1.36 fewer trips per respondent with 78 percent reporting no change in trips. When an erosion control program was introduced to prevent the stated erosion and some potential negative effects of erosion control device were presented, respondents still took fewer trips but the impact was attenuated – respondents now reported taking on average 1.01 fewer trips with 82 percent reporting no change in trips. The responses indicate that erosion control can be desirable but the potential negative impacts on the beach environment can offset the benefits of erosion control.

The beach recreation activity groups (A1–A7) are also summarized in Table 9.2. Respondents may participate in more than one activity group during the same beach visit. The majority of the survey respondents did on-beach activities (A3). Observing wildlife, sightseeing, and walking/jogging constituted the second most popular group of activities (A1). Table 9.3 provides additional summary of characteristics and activities by beaches. The eight beaches in the survey are, from south to north, Hampton Beach State Park, Hampton Main Beach, Wallis Sands State Park, Long Sands, Ferry Beach, Old Orchard Beach, Crescent Beach, and Reid Beach State Park. Seven of these beaches currently have some erosion control device in place including seawalls, jetties, and sand dunes. By examining the summary of activities of survey respondents at the eight beaches, the beaches differ by activities that the visitors engaged in. For example, visitors at Ferry Beach and Old Orchard Beach are more likely to engage in activities in the A4 group (fishing, etc.) and visitors at Wallis Sands are noticeably less likely to have activities in the A1 group (wildlife viewing, sightseeing, etc.). In addition, four of the beaches have over half of their visitors from out of state. The average travel distance of visitors varies from 39 miles (Ferry Beach) to over 100 miles (Old Orchard Beach). It is perceivable that beach trip decisions are influenced by different characteristics and activities of beaches. If erosion and erosion control alter beach characteristics and activities, then the recreational impact of erosion and erosion control can differ across beaches. This is examined in the regression analysis.

Empirical model and welfare measures

Our analysis involves three steps. First, we estimate a pooled single site recreation demand model using data on the total number of recreation trips during the year as our dependent variable. Our focus in this step is on estimating the coefficient on travel cost which is used in our welfare analysis in step three. Second, we estimate two trip-change equations to predict how the demand for trips shifts with changes in erosion and erosion control programs. These models use the changes in day trips from our contingent behavior questions as dependent variables. Third, we use the quantity changes predicted in the second step and the travel cost coefficient in the first step to compute welfare measures using conventional welfare analytic methods.

We use a Poisson regression to estimate the demand function in the first step. [4]

$$\Pr ob(Y_i = y_i) = \frac{e^{-\lambda_i} \lambda_i^{y_i}}{y_i!}$$

$$y_i = 1, 2, \ldots \tag{9.1}$$

where Y_i is the quantity demanded for beach trips by individual i and λ_i is the expected value of Y_i that depends on the price of Y and individual characteristics. Since our survey was conducted in eight different beaches in New Hampshire and Maine, we have a "pooled" model which allows for variation in site characteristics. Hence, λ_i is specified to depend on beach characteristics as well.

$$\ln \lambda_i = \alpha + \beta_p \text{Cost}_i + \beta' X_i + \gamma' W_i \tag{9.2}$$

where Cost_i is the total travel cost per trip; X_i is a vector of individual i's characteristics including recreation activities at the beach; W_i is a vector of beach characteristics faced by the individual i; and α, β_p, β, and γ are parameters to be estimated.

As noted earlier, each respondent was asked a contingent behavior question about increased erosion and then two more questions about the installation of erosion control devices to forestall the erosion. In all cases, respondents were asked how they would adjust their trips in response to the hypothetical changes. We estimate two Poisson trip-change equations in step two – one for the erosion scenario and one for the two erosion control programs that prevent the erosion.

The basic form of the Poisson trip change models is

$$\Pr(M_{ji} = m_{ji}) = \frac{e^{-\omega_{ji}} \omega_{ji}^{m_{ji}}}{m_{ji}!},$$

Table 9.2 Variable definition and summary statistics

Variable	Definition	N	Mean	Std. dev.
DTripTY	Number of day trips taken this year	459	16.373	32.545
C1	Decline in number of day trips due to erosion (22.2% of respondents reported nonzero decline)	459	1.362	5.200
C2	Decline in number of day trips due to negative impacts of erosion control devices on beach environment (18.5% of respondents reported nonzero decline)	918	1.021	3.315
TtripTY	Total number of trips in the year of interview	459	17.431	33.460
TimeCost	Travel time cost ($) [=(income/2080)*hours*2]	459	14.428	16.345
TranCost	Out-of-pocket travel cost ($) [=$0.35*distance*2]	459	35.616	26.410
Cost	Total travel cost ($) [=TimeCost+TranCost]	459	50.044	38.427
SmlKids	Number of children under 13 of age in the household	459	0.625	0.955
Adults	Number of adults in the household	459	2.102	1.118
Income	Annual household income	459	59489	28088
NH	=1 if NH resident	459	27.7%	
ME	=1 if ME resident	459	39.7%	
Resident	=1 if resident of the state where the beach is located in	459	60.6%	
Distance	Travel distance (100 miles)	459	0.509	0.377
Ocean	=1 if own ocean-front property	459	3.9%	
Retire	=1 if retired	459	10.0%	
A1	=1 if trip involved wildlife observation, photography, sightseeing, walking/jogging, bicycling, driving	459	61.9%	
A2	=1 if trip involved sports, concerts/plays, festivals, museums, hiking/trailing, horseback riding, backpacking	459	19.2%	

Variable	Description	N		
A3	=1 if trip involved swimming, surfing, picnicking, family gathering, sunbathing, shell collecting	459	94.8%	
A4	=1 if trip involved camping, fishing	459	9.2%	
A5	=1 if trip involved pool swimming, golfing, tennis	459	8.9%	
A6	=1 if trip involved boating, canoeing, kayaking, sailing, water skiing	459	11.3%	
A7	=1 if trip involved theme parks, casinos	459	12.6%	
SandDune	=1 if sand dunes present at site	459	3 beaches	
Seawall	=1 if seawalls present at site	459	4 beaches	
Jetty	=1 if jetties present at site	459	2 beaches	
BathSuf	=1 if bath facilities sufficient according to beach manager	459	6 beaches	
Length	Length of beach (1000 ft)	459	5.101	5.104
WidthLT	Width of beach at low tide (100 ft)	459	2.858	1.356
WidthHT	Width of beach at high tide (100 ft)	459	0.761	0.356
SandQ	=1 if sand quality is good according to beach manager =0 if sand quality is okay or poor	459	86.5%	
Erosion	Proposed level of erosion [=1,4,7,10,15,25 ft]	459	10.211	7.646
EroRtLT	Ratio of proposed erosion to width of beach at low tide	459	0.051	0.060
EroRtHT	Ratio of proposed erosion to width of beach at high tide	459	0.179	0.189

Table 9.3 Summaries of characteristics and activities by beaches

	Hampton Beach State Park	Hampton Main Beach	Wallis Sands	Long Sands	Ferry	Old Orchard	Crescent	Reid
WidthHT (width at high tide (ft))	82.5	82.5	100	35	50	150	30	115
Resident (% of visitors are residents)[1]	32.8	13.0	71.0	7.6	84.4	33.7	79.7	96.7
Distance (average travel distance, 100 miles)[1]	0.601	0.673	0.667	0.751	0.390	1.001	0.462	0.493
A1 (nature %)[1]	62.6	62.9	34.5	50.3	73.1	73.1	52.9	71.7
A2 (sports %)[1]	13.1	38.4	17.6	8.1	41.4	21.2	10.2	20.5
A3 (sunbath %)[1]	95.8	98.4	97.1	83.9	100.0	100.0	96.7	90.7
A4 (fish %)[1]	6.1	2.2	4.7	3.8	15.7	17.1	9.2	13.1
A5 (golf %)[1]	6.5	12.7	2.8	5.6	10.2	18.4	6.5	13.1
A6 (boat %)[1]	14.9	6.0	2.1	1.4	14.8	7.8	11.1	15.3
A7 (park %)[1]	6.7	38.3	5.3	7.4	6.0	12.6	0.7	12.2
Sea Wall (=1 if seawalls present)	1	1	1	1	0	0	0	0
Sand Dune (=1 if sand dunes present)	1	0	0	0	0	0	1	1
Jetty (=1 if jetties present)	0	0	1	0	1	0	0	0

Note

1 The summary statistic is weighted by the visit frequency: $\sum_{i=1}^{n} \frac{x_i}{trip_i} / \sum_{i=1}^{n} \frac{1}{trip_i}$, where x_i is the characteristic or activity variable, and $trip_i$ is the total number of trips taken by individual i.

$j = 1, 2$. Let C_{1i} be the change in number of day trips due to erosion and C_{2i} be the change in number of day trips assuming the erosion is mitigated by erosion control and that there are some (negative) impacts associated with that control. The expected values of the trip changes are specified as follows:

$$\omega_{1i} = \ell n(\overline{C}_{1i} + 1) = \delta_1 E_i + \delta_2 E_i / \text{Width}_i + \eta'(E_i {}^* W_i) + \phi'(E_i {}^* X_i) \tag{9.3}$$

$$\omega_{2i} = \ell n(\overline{C}_{2i} + 1) = \kappa' \text{ATT}_i + \theta'(\text{ATT}_i {}^* A_i) + \nu'(\text{ATT}_i {}^* W_i) + \psi'(\text{ATT}_i {}^* X_i) + \tau E_i / \text{Width}_i \tag{9.4}^{5}$$

where $\overline{C}_{1i}$ is the expected value of C_{1i}; E_i is the hypothesized level of beach erosion faced by individual i and Width_j is the width of beach j in high tide to assess the severity of suggested erosion; A_i is a vector of beach activity groups (that in this study, seven beach activity groups $A = [A1, A2, \ldots, A7]'$ are identified); $\overline{C}_{2i}$ is the expected value of C_{2i}; ATT is the vector of impact attributes appearing in the conjoint question (visible structure, swim danger, wildlife impact, water quality, and sand quality); and δ_1, δ_2, η, μ, ϕ, κ, θ, ν, and ψ are parameters to be estimated.

The stated level of erosion (E) and the vector of impact attributes of an erosion control program (ATT) are the sole factors to induce the changes in trips in our conjoint questions. Consequently E is interacted with all explanatory variables in equation (9.3) and ATT is interacted with all explanatory variables in equation (9.4) except for the erosion severity variable E/Width. In the survey, respondents were told that the implementation of an erosion control program would prevent the occurrence of the stated erosion. However, the respondents could still be influenced by the stated severity of erosion even though it was eradicated by erosion control. For example, some survey respondents could be skeptical about the effectiveness of the proposed erosion control program if the stated severity of erosion was high. Because of the order of questions in the survey, the response to erosion control could also be influenced by the previous response to erosion. There might be other unobserved factors associated with the stated erosion level that affected the response to erosion control. Therefore, the erosion severity variable E/Width is included in equation (9.4) as a testable hypothesis whether the trip change in response to erosion control is influenced by the hypothesized severity of erosion.

There is no intercept term in each of the trip change equations; this coupled with the addition of 1 on the left hand side of the equations to ensure that $\overline{C}_{1i} = 0$ when $E = 0$ and $\overline{C}_2 = 0$ when $\text{ATT} = 0$. Beach erosion and negative impacts of erosion control on the beach environment are in general perceived as "bad" in that the vast majority of beach goers responded by taking fewer trips. Less than 1 percent of the sample reported that they would increase their trips if erosion occurred. We deleted these observations from our sample.[6] The predicted trip changes (reductions) are computed from the estimation results of equations (9.3) and (9.4) as $\hat{C}_{ji} = e^{\hat{\omega}_{ji}} - 1$, where $j = 1, 2$.

The expected quantity demanded for beach trips takes on a semi-log functional form (equation (9.2)). As Hellerstein and Mendelsohn (1993) and Whitehead *et al.* (2000) show with this form of demand, the change in consumer surplus (ΔCS) due to a quality change is

$$\Delta CS = \frac{\hat{C}}{\hat{\beta}_p} \tag{9.5}$$

where $\hat{C}$ is the predicted change in the number of beach trips due to the introduction of the hypothetical erosion or erosion control scenario, estimated using equations (9.3) and (9.4) and $\hat{\beta}_p$ is the coefficient on travel cost and is estimated using equation (9.1). In the final step of our analysis, a variety of scenarios, varying degrees of erosion and impact of erosion control will be considered for each of the eight studied beaches. Each scenario gives rise to a $\hat{C}$ and all use equation (9.5) to compute the welfare change.

Estimation results

We estimate the demand for trips using the equations (9.1) and (9.2). The results are reported in Table 9.4. The coefficient of the travel cost variable is negative and significant as expected. Activity groups (A1–A7) are included in the models. Each activity group is indicated by a keyword in Table 9.4, and the subsequent tables. The complete list of activities in each group is given in Table 9.2. All groups of beach activities significantly influence the demand for trips in different degrees. Ocean-front property owners and retirees take significantly more beach trips. Households with more adults or more children under an age of 13, take fewer beach trips. Sufficient bathhouse facilities (BathSuf) are important to trip decisions. The width of beach at high tide also matters. Beach goers tend to take fewer trips to those beaches with sand dunes and jetties, providing evidence that beach trip decisions are affected by the impacts of erosion control on the beach environment. Finally, the estimated coefficient on the travel cost variable is –0.014. The estimated coefficient of the cost variable is used to perform the subsequent welfare analysis.

The trip change equation associated with erosion (equation (9.3)) is estimated with two specifications. The explanatory variables in the *basic* model include only the proposed level of erosion and the relative size of erosion (as a proportion of the width of the beach at high tide). It describes the average impact of erosion on recreation for all beaches. The augmented *activity specific* model explores the differential effects of erosion on trip decisions according to individual specific beach uses by adding explanatory variables that interact erosion with groups of beach activities, as well as the interactions of erosion with location of the respondent's home and the presence of erosion control device. The estimation results are reported in Table 9.5. Note that the dependent variable indicates *fewer* trips taken as a result of beach erosion, so a positive coefficient on the erosion variable implies a reduction in beach trips when erosion occurs.

Table 9.4 Estimated demand for beach trips[1,2]

Dependent variable	DTripTY	Dependent variable	DTripTY
Intercept	3.167***	Adults	−0.102***
	(0.109)		(0.013)
Cost	−0.014***	Retire	0.415***
	(0.0005)		(0.030)
A1 (nature)	0.147***	Resident	0.544***
	(0.028)		(0.035)
A2 (sports)	0.286***	SandDune	−1.116***
	(0.031)		(0.123)
A3 (sunbath)	−0.496***	SeaWall	0.158
	(0.045)		(0.166)
A4 (fish)	0.287***	Jetty	−0.501***
	(0.044)		(0.080)
A5 (golf)	−0.470***	BathSuf	0.531***
	(0.050)		(0.105)
A6 (boat)	0.218***	Length	0.021**
	(0.038)		(0.009)
A7 (parks)	0.127***	WidthHT	0.032
	(0.040)		(0.052)
Ocean	0.903***	LLF	−5,032.168
	(0.036)	N	459
SmlKids	−0.063***		
	(0.015)		

Notes
1 Standard errors are in parentheses.
2 *, ** and *** indicate significance levels at 0.1, 0.05, and 0.01, respectively.

As seen, erosion significantly reduces recreation trips. The relative size of erosion is not significant in the *basic* model but it becomes significant with twice as large magnitude in the *activity specific* model in which the heterogeneity of beaches is addressed. Most of the interaction terms are significant in the activity specific model, indicating that the magnitude of erosion impact on trip decisions depends on the individual beach activities and beach characteristics.

Based on the estimation results in Tables 9.4 and 9.5, and the summary of beach characteristics in Table 9.3, we compute the average changes in consumer surplus for two levels of beach erosion: one foot (slight) and ten feet (moderate) erosion, and report the estimates by beaches in Table 9.6.[7,8] According to the *basic* model, the average change in consumer surplus per visitor per year is approximately $4 for one foot of erosion and $50 for ten feet of erosion. The welfare measures do not vary significantly across beaches since they are distinguished only by the relative size of erosion in the *basic* model. The *activity specific* model differentiates the beaches by the corresponding activities and characteristics. Based on the *activity specific* model, the average changes in consumer surplus are quite different among the studied beaches. The benefits per visitor per year range from $1.70 (Hampton Main Beach) to $6.80 (Ferry Beach) for preventing one foot of erosion, and from $19.50 to $105.40 for preventing

Table 9.5 Estimated trip changes when erosion occurs[1,2]

Dependent Variable: log($C_1 + 1$)

Variable	Basic model	Activity specific model
Erosion	0.050***	0.043**
	(0.004)	(0.017)
Erosion/WidthHT	0.294	0.647**
	(0.204)	(0.271)
Erosion*A1 (nature)	–	0.006
		(0.005)
Erosion*A2 (sports)	–	0.001
		(0.006)
Erosion*A3 (sunbath)	–	0.023*
		(0.012)
Erosion*A4 (fish)	–	–0.016**
		(0.008)
Erosion*A5 (golf)	–	–0.024***
		(0.009)
Erosion*A6 (boat)	–	0.068***
		(0.006)
Erosion*A7 (parks)	–	–0.027***
		(0.009)
Erosion*Resident	–	–0.009
		(0.006)
Erosion*Distance	–	–0.038***
		(0.008)
Erosion*SeaWall	–	–0.016***
		(0.005)
Erosion*SandDune	–	–0.014**
		(0.007)
Erosion*Jetty	–	0.027***
		(0.007)
LLF	–1,452.370	–1,355.272
N	459	459

Notes
1 Standard errors are in parentheses.
2 *, ** and *** indicate significance levels at 0.1, 0.05, and 0.01, respectively.

ten feet of erosion. In general, the change in consumer surplus differs significantly across beaches. Every beach has its own characteristics and endowments, and attracts visitors to come for different activities. Taking into account the beach activities and characteristics helps discern the welfare effects of erosion on different beaches.

The regression analyses for trip reductions from the possible negative beach effects of erosion control (equation (9.4)) are given in Table 9.7. The dependent variable indicates *fewer* trips taken due to the negative effects of erosion control so a positive coefficient estimate indicates a trip reduction. We first report a *basic* model that only includes the impact attributes (ATT1–ATT5) of

Table 9.6 Annual per-person losses from beach erosion ($)[1]

	Hampton Beach State Park	Hampton Main Beach	Wallis Sands	Long Sands	Ferry	Old Orchard	Crescent	Reid
The Basic Model								
1 foot of erosion	3.932	3.932	3.885	4.300	4.108	3.810	4.406	3.856
	(0.236)	(0.236)	(0.251)	(0.270)	(0.218)	(0.281)	(0.320)	(0.262)
10 feet	50.565	50.565	49.803	56.638	53.437	48.615	58.452	49.337
	(3.549)	(3.549)	(3.795)	(4.235)	(3.259)	(4.272)	(5.178)	(3.970)
The Activity Specific Model								
1 foot of erosion	1.818	1.746	3.702	2.529	6.791	2.028	3.988	2.389
	(0.410)	(0.390)	(0.405)	(0.470)	(0.468)	(0.596)	(0.365)	(0.435)
10 feet	20.392	19.498	46.897	29.693	105.445	23.059	51.479	27.805
	(5.119)	(4.832)	(6.235)	(6.384)	(9.729)	(7.642)	(5.756)	(5.806)

Note
1 Standard errors are in parentheses.

erosion control and the relative size of erosion as explanatory variables. In the *basic* model, all five impacts of erosion control significantly cause reduction of beach trips. The effect of erosion control on reduction of wildlife viewing has the largest impact on reducing beach trips. The variable of relative size of erosion is also significant, indicating that there are unobserved factors associated with the stated erosion to cause a significant reduction of future beach visits even when erosion control is in place to prevent the stated erosion. An augmented *activity specific* model interacting impact attributes with beach activities and characteristics is also reported.[9] The results show that if sand dunes are currently present, the trip reduction caused by visible structure due to erosion control is enhanced (positive coefficient on ATT1*SandDune). Conversely, beach visitors are less concerned about visible structure from erosion control when a seawall is already present at the beach (negative coefficient on ATT1*SeaWall) possibly because visitors have grown accustomed to the visible seawall. The impact of erosion control attributes on trip changes depends on individual beach uses. For examples, those who come to beach to fish and camp are not adversely affected by visible erosion control devices (negative coefficient on ATT1*A4); those who come to enjoy the nature will take fewer trips if erosion control will result in significantly less wildlife sighting (positive coefficient on ATT3*A1); those who engage in boating and kayaking will take fewer trips if water quality is affected by erosion control (positive coefficient on ATT4*A6). Similar to the *basic* model, the change in beach visits in response to erosion control is significantly affected by the stated relative size of erosion.

The changes in consumer surplus from the effects of erosion control by beaches based on the *basic* model are computed and reported in Table 9.8. For comparison, we again compute welfare measures for two levels of stated erosion, one foot and ten feet. According to the *basic* model, given the stated erosion level to be one foot, on average the annual loss of consumer surplus per visitor from an erosion control program is approximately $15 if the program requires building a visible structure (ATT1), $19 if it results in a chance of minor injury to swimmers (ATT2), $23 if it reduces wildlife viewing (ATT3), $9 if deterioration of salt water quality results (ATT4), and $20 if sand quality is affected (ATT5). An erosion control device may have multiple impacts. For example, if a jetty is visible and can affect water quality (ATT1 and ATT4) then on average the change in consumer surplus is about $25. If an erosion control device affects wildlife viewing and sand quality (ATT3 and ATT5) such as sand dunes, then the overall change in consumer surplus per visitor per year is approximately $49. Welfare effects for other combinations of impact attributes can also be computed. Note that the change in consumer surplus of multiple impacts is not the sum of welfare changes from the individual impacts because of the nonlinearity in the Poisson model. Also, there is no significant difference of surplus changes across beaches for a hypothesized one-foot erosion. For a stated ten-foot erosion, on average the loss of consumer surplus for each of the erosion control impacts increases to about $22, $28, $32, $17,

Table 9.7 Estimated trip changes in response to effects of erosion control on beach environment[1,2]

Dependent Variable: log(C2+1)

Variable	Basic model	Activity specific model
ATT1 (=1, visible structure)	0.179***	0.217**
	(0.045)	(0.093)
ATT2 (=1, swim danger)	0.230***	0.260***
	(0.045)	(0.046)
ATT3 (=1, wildlife viewing ↓)	0.268***	0.089
	(0.045)	(0.069)
ATT4 (=1, water quality ↓)	0.115**	0.138*
	(0.045)	(0.076)
ATT5 (=1, sand quality ↓)	0.245***	0.173***
	(0.047)	(0.052)
ATT1*A4 (fish)	–	−0.357***
		(0.136)
ATT1*SeaWall	–	−0.175**
		(0.074)
ATT1*SandDune	–	0.167**
		(0.085)
ATT1*Jetty	–	0.101
		(0.106)
ATT2*A7 (parks)	–	−0.230**
		(0.108)
ATT3*A1 (nature)	–	0.316***
		(0.080)
ATT4*A1 (nature)	–	−0.147*
		(0.082)
ATT4*A4 (fish)	–	−0.222
		(0.137)
ATT4*A6 (boat)	–	0.354***
		(0.101)
ATT4*Jetty	–	0.244***
		(0.092)
ATT5*A2 (sports)	–	−0.382***
		(0.089)
ATT5*A4 (fish)	–	0.968***
		(0.131)
Erosion/WidthHT	0.617***	0.520***
	(0.105)	(0.108)
LLF	−2,138.326	−2,072.547
N	918	918

Notes
1 Standard errors are in parentheses.
2 *, ** and *** indicate significance levels at 0.1, 0.05, and 0.01, respectively.

Table 9.8 Annual per-person losses due to effects of erosion control on beach environment ($): the basic model[1,2]

	Hampton Beach State Park	Hampton Main Beach	Wallis Sands	Long Sands	Ferry	Old Orchard	Crescent	Reid
Losses due to negative effect(s) of erosion control to prevent 1 foot of erosion								
ATT1 (=1, visible structure)	14.720	14.720	14.606	15.603	15.142	14.429	15.861	14.537
	(3.950)	(3.950)	(3.947)	(3.981)	(3.964)	(3.941)	(3.991)	(3.945)
ATT2 (=1, swim danger)	19.207	19.207	19.088	20.136	19.651	18.901	20.407	19.015
	(4.098)	(4.098)	(4.095)	(4.128)	(4.111)	(4.090)	(4.137)	(4.093)
ATT3 (=1, wildlife viewing ↓)	22.738	22.738	22.614	23.703	23.199	22.420	23.985	22.538
	(4.293)	(4.293)	(4.289)	(4.324)	(4.307)	(4.284)	(4.335)	(4.287)
ATT4 (=1, water quality ↓)	9.354	9.354	9.248	10.182	9.750	9.081	10.424	9.182
	(3.688)	(3.688)	(3.684)	(3.716)	(3.700)	(3.679)	(3.725)	(3.682)
ATT5 (=1, sand quality ↓)	20.647	20.647	20.526	21.591	21.098	20.336	21.866	20.452
	(4.386)	(4.386)	(4.382)	(4.420)	(4.402)	(4.377)	(4.431)	(4.380)
ATT1=1 and ATT4=1	25.261	25.261	25.134	26.252	25.735	24.935	26.541	25.056
	(5.805)	(5.805)	(5.801)	(5.841)	(5.822)	(5.795)	(5.852)	(5.799)
ATT3=1 and ATT5=1	49.014	49.014	48.856	50.248	49.604	48.608	50.607	48.759
	(7.209)	(7.209)	(7.204)	(7.248)	(7.227)	(7.197)	(7.260)	(7.201)

Losses due to negative effect(s) of erosion control to prevent 10 feet of erosion

ATT1 (=1, visible structure)	20.749	20.749	19.545	30.645	25.363	17.684	33.702	18.812
	(4.275)	(4.275)	(4.189)	(5.336)	(4.696)	(4.077)	(5.773)	(4.142)
ATT2 (=1, swim danger)	25.549	25.549	24.282	35.958	30.402	22.325	39.173	23.511
	(4.420)	(4.420)	(4.333)	(5.511)	(4.849)	(4.221)	(5.964)	(4.286)
ATT3 (=1, wildlife viewing ↓)	29.326	29.326	28.010	40.138	34.368	25.977	43.479	27.209
	(4.632)	(4.632)	(4.541)	(5.767)	(5.080)	(4.423)	(6.238)	(4.491)
ATT4 (=1, water quality ↓)	15.009	15.009	13.880	24.291	19.337	12.134	27.159	13.192
	(3.988)	(3.988)	(3.908)	(4.983)	(4.382)	(3.804)	(5.393)	(3.864)
ATT5 (=1, sand quality ↓)	27.089	27.089	25.803	37.663	32.020	23.814	40.929	25.020
	(4.731)	(4.731)	(4.641)	(5.843)	(5.172)	(4.522)	(6.301)	(4.591)
ATT1=1 and ATT4=1	32.025	32.025	30.674	43.126	37.201	28.586	46.556	29.852
	(6.141)	(6.141)	(6.056)	(7.159)	(6.545)	(5.943)	(7.581)	(6.009)
ATT3=1 and ATT5=1	57.433	57.433	55.751	71.250	63.876	53.153	75.519	54.728
	(7.589)	(7.589)	(7.491)	(8.792)	(8.063)	(7.362)	(9.299)	(7.437)

Notes
1 Standard errors are in parentheses.
2 By comparing the benefits and losses in Tables 9.6 and 9.8, the cells with bold text indicate the cases where recreation losses of erosion outweigh the losses from the negative effects of erosion control that preventing erosion generates overall positive recreational benefits.

and $30, respectively. The annual per-person loss in consumer surplus averages about $35 if an erosion control program results in both visible structure and deteriorated water quality, and the average loss of per-person consumer surplus is close to $61 if reduced wildlife viewing and lower sand quality result from the erosion control program. We also see differences in surplus changes across beaches. Under the hypothesized ten feet of erosion, the negative effects of erosion control will result in the largest losses at Crescent Beach and smallest losses at Old Orchard Beach.

Comparing the changes in consumer surplus from erosion in Table 9.6 and from erosion control in Table 9.8, it is clear that when the erosion is slight (e.g. one foot), erosion control is not beneficial since the losses of erosion do not outweigh the losses from the negative effects of erosion control. When erosion is moderate, erosion control can be beneficial. The cells with bold text in Table 9.8 indicate the cases where losses of erosion are larger than the losses from the negative effects of erosion control. When erosion is ten feet, any erosion control device that causes only one of the five negative effects generates an overall positive benefit at any of the beaches. However, erosion control programs that induce multiple negative effects are not necessarily desirable. For example, an erosion control program with a visible structure and reduced water quality is still beneficial at all eight beaches, while an erosion control program with reduced wildlife viewing and sand quality is not. The results show that certain negative impacts of erosion control are worse than others. Reducing wildlife viewing is considered by beach visitors the most negative impact of erosion control. The findings suggest that certain erosion control devices are preferred by visitors for their less negative effects on the beach environment.

Based on the *activity specific* model, the computed changes in consumer surplus associated with impact attributes of erosion control by beaches are reported in Table 9.9. Among the five impact attributes, reduced wildlife viewing remains to be the most devastating impact of erosion control on recreation. The average annual per-person loss of reduced wildlife viewing due to erosion control is about $24 for a stated one-foot erosion and $31 for a ten-foot erosion.[10] Comparing across beaches, the recreation impact of the five effects of erosion control differs. For example, adding a visible structure for erosion control causes the smallest loss in recreation value at Hampton Main Beach where a seawall is already present and incurs the largest loss at the more natural Crescent Beach; deterioration of water quality results in more losses of recreation values at Wallis Sands and Ferry Beaches than at Old Orchards Beach; Ferry Beach incurs the largest loss of recreation value with a combination of visible structure and lower water quality from erosion control.

Comparing the welfare losses of erosion and losses from the negative effects of erosion control (the bottom halves of Tables 9.6 and 9.9), the net welfare effect depends on the amount of erosion that is controlled. The net welfare effects of erosion control to prevent one foot of erosion will always be negative since the estimated losses of erosion control are larger than the losses of erosion. When erosion is ten feet, the cells with bold text in Table 9.9 indicate the cases where erosion control generates overall positive recreational benefits. For example, an erosion control program with a visible device will have positive recreational benefits at most beaches except for Hampton Beach State Park and Reid State Park; a program that reduces wildlife viewing will not be beneficial at five out of the eight beaches; all beaches will benefit from erosion control if the only negative effect is slight deterioration of water quality; half of the beaches will still have positive recreational benefits from erosion control when it results in visible structure and reduced water quality but only two beaches benefit from erosion control if it affects wildlife viewing and sand quality.[11] In sum, erosion control can be beneficial to prevent moderate to severe erosion that the welfare loss associated with the erosion is likely to exceed the loss due to erosion control disamenities. However, for small amounts of erosion, erosion control programs may bring on larger negative effects than the erosion itself.

Conclusion

We designed the trip frequency, in-person survey to value beach erosion control and employed a conjoint design in formulating the hypothetical erosion control to take into account the impacts of erosion control on the beach environment. The differential effects of erosion and erosion control on individual trip decisions due to varying trip activities and beach characteristics were demonstrated. We find that on average the loss of consumer surplus for a ten-foot erosion is approximately $50 per person, per year. However, this welfare loss is not completely recovered by erosion control due to potential negative effects of erosion control on the beach environment. The benefits of erosion control can be exaggerated if these negative erosion control effects are ignored. Further, the changes in consumer surplus due to erosion and erosion control vary with individual beach activities and characteristics. Our findings reiterate the importance of distinguishing the purposes of recreational trips and incorporating beach characteristics in the welfare analysis of beach erosion control. The proposed survey questioning format and estimation strategies give rise to program- and beach-specific welfare measures that may be used by policy makers to design economically efficient erosion control programs at locations facing different beach uses.

In this study, we examine the impact of erosion control on the demand for day trips. It is expected that the effects of erosion on the demand for overnight trips will differ. Also, the focus here is the use value of beach erosion control. Huang *et al.* (2007) find that beach preservation is valued by the general public for its contribution to property protection, protection of wildlife habitat, etc. The total benefits of beach erosion control must take into account both the use and non-use values, and further research to combine these values is warranted.

Table 9.9 Annual per-person losses due to effects of erosion control on beach environment ($): The activity-specific model

Losses due to negative effect(s) of erosion control to prevent 1 foot of erosion

	Hampton Beach State Park	Hampton Main Beach	Wallis Sands	Long Sands	Ferry	Old Orchard	Crescent	Reid
ATT1 (=1, visible structure)	15.363 (6.780)	2.997 (5.387)	10.073 (7.299)	3.211 (5.379)	22.444 (9.082)	12.421 (7.699)	31.996 (6.497)	29.252 (6.325)
ATT2 (=1, swim danger)	20.472 (4.237)	14.008 (4.736)	20.648 (4.259)	21.100 (4.245)	20.996 (4.258)	18.965 (4.172)	22.791 (4.410)	19.150 (4.176)
ATT3 (=1, wildlife viewing ↓)	24.473 (4.450)	24.544 (4.453)	16.184 (4.576)	21.601 (4.425)	28.118 (4.666)	27.426 (4.647)	22.585 (4.428)	27.104 (4.615)
ATT4 (=1, water quality ↓)	6.896 (4.049)	5.092 (4.059)	28.414 (8.351)	5.644 (4.206)	25.359 (8.276)	1.734 (3.835)	7.285 (4.106)	4.604 (3.883)
ATT5 (=1, sand quality ↓)	14.849 (4.232)	3.921 (4.153)	12.152 (4.139)	15.288 (4.324)	13.881 (4.508)	21.358 (4.514)	19.487 (4.413)	18.199 (4.334)
ATT1=1 & ATT4=1	23.133 (8.064)	7.797 (6.390)	41.880 (10.828)	7.913 (6.394)	54.407 (13.201)	14.156 (8.752)	40.560 (8.451)	35.245 (8.100)
ATT3=1 & ATT5=1	43.651 (7.026)	29.166 (6.579)	30.540 (6.749)	39.815 (6.950)	46.198 (7.603)	56.493 (7.910)	46.135 (7.223)	51.612 (7.528)

Losses due to negative effect(s) of erosion control to prevent 10 feet of erosion

ATT1 (=1, visible structure)	20.457 (7.240)	**7.368** (5.759)	**14.001** (7.713)	**13.956** (6.616)	**31.702** (10.100)	**15.093** (7.912)	**49.540** (8.192)	33.454 (6.523)
ATT2 (=1, swim danger)	25.864 (4.499)	19.023 (5.058)	25.083 (4.448)	34.407 (5.490)	30.112 (4.899)	**21.844** (4.273)	**38.780** (6.071)	**22.932** (4.329)
ATT3 (=1, wildlife viewing ↓)	30.098 (4.743)	30.174 (4.746)	20.405 (4.793)	34.980 (5.711)	37.934 (5.393)	30.574 (4.767)	38.539 (6.148)	31.217 (4.793)
ATT4 (=1, water quality ↓)	**11.494** (4.298)	**9.585** (4.301)	**33.221** (8.799)	**16.738** (5.240)	34.903 (9.357)	**4.067** (3.933)	**20.654** (5.516)	**7.782** (4.030)
ATT5 (=1, sand quality ↓)	**19.913** (4.528)	**8.346** (4.425)	**16.179** (4.353)	27.763 (5.593)	22.298 (5.135)	24.314 (4.629)	34.917 (6.125)	**21.941** (4.503)
ATT1=1 & ATT4=1	28.680 (8.503)	12.449 (6.730)	47.332 (11.398)	19.332 (7.530)	66.804 (14.610)	**16.883** (8.963)	59.552 (10.026)	39.697 (8.295)
ATT3=1 & ATT5=1	50.397 (7.330)	35.066 (6.874)	**35.449** (6.982)	55.802 (8.261)	57.789 (8.300)	60.564 (8.034)	66.069 (9.000)	56.743 (7.708)

Notes
1 Standard errors are in parentheses.
2 By comparing the benefits and losses in Tables 9.6 and 9.9, the shaded cells with bold text indicate the cases where recreation losses of erosion outweigh the losses from the negative effects of erosion control that preventing erosion generates overall positive recreational benefits.

Acknowledgements

The research is partially supported by the New Hampshire Sea Grant #NA16RG1035.

Appendix: Sample conjoint-contingent behavior questions in the survey

Suppose that this beach were to erode by one foot next year if no erosion controls were undertaken. Would this affect the number of trips you take to this beach next year?

1   YES
2   NO

How would this affect the number of trips you take to this beach next year?

1   Take fewer trips ⇒ How many fewer? _____ FEWER TRIPS
2   Take more trips ⇒ How many more? _____ MORE TRIPS

As you have seen in the booklet and the impact information sheet, erosion control programs can help prevent erosion but at the same time they can also result in other impacts on the beach environment.

   Suppose by the end of this year an erosion control program (program A) were implemented at this beach to prevent the one foot of erosion from occurring. However, this erosion control program would also result in the following impacts on the beach environment at this beach.

   Given the implementation of this erosion control program and its impacts, would it affect your trip decision(s) to this beach next year?

1   YES
2   NO ® (Skip to B_9)

How would the implementation of this erosion control program affect the number of trips you take to this beach next year?

1   Take fewer trips ⇒ How many fewer? _____ FEWER TRIPS
2   Take more trips ⇒ How many more? _____ MORE TRIPS

Table 9.a.1 Sample program details

Program A

Impact:

   1 Beach aesthetics: Visible structure/device installed
   2 Swimmer impact: No danger to swimmers
   3 Wildlife viewing: 50% less
   4 Salt water quality: No change
   5 Sand quality: Coarser sand with small rocks

Notes

1 See the website of Program for the Study of Developed Shorelines at Western Carolina University (formerly at Duke University) for a description of erosion control devices and potential effects, www.wcu.edu/1043.asp.
2 Specifically, a two-factorial main effects with five factors experimental design, accompanying six levels of erosion, is employed.
3 The opportunity costs of on-site time are not computed due to unavailability of data.
4 For comparison, we also estimated the Poisson model with a correction for on-site sampling bias (Shaw 1988). The results were very similar.
5 In equation (9.4), the notations are used for easier comprehension. Algebraically the expressions (ATT_i*A_i), (ATT_i*W_i), and (ATT_i*X_i) should be written as (ATT_iA_i'), (ATT_iW_i'), and (ATT_iX_i'), respectively.
6 It is debatable to exclude those who wanted to take more trips in response to the increased erosion in the analysis. In this study, we exclude these observations to enable the use of the Poisson model to analyze the trip reductions due to erosion and erosion control.
7 The general formula to compute the change in consumer surplus is:
$(e^{\delta_1 E + \delta_2 E\,Width + \tilde{\eta}'E^*A + \tilde{\mu}'E^*W + \tilde{\phi}E^*X} - 1)/\hat{\beta}_p$, where average values of the variables for each beach, as described in Table 9.3, are inserted in the formula.
8 Instead of welfare measures by beaches, we may compute changes in consumer surplus by activities. We report welfare measures by beaches to demonstrate the feasibility of using our models to derive welfare measures for any beach with a set of characteristics.
9 In total, 35 attribute-activity interaction terms can be included in the estimation. We "trimmed" the specification by including the terms that are plausible and significant.
10 As discussed previously, we find that relative size of erosion affects trip decisions even after the alleged erosion is to be prevented by erosion control. Consequently welfare measures associated with the negative effects of erosion control vary with the relative size of erosion.
11 We also compute the changes in consumer surplus for a 25-foot (severe) erosion. As expected, erosion control generates overall positive recreational benefits at all beaches. We also examine the "critical size" of erosion at which a specific erosion control program becomes beneficial for each of the studied beaches. For example, for the erosion control program that causes lower sand quality to be beneficial at Crescent Beach, the erosion has to be at least 6.5 feet. All these results are available upon request from authors.

References

Bishop, R.C. and K. Boyle (1985) "The economic value of Illinois Beach State Nature Preserve," final report to Illinois Department of Conservation, Madison, WI: HBRS.

Curtis, T.D. and E.W. Shows (1984) "A comparative study of social economic benefits of artificial beach nourishment: Civil works in Northeast Florida," Tampa, FL: Department of Economics Report, University of South Florida.

Dobkowski, A.H. (1998) "Dumptrucks versus dredges: An economic analysis of sand sources for beach nourishment," *Coastal Management*, 26(4): 303–314.

Freeman III, A.M. (1995) "The benefits of water quality improvement for marine recreation: A review of the empirical evidence," *Marine Resource Economics*, 10(4): 385–406.

Hellerstein, D. and R. Mendelsohn (1993) "A theoretical foundation for count data models," *American Journal of Agricultural Economics*, 75(3): 604–611.

Huang, J.-C., P.J. Poor, and M.Q. Zhao (2007) "Economic valuation of beach erosion control," *Marine Resource Economics*, 22(3): 221–238.

Lindsay, B.E., J.M. Halstead, H.C. Tupper, and J.J. Vaske (1992) "Factors influencing the willingness to pay for coastal beach protection," *Coastal Management*, 20(3): 291–302.

Lorenzen, T.J. and V.L. Anderson (1993) *Design of Experiments: A No Name Approach*, New York: Marcel Dekker, Inc.

Parsons, G R. (2003) "The travel cost model," in P. Champ, K. Boyle, and T. Brown (eds.), *A Primer on NonMarket* Valuaiton, Chapter 9.

Shaw, D. (1988) "On-site samples' regression: Problems of non-negative integers, truncation, and endogenous stratification," *Journal of Econometrics*, 37(2): 211–223.

Smith, V.K. (1991) "Household production functions and environmental benefit estimation," in John B. Braden and Charles D. Kolstad (eds.), *Measuring the Demand for Environmental Quality*, Amsterdam: Elsevier/North-Holland.

Stronge, W.B. (1995) "The economics of government funding for beach nourishment projects: The Florida case," *Shore and Beach*, 63(3): 4–6.

U.S. Army Corps of Engineers (1994) "Shoreline protection and beach erosion control study: Phase I: Cost comparison of shoreline protection projects of the U.S. Army Corps of Engineers," Alexandria, VA: WRSC-IWR, online, available at: www.iwr.usace.army.mil/docs/iwrreports/94-PS-1.pdf.

Whitehead, J.C., T.C. Haab, and J.-C. Huang (2000) "Measuring recreation benefits of quality improvements with revealed and stated behavior data," *Resource and Energy Economics*, 22(4): 339–354.

10 Using revealed and stated preference methods to value large ship artificial reefs

The Key West *Vandenberg* sinking

O. Ashton Morgan and William L. Huth

Introduction

This chapter provides an application for jointly estimating revealed and stated preference data in a non-market valuation framework. The purpose of the application is threefold. First, a single-site count data travel cost model is developed to estimate the value of diving on natural and artificial reefs in the Florida Keys. Second, the marginal effects of changes in site quality are evaluated by considering jointly divers' actual and anticipated trips. Specifically, the value of increasing site scope by sinking the USS *General Hoyt S. Vandenberg*, a 520-foot long decommissioned missile tracking vessel at the site, is considered. Scope effects are tested by combining data that evaluate divers' stated preferences for two wreck/reef systems in which one system is a subset of the other. Scope effects have been tested in a contingent valuation framework with some research finding that individuals' willingness to pay increases with the scope of the public good (Carson 1997; Powe and Bateman 2004) while others have found scope insensitivity with willingness to pay for a public good of greater quantity or quality not significantly different from existing measures (Schkade and Payne 1994; Whitehead and Finney 2003). In this chapter, scope effects are examined in a revealed and stated preference framework to assess whether adding a large ship artificial reef to the existing system impacts anticipated trip behavior. This component of the analysis addresses a specific reef management policy. As the number of decommissioned military vessels in the US Maritime Administration (MARAD) vessel disposal program increases, sinking vessels as artificial reefs has become a viable disposal option.[1] Further, in addition to providing a new diving and fishing attraction in the area, it is expected that this artificial reef will also relieve some of the SCUBA diving pressure off the area's natural coral reefs. As a substantial amount of time, effort, and expense is involved in sinking a vessel, measuring the marginal diving value of adding a large vessel near the existing reef system will provide important valuation feedback to reef managers concerning the benefits of such actions. Finally, as previous research has questioned the assumption of using a single preference structure when combining revealed and stated preference data (see Huang *et al.* 1997), we also estimate additional model specifications that allow travel cost preferences to vary across the different trip counts to examine whether preferences are impacted by stated preference elicitation strategies or changes in site quality attributes.

Demand for recreational diving

While travel cost models have been used extensively to measure recreational value associated with many leisure activities (such as general beach trips, fishing, bird watching, hiking, etc.), relatively few studies have examined recreational diving use values. Since most economic development groups are interested in examining the regional economic benefit from individuals traveling to the area to dive or fish at a wreck/reef system, diving valuation estimates have been mainly generated from expenditure-driven economic impact models. Further, these studies have tended to cluster activities (diving, fishing, boating) at the sites to generate aggregate measures of the local output, employment, and labor income impacts associated with reef visitation (Johns et al. 2001; Ditton and Baker 1999; Ditton et al. 2001; Heitt and Milon 2002; and Leeworthy et al. 2006). From a non-market valuation perspective, estimates of dive site consumer surplus are theoretically preferred. The majority of non-market valuation studies use contingent valuation methods to elicit divers' willingness to pay for recreational diving opportunities (Roberts et al. 1985; Ditton et al. 2001; and McGinnis et al. 2001) while only four studies focus specifically on artificial reefs (Milon 1989; Johns et al. 2001; Bell et al. 1998; Morgan et al. 2009). Of these, Morgan et al. (2009) is the closest in design to this study as they analyzed the value of diving the world's largest artificial reef (the aircraft carrier USS *Oriskany*) sunk in the Gulf of Mexico off the Florida Panhandle in 2007. Results from their truncated at zero negative binomial model indicated that the annual use value from diving the USS *Oriskany* was between $1,100 and $1,900 depending on the model specification used.

Sinking the USS *General Hoyt S. Vandenberg* and the site of interest

The USS *General Hoyt S. Vandenberg* was sunk at 10:21 AM EST on May 27, 2009 about seven miles south of Key West, Florida ending its long and interesting career as a military ship and beginning a new life as an artificial reef. The *Vandenberg* was christened in 1944 as the troop transport General Taylor and saw military action in the South Pacific. The ship was sent to the reserve fleet in 1958 and then transferred to the US Air Force in 1961. It was then converted into an advanced range instrumentation ship (ARIS) to serve as a mobile electronic missile tracking station. That conversion was completed and the ship was commissioned as the USS *Vandenberg* in July of 1963 at Cape Canaveral in Florida. The *Vandenberg* served as a missile tracker for 20 years and was retired to the reserve fleet again in 1983 where it was subsequently struck from the Navy Vessel Register in 1993.[2]

MARAD received the *Vandenberg* in 1999 and it was put into the disposal inventory at the James River Naval Reserve Fleet in Norfolk, Virginia. In response to a Florida reefing request the title was transferred to Florida in 2007 (although Horn (2007) suggested the work towards a Florida reefing actually began in 1998) and it was scheduled for sinking in the Florida Keys National Marine Sanctuary (FKNMS) near Key West in May of 2008. Due to financial issues it was placed under federal arrest by a US Federal Court for failure to pay cleanup and other sinking costs and ordered to be auctioned. With additional funding from several sources including the State of Florida, the ship's title was transferred to the City of Key West and the ship was towed from Norfolk, Virginia and arrived in Key West on April 22, 2009 after a ten-day tow. The total cost of the project was approximately $8.6 million. Major contributions to those costs were a $1.25 million grant to the Florida Fish and Wildlife Conservation Commission (FWC) from MARAD, a $1 million grant from the Florida legislature to FWC, and a $1.6 million grant from the Florida Governor's Office of Tourism, Trade, and Economic Development to the City of Key West. The remaining funds were provided from Monroe County in Florida, the City of Key West, and donations from various sources (Dodrill *et al.* 2009). Justification for the public allocation of funds came from work by Leeworthy (2007) that documented an expected $8 million annual economic impact from an increase of about $7.5 million in visitor and residential reef spending. Leeworthy's advice to the State of Florida was that it could afford to invest $5.6 million in the *Vandenberg* based on the net present value of expected tax revenue flows (Leeworthy 2007). Another justification for the spending on the Vandenburg was that the sinking would reduce use pressure from SCUBA diving on the fragile natural coral reef systems that are near Key West including areas in the Key West National Wildlife Refuge and the Western Sambo Ecological Reserve. The natural reef pressure reduction attribute of an artificial reef was suggested by Leeworthy *et al.* (2006) in their work on the *Spiegel Grove* that was reefed just off Key Largo in 2002 and used extensively in the campaign to sink the *Vandenberg*.

Now placed as an artificial reef, the *Vandenberg* serves as a foundation for a developing ecological system and as an economic engine for Key West travel and tourism. The ship is close to shore and rests in about 140 feet of water giving it a vertical clearance of about 45 feet from the surface (Figure 10.1). During the "under two-minute" sinking event the large radar antennas broke loose and are now chained to the vessel to prevent further movement. The ship is 520 feet long

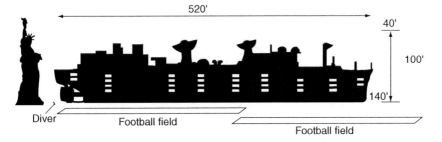

Figure 10.1 Sinking of the world's second largest artificial reef (Image Courtesy of Artificial Reefs of the Keys, www.bigshipwrecks.com).

and has been called "the world's second largest artificial reef." The largest is the aircraft carrier USS *Oriskany* (888 feet long), reefed off of Pensacola, Florida in 2007 (see Morgan *et al.* 2009).

The Florida Keys have long been the main focus for SCUBA diving in the US as its warm waters and coral reefs serve as a major draw. From Key Biscayne, located just south of Miami, stretching comma-like to Key West and beyond to the Dry Tortugas is the FKNMS. The sanctuary is divided into an upper and lower region and also contains the Tortugas Ecological Preserve. Each region consists of a set of zones; 24 in the upper region and 13 in the lower region that contains Key West. Each zone has a natural coral reef structure and there are numerous shipwreck reefs that are both natural and artificial. Within the sanctuary a "Shipwreck Trail" has been developed that includes nine historic wrecks; *City of Washington, Benwood, Duane, Eagle, San Pedro, Adelande Baker, Thunderbolt, North America,* and *Amesbury.* Just north and east of the sanctuary is Key Biscayne National Park that also houses a Maritime Heritage Trail that showcases five shipwrecks; the *Arratoon Apcar* (1878), *Erl King* (1891), *Alicia* (1905), *Lugana* (1913), and *Mandalay* (1966). Also within the sanctuary, near Key Largo, is John Pennekamp Coral Reef State Park, part of the Florida State Park system. This was the first underwater park in the U.S. and is where the "Christ of the Abyss" statue is located.

In addition to the historical maritime shipwrecks there have been a number of ships that have been intentionally sunk as artificial reefs in the sanctuary and several have become very popular dive sites for both recreational and technical divers. The USS *Wilkes-Barre* was a 608-foot long Cleveland Class cruiser built in 1942. On May 12, in 1972 the ship was intentionally sunk during an underwater explosion test. The ship broke into two parts and the stern sank quickly while the bow section required additional explosives to complete the sinking. Both sections are in 250 feet of water with the stern encountered at 140 feet and the bow encountered at 200 feet. The stern sits upright on the bottom while the bow is lying on its starboard (right) side. Because of the depth, the *Wilkes-Barre* has been considered one of the best technical (below 130 feet) dives in the Florida Keys. The *Spiegel Grove*, a landing ship dock was sunk in June 2002 in 134 feet of water 5.5 miles off of Key Largo, Florida within the FKNMS. The Key Largo Chamber of Commerce spearheaded the effort to sink the ship with the agenda to increase diving related tourism in the area. The *Spiegel Grove* is 510 feet long with a beam of 84 feet and until the *Oriskany* was sunk it was the largest ship ever intentionally reefed. Now that the *Vandenberg* has also been sunk, the *Spiegel Grove* has been eclipsed again, this time by just 10 feet.[3]

Large ship artificial reefing was considered in a 2001 Rand report (Hess *et al.* 2001) on disposal options for ships and it was concluded that reefing was the least expensive of the various options for ship disposal and that reefing was the only option that had the potential to create revenue to the government. That revenue was in the form of taxes from businesses engaged in reef use. Hess *et al.* (2003), in their examination of the reefing disposal option reported results from a convenience survey of seven states, and concluded that there was demand for more than 540 ships of the sizes they considered (55 feet to over 400 feet in length). Thus, they concluded there was sufficient demand for all the 358 ships awaiting disposal in Navy and MARAD inventories at the time. The Rand ad hoc demand survey did not consider ship demand for reefing off the west coast or any other Pacific Ocean locations. With regard to large ship disposal as reefs Hess *et al.* (2003: 80) pointed out that "the Navy and MARAD will need to work out the details of how to administer such a program so that ships are fairly distributed among the many parties likely to request them." The process developed here is a step in that direction.

Florida has long been engaged in the development of artificial reefs around its coastline. Hess *et al.* (2003: 62) stated that "Florida is in many ways an ideal state for engaging in reef building. Its comparative advantage relative to other geographic locations includes the fact that its coastal waters are warm and shallow for many miles out toward sea," and that "Large areas of its coastal ocean have barren sand and mud bottoms with a surface climate suitable for nearly year-round marine activities." It is not surprising that the first two large ship reefings were in the Sunshine State.

A comprehensive look at economic activity associated with Florida's ocean and coastal resources was provided by Kildow (2006) under a contract from the Florida Department of Environmental Protection. That report briefly addressed the non-market valuation of SCUBA diving as a part of coastal recreation and noted a dearth of diving specific valuation studies. The conclusion was that most diving measures were indirect ones from studies that focused on other activities and might well misrepresent actual diver valuations. Kildow (2006) suggested that additional work was necessary on a variety of maritime activities including diving.

In its April 2005 Report to Congress, MARAD (2005: 6) stated that

> Reefing has potential that is currently constrained by limited demand for ships by the coastal States. The limited demand is a result of a general reluctance of States to be responsible for the preparation, tow, and sinking of the ships, and to share in the significant costs associated with reefing activities.

While the costs are relatively clear it is the benefit side that produces uncertainty for the public sector.

Survey design

The survey was designed to elicit information on diver's personal characteristics (such as age and income), diving experience and qualifications, and actual/ expected trip counts to the site under existing and quality change conditions. To derive the sample diving population, we posted the survey on five online diving forums for three weeks asking those that dive in the Key West area if they would be willing to participate in the survey. Individuals were provided with a link to the survey instrument and informed that the survey should take approximately eight minutes to complete.[4] Upon completing the survey, responses were automatically uploaded in a spreadsheet format and available to the authors. In the survey, respondents were asked both revealed and stated preference questions related to trip count. In terms of diving behavior, each diver was first asked how many trips were taken to dive the Key West site over the previous 12 months (which we term the 2008–2009 dive season).[5] This was labeled revealed preference trip count TRP_RP. Next, two separate stated preference trip-count questions were asked to elicit divers' expected trips over the next 12 months, under both current conditions and with a change in site-quality conditions. Specifically, each diver was asked how many trips they expected to take over the next 12 months (TRP_SP). At this point the respondents were informed that

> after several years of planning, it is anticipated that the *General Hoyt S. Vandenberg* will be reefed off the Key West coastline this year and will become a signature wreck dive in the Key West area. However, we would first like you to assume that there is another delay in the reefing process and the *Vandenberg* is **NOT** sunk this year.

Eliciting the status quo stated preference response and including a stated preference elicitation dummy in the empirical model provides a means to control for hypothetical bias (Whitehead 2005; Egan and Herriges 2006).

In the final trip-count question, respondents were told to

> assume that the reefing of the *Vandenberg* goes ahead as planned and the 520-foot vessel is reefed about 6 miles offshore. The keel and screw will rest at 140 feet. The tops of the bridge, com rooms, crow's nest, and the vast dish antennas will be only 40 feet below the surface in normally clear Gulf Stream water. All 4 upper decks will be open to divers, with access vertically through the 18 stair towers, elevator shafts, and cargo holds. The spaces will also be accessible horizontally through 7'×10' holes in the hull. The fuel tanks, tank-top, and first platform will be sealed and ballasted to insure upright positioning.

Respondents were then asked if the *Vandenberg* was sunk and available to dive today, do you think it would change the number of diving trips you expect to take to the Key West area over the next 12 months? If the respondent answered yes they were then prompted to state how many trips, more or less, they would take to the site given its sinking. This stated preference trip count was termed TRP_SP_VAN.

In total 156 completed surveys were received. Due to the geographical location of Key West, most trips taken to the site were overnight trips. In the travel cost literature this can create a problem with regard to dealing with multipurpose trips. These refer to trips where individuals no longer purchase a single recreation experience. Instead, they purchase a package of recreational experiences. Many researchers avoid this problem by omitting any overnight trips from the dataset; however, in this study doing so would result in too few observations for a meaningful analysis. As such, we included both day and overnight trips but dropped any observations for overnight trips (n=22) where respondents stated that diving was not the primary reason for the trip. Because we might be bundling other experiences in with the diving trip expenses, we viewed our diving use value estimates as an upper bound.[6] A further eight responses were dropped from the dataset due to incomplete surveys leaving 126 completed and usable surveys for estimation. Table 10.1 provides detailed descriptive statistics of the sample.

To allay concerns regarding the use of an internet-based survey instrument regarding generating a representative sample of the diver population, a recent report released by Harris Interactive (2008) indicated that 81 percent of US adults are now online with only individuals over the age of 65 and living in rural areas likely to be under-represented by an online sample. Also, the average diver in our sample earned a household income in excess of $100,000. These earnings are in line with the findings in Ditton *et al.* (2001) who reported average diver incomes close to $100,000. The mean age of a diver was 42 years. In terms of diving characteristics, the average diver in the sample had close to 15 years experience with open water, advanced open water, and nitrox certification levels.

The average travel cost to the site is $1,433 and 95 percent of the respondents are male.[7] The Fort Lauderdale area substitute site includes a number of near shore wrecks/reefs including the 198-foot freighter *Mercedes I* in 100 feet of water plus the *Lowrance* and *Hydro Atlantic* that are upright and intact on the bottom. The trip count statistics show that the average diver in the sample took approximately one trip to the Key West site in the 2008–2009 dive season. Divers stated that they expect to take almost one more trip to the site in the following season. This may be due to hypothetical bias in the survey framework and/or perhaps due in part to habit formation. Other research in recreation demand modeling has found that past visits or experience have a positive effect on the probability of choosing to visit a site again in future choice occasions (Adamowicz *et al.* 1994; Provencher and Bishop 1997; Moeltner and Englin 2004). Finally, with the additional sinking of the *Vandenberg* at the site, the average number of expected dive trips more than doubles to over four trips in the year following its sinking. As the sample used in this study consisted of divers who had previously dived in Key West, they therefore may be more likely than the general diving public to dive at the site in a future season.

Single-site travel cost model

A single-site travel cost model is developed to estimate (1) the economic value associated with diving in the Key West area; and (2) the marginal value of adding a decommissioned military vessel at the site. The travel cost model exploits the tradeoff a recreator makes between site quality and visitation costs when choosing where, and how often, to recreate. In the model, travel cost for accessing the site is interpreted as the price, and the number of trips taken in the

Table 10.1 Variable definitions and descriptive statistics (n = 378)

Variable	Definition	Mean	Std. dev.	Minimum	Maximum
TRP_RP	Number of actual dive trips taken to Key West during the 2008–2009 dive season	0.96	2.32	0.00	20.00
TRP_SP	Expected number of dive trips to be taken to Key West during the 2009–2010 dive season	1.93	6.00	0.00	60.00
TRP_SP_VAN	Expected number of dive trips to be taken to Key West during the 2009–2010 dive season if the USS *Vandenberg* is sunk in the area	4.21	10.47	0.00	90.00
TC_KW	Per-person travel costs to access Key West	$1,433.51	1,201.57	$30.00	$6,325.65
TC_SUB	Per-person travel costs to access a substitute site (Fort Lauderdale)	$1,412.68	1,303.94	$3.45	$6,815.56
AGE	Age of respondent	41.83	10.09	18.00	62.00
MALE	Dummy variable denoting respondent gender (Male = 1)	0.95	0.21	0.00	1.00
INC	Respondent income ($1000s)	$102.08	47.70	$20.00	$200.00
OPEN	Dummy variable = 1 if respondent has a basic open water certification	0.76	0.43	0.00	1.00
ADV_OPEN	Dummy variable = 1 if respondent has an advanced open water certification	0.79	0.41	0.00	1.00
NITROX	Dummy variable = 1 if respondent has a basic nitrox certification level	0.78	0.42	0.00	1.00
EXPER	Number of years of dive experience	14.67	10.93	0.00	42.00
SP	Dummy variable denoting the trip count was elicited through a stated preference question	0.67	0.47	0.00	1.00
VAN	Dummy variable denoting trip counts elicited under the assumption that the *Vandenberg* is available to dive at Key West	0.33	0.47	0.00	1.00

season is the quantity demanded at that price. The main strength of the travel cost method is that it is based on actual choices (revealed preference) as a recreator considers the benefits and costs of participation and experience along with the consequences of their actions (Whitehead *et al.* 2009). However, a primary weakness of the travel cost method is that it relies on historical data so analyzing site quality changes, such as changes in the size of a site or improved site access, might not be feasible because individuals may not be able to form preferences due to lack of an actual experience. To overcome this constraint, stated preference methods can be used to estimate site quality benefits beyond the range of an individual's experience (see McConnell *et al.* 1995; Loomis 1993; Whitehead and Finney 2003). A major strength of a stated preference approach is its flexibility; however, the hypothetical nature of the approach has also been recognized as a weakness. Overall, the strengths of both approaches can be exploited through joint estimation of revealed and stated preference data. Essentially, joint estimation has the advantage of allowing the measurement of preferences outside of an individual's historical experience while anchoring the stated preference responses to actual behavior (Rosenberg and Loomis 1999; Grijalva *et al.* 2002; Whitehead 2005; Egan and Herriges 2006).

Following Haab and McConnell (2003), the basic model is written as

$$y_i = f(TC_{y_i}, TC_{sub_i}, z_i, q, SP) \tag{10.1}$$

where the actual/expected number of trips taken to site y, by diver i, is a function of the travel costs to access the site, TC_{y_i}, travel costs to a substitute site, TC_{sub_i}, a vector of socio-demographic and dive experience-related variables, z_i, a site quality attribute, q, and a stated preference elicitation dummy variable, SP. Within the stated preference literature, research has shown that values for non-market goods derived from stated preference survey techniques often exceed revealed values (List and Gallet 2001; Murphy *et al.* 2005). Therefore, a stated preference elicitation dummy variable is included to account for and measure any hypothetical bias that might be present in the stated preference trip counts (Egan and Herriges 2006; Whitehead 2005).

The diving demand data collected in this study poses unique features. First, the dependent variable is a non-negative integer with a high frequency of low trip counts. Therefore, a linear count panel data specification is estimated. Second, we collected diving demand data from the same set of individuals under different site quality conditions (i.e. status quo versus diving at the site with the addition of the *Vandenberg*). The dependent variable is therefore constructed by stacking the three trip count measures (TRP_RP, TRP_SP, and TRP_SP_VAN). This generates a pseudo-panel dataset enabling the joint estimation of both revealed and stated preferences. The panel nature of the data indicates that in addition to the explanatory variables, persistent individual differences may also influence diving demand. As such, while divers may share identical observed characteristics, they reveal and/or state systematically different trip counts. We estimate a Poisson model with a random effect error term that assumes the mean number of trips depends on an error term, u_{it}, to allow for variation across divers that cannot be explained by the independent variables. As the actual/expected number of diving trips, λ, typically takes a log-linear form to ensure non-negative trip counts, the basic diving demand model can be specified as

$$\ln \lambda_{it} = \beta_0 + \beta_1 TC_{y_i} + \beta_2 TC_{sub_i} + \beta_3 AGE_i + \beta_4 MALE_i + \beta_5 INC_i + \beta_6 OPEN_i$$
$$+ \beta_7 ADV_{OPEN_i} + \beta_8 NITROX_i + \beta_9 EXPER_i + \beta_{10} SP + \beta_{11} VAN + u_{it}$$

$$(10.2)$$

where *AGE*, *MALE*, and *INC* are socio-demographic diver descriptor variables; *OPEN*, *ADV_OPEN*, and *NITROX* are dummy variables denoting dive certification levels earned by each individual; *EXPER* represents the diver's experience level (in years of diving experience); β_0 to β_{11} are coefficients to be estimated; individual divers are indexed $i=1,\ldots,$ 126; $t=1,\ldots,$ 3 indicates annual trip demand under RP current conditions, SP current conditions, and SP *Vandenberg* sinking; *SP* is a stated preference elicitation dummy variable equal to one when $t=2$ and 3; and *VAN* is a site quality dummy variable equal to one when $t=3$.

For each model we use the estimated coefficients to calculate per-person per-trip consumer surplus (CS), or use value measures. These are estimated as the difference between a diver's total willingness to pay for the trips and the total travel cost (or trip price). Using the specified log-linear model, per-person per-trip CS is estimated as

$$\text{Per trip CS} = \int_{TC_y^0}^{TC_y^{choke}} f(TC_{y_i}, TC_{sub_i}, z_i, q, SP) dTC_y = \frac{1}{-\beta_1} \qquad (10.3)$$

Where TC_y^0 is the diver's round-trip cost to access the site and TC_y^{choke} is the choke price that makes the number of trips decline to zero. The change in per-person per-trip consumer surplus is then calculated due to the proposed change in site quality. Following Whitehead *et al.* (2008) the economic benefit of adding the *Vandenberg* at the site is

$$\text{Marginal Annual Value of Sinking the } \textit{Vandenberg} = \frac{\lambda^* - \lambda}{-\beta_1} \qquad (10.4)$$

where λ^* is the number of trips associated with adding the *Vandenberg* at the site.

As discussed by Huang *et al.* (1997), when pooling data to jointly estimate revealed and stated preference behavior, a critical issue is "whether the two types of discrete choices can be pooled together under a single preference structure." We test whether diver travel cost preferences vary across revealed and stated preference trip counts by estimating a second model that includes an interaction term between the stated preference dummy and the travel cost variable. Model 2 is written as

$$\ln \lambda_{it} = \beta_0 + \beta_1 TC_{y_i} + \beta_2 TC_{sub_i} + \beta_3 TC_{y_i} * SP + \beta_4 AGE_i + \beta_5 MALE_i + \beta_6 INC_i$$
$$+ \beta_7 OPEN_i + \beta_8 ADV_{OPEN_i} + \beta_9 NITROX_i + \beta_{10} EXPER_i + \beta_{11} SP + \beta_{12} VAN + u_{it}$$

$$(10.5)$$

where β_3 is the marginal effect of the stated preference elicitation strategy on revealed travel cost parameters. The annual per-person change in consumer surplus is then calculated as

$$\text{Marginal Annual Value of Sinking the } \textit{Vandenberg} = \frac{\lambda *}{-(\beta_1 + \beta_3)} - \frac{\lambda}{-(\beta_1)} \quad (10.6)$$

For each model an uncorrected version (where SP=1) and a hypothetical bias-corrected version (where SP=0) is also estimated and the change in economic benefit measures is calculated for both model versions. In Model 2, this implies that the marginal economic benefit of adding the *Vandenberg* under the assumption that SP=0 is given by equation (10.4) and by equation (10.6) for the uncorrected model.

Finally, as Huang *et al.* (1997) also indicated that assuming a single preference structure when combining revealed and stated preference data embodying large changes in site attributes and quality can lead to biased estimates, a third model is also estimated that interacts the demand quality shift variable, VAN, with diver travel cost to examine the marginal effect on baseline preferences due to an improvement in site quality by sinking the *Vandenberg* alongside the nearby reefs at the site. Model 3 is written as

$$\ln \lambda_{it} = \beta_0 + \beta_1 TC_{y_i} + \beta_2 TC_{sub_i} + \beta_3 TC_{y_i} * SP + \beta_4 TC_{y_i} * SP * VAN + \beta_5 * AGE_i$$
$$+ \beta_6 MALE_i + \beta_7 INC_i + \beta_8 OPEN_i + \beta_9 ADV_{OPEN_i} + \beta_{10} NITROX_i + \beta_{11} EXPER_i$$
$$+ \beta_{12} SP + \beta_{13} VAN + u_{it}$$

$$(10.7)$$

In Model 3, the marginal annual value of adding the *Vandenberg* accounting for the stated preference bias (uncorrected model) is computed as

Marginal Annual Value of Sinking the *Vandenberg*
$$= \frac{\lambda *}{-(\beta_1 + \beta_4 + \beta_{13})} - \frac{\lambda}{-(\beta_1 + \beta_4)} \quad (10.8)$$

Likewise, the marginal annual value of adding the *Vandenberg* where SP=0 is

Marginal Annual Value of Sinking the *Vandenberg*
$$= \frac{\lambda *}{-(\beta_1 + \beta_{13})} - \frac{\lambda}{-(\beta_1)} \quad (10.9)$$

Results

In total, we run three Poisson regressions with a random effect error term. Results across all three models are largely consistent. The pseudo-panel data set has 126 survey respondents and 3 scenarios: RP status quo, SP status quo, and SP with the *Vandenberg*. Model 1 is the basic (restricted) model. Model 2 tests whether diver travel cost preferences vary across revealed and stated preference counts, while Model 3 tests whether travel cost preferences are influenced by a site quality change (Table 10.2).

Across all models, the travel cost parameter (TC_KW) is negative and significant indicating that divers living farther from the site take fewer trips. The travel cost parameter on the substitute site (TC_SUB) also has the expected positive sign indicating that divers living farther from the substitute site take more dive trips to Key West. The high level of significance also indicates that the diving site near Fort Lauderdale, Florida (the *Hydro Atlantic* wreck) is a strong substitute site for Key West. Results also indicate that older males take more trips, as do divers with more disposable income, so diving is a normal good. In terms of certification level, divers with an advanced open certification take more dives, illustrating that divers who have invested in additional training dive more. In terms of experience, perhaps surprisingly, divers with more years diving experience take fewer trips.

The stated preference coefficient across all models is positive and significant suggesting the presence of hypothetical bias in the stated preference methodology, although habit formation may also be an influence.[8] Finally, the coefficient on our site quality dummy variable, VAN, is positive and highly significant, so sinking the *Vandenberg* at the site increases the expected number of diving trips.

Table 10.2 Results: Poisson regression with random effects

Variable	Model 1		Model 2		Model 3	
	Coeff.	p-value	Coeff.	p-value	Coeff.	p-value
CONSTANT	0.8473	0.0000	0.7264	0.0000	0.7256	0.0000
TC_KW	−0.0012	0.0000	−0.0010	0.0000	−0.0010	0.0000
TC_SP	–	–	−0.0002	0.0435	−0.0001	0.1199
TC_SP_VAN	–	–	–	–	−0.0000	0.5948
TC_SUB	0.0003	0.0000	0.0003	0.0000	0.0003	0.0000
AGE	0.0092	0.0000	0.0093	0.0000	0.0092	0.0000
MALE	0.6724	0.0000	0.6677	0.0000	0.6679	0.0000
INC	0.0022	0.0000	0.0022	0.0000	0.0022	0.0000
OPEN	−1.4609	0.0000	−1.4624	0.0000	−1.4635	0.0000
ADV_OPEN	0.8195	0.0000	0.8241	0.0000	0.8252	0.0000
NITROX	−0.1721	0.0687	−0.1693	0.0690	−0.1672	0.0737
EXPER	−0.0009	0.0011	−0.0009	0.0022	−0.0009	0.0021
SP	0.4884	0.0000	0.6208	0.0000	0.6066	0.0000
VAN	0.3730	0.0000	0.3748	0.0000	0.3961	0.0000
Obs	378	–	378	–	378	–
LOG LIK	−986.3	–	−984.7	–	−984.7	–

Now considering whether diver preferences change across revealed and stated preference trip counts, in Model 2 the interaction term (TC_SP) is negative and significant. This indicates that divers' travel cost preferences do change across elicitation methods and that they perceive an increasing disutility with accessing the site in the future. However, in Model 3, the coefficient on TC_SP_VAN is not significant so the change in site quality does not influence divers' travel cost preferences (Table 10.3).

We present per-person per-trip consumer surplus measures for both an uncorrected (SP = 1) and corrected (SP = 0) model and 95 percent confidence intervals estimated using the Krinsky-Robb procedure. As the travel cost inter-action term on site quality change is not statistically significant in Model 3, we concentrate on the consumer surplus estimates provided by Models 1 and 2.[9] Baseline per-trip estimates are between $836 and $965 depending on the model and whether hypothetical bias is corrected for. Based on the number of predicted trips, this translates into annual consumer surplus values ranging between $1,681 and $2,385 with smaller annual values when correcting for hypothetical bias. Adding the *Vandenberg* at the site increases the annual per-person value of diving at the site by between $251 and $409, again depending on whether a hypothetical bias correction is used. As a point of interest, consumer surplus results from Model 3 highlights that while adding the *Vandenberg* increases annual per-trip use values, the marginal per-trip value declines (although this effect is not statistically significant). As such, even though the per-trip value declines, the expected increase in the number of trips generates a positive annual per-trip increase in economic value.

Finally, to specifically address the policy-based component of the research, we estimate the aggregate marginal value associated with sinking the *Vandenberg* at the Key West site. To do this, our estimate is based on the approximate 150,000 dives estimated by Leeworthy *et al.* (2006) taken annually in the Key West area. Based on this trip count, the predicted trip estimates, and our consumer surplus estimates, sinking the *Vandenberg* at the Key West site adds a marginal annual aggregate value of between approximately $16.5 and $18.5 million. It is worth emphasizing that this estimate represents just one year's marginal economic value. While the marginal aggregate annual values may diminish over time as the allure of diving a newly reefed vessel weakens, and our estimates can be viewed as an upper bound due to the inclusion of overnight trips in the sample, overall, when considering the potential discounted flows of all future values against an approximate reefing cost of $8.6 million, sinking the *Vandenberg* provides a clear net economic benefit.

Conclusions

This chapter provides an application for jointly estimating revealed and stated preference data to value the economic benefit associated with diving natural and artificial reefs in Key West, Florida. Using coefficient estimates from a Poisson model with a random effect error term, per-person per-trip consumer surplus

Table 10.3 Consumer surplus estimates

	Model 1		Model 2		Model 3	
	Uncorrected ($SP=1$)	Corrected ($SP=0$)	Uncorrected ($SP=1$)	Corrected ($SP=0$)	Uncorrected ($SP=1$)	Corrected ($SP=0$)
Predicted trips						
Baseline	2.80	1.98	2.72	1.73	2.67	1.72
Adding *Vandenberg*	3.29	2.27	3.20	1.99	3.17	1.99
Baseline consumer surplus						
Per-trip	$849.81	$849.81	$835.92	$965.06	$849.35	$963.94
95% CI–LB	$766.43	$766.43	$752.16	$812.23	$813.78	$906.49
95% CI–UB	$954.10	$954.10	$936.70	$1,184.72	$978.05	$1,185.43
Annual	$2,384.98	$1,680.95	$2,271.76	$1,668.00	$2,266.06	$1,653.99
95% CI–LB	$2,146.29	$1,513.55	$2,044.07	$1,402.97	$2,169.80	$1,557.77
95% CI–UB	$2,678.44	$1,897.14	$2,553.83	$2,061.33	$2,612.43	$2,045.56
Marginal value of Vandenberg						
Per-trip	$0	$0	$0	$0	–$20.31	–$26.07
95% CI–LB	–	–	–	–	–$46.01	–$56.44
95% CI–UB	–	–	–	–	$51.94	$80.38
Annual	$408.89	$250.89	$403.75	$250.54	$364.73	$213.62
95% CI–LB	$368.76	$225.67	$363.93	$211.23	$289.74	$151.28
95% CI–UB	$459.56	$282.01	$453.68	$309.88	$581.24	$447.43

values are between $836 and $965 depending on the model and whether hypothetical bias is corrected for. This equates to annual consumer surplus values ranging between $1,681 and $2,385. As the number of aging vessels in the MARAD fleet increase and coastal counties acknowledge the potential regional economic benefit from sinking vessels as artificial reefs, stated preference questions regarding anticipated dive trips following the sinking of the *Vandenberg* at the Key West site enable the value of diving a new wreck to be estimated, while anchoring responses to actual diving behavior. We find that adding the *Vandenberg* at the site increases the annual per-person value of diving at the site by between $251 and $409, again depending on whether a hypothetical bias correction is used. Based on expected visitation rates and the known cost of reefing, our estimates indicate that sinking the *Vandenberg* at the Key West site generates a substantial increase in net economic benefit. Given the net economic benefit flows, one would expect a larger willingness to invest by the public sector in artificial reefs.

Finally, by allowing travel cost preferences to vary across the different trip counts, we found that divers' travel cost preferences do change across elicitation methods, implying that they perceive an increasing disutility with accessing the site in the future. However, the marginal effect on baseline preferences due to sinking the *Vandenberg* at the site did not influence divers' travel cost preferences.

Notes

1 Several decommissioned military vessels have been sunk off coastal states to enhance aquatic habitat and marine resources, as well as to increase demand for local diving and fishing recreation.
2 The *Vandenberg* also starred in the 1999 film *Virus* where it was renamed the *Akademic Vladislav Volcov*, after a Soviet cosmonaut, and portrayed as a Russian science ship that inadvertently downloaded an alien life form from the MIR space station and became a "ghost ship" with the intent to eliminate humans as a "virus" infecting the planet.
3 The *Spiegel Grove* has had an interesting history since its sinking. It was originally scheduled for sinking on May 17, 2002 but when doors were opened to flood it, the entering water rolled it upside down where it remained until June 10 when divers using lift bags were able to roll it on its side so that it sank. It sank on its starboard side with a 15 degree list and remained so until July 2005 when Hurricane Dennis wave and water action caused it to roll upright into a trench that had been scoured out underneath the ship by the strong currents in the area.
4 The five forums were the Decostop, Scuba Board, Spearboard, Rebreather World, and the Cave Diving Forum. There are a total of 216,000 registered users at these dive forums although some divers may be registered at all sites, and others may have multiple accounts at one site.
5 In the survey, the Key West area was defined to be the adjacent waters from Biscayne National Park on the eastern side down Highway 1 through Key Largo, Marathon, and on to Key West. We also considered Dry Tortugas National Park to be a part of the area as well.
6 Due to the time-intensive nature of diving and general avidity levels of the diving population, the large majority of overnight divers will maximize their time in the area by diving only.

7 Travel costs are calculated as round trip travel expenses, plus site fees, plus the opportunity cost of time estimates. Roundtrip distance is estimated using the PC*Miler software. Based on AAA's *Your Driving Costs 2006* brochure (www. viainfo.net/FaresAndPasses/YourDrivingCosts2006.pdf) per-mile travel costs are assumed to be $0.48. The opportunity cost of time for the roundtrip travel is calculated as one-third the hourly wage foregone assuming the average diver works 2,080 hours per year.

8 The positive coefficient on the SP parameter may also indicate that the counter factual did not work. That is, perhaps respondents believed that the *Vandenberg* would be sunk for the upcoming season and factored this into their anticipated trips even though the survey asked them to first assume that there was another delay in the reefing process and the *Vandenberg* would not be sunk this year.

9 Also, log likelihood tests indicate that both Modes 1 and 2 are preferred to Model 3.

References

Adamowicz, W., Louviere, J. and Williams, M. (1994) "Combining revealed and stated preference methods for valuing environmental amenities," *Journal of Agricultural and Resource Economics*, 19(1): 19–31.

Bell, F.W., Bonn, M.A. and Leeworthy, V.R. (1998) *Economic Impact and Importance of Artificial Reefs in Northwest Florida*, Tallahassee, FL: Office of Fisheries Management and Assistance Service, Florida Department of Environmental Protection.

Carson, R.T. (1997) "Contingent valuation surveys and tests of insensitivity to scope," in Kopp, R.J., Pommeerehne, W.W., Schwarz, N. (eds.), *Determining the Value of Non-Market Goods: Economic, Psychological, and Policy Relevant Aspects of Contingent Valuation Methods*, London: Kluwer Academic Publishers.

Ditton, R. and Baker, T.L. (1999) *Demographics, Attitudes, Management Preferences, and Economic Impacts of Sport Divers Using Artificial Reefs in Offshore Texas Waters*, Austin, TX: Texas Parks and Wildlife Department.

Ditton, R., Thailing, C., Reichers, R. and Osburn, H. (2001) "The economic impacts of sport divers using artificial reefs in Texas offshore waters," *Proceedings of the Annual Gulf and Caribbean Fisheries Institute*, 53: 349–360.

Dodrill, J., Horn, B. and Mille, K. (2009) *State of Florida Artificial Reef Activity Summary FY 08/09*, presentation at the Joint Artificial Reef Meeting of the Atlantic and Gulf States Marine Fisheries Commissions in St. Petersburg, FL.

Egan, K. and Herriges, J. (2006) "Multivariate count data regression models with individual data from an on-site sample," *Journal of Environmental Economics and Management*, 52(2): 567–581.

Grijalva, T.C., Berrens, R.P., Bohara, A.K. and Shaw, W.D. (2002) "Testing the validity of contingent behavior trip responses," *American Journal of Agricultural Economics*, 84(2): 401–414.

Haab, T.C. and McConnell K.E. (2003) *Valuing Environmental and Natural Resources: The Econometrics of Non-Market Valuation*, Northampton, MA: Edward Elgar.

Harris Interactive (2008) *Four Out of Five Adults Now Use the Internet*, online, available at: www.harrisinteractive.com/harris_poll/index.asp?PID=973.

Heitt, R. and Milon, J.W. (2002) *Economic Impacts of Recreational Fishing and Diving Associated with Offshore Oil and Gas Structures in the Gulf of Mexico*, New Orleans, LA: Department of the Interior Mineral Management Service.

Hess, R., Rushworth, D., Hynes, M., and Peters, J. (2001) *Disposal Options for Ships*, Rand Monograph Report.

Hess, R., Rushworth, D., Hynes, M., and Peters, J. (2003) *Disposal Options for Ships*, Rand Monograph Report, online, available at: www.rand.org/pubs/monograph_reports/MR1377.html

Horn, B. (2007) *Towing of the ex-Hoyt Vandenberg*, Tallahassee, FL: Division of Marine Fisheries Management, Artificial Reef Program, Florida Fish and Wildlife Conservation Commission.

Huang, J.-C., Haab, T.C. and Whitehead, J.C. (1997) "Willingness to pay for quality improvements: Should revealed and stated preference data be combined?" *Journal of Environmental Economics and Management*, 34(3): 240–255.

Johns, G., Leeworthy, V.R., Bell, F.W. and Bonn, M.A. (2001) *Socioeconomic Study of Reefs in Southwest Florida*, Miami, FL: Hazen and Sawyer.

Kildow, J. (2006) *Florida's Ocean and Coastal Economies Report*, Tallahassee, FL: National Ocean Economics Program, Florida Department of Environmental Protection.

Leeworthy, V.R. (2007) *Projected Economic Impacts of U.S.S. Vandenberg.* Memorandum to Weatherby and Dey, Key West, FL: Artificial Reefs of the Keys (ARK).

Leeworthy, V.R., Maher, T. and Stone, E. (2006) "Can Artificial Reefs Alter User Pressure on Adjacent Natural Reefs?" *Bulletin of Marine Science*, 78(1): 29–37.

List, J.A. and Gallet, C.A. (2001) "What experimental protocol influence disparities between actual and hypothetical stated values?" *Environmental and Resource Economics*, 20(3): 241–254.

Loomis, J.B. (1993) "An investigation into the reliability of intended visitation behaviour," *Environmental and Resource Economics*, 3(2): 183–191.

MARAD (US Department of Transportation Maritime Administration) (2005) "Report to Congress on the Progress of the Vessel Disposal Program," online, available at: www.marad.dot.gov/documents/April2005ReportToCongress.pdf.

McConnell, K.E., Strand, I.E. and Blake-Hedges, L. (1995) "Random utility models of recreational fishing: Catching fish using a poisson process," *Marine Resource Economics*, 10(3): 247–262.

McGinnis, M., Fernadez, L. and Pomeroy, C. (2001) *The Politics, Economics, and Ecology of Decommissioning Offshore Oil and Gas Structures*, New Orleans, LA: Department of the Interior Mineral Management Services.

Milon, J. W. (1989) "Contingent valuation experiments for strategic behavior," *Journal of Environmental Economics and Management*, 17(3): 293–308.

Moeltner, K. and Englin, J. (2004) "Choice behavior under time-variant quality: State dependence versus 'play-it-by-ear' in selecting ski resorts," *Journal of Business and Economic Statistics*, 22(2): 214–224.

Morgan, O.A., Massey, D.M. and Huth, W.L. (2009) "Diving demand for large ship artificial reefs," *Marine Resource Economics*, 24(1): 43–59.

Murphy, J.J., Allen, P.G., Stevens, T.H. and Weatherhead, D. (2005) "A meta-analysis of hypothetical bias in stated preference valuation," *Environmental and Resource Economics*, 30(3): 313–325.

Powe, N.A. and Bateman, I.J. (2004) "Investigating insensitivity to scope: A split-sample test of perceived scheme realism," *Land Economics* 82(2): 258–271.

Provencher, B. and Bishop, R. (1997) "An estimable dynamic model of recreation behavior with an application to great lakes angling," *Journal of Environmental Economics and Management*, 33(1): 107–127.

Roberts, J., Thompson, M.E. and Pawlyk, P.W. (1985) "Contingent valuation of recreational diving at petroleum rigs, Gulf of Mexico," *Transactions of the American Fisheries Society*, 114(2): 214–219.

Rosenberg, R.S. and Loomis, J.B. (1999) "The value of ranch open space to tourists: Combining observed and contingent behavior data," *Growth and Change*, 30(3): 366–383.

Schkade, D.A. and Payne, J.W. (1994) "How people respond to contingent valuation questions: A verbal protocol analysis of willingness to pay for an environmental regulation," *Journal of Environmental Economics and Management*, 26(1): 88–109.

Whitehead, J.C. (2005) "Environmental risk and averting behavior: Predictive validity of jointly estimated revealed and stated behavior data," *Environmental and Resource Economics*, 32(3): 301–316.

Whitehead, J.C. and Finney, S.S. (2003) "Willingness to pay for submerged maritime cultural resources," *Journal of Cultural Economics*, 27(3): 231–240.

Whitehead, J.C., Dumas, C.F., Herstine, J., Hill, J., and Buerger, B. (2008) "Valuing beach access and width with revealed and stated preference data," *Marine Resource Economics*, 23(2): 119–135.

Whitehead, J.C., Phaneuf, D., Dumas, C.F., Herstine, J., Hill, J., and Buerger, B. (2009) "Convergent validity of revealed and stated recreation behavior with quality change: A comparison of multiple and single site demands," *Environmental and Resource Economics*, 45(1): 91–112.

11 Combining revealed and stated preferences to identify hypothetical bias in repeated question surveys

A feedback model of seafood demand

Timothy C. Haab, Bin Sun and John C. Whitehead

There are numerous valuation methodologies available to estimate the economic values of environmental changes for benefit-cost and other policy analyses. As this book has pointed out repeatedly, these methodologies can be roughly classified as revealed preference and stated preference approaches. The strengths of the revealed preference approach are the weakness of the stated preference approach, and vice versa. The joint estimation of revealed and stated preference data seeks to exploit the contrasting strengths of both approaches while minimizing their weaknesses.

While there are benefits, experimental evidence also suggests some problems with the use of combined revealed and stated preference data. Among these problems, two crucial characteristics of the joint data tend to be ignored or misspecified. The first is hypothetical bias (Cummings *et al.* 1997; Whitehead *et al.* 2000). Hypothetical bias exists when stated preference questions are not incentive compatible, i.e. the respondent's answer is not "independent of the use of a real or hypothetical referendum mechanism" (Cummings *et al.* 1997: 611). When hypothetical bias exists, answers to stated preference questions do not reflect the respondent's actual behavior and predictions are inaccurate whether the stated preference data is used alone or in combination with revealed preference data.

The second oft-overlooked problem is correlation among answers offered by the same respondent to different scenarios offered in sequential questions. Many revealed and stated behavior studies attempt to take advantage of economies of scale and extract as much information as possible from a single respondent by offering multiple questions. Correlation between responses seems obvious although many studies ignore such a connection, treating every response as independent.

To incorporate correlation between responses in multiresponse surveys, panel data techniques (Whitehead *et al.* 2000; Whitehead *et al.* 2003) and first-order autocorrelation models (Boxall *et al.* 2003) have been used in estimation of combined revealed and stated preference data. The panel data models include an additional unobserved individual specific error in the estimation error, while the first-order autocorrelation model assumes the error term between responses for a given individual is first-order serially correlated. However, both models ignore another connection between responses; the direct correlation between the answers. The answer to follow-up questions may be affected by the answer to previous questions.

Data

Before introducing the model we propose for investigating the degree to which serial correlation is present in multiresponse surveys, it is useful to first describe the data we will be using. In 1992, researchers at North Carolina State University identified the toxic dinoflagelate, *Pfiesteria Piscicida* (pfiesteria), as a possible cause of fish kills in eastern North Carolina's estuarine systems (Burkholder *et al.* 1992). Pfiesteria belongs to a larger class of potential causes of fish kills termed Harmful Algal Blooms (HAB). In addition to scientific questions concerning the effects of Pfiesteria on the ecological (and public) health of the Mid-Atlantic region's estuary system, public perception of Pfiesteria and other harmful algal blooms can lead to significant economic losses in affected areas including: losses due to the perceived risk of seafood consumption, lost use of recreational resources, lost tourism revenues, lost fishing time due to estuary closures, possible medical costs for treatment and increased regulation of industries that impact the estuary systems. Past research suggests that information about seafood safety may change behavior; consumers may self-protect against seafood risk by reducing consumption.

The current data comes from a National Oceanic and Atmospheric Administration-sponsored research project to measure the potential economic losses from a Pfiesteria related fish kill event (Haab *et al.* 2002). The data is from a telephone-mail-telephone survey of seafood consumers in Delaware, Maryland (including the District of Columbia), North Carolina and Virginia. The survey was conducted during fish kill season: June through November, 2001.

The East Carolina University Survey Research Laboratory conducted the first telephone interviews from August to October. Of relevance for the current chapter, the full Pfiesteria survey included a series of nine seafood consumption questions (Table 11.1). The intial phone interview collected preliminary information about attitudes towards seafood risk (for example, do you think your chances of getting sick are greater or less than 1 percent, and what do you think your chances of getting sick from eating these meals are) and socioeconomic information of the respondents (for example, household size, household income, *inter alia*). In addition, the initial phone survey contained four questions about seafood consumption. The first is a revealed behavior question asking the number of seafood meals eaten in the past month. Questions two through four are stated preference question about intended seafood consumption behavior next month at current, higher, and lower prices.

Following the initial phone contact, an informational packet was mailed to those respondents who agreed to participate in a second telephone survey. The information mail-out included some combination of a Pfiesteria brochure, a

Table 11.1 Scenarios and statistics for seafood demand

t	Scenario for seafood demand	RP, SP	Mean (quantity)	Std. dev. (quantity)
1	1st survey, last month, current price	RP	4.87	4.92
2	1st survey, next month, current price	SP	4.93	5.04
3	1st survey, next month, higher price	SP	3.93	4.71
4	1st survey, next month, lower price	SP	6.13	5.68
5	2nd survey, last month, current price	RP	4.27	4.45
6	2nd survey, next month	SP	4.25	4.46
7	2nd survey, after fish kill, next month	SP	3.34	4.33
8	2nd survey, after fish kill, seafood inspection, next month	SP	4.13	4.42
9	2nd survey, after fish kill, seafood inspection, next month, higher price	SP	3.40	4.39
	Total		4.36	4.80

counter-information insert describing seafood safety, a seafood inspection program insert, and a hypothetical fish kill insert (details below).

The second phone survey (roughly a month after the mailing), asked an additional sequence of five seafood consumption questions. One revealed behavior question about seafood consumption in the previous month, and four stated preference questions about seafood consumption next month under various fish kill, seafood inspection, and price treatments. Table 11.1 summarizes the demand scenarios and reports the means and standard deviations of the responses.

Informational treatments

The Pfiesteria brochure was based on a brochure published by US Environmental Protection Agency's Office of Water titled "What you should know about Pfiesteria Piscicida." Each section of the Pfiesteria brochure included one or two short paragraphs. Full color photographs accompanied the text. The first page includes three sections. The first section of the brochure began with a simple definition of Pfiesteria. The second section explained that Pfiesteria stuns with released toxics and that the toxins are believed to cause sores on fish. The third section stated that toxic outbreaks of Pfiesteria are short but Pfiesteria-associated fish kills can last for days or weeks. The second page included three sections. The fourth section of the brochure described other sources of fish kills and sores. The fifth section then described in detail where Pfiesteria has and has not been found with an illustrative map. The sixth section emphasized the scientific uncertainty about Pfiesteria by using qualifiers to describe each source of outbreak including the presence of a large number of fish, pollutants, and excess nutrients. The back page of the brochure contained three sections. The seventh section of the brochure discussed health effects and includes the statement: "There is no evidence that Pfiesteria-associated illnesses are associated with eating finfish or shellfish." The eighth section stated that brown and red tides and Pfiesteria are types of harmful algal blooms. The ninth section provided state-level Pfiesteria hotline numbers.

The counter-information is intended to enforce the notion of the safety of seafood. The information states "Yes. In general, it IS safe to eat seafood." It further reports that there has never been a case of illness from eating finfish and shellfish exposed to Pfiesteria and that swimming and boating and other recreational activities in costal waters are generally safe. Finally, it has information on what is being done about Pfiesteria by the collaboration of state, federal, and local government and academic institutions. The expectation is that respondents who received this counter-information are less likely to worry about seafood safety.

The fish kill scenarios differ in two ways: (1) geographic location depending on where respondents live (North Carolina or other), and (2) the size of the fish kill: major (hundreds of thousands of fish over large areas of river surface) or minor (less than ten thousand menhaden). The respondents in North Carolina were asked to consider a hypothetical press release about a fish kill in the Neuse

River near New Bern, North Carolina. Respondents in Delaware, Maryland and Virginia were asked to consider a hypothetical fish kill in the Pocomoke River on the eastern shore of Maryland.

A seafood inspection insert provided further information about fish kills and a proposed mandatory seafood inspection program. The fish kill information includes a bar chart defining major and minor fish kills. The other side of the insert proposes a mandatory inspection program by the US Department of Commerce instead of the voluntary inspection services of seafood producers and processors (under the authority of the Agricultural Marketing Act of 1964).

The experimental treatment consists of a split sample design. All respondents received a version of the hypothetical fish kill (48 percent received minor fish kill information and 52 percent received major fish kill information) and the seafood inspection program information. In addition, 73 percent of the sample received the Pfiesteria brochure and 36 percent of these people received the counter-information. Twenty seven percent received neither.

About three weeks after the mailing, the respondents were called for a second survey. Questions in the second survey were similar to those in the first survey. One thousand four hundred and three respondents agreed to participate in the second survey. This represents 77 percent of respondents to the first survey and 46.9 percent of those who were contacted for the first survey. Of the 1403 respondents who were contacted for the second survey, 842 completed the interview, which accounts for 60 percent of those who were contacted for the second survey and 22 percent of those contacted for the first survey.

Theory

The joint revealed and stated preference study allows the researcher to use revealed preference data as the baseline for introducing contingent scenarios and to measure the potential welfare changes given hypothetical scenario changes. Combining stated preference data with revealed preference data allows both the detection of hypothetical bias and the calibration of hypothetical choices with real choice behavior, which could lead to improvement in forecast accuracy and predictive validity (Grijalva *et al.* 2002).

One approach to testing hypothetical bias is to include a dummy variable in the regression indicating whether the question is hypothetical or real. Assume the econometric model to be estimated is

$$y_{it} = f(\beta' x_{it} + \gamma D_{it} + \mu_{it}) \tag{11.1}$$

Where $i = 1, \ldots, I$ indexes the respondents, $t = 1, \ldots, T$ indexes the multiple responses by each respondent, and D_{it} is the dummy variable equal to one if the question asked is hypothetical and equal to zero if real. Detecting hypothetical bias simplifies to a Z-test for $H_0: \gamma = 0$. If the null hypothesis is rejected, hypothetical bias exists and the prediction based on stated preference tends to be inaccurate.[1] Many jointly estimated demand studies find that the stated preference data suffers from hypothetical bias ($\gamma > 0$), which indicates that the stated preference quantity is greater than the revealed preference quantity.

Some research finds no hypothetical bias in joint data because it ignores the fact that there are multiple observations from the same respondent. Eiswerth *et al.* (2000) estimate a pooled data model, where the regression errors μ_{it} are identically and independently distributed. Recognizing that observations within each respondent are correlated by the individual effects leads to the treatment of the data as cross-section, time-series data (i.e. panel data). Whitehead *et al.* (2000) and Whitehead *et al.* (2003) estimate random-effect panel data models on combined stated and revealed preference data, which decompose the error term μ_{it} into the sum of a within-respondent constant error component η_i and an independently and identically distributed error term ε_{it}, i.e. $\mu_{it} = \eta_i + \varepsilon_{it}$.

Treating the correlation of observations within each individual as fixed or random effects in a panel data model solves the problem of heteroskedasticity that exists among respondents. However, this approach cannot capture the serial correlation between multiple answers within each respondent. Boxall *et al.* (2003) use a first-order serially correlated error model as an alternative to the panel data model. The serially correlated error model employs a decomposition in which the error for each question is correlated with the error from the previous question, i.e. $\mu_{it} = \rho\mu_{it-1} + \varepsilon_{it}$. This specification suggests that the error term follows an AR(1) process: the current estimation error has a persistent effect on future choices, and the strength of such persistency depends on the coefficient ρ.

In fact, individual specific effects and serial correlation can exist at the same time. When a respondent provides multiple answers, it is possible that not only the unobserved individual specific effect is carried across, but also the error term existing in previous questions is carried forward. To allow for this, we estimate a model that assumes the unobserved error term is composed of two parts: A respondent-constant individual specific effect and a respondent-varying within-individual first-order autocorrelated error term: $\mu_{it} = \eta_{it} + \rho\mu_{it-1} + \varepsilon_{it}$.

However, assuming an error term structure composed of the individual effects and serial correlation still cannot convey the full information about the interdependence of multiple responses in the joint data. For example, if a respondent is asked about his/her consumption choices given contingent scenarios, such as price changes, food safety, and so on, his/her responses tend to be influenced by the answers he/she provided to the previous questions. Assuming a correlated error term structure is not enough to describe the dynamics because the lagged dependent variable may be an explanatory variable. If lagged values of the dependent variable become explanatory variables, not only are the previous error terms carried forward, but also all of the previous independent variables become explanatory variables for the current response. Failure to include the lagged dependent variable as one of the explanatory variables may lead to omitted variable bias. To account for the dynamics among answers, a more general model that includes lagged dependent variables and allows response feedback is needed.

Econometric models

Since the number of seafood meals is "count" data (i.e. non-negative integers), the first model estimated is a panel Poisson model. Assume that y_{it}, the number of seafood meals consumed by respondent i in scenario t, is drawn from a Poisson distribution with mean $E(y_{it})$:

$$Pr(Y_{it}=y_{it})=\frac{e^{-E(y_{it})}E(y_{it})y_{it}}{y_{it}!} \quad y_{it}=0, 1, 2,\ldots \tag{11.2}$$

The positive mean $E(y_{it})$ is expressed by an exponential function in an error component model (ECM):

$$E(y_{it})=e^{\beta'x_{it}+\gamma D_{it}+\mu_{it}}$$
$$\mu_{it}=\eta_i+\rho\mu_{it-1}+\varepsilon_{it} \tag{11.3}$$

where D_{it} is the dummy variable indicating whether the question is hypothetical; x_{it} is the vector of all other explanatory variables, η_i is the unobserved individual specific effect that is carried across each answer by each respondent; ρ is the first-order autocorrelation coefficient that measures the strength of the serial correlation; μ_{it-1} is the first-order lagged error term and ε_{it} is the identically and independently normally distributed error term, $i=1,\ldots, 723$ indexes the number of respondents and $t=1,\ldots, 9$ indexes the number of observations for each respondent. This model relaxes the assumption of identical and independent errors and assumes the residuals have a fixed individual effect as well as an error component which is first-order correlated within the individual.

The dynamics of the multiple "count" responses is modeled by the linear feedback Poisson model (LFM):

$$E(y_{it})=\phi y_{it-1}+e^{\beta'x_{it}+\gamma D_{it}+\mu_{it}} \tag{11.4}$$

Now, the first-order lagged dependent variable y_{it-1} is included as an explanatory variable.

LFM has its foundations in the integer valued autoregressive (INAR) generalization of the Poisson model to the ARMA process developed by Al-Osh and Alzaid (1987) and McKenzie (1988). It incorporates the autocorrelation of the dependent variables and heteroskedasticiy when the data is a count process (Blundell *et al.* 2002). In this model, the conditional mean of the count variable is modeled linearly in its history and exponentially of other explanatory variables. Blundell *et al.* (2002) use this specification to explain the relationship between the number of patents and R&D expenditures. The result in their research shows the LMF is well adapted to economic applications for understanding the dynamic properties of count data processes.[2]

Obviously, the LFM generalizes the ECM. Unlike the ECM, which only incorporates the persistent effects of the error term, the LFM explicitly captures the influence of previous answers of seafood consumption by adding the first-order lagged dependent variable as one of the independent variables. Both the independent variables and the error terms can have persistent effects on the current answer of seafood demand.

Results and discussion

The ECM is estimated using a fixed-effect rather than a random-effect specification for two reasons. First, Blundell *et al.* (2002) suggest the fixed-effect estimator because the Poisson fixed-effect estimator is consistent for a panel data structure. Second, a simple Hausman test rejects random effects. Robust standard errors are estimated to correct the first order autocorrelation in the error terms.

To estimate the LFM, Blundell *et al.* (1995), Blundell *et al.* (2002), and Windmeijer (2002) suggest two estimators: a quasi-differenced Generalized Method of Moments estimator (QDGMM) and a pre-sample mean GMM estimator (PSMGMM). Both estimators use a maximum likelihood algorithm, with the difference between them lying in how to deal with the unobserved individual effects. QDGMM uses "quasi-difference" techniques to eliminate the unobserved individual effects. PSMGMM instead uses the pre-sample history of the dependent variable to measure these effects. Using data of the influence of market structure on technical innovation activity, Blundell *et al.* (1995) show that PSMGMM is adequate to control for fixed effects and is superior to QDGMM. Furthermore, Blundell *et al.* (2002) show that PSMGMM improves the efficiency of the estimator.

In this chapter, PSMGMM is used to estimate Model 2. The first two responses are split out of the sample as the pre-sample and an additional variable

$$LQUANTITY = \ln \left(\frac{\sum_{j=1}^{2} QUANTITY_{ij}}{2} \right)$$ is created to measure the unobserved

individual effects. The estimation is performed using the GAUSS add-on program "EXPEND" (Windemeijer 2002). "EXPEND" uses maximum likelihood algorithm to estimate a non-linear GMM exponential model with endogenous regressors for cross section and panel data.

The estimation results are presented in Table 11.2. Column 1 contains the names of all explanatory variables, the next two columns are the estimation results of the ECM and the last two columns are the estimation results of the LFM.

Column 2 and column 4 in Table 11.2 are the results including the Pfiesteria-related information variables and price variables only. For comparison purposes, the selection of these variables is similar to the work of Whitehead *et al.* (2003), who estimate the seafood demand changes using a random-effects Tobit model. The principal findings of their work are (1) the price changes and fish kill information

Table 11.2 Parameter estimates[1,2]

	Robust (poi+dum)	Robust (poi+dum)	Robust (LFM)	Robust (LFM)
Quantity_1	–	–	0.56*** (0.05)	0.56*** (0.04)
Lquantity	–	–	0.75*** (0.05)	0.68*** (0.05)
Constant	2.03*** (0.12)	1.25*** (0.08)	0.39*** (0.13)	0.42*** (0.11)
D	0.04*** (0.01)	0.02*** (0.01)	0.91*** (0.16)	0.65*** (0.14)
House	–	-0.14*** (0.01)	–	-0.01 (0.05)
Children	–	0.14*** (0.01)	–	0.03 (0.07)
Educ	–	0.11*** (0.003)	–	0.01 (0.02)
Age	–	0.00 (0.0004)	–	0.01** (0.003)
Male	–	0.50*** (0.02)	–	0.03 (0.08)
White	–	-0.57*** (0.02)	–	-0.002 (0.10)
Income	–	0.006*** (0.0002)	–	0.001 (0.002)
Minor	-0.30*** (0.04)	-0.23*** (0.03)	-1.11*** (0.19)	-0.82*** (0.18)
Major	-0.33*** (0.04)	-0.26*** (0.04)	-1.08*** (0.17)	-0.80*** (0.16)
Pfiebroc	-0.12 (0.05)	0.04 (0.07)	-0.29*** (0.09)	-0.06 (0.11)
Counter	0.02 (0.08)	0.02 (0.08)	0.02 (0.12)	-0.01 (0.11)
NC	–	-0.82*** (0.02)	–	-0.28 (0.09)
SIP	0.24*** (0.02)	0.23*** (0.02)	0.70*** (0.16)	0.72*** (0.17)
Safe	–	-0.04** (0.01)	–	-0.16** (0.08)
Price	-0.06*** (0.004)	-0.06*** (0.004)	-0.01 (0.01)	-0.003 (0.01)
Corr. (w/in ID)	–	–	M1 = -0.31 M2 = 2.55**	M1 = 0.08 M2 = 2.06**

Notes
1 Standard errors are reported in parentheses.
2 Significance at the 90%, 95% and 99% levels is indicated by *, ** and *** respectively.

have significantly negative effects on the seafood demand changes; (2) the seafood inspection program has positive effects on the demand changes but the Pfiesteria brochure and the counter-information do not have a significant effect.

In column 2 and column 4, both coefficients of the stated preference dummy variable are positive and significant. Hypothetical bias exists and estimation using the stated preference data alone will overestimate the seafood demand. Also, the coefficient of D in column 4 is much larger than that in column 2 (0.91 vs. 0.04). Both models produce the same signs and the same level of significance for the coefficients of minor fish kill (MINOR), major fish kill (MAJOR), the presence of Pfiesteria brochure (PFIEBROC), the presence of positive counter information eschewing the safety of seafood even in the presence of Pfiesteria (COUNTER) and the presence of a mandatory seafood inspection program (SIP) as well. But all coefficients in column 4 are larger in absolute value. The findings show that fish kill information and Pfiesteria brochure reduce seafood demand, while a seafood inspection program increases seafood demand. However, counter-information does not have a significant effect on seafood demand. Both models find that price is negatively associated with seafood demand. The price effect is significant in column 2 while it is not significant in column 4.

The analysis so far has not included the socioeconomic variables: HOUSE, CHILDREN, EDUC, AGE, MALE, WHITE, INCOME and NC, and prior safety consideration variable, SAFE. These variables have been found to have significant impacts on seafood demand in previous work. To get a clearer description of the causes of seafood demand changes, we estimate both models by adding these variables. The estimation results are reported in column 3 (ECM) and column 5 (LFM). Both coefficients of stated preferences remain positive and significant. Again, hypothetical bias exists and the estimation using the stated preference data alone will overestimate the seafood demand. Both coefficients of SAFE are significantly negative, which suggests that respondents with previous unsafe experiences consume less seafood than those with safe experiences.

In both models, minor and major fish kill information still reduces seafood demand, although the magnitude is smaller after we control for socioeconomic factors. The positive impact of seafood inspection program information is mitigated in the ECM, while the positive impact of seafood inspection program information is strengthened in the LFM. The coefficient on the Pfiesteria brochure variable turns out to be insignificant when socioeconomic variables are included. This result is not surprising as the purpose of brochure is educational instead of influential. The effects of respondents' personal knowledge, prior safety consideration, etc. may dampen the impacts of Pfiesteria brochure.

It is worth noting that the coefficient estimation of the lagged dependent variable QUANTITY_1 and the pre-sample mean indicator LQUANTITY in Model 2 are both significantly positive at the 99 percent level. The significant positive sign of the QUANTITY_1 coefficient implies that the previous answer of consumption choices has a positive impact on the current answer. The fact that the coefficient of LQUANTITY is significant indicates the existence of heteroskedasticity among individuals.

Conclusions

This chapter uses a linear feedback count data model and pre-sample mean estimator to estimate the effects of fish kill information on seafood consumption behavior. This choice of model and estimator is based on the data used in this research, which includes a long series of answers, relative to past studies, to both revealed and stated preference questions. Combining revealed and stated preference data to value the non-market changes has been shown to outperform using revealed or stated preference data alone in terms of the predictive ability. Existing studies with combined data use naïve pooled, panel data, or serial correlation models in estimation. However, these models only focus on the unobserved individual characteristics, but ignore one important source of the dynamics between multiple answers within each respondent, i.e. the previous answers influence the following answers.

This paper is a first trial to capture such dynamics, using a linear feedback count data model, which incorporates both the correlation between error terms and the effect of previous independent variables. For comparison purposes, we also estimate a fixed effects Poisson model assuming first-order autocorrelation of the error term.

In contrast to previous analyses of these data (e.g. Chapter 4 of this book), the results show that hypothetical bias exists (t-tests of $D=0$ are rejected at 99 percent significance level for all estimations). The coefficient estimation of D is positive, which indicates that the answers to hypothetical questions tend to overestimate the seafood demand, *ceteris paribus*.

Both models show similar effects of Pfiesteria-related information on seafood demand, that is, hypothetical fish kill information, minor or major, significantly decreases seafood demand, while seafood inspection program information significantly increases seafood demand. The negative impacts of Pfiesteria brochure on seafood demand disappear when socioeconomic variables are included in the regression, which shows that respondents' personal knowledge, prior safety consideration, etc. may dampen the impacts of Pfiesteria brochure. Interestingly, the impacts of minor and major fish kill information, seafood inspection program information, and prior safety consideration are strengthened in the linear feedback model, that is, respondents reduce seafood consumption more when exposed to minor/major fish kill, or if previous experience make them feel eating seafood is unsafe and increase seafood consumption more when exposed to seafood inspection program information. Price effects are significant in the panel data model but insignificant for feedback model.

The estimation results offer important recommendations for information conveyance mechanism design. In both models, when we exclude the impacts of socioeconomic variables, the Pfiesteria brochure significantly reduces seafood demand. However, its effects are insignificant when socioeconomic variables are included. This suggests that educationally-purposed information, such as the Pfiesteria brochure, may not be effective with regard to respondents' own knowledge and safety beliefs. Counter-information designed to alleviate negative effects associated with Pfiesteria-related fish kill information has no significant effects on seafood consumption. A mandatory seafood inspection program is an effective mechanism for alleviating these negative effects: Actions speak louder than words.

168   *T.C. Haab* et al.

Notes

1 The regression can also include interactions of D_t with all other explanatory variables, then the model changes to $y_{it}=f(\beta'x_{it}+\phi'x_{it}D_t+\gamma D_t+\mu_{it})$. And the task of detecting hypothetical bias changes to a Chi-squared test for H_0: $\phi=\gamma=0$ accordingly.
2 It is natural to consider putting the lagged dependent variable in the exponential, so that the model is $E(y_{it})=e^{\beta'x_{it}+\phi\gamma_{it-1}+\gamma D_{it}+\eta_i}$. This model was also examined and showed poor performance on prediction.

References

Al-Osh, M.A. and A.A. Alzaid (1987) "First-order integer valued autoregressive (INAR(1)) process," *Journal of Time Series Analysis*, 8: 261–275.

Blundell, R., R. Griffith, and J. Van Reenen (1995) "Dynamic count data models of technological innovation," *The Economic Journal*, 105: 333–344.

Blundell, R., R. Griffith, and F. Windmeijer (2002) "Individual effects and dynamics in count data models," *Journal of Econometrics*, 108: 113–131.

Boxall, P.C., J. Englin, and W.L. Adamowicz (20030 "Valuing aboriginal artifacts: A combined revealed-stated preference approach," *Journal of Environmental Economics and Management*, 45: 213–230.

Burkholder, J.M., E.J. Noga, C.W. Hobbs, H.B. Glasgow Jr., and S.A. Smith (1992) "New 'phantom' dinoflagellate is the causative agent of major estuarine fish kills," *Nature*, 358: 407–410.

Cummings, R.G., S. Elliott, G.W. Harrison, and J. Murphy (1997) "Are hypothetical referenda incentive compatible?" *Journal of Political Economy*, 105: 609–621.

Eiswerth, M.E., J. Englin, E. Fadali, W.D. Shaw (2000) "The value of water levels in water-based recreation: A pooled revealed preference/contingent behavior model," *Water Resources Research*, 36: 1079–1086.

Grijalva, T.C., R.P. Berrens, A.K. Bohara, and W.D. Shaw (2002) "Testing the validity of contingent behavior trip responses," *American Journal of Agricultural Economics*, 84: 404–414.

Haab, T.C., J.C. Whitehead, G.R. Parsons, J. Kirley, and D. Lipton (2002) "The economic effects of Pfiesteria in the mid-Atlantic region," report to the National Oceanic and Atmospheric Administration, online, available at: www.appstate.edu/ ~whiteheadjc/ research/ecohab/pdf/report.pdf.

McKenzie, E. (1988) "Some ARMA models for dependent sequences of Poisson counts," *Advances in Applied Probability*, 20: 822–835.

Whitehead, J.C., T.C. Haab, and J.-C.Huang (2000) "Measuring recreation benefits of quality improvements with revealed and stated behavior data," *Resource and Energy Economics*, 22: 339–354.

Whitehead, J.C., T.C. Haab, and G. Parsons (2003) "Economic effects of Pfiesteria," *Ocean and Coastal Management*, 46: 845–858.

Windmeijer, F. (2002) *ExpEnd, a Gauss Programme for Non-Linear GMM Estimation of Exponential Models with Endogenous Regressors for Cross Section and Panel Data*, CEMMAP working paper CWP14/02, online, available at: www. cemmap.ac.uk/wps/ cwp0214.pdf.

Part III
Mixed data

12 Joint estimation and consumers' responses to pesticide risk

Young Sook Eom and V. Kerry Smith

Introduction

Sometimes a paper has a long gestation period, but nearly 20 years is probably too long. We started this research as part of the first author's PhD thesis in the late 1980s, completed the survey providing the data for this analysis in 1990, and then circulated earlier drafts of the paper in the early 1990s. Fortunately for us the problems associated with consumers' responses to risk have remained a continuing intellectual interest of environmental economists and there have been few efforts to combine revealed and stated preference responses to choices involving risk.[1] Equally important, food safety is once again in the news. In 2006 it was e-coli and spinach. Two years later it was salmonella linked to raw tomatoes, and jalapeño peppers.[2]

The literature in the intervening years has not been able to deal convincingly with food safety. Indeed, a recent session (2007) on the demand for food safety at the American Agricultural Economics Association finds stark contrasts in the authors' confidence in estimates of consumers' willingness to pay to reduce risk of food borne illness. For example, in the papers published based on this session, Lusk (2007) notes one study's estimates (Hammitt and Haninger 2007) are over five times larger than earlier results from Hayes *et al.* (1995) based on comparable risk changes. Moreover, initial survey research by Shogren and Stamlund (2007) raises concerns with respondents' ability to understand risk information and thus with analysts' ability to include models of the perception/adjustment process in those models. While this research was designed and completed before these issues were raised, we believe it nonetheless offers some information that is responsive to both concerns.

There are other reasons why we were lucky. At the time our survey was conducted there was no organic produce in major supermarkets in Raleigh, North Carolina (the site of our survey). As a result, the choices available to consumers were more limited than they are today. One final aspect in which our results may have relevance a decade after initial draft of the work was circulated stems from the model. It appears that no one has considered a mixed discrete/continuous demand model interpreting a demand function describing the determinants of the amount consumed with a random utility framework for the choice of the type of commodity when the choices involve risk. Our application is to risks due to pesticide residues on fresh fruits and vegetables.[3]

Our results indicate that the stated preference models recover statistically significant estimates for all variables where a priori hypotheses suggested there should be effects. Revealed preference data are incapable of measuring some of these influences. Joint estimation assures compatibility in price and income responses. Of course, to do so we must accept the maintained assumptions about how pesticide residues influence consumers' food purchasing choices. We are able to estimate separate effects for price, income, and the perceived risk of pesticide residues on the typical consumer's fresh produce demand. Moreover, our models do *not* reject the null hypothesis that RP and SP information would be judged consistent. To our knowledge, this is also one of the few applications where the two types of data have been found compatible in the sense that we fail to reject the null hypothesis of consistent shared parameters.[4] Of course, this conclusion is conditioned by the shared parameters our models can identify and estimate.

The next section outlines the theoretical framework used to combine revealed and stated preference choices. It has three elements: (1) a continuous demand model for a consistently aggregated measure of fresh produce; (2) a model of individual risk perception that recognizes both prior beliefs and new information (see Viscusi 1989); and (3) an expected utility model of the stated choices between existing and "new" produce tested for pesticide residues (based on those subjective risk perceptions). The models used in steps (1) and (3) are derived from a common preference structure. The subsequent section describes the collection of the data used in estimating our model. The last section discusses the prospects for joint estimation in general and the relevance of our early results for current policy questions.

Modeling revealed and stated preference responses

There are a variety of models that have been used in combining revealed (RP) and stated choices (SP). Our approach combines a continuous random variable— a measure of the quantity demanded of fresh produce with a discrete choice between two types of the respondent's "favorite" produce. The types refer to whether or not the produce is described as having health risks due to pesticide residues. We selected an aggregate of all produce varieties because to consider a specific fresh fruit or vegetable would have required quite a large sample and a multi-stage discrete-continuous model. Our approach fits the Whitehead *et al.* (2008) category of continuous RP with discrete SP that cannot be stacked. Our framework estimates the model in two ways. One assumes the errors associated with the discrete choice for selections between pesticide tested and non-tested and amount purchased are independent and identically distributed. The second allows for correlation between the errors. In both cases a subset of the parameters that can be identified from either the RP or the SP data are restricted to be equal. The set of parameters that can be restricted is limited because some attributes of the objects of choice are not observed within the RP data. They were not a part of the current produce choices of consumers at the time of our survey so they do not vary in the RP data.

There are three important assumptions in our model for describing mixed discrete and continuous decisions. First, we assume a Stone price index can be used to describe the price for an aggregate measure of produce. This specification allows us to use a Fisher consistency requirement for index numbers to estimate the quantity index for produce. The Fisher condition implies that the product of the index for the aggregate of the prices and the index for the aggregate of the quantities of a set of goods within a separable sub-function in a consumer's preference function implies the same total expenditures as the sum of the disaggregated expenditures. Thus, the index for quantity demanded of fresh produce is derived by dividing the Stone price index into each household's total expenditures on produce. The second assumption maintains that the two types of fresh produce compared in our stated choice question are distinguished by only two attributes—each type's price and the health risk each poses to its consumers due to the pesticide residue present with the produce. Taste, appearance, and freshness are assumed to be interpreted as equivalent across the varieties by the survey respondents. Thus, an important maintained assumption is that any differences in these factors are not relevant to consumers' decisions. Finally, the last assumption relates to the process people use to form risk perceptions. We maintain that Viscusi's (1989) Bayesian learning model for risk perceptions adequately describes how people evaluate the new information provided in the survey about pesticide related risks.

Our description of individual preferences begins with a demand specification. This function is used to recover the implied quasi-indirect utility function (following Hausman 1981). A semi-log demand specification, as given in equation (12.1) below, is used because it offers the best description of produce demand at the household level.

$$q = \gamma \exp(-\phi p + \tau m + \theta) \tag{12.1}$$

where q is the quantity index for fresh produce, p is the price index for fresh produce, m is income (total expenditures) and γ, ϕ, τ, and θ are parameters. Equation (12.2) is the associated quasi-expenditure function.[5]

$$m = -\frac{1}{\tau} \ln \left[\tau \left(\frac{\gamma}{\phi} \exp(\theta - \phi p) - k \right) \right] \tag{12.2}$$

In this derivation the parameter k is sometimes treated as an index of utility. It is actually a composite of everything that is assumed constant in the integration of the differential equation defined by Roy's identity. This relationship is integrated over price to recover a function used to define the quasi-indirect utility function. Thus, when we maintain that k is constant (to define Hicksian consumer surplus measures) for price changes from equation (12.2) the process is also implicitly assuming these other factors are held constant as well. This issue would be important if the objective of the demand analysis was to measure consumer surplus for a quality change (see Bullock and Minot 2006). In our case, the objective is to select a preference function that yields a conventional demand function, similar to what is routinely estimated in describing single commodity demands for market data. We use that function to frame our model for how each consumer responds to risk. The actual market conditions at the time did not offer varieties with these differences. People were aware of the potential risks in general terms but did not have access to commodities that allowed them to respond. By construction, the function yields the original demand function and thus can also be used to describe the RP responses. We rely on a composite of the RP and SP information to estimate the tradeoffs consumers would make in order to realize a change in the pesticide risks by selecting one of the two (hypo-thetical) types of produce. These could not be learned from observed behavior. The next step in our derivation is to adapt the parameters in equation (12.2) to meet the conditions of the RP data and the SP questions.

As we noted, at the time of our survey conventional retail food stores in Raleigh, North Carolina did not offer consumers other types of produce. The only way to avoid the risk of pesticide residues would be to forego any con-sumption of fresh produce. A stated preference question was the only way to recover how consumers would react to some way to reduce the residues and the risk was to suggest a hypothetical choice with a new set of produce. To adapt the indirect utility function derived from (12.2) so that it takes account of consum-er's perceptions of the effects of pesticide residues we allow the level of well-being and the marginal utility of income to vary with the health consequences of pesticides. Solving (12.2) for the constant of integration, k, which we treat as an index of utility we add a parameter to equation (12.2), α_j, j=G, B (with G=a good health state, B=a bad health state) to the marginal utility of income. By construction, this parameter could not be identified from the demand function alone. Roy's identity implies it would not be present in the demand. We also assume θ reflects the expected impact of the health state attributed to pesticide residues as developed in the equation below:

$$k_j = V_j = -\frac{\alpha_j}{\tau}\exp(-\tau m) + \frac{\gamma}{\phi}\exp(\theta - \phi p) \tag{12.3}$$

Now equation (12.3) provides the basis for distinguishing the effects of pesticide residues. α_j allows the marginal utility of income to vary by health state.

Using equation (12.3) we can define the expected utility an individual would associate with the possibility of experiencing the two health states. This descrip-tion assumes each person has a subjective probability of a specific health state. We label this subjective assessment as Π. Equation (12.4) defines the expected utility associated with a situation with these two states and the subjective beliefs. The next step is to use the model to describe a choice where it is possible to observe how each individual would respond to information that causes an update in these subjective beliefs. In our survey the information arises when each respondent is presented with a new choice situation that offers produce with different risks and different prices. Before turning to these details it is important to recognize that equation (12.3) remains consistent with the original demand function that we could observe and associate with *ex post* consumption levels for *q*. More specifically, this conclusion follows by applying Roy's identity to equation (12.4).

$$\Pi V_B + (1-\Pi)V_G = -\left(\frac{\Pi\alpha_B + (1-\Pi)\alpha_G}{\tau}\right)\exp(-\tau m) + \frac{\gamma}{\phi}\exp(\theta - \phi p) \quad (12.4)$$

We recover the original demand. With this information we could not separately estimate the parameter, γ from the composite of $\frac{\gamma}{\phi}$. Moreover, there remains an added limitation in equation (12.4), especially if the ultimate objective is to recover a description of the role of new information in the updating of risk perceptions and decisions leading to the amounts of produce consumption. The demand for produce reflects a person's beliefs about both the subjective risk and the health effects but we simply cannot recover these distinctive effects. We observe a consumption pattern. The consumer has no ability to change the *ex ante* conditions once he (or she) consumes. We would expect the level of consumption does reflect these concerns. We can incorporate this effect in our model by assuming that:

$$\theta = \ln\left[\left(\Pi\alpha_B + (1-\Pi)\alpha_G\right)\left(\frac{\phi}{\gamma}\right)\right] \quad (12.5)$$

With this addition we can use equation (12.4), including this change to θ to derive a discrete choice equation. Expected utility with given subjective beliefs about the odds of health states becomes:

$$\Pi V_B + (1-\Pi)V_G = \Pi\left(\frac{\alpha_B}{\tau}\exp(-\tau m) + \frac{\gamma}{\phi}\exp(\theta - \phi p)\right) +$$
$$(1-\Pi)\left(\frac{\alpha_G}{\tau}\exp(-\tau m) + \frac{\gamma}{\phi}\exp(\theta - \phi p)\right) \quad (12.6)$$

Now using our assumed form for θ we have

$$\Pi V_B + (1-\Pi)V_G = \Pi\left(\frac{\alpha_B}{\tau}\exp(-\tau m)\right) + (1-\Pi)\left(\frac{\alpha_G}{\tau}\exp(-\tau m)\right) +$$
$$\Pi\alpha_B + (1-\Pi)\alpha_G + \frac{\gamma}{\phi}\exp(-\phi p) \quad (12.7)$$

There are several alternative assumptions about the form of these parameters that would yield equivalent results. Thus, the interpretations and our conclusions about the estimates derived by linking RP and SP data are conditional to these maintained assumptions. What we believe is important about spelling out these details is that it forces us (the modelers) to describe specifically what can be recovered using each type of information and how this added information is reflected in the specific parametric form of our choice model.

In equation (12.4) we see that in the absence of additional information τ and $\Pi\alpha_B + (1-\Pi)\alpha_G$ cannot be separately identified. This is simply an algebraic description of the information that can be provided through a stated preference survey. It must be designed to provide choices that reveal different responses to the perceived risks associated with produce with pesticide residues versus that without the residues. To complete the link to what is presented to our sample respondents we need to describe how the information presented in the survey relates to their subjective beliefs.

We assume the subjective probability, Π, is a weighted average of each individual's prior beliefs about the health risk associated with pesticide residues on conventional produce and the "technical" or experts' assessments of the risk. This later variable is explained to each respondent as part of our stated preference survey. This composite is defined in equation (12.8). We follow the framework developed in Viscusi (1989). A person's current subjective risk perception, Π, is a weighted average of his (or her) prior beliefs and the new information our survey provides about the risks. We described this new information as being associated with scientists' estimates for pesticide residues. We assume this information is treated as a probability. These estimates are labeled here as the "technical risk estimates" to distinguish them from each respondent's initial subjective beliefs. The updates for subjective beliefs are hypothesized to combine prior and sample information using a Bayesian learning model. Viscusi has described the model using this form of learning together with an expected utility model as prospective reference theory.

$$\Pi = a_1 r_0 + a_2 r_c \tag{12.8}$$

where r_0 is initial risk perception of pesticide residues, r_c is technical risk explained to be associated with pesticide residues and a_1, a_2 are weights attracted to each type of risk information.

Our extension to the basic framework now accommodates the two types of behavior that our model must recognize in order to combine the revealed and stated choice information. For produce purchases in markets where there is no opportunity to select produce screened for pesticide residues, the variation in Π arises from each individual's prior beliefs and is not separately observed. Our analytical model has it appear in the term $\dfrac{\gamma}{\left(\Pi\alpha_B + (1-\Pi)\alpha_G\right)}$ in the produce demand derived from (12.7) with Roy's identity. Assuming the denominator is a function of consumers' attitudes toward risk and stated risk perceptions, the model provides a direct rationale for including these variables in the specification for the demand function. They describe beliefs at the time produce was purchased, *before* the information provided in the stated preference survey. Thus the revealed preference information relates to purchases of produce before they received the information in the survey.

Once consumers are offered a new choice it is possible to use equations (12.7) and (12.8) to describe how the values of r_c, the prices, and the other individual characteristics influence those decisions. However, there is an important difference in our model. We combine a model for a continuous variable, the quantity demanded of fresh produce, with a discrete choice framework for selecting among types of produce. Because we have assumed the latter decision involves a corner solution (i.e. only one type is selected), individual decisions are based on the values for expected utility defined by (12.4) with the choice alternatives corresponding to the risk-price combinations for each of the two produce types (conventional and screened for the residues).[6] A description consistent with equation (12.7) involves selecting the highest expected utility among two choice alternatives or Max$[V_{r_t}, V_{r_T}]$. The specific estimating equation is derived assuming each person's choice can be defined by the difference in the expected utilities with each of these possible produce selections, as in equation (12.9).

$$V_{r_T} - V_{r_C} = \frac{\gamma}{\phi} [\exp(-\phi P_T) - \exp(-\phi P_C)] - \frac{1}{\tau}(\alpha_G - \alpha_B)(r_C - r_T)a_2 \exp(-\tau m) + (\alpha_G - \alpha_B) a_2 (r_C - r_T) \tag{12.9}$$

where r_T designates the lower risk from tested produce.

Each person's initial risk perceptions (r_0) does not affect choices, because it relates to each consumer's starting point for updating. As a result it is the same starting point in comparing the commercial with the tested produce and do not influence the gain (reduced risk) from the new type of produce. Equation (12.9) indicates that choices will be based on the differences in the risk information provided in the stated preference questions. While separate estimates of a_2 and $(\alpha_G - \alpha_B)$ cannot be recovered, equation (12.6) does illustrate the opportunities for parametric restrictions. Both ϕ and τ are common parameters to (12.1) and (12.9).

The basic logic used in formulating our model is similar to the earliest applications of combined RP/SP models by Morikawa *et al.* (1990) and Cameron (1992). There are, however, several differences. Morikawa *et al.* treat the task of combining RP and SP as one that involves expanding the set of choice alternatives in a random utility framework. Cameron's model, by contrast, is a mixture of discrete and continuous responses. The stated preference responses focus on how the choke price for the recreation demand model varies across respondents.

Our analysis must also address the task of developing a consistent price index for a wide range of different types of produce for the RP application. The challenge arises in developing a consistent link between the prices stated in the SP question and those contributing to this index. In addition the SP question relates to a new set of produce that was not previously available. Finally, it is important to recognize that our model integrates an *ex post* RP model with an *ex ante* SP choice. The analysis is further complicated by the fact that consumers, when faced with new information about the risks associated with pesticide residues, may choose to avoid both the old and the new produce described to them. Thus, we need to take account of the selection effect that arises when people reject both types of produce and choose not to consume (i.e. the respondents do not report a consumption choice).[7] These details are discussed in the strategy used to adapt the model for our data as discussed in the next section.

Data and model estimates

To implement the model two types of data are needed—actual purchases of fresh produce (including quantities and prices) and people's hypothetical choices between the currently available fresh produce and a new type tested to be free of pesticide residues.[8] Our empirical analysis began with two focus groups conducted in Raleigh, North Carolina, the site of our survey. One of these focus groups recruited people likely to be sensitive to food safety issues and the other used a random sample of households based on local telephone listings.[9] The insights derived from these sessions influenced the definition of the relevant population for our survey; the strategy used to target the survey respondents; the types of information requested in the survey questionnaire; and the presentation of the CV choice questions.[10]

Our data were collected as part of a point-of-sale intercept survey between September 30 and October 28, 1990. This involved distributing mail-back questionnaires to customers of retail food stores as they left one of the 24 stores agreeing to participate. These stores were outlets for each of five different retail food chains. Interviewers collected separate price information for the produce at each location for each day the surveys were distributed. The record keeping for this process allowed these price data to be matched with questionnaires from each location. The survey also included questions to check the accuracy of the reports of produce purchases (e.g. individual expenditures and totals for sub-categories were requested). In addition, the survey included questions about food safety attitudes, demographic and economic characteristics, and the stated preference choices.

Our SP question has three primary features. First, it presents the choice using two simple "labels" (boxes with price and risk information). Respondents compare the prices (defined in per unit terms) and the stated additional lifetime risks associated with any pesticide residues on each type of produce. This formulation corresponds to the preferred framing that was derived based on the responses of the focus group participants. Our focus group participants also indicated that a choice between these two alternatives (one with pesticide screening and one without) did not accurately describe their decision process. As a result, the second aspect of the framing for our questions involves allowing respondents to decide to consume neither item after reviewing the information about risks. Finally, the risk information was described using probability estimates that are within the range reported for a variety of food related risks, including those associated with pesticide residues.[11]

Price increments were selected in the SP questions based on the average price of produce in the area. We varied both the probabilities together with the level and size of the price increments. Fifty-six different combinations of prices and probabilities were selected for our design. We used two different formats for the SP question (described below). This added variation implies there were 112 design points. A total of 1,860 questionnaires were distributed and 567 (approximately 30 percent of those accepting them at each of the food stores) returned the questionnaires.[12] Table 12.1 provides some summary statistics for the sample with complete responses for all key variables and for the sample that selected a type of produce.

The use of a mail-back format for our SP questionnaire required specific attention to the description of the new type of produce—tested to be free of pesticide residues. Past studies selected a specific fruit or vegetable, such as apples or carrots (see van Ravenswaay and Hoehn 1991b; Hammitt 1986; and Florax *et al.* 2005 for an overview of most of the literature to about 2004). A decision to select one type of produce can restrict the analysis to respondents who report that they typically consume the items. In our sample, 19 different fruits and vegetables were reported as one or more of the sampled households' favorite item of fresh produce. To accommodate this anticipated diversity in consumer tastes, we designed two versions of the stated preference question.

One version asks about the fruit or vegetable that the respondent reported to be the one his (or her) household enjoyed most. After asking about this fruit or vegetable this version then asks about the most recent purchase and the unit price paid for that item. The questionnaire presents an increment to the price for the tested produce along with the risk information for both types of produce. The second version presents specific price and risk for tested and conventional produce with the specific fruit or vegetable described as the "typical fresh produce" consumed by the respondent's household. Our focus group comparison of these wordings suggested that some people would have difficulty interpreting what "typical produce" meant for them. Others in these groups had no difficulty. To investigate the effect of this wording difference, the two versions were randomly assigned to respondents. Both formats allow individuals to report that they selected different types of produce. To account for these differences a Stone price index (defined in equation (12.10) below)[13] was constructed for produce using the respondents' reported expenditures for each produce item, the total expenditures reported on fresh fruit and vegetables, and price information collected separately for each of the shopping locations and produce types.[14]

$$\ln p_i^{FV} = \sum_{j \varepsilon C_i} s_{ji} \ln p_{ji} + \left(1 - \sum_{j \varepsilon C_i} s_{ji}\right) \ln CPI^{FV} \qquad (12.10)$$

where p_i^{FV} is the price index for respondent i for the aggregate of fresh fruits and vegetables, p_{ji} is the price for the jth fruit or vegetable consumed by individual I (price varied by where ith individual shopped), C_i is the set of fresh fruits and

Table 12.1 Summary statistics for selected variables[1]

Variable	Descriptions	Full sample	Choice sample
Dependent variables			
CHOICE	Dummy var. = 1 if responded to the contingent produce choice	0.64 (0.48)	–
CHIC	Dummy var. = 1 if responded to purchase Type II produce	–	0.66 (0.47)
QUANT1	Constructed quantity of demanded for fresh produce	14.36 (10.52)	14.12 (11.22)
Independent variables			
LPRCI, LPRCT	Stone price of Type I and Type II produce for CBM (T = tested − Type II)	0.90 (0.32)	0.90 (0.32)
		1.31 (0.78)	1.25 (0.66)
PRICE	Stone price for fresh produce in demand	0.88 (0.31)	0.89 (0.30)
DRISK	Difference between contingent risks for Type I and Type II produce	20.3 (15.1)	19.4 (14.8)
FRA2	Subjective seriousness index (1 to 10) of health risks from commercially grown produce	6.59 (2.09)	6.47 (2.07)
INCOME	Household income (annual)	48,835 (25,837)	48,748 (26,105)
VERSION	= 1 if yellow color of booklet	0.51 (0.50)	0.52 (0.50)
	Respondents reported prices for their preferred produce and add price increments for price for tested produce.		
	= 0, respondents were asked about "typical" produce and received the price and risk for the tested produce.		
EDUC	Years of education	16.0 (2.43)	16.06 (2.37)
AGE	Age of respondent	39.1 (12.5)	38.34 (12.49)
SEX	Gender of respondent (female = 1)	0.68 (0.47)	0.67 (0.47)
NO. of CHILDREN	No. of children under age 18	0.68 (0.96)	0.65 (0.91)
EAT4	Subjective seriousness index (1 to 10) from chemicals in the food supply	7.96 (2.15)	7.78 (2.21)
FRA3	Subjective seriousness index from tested produce	4.25 (2.09)	4.01 (1.95)
Food Store1, Food Store2,	Fixed effects for retail food chains(fraction of sample from each store,	0.23, 0.24	0.24, 0.23
Food Store3, Food Store4	including the omitted category)	0.24, 0.28	0.24, 0.29

Note
1 Numbers in parentheses are standard error.

vegetables reported by ith respondent, s_{ji} is the share of ith respondent's total expenditures on fresh fruits and vegetables reported for jth type of produce, and CPI^{FV} is the consumer price index component for October 1990 for general fruits and vegetables.

The quantity index for the produce aggregate was derived using this price index and the household's total reported expenditures on fresh fruits and vegetables. The same framework was used to transform the prices posed in our stated preference questions.

Two further adjustments were made in composing our final sample. The first arises from inconsistencies in respondent's reported expenditure patterns. Our questionnaire asks for typical weekly expenditures on the most frequently purchased items of fresh produce (during the preceding summer). Twenty-three items were listed, with additional space for respondents to fill in other produce items they consumed. Sixty-four individuals reported total expenditures for all of the 23 types of produce that exceeded by more than three times what they reported (in an earlier section of the questionnaire) as their typical total weekly expenditures on all fresh fruits and vegetables. Because our focus group findings indicated that this type of SP question would be most effective with respondents responsible for the household's food purchases, we interpreted this inconsistency as indicating the questionnaire was completed by someone unfamiliar with food purchases. As a result, we evaluated samples with and without these individuals.

A second adjustment to our sample arises from individuals who reported that they would not consume either type of produce. Thirty-seven percent of the sample indicated they would not select either type of produce. While these respondents were dropped in the estimation of our joint model, leaving a sample of 276 respondents, we investigated their role in modeling the stated preference responses in two ways: (1) including in our joint model an inverse Mills' ratio as a correction factor;[15] and (2) investigating the effects of this decision as a sample selection in modeling respondents' demands for produce based on actual expenditures. The RP data in our analysis involves actual purchase decisions for produce that took place before the stated purchases. As a result, it seems reasonable to assume that the errors associated with the demand equation and the choice model could be treated as independent. Based on this assumption, the likelihood function for the simplest joint estimation for the models is the product of what would be specified for each problem individually. Cross equation parameter restrictions on τ and ϕ enhance the efficiency of estimation and provide a mechanism for testing the consistency of description of consumers' produce choices with and without the restriction that these parameters are equal. Under the assumption of independent and normally distributed errors, equation (12.11) defines the log-likelihood function.

We also estimated the model assuming the errors are corrected following the framework developed in Huang *et al.* (1997). The likelihood function for our model is a straightforward adaptation of the expression given in their equation

(12.7). The specific expressions for their RP and SP are different than ours, but replacing their economic models with our semi-log demand and *ex ante* utility difference yields a comparable log-likelihood expression.

$$\log L = \left(\frac{N}{2}\right) \log(2\pi) - N \log(\sigma)$$

$$-\frac{1}{2}\sum_i (q_i - g(p_i, m_i, X_i, A)/\sigma)^2$$

$$+\sum_i I_i \ln(\Phi(f(p_{ci}, p_{Ti}, r_{Ti}, r_{ci}, m_i, Z_i, B)))$$

$$+\sum_i (1 - I_i) \ln(1 - (\Phi(f(p_{ci}, p_{Ti}, r_{Ti}, r_{ci}, m_i, Z_i, B))))$$

(12.11)

A and *B* correspond to parameter vectors that have some overlapping components. σ is the standard deviation for the error associated with the produce demand. The variance for the choice model's error is normalized to unity. I_i is an indicator variable that is unity if respondents selected the Type II produce (described as tested for pesticide residues) and zero otherwise. $\Phi(.)$ is the normal distribution function; $g(.)$ the single equation demand function (in our case the form is an expanded version of equation (12.1)); and $f(.)$ is an expression derived from difference in *ex ante* indirect utility functions (as given in equation (12.9)). X_i and Z_i correspond to vectors of independent variables that can overlap between the two models. The price terms in $g(.)$ and $f(.)$ and the risk terms entering $f(.)$ require some explanation. As we noted earlier, the prices are measured using a Stone price index for produce reported by each respondent to have been purchased in a typical week using the prices collected at the time of our interview. p_{ci} and p_{Ti} correspond to the constructed Stone price indexes, based on what the SP question offered to each respondent for conventional (c) and tested (T) produce.

The risk measures recognize that people form subjective perceptions based on the technical risk information presented to them in the questionnaire. This new description causes respondents to update their subjective risk perceptions.[16] This formulation is the way our model responds to the Shogren-Stamlund concern noted earlier. More specifically, our theoretical framework suggests that respondents' choices should be based on differences in the technical risks presented, $(r_c - r_T)$ and the relative weight, a_2, each person assigns to the survey's description information about the risk for the two produce types. We explored several ways of enhancing what the model could tell us about these weights. These included using each respondent's answers to an attitude question describing, on a 1 to 10 Likert scale, how serious the risks from consuming commercial produce with pesticides was. In the final specification the model hypothesizes that this seriousness index influences the differences in the level of expected utility and not in the marginal utilities of income across health states.

Four model specifications have been applied to the survey responses and the results are presented in Table 12.2. These models can only be applied to respondents who indicated they would select between the two types of produce. As we noted earlier, to account for this selection effect an inverse Mills ratio has been included in each equation as a correction term for effects induced by this sample selection.[17] The probit model describing these decisions is reported in the Appendix to this chapter. The first and second columns report the maximum likelihood estimates for our joint model with the assumption of independent errors between RP and SP responses. The first column reports the estimates combining in a maximum likelihood estimation with the restriction of equality of the price (ϕ) and income (τ) parameters, whereas the second column reports the joint estimation results without the equality restriction. Columns three and four report these estimates assuming the errors for the RP and SP responses are correlated. Table 12.3 reports the estimates for the single equation preference demand function.

There are several interesting elements in the results from the four models. First, the joint model yields theoretically consistent estimates for produce prices, income, and the technical risk effects described to our respondents. The last of these effects could not have been estimated without access to the stated preference responses. The estimated coefficients for price and income are close to what would have been estimated from a single demand equation, based on either the selected sample or the full sample, though the measured effect of income from the joint model is somewhat smaller. A likelihood ratio test of the null hypothesis that these parameters should be restricted to be equal (using the sample for the joint estimator) fails to reject the equality hypothesis. Thus our results contrast with the Whitehead *et al.* (2008) summary of the RP/SP literature's test results.

To understand the effects of risk we must consider two terms. Both imply that increases in the technical risk differential, $(r_c - r_T)$, will increase the likelihood that respondents would purchase the produce tested for residues over the conventional type of produce. The first of these terms, $(\alpha_G - \alpha_B) \cdot a_2$, is associated with a three way interaction—the risk differential, the income term as implied by equation (12.9), and the seriousness index—is positive as expected but insignificant. The second term including the perception of seriousness (FRA2) has significant and positive effects, suggesting a difference in the level of expected utility that would be realized with tested produce. The exact interpretation of this seriousness index will vary depending on the treatment of the prior risk perceptions in defining the *ex ante* indirect utility function. We used a separate effect for these perceptions interaction to reflect the effects of variations in respondents' weights for the risk information presented to them. This term has a positive and highly significant effect on the likelihood of selecting the tested produce.

Version is a qualitative variable identifying the questionnaire assigned to each respondent. The significant negative sign of the Version variable implies that respondents who had to construct their own per-unit price for their favorite

Table 12.2 Joint estimation results[1]

	Independent errors		With error correlation (Rho)	
	W/parameter restriction	W/O parameter restriction	W/parameter restriction	W/O parameter restriction
Stated preference				
Intercept (choice)	−0.0975 (−2.571)	−1.024 (−2.651)	−0.942 (−2.520)	−0.0995 (−2.622)
Price ϕ	−0.780 (−4.570)	−0.518 (−1.092)	−0.817 (−4.797)	−0.511 (−1.183)
Income τ	0.366×10^{-4} (1.724)	0.239×10^{-4} (0.450)	0.361×10^{-4} (1.709)	0.249×10^{-3} (0.451)
$(\alpha_G - \alpha_B)\,a_2\,{}^*$Fra2	0.0003 (0.634)	0.0039 (0.301)	0.0003 (0.659)	0.0044 (0.301)
Perceived risk of fresh produce (Fra2)	0.206 (4.049)	0.203 (4.031)	0.205 (4.133)	0.202 (4.098)
Version	−0.485 (−2.340)	−0.483 (−2.338)	−0.503 (−2.488)	−0.508 (−2.521)
IMR (choice)	0.816 (1.236)	0.935 (1.384)	0.774 (1.192)	0.918 (1.382)
Revealed preference				
Price ϕ	—	−0.818 (−4.526)	—	−0.866 (−4.806)
Income τ	—	0.359×10^{-4} (1.689)	—	0.365×10^{-4} (1.737)
Age	0.0082 (1.609)	0.0083 (1.653)	0.0075 (1.519)	0.0078 (1.578)
No. of children	0.186 (3.020)	0.187 (3.036)	0.169 (2.747)	0.169 (2.754)
Food store 1	0.0253 (0.160)	0.0239 (0.151)	0.0007 (0.005)	−0.0018 (−0.012)
Food store 2	0.0007 (0.005)	−0.0023 (−0.015)	−0.0196 (−0.132)	−0.023 (−0.154)
Food store 3	−0.213 (−1.381)	−0.215 (−1.392)	−0.246 (−1.604)	−0.252 (−1.645)
IMR (demand)	0.777 (2.010)	0.756 (1.950)	0.791 (2.052)	0.764 (1.977)
Intercept (demand)	2.089 (6.837)	2.130 (6.833)	2.168 (7.072)	2.216 (7.109)
σ	0.933 (33.216)	0.933 (33.226)	0.933 (33.191)	0.933 (33.171)
Rho (correlation)	—	—	0.245 (2.079)	0.255 (2.164)
N	276	276	276	276
Log L	−206.44	−206.08	−204.51	−204.00
LR test statistic		0.72		1.02

Note
1 The numbers in parentheses below the estimated coefficients are the ratios of the estimated coefficient to the estimated standard error

Table 12.3 Demand models for fresh produce and risks due to pesticide residues[1]

	Revealed preference	
	Semi-log demand selected sample	Semi-log demand full sample
Price ϕ	−0.788 (−5.65)	−0.795 (−8.01)
Income τ	0.378×10^{-4} (2.27)	0.477×10^{-4} (3.81)
No. of children	0.166 (2.84)	0.169 (5.32)
Seriousness of food risks (EAT4)	0.017 (0.90)	0.043 (3.05)
Food store type 1[2]	0.050 (0.32)	0.076 (0.87)
Food store type 2	0.012 (0.08)	−0.066 (−0.79)
Food store type 3	−0.226 (−1.48)	−1.54 (−1.79)
Inverse Mills ratio	1.019 (3.14)	0.001 (0.02)
Intercept	1.770 (3.75)	2.060 (8.31)
Education	0.023 (1.00)	−0.026 (1.96)
R^2	0.292	−0.219
Σ	0.619	−0.623
Log (L)	−259.39	−406.40
Sample size	276	430

Notes

1 The numbers in parentheses by the estimated coefficients are the ratios of the estimated coefficient to the estimated standard error. For the maximum likelihood models, these are based on asymptotic standard errors. Computations used standard procedures in LIMDEP and the MINIMIZE procedure for the jointly estimated model.

2 The food store type 1 are qualitative variables identifying each of three national food chains. A fourth national chain along with a local outlet with a very small number of sample respondents were combined as the omitted category. As one of the conditions allowing us to recruit respondents at each chain's food stores, we agreed not to identify them in widely circulated results from the analysis. This requirement precludes us from identifying the names of the chains.

produce in the contingent choice were less inclined to state purchase intentions for tested produce. The remaining demographic, attitude, and food store descriptive variables enter only the produce demand model. For the most part their effects parallel the estimates based on the model for produce demand alone. Older households with children under 18 seem to demand more fresh produce. Qualitative variables for three of the five food store types in our sample were included because of distinct differences in the perceived quality of the produce across each chain.[18] The negative and significant effect (at a 0.10 *p-value*) corresponds to the food chain that focus group respondents consistently identified as having poor quality produce.

One of the inverse Mills ratios included to take account of selection effects is significant. It is for the RP equation. This term is not a significant factor in *both* the choice equation and the model for produce demand. These results seem to suggest that ignoring the selection has greater implications for our ability to describe the amount demanded than the stated choice between conventional and tested produce.

Overall then, our analysis confirms that combining the RP and SP data sources improves the model's ability to incorporate the effects of income, allows more consistent treatment of the demand for the commodities hypothesized to convey the risk. It also influences the estimated parameters for price and risk effects.

Implications

Our research was designed in response to the innovations in joint or combined estimation with revealed and stated preference data. The first proposals for joint estimation were made over 20 years ago (1988) simultaneously by Cameron (in an unpublished version of her 1992 paper) and Morikawa as part of his thesis (1989). This volume was designed to explain the theory and current econometric methods for joint estimation. Examples such as this paper have been elicited to illustrate what can be learned from combined estimates. Several important lessons emerged from our research. The first stems from a recognition that the control allowed when stated preference data enable the researcher to collect choice data must be tempered and adapted when the stated choice information is to be part of a combined SP/RP model. More specifically, if the SP responses are to be used with RP data they must be "nested" or cast within the framework conventionally used to interpret revealed preference data. Often this structure involves a wide array of maintained assumptions—whether price indexes (and associated separability assumptions) or specific assumptions about Marshallian demand functions— they need to be linked to the models intended for the SP data. This process can result in changes in survey design, including the information aside from the specifc choice question that is collected from sample respondents. It can also lead to changes in how the RP and SP models are formulated to describe consumers' behavior.

A second issue concerns the fact that behavioral models need not be directly linked to choice. In our case more detailed information on the formation of subjective probabilities and the role of new information in altering these perceptions would have been especially helpful. Our RP responses described a situation where private mitigation (aside from no consumption of produce) was not possible. The stated preference questions offered "new" prospects for adjustment. As a result, the analytical structure had to reconcile *ex ante* and *ex post* beliefs and the role of information and learning for how each person responds.

Finally, joint data collection designed within a consistent structure offers opportunities to cross check or validate models by eliciting behaviors that should be associated with choices.[19]

Our results would suggest that Lusk's (2007) qualification to the pessimistic conclusions of Shogren and Stamlund (2007) may well be warranted. When respondents are offered credible choices to reduce risks of premature death and an economic model consistently integrates these decisions in a

framework that acknowledges the distinction between technical risk information and subjective risk perceptions it is possible to recover consistent risk/
resource tradeoffs.

Acknowledgments

Partial support of this research was provided by several sources including
Resources for the Future, the National Science Foundation (grant number SES-
8911 372), the North Carolina State University Agricultural Research Service,
and a Cooperative Agreement with the Economic Research Service, US
Department of Agriculture. Thanks are due Ed Estes for help in arranging the
survey and in designing the research; to Richard Carson, Bill Desvousges,
Michael Hanemann, and Robert Mitchell for comments on drafts of the questionnaire and to the editors for constructive comments on several earlier drafts;
to Richard Laborin and Jon Valentine for preparing the recent draft of this
manuscript.

Appendix

Table 12.a.1 Probit selection model[1]

	Probit selection model
Intercept (choice)	1.176 (2.22)
No. of children	−0.082 (−1.22)
Age	−0.011 (−2.14)
Food store type 1[2]	0.192 (1.04)
Food store type 2	0.238 (1.36)
Food store type 3	0.037 (0.21)
Education	0.309×10^{-2} (0.12)
$(r_c - r_t)$	0.434×10^{-2} (0.99)
Δ Stone price	−0.248 (−2.73)
Perceived risk of tested produce (FRA3)	−0.107 (−3.51)
R^2	0.048
Log (L)	−266.92
N	430

Notes
1 The numbers in parentheses below the estimated coefficients are the ratios of the estimated coefficient to the estimated standard error. For the maximum likelihood models, these are based on
asymptotic standard errors. Computations used standard procedures in LIMDEP and the MINI-
MIZE procedure for the jointly estimated model.
2 The food store type 1 are qualitative variables identifying each of three national food chains. A
fourth national chain along with a local outlet with a very small number of sample respondents
were combined as the omitted category. As one of the conditions allowing us to recruit respondents at each chain's food stores, we agreed not to identify them in widely circulated results from
the analysis. This requirement precludes us from identifying the names of the chains.

Notes

1 See Whitehead *et al.* (2008) for a review of the joint estimation research in environmental economics. Based on their review it appears that no one has attempted to combine RP and SP in a framework that acknowledges the risk perception process.

2 The CDC reported a multi-state outbreak of Salmonella associated with raw tomatoes that involved 28 states and the District of Columbia. See CDC (2008) for details. A smaller, but similar episode involving fresh spinach and e-coli took place in 2006 involving 26 states see CDC (2006) for further details.

3 See Florax *et al.* (2005) for a meta analysis of the non-market valuation studies involving pesticide risks.

4 Whitehead *et al.* (2008) suggest that the record in combining continuous RP responses with SP is not good. As a rule, they suggest, the findings of studies combining RP and SP find that the two information sources are not consistent. However, as they also note the mechanism linking the models has often been limited. The tests have also been confined to a few parameters and may well have ignored *ex ante/ex post* distinctions in the two choice processes that we describe in our application developed below.

5 p and m are implicitly assumed to be normalized by an index of all other goods' prices which is taken to be unity because all consumers come from the same small market area Raleigh, North Carolina.

6 Deaton (1981) offers an alternative approach that would be to allow modeling those choosing to consume neither the tested nor conventionally grown produce with a more disaggregate description of demand by type of fruit or vegetable. Unfortunately, this would require a larger sample to assure sufficient sample size for each commodity.

7 There are at least two interpretations of this approach. The first follows from an economic argument paralleling Dubin and McFadden (1984) that suggests a corner solution with no consumption. The second treats the observed demand (choices) of those who do not report a choice as protest responses and applies a selection model following the practice of past literature.

8 Focus group respondents indicated reports of expenditures would be easier to prove and likely to be more accurate than the amount purchased. The latter also raised difficulties with the units of measurement for these reports—pounds, a count or bunch. The packaging will vary greatly with fresh produce.

9 The group of individuals concerned about food safety was recruited from a food cooperative offering organic produce in Raleigh, North Carolina. See Eom (1992) for summary of the design and highlights of the findings from these two groups.

10 A copy of a data appendix describing features of the sample along with the text of the questionnaires is available from the authors.

11 Focus group participants perceived the risks reported per million as more threatening than per ten thousand consumers. When we explained to them that each presentation implied the same probability, they acknowledged that there were no genuine differences but suggested that they found the use of thousands easier to comprehend than millions. We used the range of estimates defined by the National Academy of Sciences to structure our experimental design (i.e. 50 per 50,000 to one per 50,000).

12 The interviewers distributing questionnaires were undergraduates recruited from advanced marketing methods class. They were given approximately two hours of training and reported weekly on their activities and problems. Because each questionnaire had a unique identification number and a detailed log was kept of where they were to be distributed, it was possible to monitor activities of each interviewer with each new assignment. To enhance responses, we offered those returning completed questionnaires within ten days a chance at one of two $25 bonuses for participating. Most of the questionnaires returned were received within ten days of being distributed.

13 See Deaton and Muelbauer (1980) for further discussion.

14 Respondents receiving questionnaires that required they compute price were converted to aggregate price indexes by substituting the proposed prices of each version (i.e. the currently available variety and the "tested" variety) in the relevant argument in equation (12.10) with all other components unchanged. Those receiving the version with stated prices used $\sum_{j \in C_i} s_{ji}$ as the weight for the prices posed in the contingent behavior questions.

15 White's (1982) development of the asymptotic properties of quasi-maximum likelihood estimators provides the justification for our adaptation of a Heckman (1979) selection rule to this case and avoids the need for a trivariate normal model to estimate the joint system with selection effects. White's analysis established that when the true model and the mis-specified model are identical for certain parameter values, ML estimates from the mis-specified model are consistent. We are grateful to Xiaolong Zhang for suggesting this argument.

16 This is the basic rationale for Viscusi's (1989) proposal to use a Bayesian learning model describing the formation of subjective probabilities as an exogenous process to choice. They are a weighted average of prior beliefs and the probabilities implied by new information. In his prospective reference theory, these subjective probabilities replace the known probabilities. There have been a number of empirical tests of the risk updating component of Viscusi's model using both hypothetical situations (see Viscusi and O'Connor 1984) and real risks and technical information explaining them (see Smith *et al.* 1990 and Viscusi 1989 as examples).

17 To our knowledge there have been no efforts to deal with selection within the context of mixed discrete/continuous models as described here. The Monte Carlo evidence available would, loosely interpreted, favor our strategy over ignoring the problem completely. Building the selection model into the choice process would require a full specification of the demand for other food items that become the outside alternative when produce is not selected. This was beyond the scope of our survey and thus could not be considered in the modeling. See Schmertmann (1994) and Bourguignon *et al.* (2001) for further details on sampling experiments with related models.

18 The major food chains with retail outlets in Raleigh include: Kroger, Sav-A-Center (A&P), Winn-Dixie, Harris-Teeter, and Food Lion. Other chains with outlets include: Food Carnival, Fresh Market, and Well Spring Grocery. Five of this group agreed to have questionnaires distributed at their stores in Raleigh.

19 This is discussed in more detail in Smith (2007).

Bibliography

Alberini, Anna, Maureen Cropper, Alan Krupnick, and Nathalie B. Simon (2004) "Does the value of a statistical life vary with age and health status? Evidence from the U.S. and Canada," *Journal of Environmental Economics and Management*, 48(1): 769–792.

Bourguignon, Francois, Martin Fournier, and Marc Gurgand (2001) "Selection bias correction based on the multinomial logit model," CREST working paper, online, available at: www.econometricsociety.org/meetings/esem02/cdrom/papers/403/ Lee531.pdf.

Bourguignon, François, Martin Fournier, and Marc Gurgand (2007) "Selection bias corrections based on the multinomial logit model: Monte Carlo comparisons," *Journal of Economic Surveys*, 21(1): 174–205.

Bradley, M.A. and A.J. Daly (1992) "Estimation of logit choice models using mixed stated preference and revealed preference information," in P.R. Stopher and M. Lee-Goslin (eds.), *Understanding Travel Behaviour in an Era of Change*, Oxford: Pergammon Press.

Bullock, David S. and Nicholas Minot (2006) "On measuring the volume of a non-market good using market data," *American Journal of Agricultural Economics*, 88(4): 961–973.

Cameron, Trudy Ann (1988) "Auto validation: Empirical discrete/continuous choice modeling with contingent valuation referendum survey data," unpublished paper, Department of Economics, University of California at Los Angeles.

Cameron, Trudy Ann (1992) "Combining contingent valuation and travel cost data for the valuation of nonmarket goods," *Land Economics*, 68(3): 302–317.

CDC (Centers for Disease Control and Prevention) (2006) *Update on Multi-State Outbreak of* E. coli *O157:H7 Infections from Fresh Spinach*, online, available from: www.cdc.gov/ecoli/2006/september/updates/092406.htm.

CDC (Centers for Disease Control and Prevention) (2008) *Investigation of Outbreak of Infections Caused by Salmonella Saintpaul*, online, available from: www.cdc.gov/salmonella/saintpaul/jalapeno/archive/082008.html.

Conklin, Neilson C., and Pamela A. Mischen (1992) *Quality Standards and Pesticide Use: A Review of Research*, Tempe, AZ: Center for Agribusiness Policy Studies, Arizona State University.

Conklin, Neilson C., Gary D. Thompson, and Lyle D. Riggs (1991) *Price and Quality Differentials in Organic and Conventional Produce*, final report prepared for the Fruit and Vegetable Division Agricultural Marketing Service, Cooperative Agreement No. 12–25-A3202.

Cook, Phillip J. and Daniel A. Graham (1977) "The demand for insurance and protection: The case of irreplaceable commodities," *Quarterly Journal of Economics*, 91(1): 143–156.

Deaton, Angus (1981) "Theoretical and empirical approaches to consumer demand under rationing," in A.Deaton (ed.), *Essays in the Theory and Measurement of Consumer Demand in Honour of Sir Richard Stone*, Cambridge: Cambridge University Press.

Deaton, Angus, and John Muellbauer (1980) *Economics and Consumer Behavior*, New York: Cambridge University Press.

Desvousges, William H. and V. Kerry Smith (1988) "Focus groups and risk communication: The 'science' of listening to data," *Risk Analysis*, 8(4): 479–484.

Dillman, Don A. (1978) *Mail and Telephone Surveys: The Total Design Method*, New York: John Wiley & Sons.

Dubin, Jeffrey A. and Daniel L. McFadden (1984) "An econometric analysis of residential electric appliance holdings and consumption," *Econometrica*, 52(2): 346–362.

Eom, Young Sook (1992) *Averting Behavior and Consumers' Responses to Environmental Risks: The Case of Pesticide Residues*, unpublished doctoral dissertation, Raleigh, NC: North Carolina State University.

Evans, William N. and W. Kip Viscusi (1993) "Income effects and the value of health," *Journal of Human Resources*, 28(3): 497–518.

Florax, Raymond J.G.M., Chiara M. Travisi and Peter Nijkamp (2005) "A meta-analysis of the willingness to pay for reductions in pesticides risk exposure," *European Review of Agricultural Economics*, 32(4): 441–467.

Hammitt, James (1986) *Organic Carrots: Consumer Willingness to Pay to Reduce Food Borne Risks*, R-3447-EPA, Santa Monica, CA: The Rand Corp.

Hammitt, James K. and Kevin Haninger (2007) "Willingness to pay for food safety: Sensitivity to duration and severity of illness," *American Journal of Agricultural Economics Proceedings*, 89(5): 1170–1175.

Hanemann, W. Michael (1984) "Welfare evaluations in contingent valuation experiments with discrete responses," *American Journal of Agricultural Economics*, 66(3): 332–341.

Hanemann, W. Michael (1989) "Welfare evaluations in contingent valuation experiments with discrete response data: Reply," *American Journal of Agricultural Economics*, 71(4): 1057–1061.

Hausman, Jerry (1981) "Exact consumer's surplus and deadweight loss," *American Economic Review*, 71(4): 662–676.

Hayes, Dermot, Jason Shogren, Seung Youll Shin, and James Kliebenstein (1995) "Valuing food safety in experimental auction markets," *American Journal of Agricultural Economics*, 77(1): 40–53.

Heckman, James J. (1979) "Sample selection bias as a specification error," *Econometrica*, 47(1): 153–161.

Huang, Ju-Chin, Timothy C. Haab, and John C. Whitehead (1997) "Willingness to pay for quality improvements: Should revealed and stated preference data be combined?" *Journal of Environmental Economics and Management*, 34(3): 240–255.

Larson, Douglas M. (1991) "Recovering weakly complementary preferences," *Journal of Environmental Economics and Management*, 21(2): 97–108.

Lusk, Jason L. (2007) "New estimates of the demand for food safety: Discussion," *American Journal of Agricultural Economics Proceedings*, 89(5): 1176–1182.

Mitchell, Robert C. and Richard T. Carson (1989) *Using Surveys to Value Public Goods—the Contingent Valuation Method*, Washington, DC: Resources for the Future.

Morikawa, Takayuki (1989) *Incorporating Stated Preference Data in Travel Demand Analysis*, unpublished PhD Thesis, of Civil Engineering, Massachusetts Institute of Technology.

Morikawa, Takayuki, Moshe Ben-Akiva, and Daniel McFadden (1990) "Incorporating psychometric data in econometric travel demand models," unpublished paper, Cambridge, MA: Department of Civil Engineering, Massachusetts Institute of Technology.

National Academy of Science (1987) *Regulating Pesticides in Food: The Delaney Paradox*, report by Board on Agriculture, National Research Council, Washington, DC: National Academy Press.

Schmertmann, Carl P. (1994) "Selectivity bias correction methods in polychotomous sample selection models," *Journal of Econometrics*, 60(1): 101–132.

Shogren, Jason F. and Tommy Stamlund (2007) "Valuing lives saved from safer food—A cautionary tale revisited," *American Journal of Agricultural Economics Proceedings*, 89(5): 1176–1182.

Smith, V. Kerry (1991) "Household production functions and environmental benefit measurement," in John Braden and Charles Kolstad (eds.), *Measuring the Demand for Environmental Improvement*, Amsterdam: North Holland.

Smith, V. Kerry (2007) "Judging quality," in B.J. Kanninen (ed.), *Valuing Environmental Amenities Using Stated Choice Studies*, Dordrecht: Springer, pp. 297–333.

Smith, V. Kerry, William H. Desvousges, F. Reed Johnson, and Ann Fisher (1990) "Can public information programs affect risk perceptions?" *Journal of Policy Analysis and Management*, 9(1): 41–59.

Tversky, Amos, Samuel Sattath, and Paul Slovic (1988) "Contingent weighting in judgment and choice," *Psychological Reviews*, 95(3): 371–384.

Van Ravenswaay, Eileen O. and John P. Hoehn (1991a) "The impact of health risk on food demand: A case study of Alar and apples," in Julie Caswell (ed.), *Economics of Food Safety*, New York: Elsevier.

Van Ravenswaay, Eileen O. and John P. Hoehn (1991b) "Contingent valuation and food safety: The case of pesticide residues in food," Discussion Paper No. 91–13, Lansing, MI: Department of Agricultural Economics, Michigan State University.

Van Ravenswaay, Eileen O. and John P. Hoehn (1991c) "Consumer perspectives on food safety issues: The case of pesticide residues on fresh produce," Discussion Paper No. 91–20, Lansing, MI: Department of Agricultural Economics, Michigan State University.

Viscusi, W. Kip (1989) "Prospective reference theory: Toward an explanation of the paradoxes," *Journal of Risk and Uncertainty.* 2(3): 235–264.

Viscusi, W. Kip, and William N. Evans (1990) "Utility functions that depend on health status: Estimates and economic implications," *American Economic Review*, 80(3): 353–374.

Viscusi, W. Kip and Charles J. O'Connor (1984) "Adaptive responses to chemical labeling: Are workers Bayesian decision makers?" *American Economic Review*, 74(5): 942–956.

White, Halbert (1982) "Maximum likelihood estimation of misspecified models," *Econometrica*, 50(1): 1–26.

Whitehead, John C., Subhrendu K. Pattanayak, George L. Van Houtven and Brett R. Gelso (2008) "Combining revealed and stated preference data to estimate the nonmarket value of ecological services: An assessment of the state of the science," *Journal of Economic Surveys*, 22(5): 872–908.

13 Local impacts of tropical forest logging

Joint estimation of revealed and stated preference data from Ruteng, Indonesia

David T. Butry and Subhrendu K. Pattanayak

Introduction

Currently, forests constitute 25 percent of the earth's land surface area, but this is a reduction, possibly of up to a half, of that existing during pre-agricultural times (World Resources Institute 2000). Tropical deforestation, in particular, is of global concern, prompting leaders to seek protection for these natural resources. Forested ecosystems provide a plethora of goods and services. The World Resources Institute (WRI) distinguishes between the two—goods include timber, fuelwood, drinking and irrigation water, fodder, non-timber forest products (such as vines, bamboo, leaves), food (honey, mushrooms, fruits), genetic resources; whereas services consist of the removal of air pollutants, emission of oxygen, cycling of nutrients, maintenance of watershed functions and biodiversity, the sequestering of carbon, the moderation of weather extremes, the generation of soil, providing employment opportunities, provide human and wildlife habitat (two-thirds of all terrestrial species reside within the forest), contribute to aesthetic beauty, and provide recreation. However, sometimes the ideals of protection and preservation are at odds with the rights of those indigenous peoples residing in or around these tropical forests.

The debate over tropical forest conservation is contentious in part because there is little or no information on whether or how tropical forest conservation affects local economic development. This study takes a quantitative approach to fill this policy gap by estimating models and testing hypotheses regarding local use and reliance on tropical forests in the Manggarai region of eastern Indonesia. The goal is to provide some policy information on the highly charged debate regarding the unequal distribution of costs and benefits of environmental conservation in tropical developing countries. Critics of tropical forest protection contend that it generates largely global benefits, such as biodiversity conservation, recreation, and ecological services, while it imposes sizeable opportunity costs on local people who are denied access to or use of forest resources (Kremen et al. 2000). Local benefits of biodiversity, recreation, and ecological services are typically indirect and latent, in contrast to seemingly transparent and sizeable opportunity costs of protection borne by local economies.

Thus, we use microeconomic data from surveys of logging households in the buffer zone of Ruteng Park to estimate welfare effects of forest conservation. Quantitative estimates of this nature can provide the starting point for policy discussions about compensation or charges. As this book shows, revealed preference (RP) or stated preference (SP) data can be used to examine and estimate the welfare impacts of environmental policies. In particular, joint estimation by combining RP and SP data can result in at least three benefits (see Whitehead *et al.* (2008) for a review of this literature). Combining RP data with SP data (1) allows an extension of the behavioral model beyond the limited range of historical experience, (2) breaks the multi-collinearity among characteristics in revealed preference data, and (3) grounds hypothetical choices with real choice behavior and may mitigate hypothetical bias.

Our chapter is unique because we present a rare empirical application of producer welfare impacts in developing countries (Pattanayak and Kramer 2001a), but more importantly are among the first to apply the RP-SP data combination strategy to producer based welfare estimation (Pattanayak (2001) represents another exception). Additionally, we explore the potential use of policy levers to more effectively conserve forests and mitigate economic impacts. We investigate the potential for "green market initiatives" as alternatives to total restrictions on forest use by measuring price responsiveness from profit analysis and contingent valuation data on timber permits. Hard evidence on the size of the welfare losses of conservation as well as on potential policy mechanisms to mitigate such impacts can be valuable for the policy discourse on climate change mitigation efforts such as REDD–reduced emissions from deforestation and forest degradation (Angelsen *et al.* 2009).

Background

Forest dependency

One of the most significant and consistent efforts to reduce tropical deforestation has included public efforts for establishing nature reserves and parks, usually to protect against deforestation, species habitat destruction, and biodiversity loss, or to provide watershed protection, through the setting aside forested lands. By definition, these reserves and parks limit the use (access) of the resource, affecting the lives and economic livelihoods of those indigenous peoples living within proximity of the park. Many of these communities are quite dependent on the forest and the multitude of goods and services that it provides. Worldwide, these "forest dependent" communities total anywhere between one million to one billion people, depending on one's definition of "forest dependence" (Byron and Arnold 1999).

While much has been made of the global benefits of curbing deforestation— carbon sequestration, biodiversity and species preservation, etc.—relatively little has been made concerning the fact that forest dependent communities will be affected. Some have questioned the pragmatism of severing the economic, social, and cultural ties between these communities and the forests around which they reside. "Forest residents—and rural people generally—are potent political actors in tropical forest regions and an essential component of the environmental political constituencies that are necessary for the long-term conservation of tropical forests" (Schwartzman *et al.* 2000: 1351). Schwartzman *et al.* (ibid.) find that in some areas indigenous people "are defending far bigger areas of tropical forest from unfettered deforestation and logging than are parks, thereby conserving the ecological services provided by these forest and the majority of their component plant and animal species." The lack of property rights is perhaps the reason we observed unsustainable timber extraction within these tropical forests at the hands of the local populations, as adjacent villages share many of these forests, which are owned in common.

Forests provide more than just a source of work and income, they also play a major role in defining the social and cultural identity of those around them (Byron and Arnold 1999). Because tropical forest protection provides global benefits that *may* outweigh the local costs of giving up forest access, this does not mean we can simply ignore the costs on these communities—the sustainability of such policies depends on them. Global efficiency does not necessarily translate into local stability, meaning if there are no incentives for forest dependent communities to abstain from forest use (if no other substitutes are available), then banning logging may have little effect. In order to develop viable long-run forest policies, we must understand these people and the economic realities (economic incentives) they face *or* would face given some policy decision. We must ask, "What happens if…?"

Socioeconomic factors

Poorer households are typically more reliant on the forest, and natural resources in general, as a source of income than are wealthier households, although in absolute terms, wealthier households tend to consume more of the forest resource (Gunatilake 1998; Byron and Arnold 1999; Cavendish 2000). Since resource extraction tends to be so labor intensive, upper income households prefer other income opportunities, as they tend to have a greater opportunity cost of time (Gunatilake 1998). Also natural resource areas tend to be open access areas, as opposed to agriculture where someone owns the land under cultivation. Because of free access, lower income households tend to be more reliant upon these areas.

Gunatilake (1998: 275) finds that while no study has examined the "theoretical relationships between forest dependence and socio-economic variables," he finds other related studies that assist in his own theory of forest dependence. Key socioeconomic variables tend to be: education, household income, labor availability, proximity to forest, and agricultural productivity. Education is expected to be inversely related to forest dependence, primarily because more education brings with it a higher opportunity cost of time (forest related income activities are usually lower wage). As mentioned above, household income is negatively related to forest dependency. Forest activities are not only low paying but also, as mentioned, time intensive, thus forest dependent families tend to be larger and have more labor available. Labor is positively related to dependence. Forest dependence is believed to be inversely related to agricultural productivity.

Understanding the socioeconomic variables related to forest dependence is important. If for instance, a policy goal is to reduce dependency and curb deforestation, knowing that education and agricultural productivity are inversely related to dependence can be helpful. A program set at reducing dependency might offer education or job training assistance, or may offer subsidies on agricultural supplies to foster a smoother, more profitable transition from logging to agriculture or other non-forest related positions.

Valuation

"As long as we are forced to make choices, we are doing valuation" (Pritchard *et al.* 1999: 36). Paraphrasing Pritchard *et al.* ecosystem valuation is done for three reasons:

1   to show that nonmarket ecosystem or natural resource goods are connected to human welfare;
2   that the valuation of ecosystems or natural resources is performed to quantify their relative importance to human welfare; and
3   that valuation may be performed to determine the merit of a decision or policy (the cost-benefit assessment).

Stated preference techniques have been used to value tropical forest protection. Contingent valuation (CV) has been used to determine the willingness-to-accept for the loss of forest access (see Shyamsundar and Kramer 1996). In Shyamsundar and Kramer (1996), respondents were asked how much rice they would be willing-to-accept to respect the boundaries of a newly established nature reserve. Conversely, Kramer and Mercer (1997) examine the willingness-to-pay for tropical forest preservation by US citizens. Pattanayak and Kramer (2001) price the value of drought mitigation (an increase in ecosystem services) to local tropical forest residents, which could result from less forest use (deforestation). Kramer *et al.* (2003) provides a review of other CV literature concerning forest protection.

However, few have examined the value of tropical forest protection using revealed preferences. This may be because of the paucity of available data. Some have attempted to quantify components of the forests, particularly the nonmarket ecosystem services they provide. Pattanayak and Butry (2003) estimate the demand for ecosystem services using Freeman's (1993) three-stage framework, a framework modified for ecosystem services by Kramer *et al.* (1997a) and Pattanayak (2004). In Pattanayak and Butry (2003), forest protection and conservation is assumed to induce a change in ecosystem services (watershed protection), which is shown to increase agricultural productivity. Using the production analog of weak complementarity, developed by Huang and Smith (1998), the change in ecosystem service can be valued. In Pattanayak and Butry (2005), the models are made spatially explicit, and find that failing to incorporate the spatial nature of the data biases the willingness-to-pay estimates of the ecosystem services.

Yet, it appears no one has examined the totality of forest protection using RP. This method should include the *costs* of protection, the loss in income provided by the forest resource (logging, fuelwood extraction, nontimber forest products, forest food products), and the local benefits (ecosystem services, etc.). Theoretically, CV and RP methods should yield about the same estimates of forest protection, although Carson *et al.* (1996), perform a meta-analysis comparing CV and RP WTP estimates, and find that the CV estimates are consistently lower.[1]

Ruteng Park

Ruteng Park was created in 1993 in Manggarai, Indonesia as part of the global and national concern regarding tropical deforestation. It was designed along the lines of an integrated conservation and development project (ICDP) with the twin goals of protecting tropical ecosystems while promoting local economic development. The park is 32,246 hectares, with a 56,000 hectare buffer zone, an area in which sustainable levels of forest product collection, agroforestry, and small-scale agriculture are permissible, as long as they are consistent with the ICDP design principle (Blomkvist 1995; Moeliono 1995). The area is mainly a subtropical forest that is rich with biodiversity, including Komodo rats, monkeys, wild boar, civets, cobra, and vipers. The terrain is extremely steep, as the park is located on the tops of several volcanic ridges and is the source of many rivers and streams. Previous research has found evidence of ecotourism potential (Kramer *et al.* 1997b) and watershed protection benefits for farming (Pattanayak and Kramer 2001b) and domestic use (Pattanayak 2004).

Although many Manggarai people are farmers, approximately 2,000 households—a sizeable subset of the local population—rely on timber logging.[2] These households process timber into boards and beams, and sell them as construction lumber to local government agencies, churches, and private builders. Timber comes from the forests managed or owned by villages, the buffer zone, and the reserve section of Ruteng Park. In 1989, the government banned concessionaire logging for timber in government forests, including Ruteng Park in 1993. Our field research shows, however, that local inhabitants have continued to log limited amounts of timber from in and around the park. They also collect a variety of nontimber forest products such as rattan, herbs, and textile coloring agents. Park managers can allow sustainable logging and nontimber forest products collection in the buffer zone since the ICDP recognizes the rights of local people. However, forest conservation policy is an evolving process, as national and local policy makers continue to ponder alternatives for forest conservation, including tougher enforcement and participatory conservation that can be reconciled with local development goals. Because inadequate information on the economics of controlling logging stymies current forest conservation efforts (Blomkvist 1995), we focus on investigating the magnitude and distribution of the economic impacts of restricted forest use.

While we do not support or argue for a complete ban on forest logging, we wish to examine the effects of various degrees of forest protection, including an effective ban on logging by local households. There are many benefits and costs of different levels of restricted forest use. The ecotourism industry will benefit by accruing amenities and profits, and downstream farming communities will realize watershed protection benefits (Pattanayak 2004; Pattanayak and Butry 2003). Carbon sequestration and biodiversity preservation will be among the major global benefits (Kremen *et al.* 2000; WRI 2000). On the cost side, clearly consumers in the region will be deprived of timber products. Moreover, loggers will gain little and instead stand to lose substantially (Blomkvist 1995; Moeliono 1995). Although a majority of loggers surveyed in the region expressed concern for the forest deterioration, 26 percent felt that the logging restrictions were not warranted. In this paper, we focus on costs to local loggers.

Model specification

A semi-log profit function is used to establish the relationship between forest access and household timber production.

$$\ln(\pi_i) = \beta_0 + \beta_p \cdot P_i + \beta_w \cdot W_i + \varepsilon_i \tag{13.1}$$

In equation (13.1), annual household profits, π_i, are estimated as a function of forest access, W_i, vector of output and input prices, P_i, and a vector of fixed inputs, Z_i. The subscript, i, refers to the household.

The change in profit, $\Delta\pi$, generated by a ban on logging measures compensating variation or willingness-to-pay (WTP) for this ecological service (Mäler *et al.* 1994). Therefore, in theory WTP for timber harvesting can be measured by directly questioning the logging households, using the CV method. In practice however, because this service is a proposal in a CV question, household stated willingness to pay, WTP_S, could diverge from $\Delta\pi$ for at least two reasons. Laughland *et al.* (1996) build a convincing case for the role of empirical work in analyzing divergences between theoretical and observable measures of WTP.

The first reason for the divergence is that household responses to the CV question depend on their perceptions of the service, θW. A perceptions process posits that the perceived forest access, θW, is reflected in the household response to the CV question. We contend that the WTP_S amount reflects households' combination of perceived value and the perceived increase, i.e. perceived $d\pi$ multiplied by θW, they expect to receive. A second reason for the divergence between theoretical and stated WTP is that households consider the context within which this contingent service is provided and take into account other commodities and conditions, not just forest access. An adjustment mechanism, ρ, by which households either discount or mark-up their perceived profit increase, $\Delta\pi_S(\theta)$, is similar to a non-use component of estimated WTP in many CV studies. In part, the adjustment is due to the public dimension of forest access, given that joint private-public features are inherent to most contingent goods evaluated in CV studies (Whittington 1998). In this case the discounting could be, for example, because the logging households are not familiar with forest access options or local timber conditions. Similarly, an example of a reason for a mark-up is the public good nature of an ecological service that benefits the entire community. Thus, households adjust their WTP$_S$ by ρ depending on the environmental conditions, R, and demographic attributes and opinions, H.

We propose a linear-in-parameters adjustment as a first approximation of a general WTP$_S$ function

$$WTP_S = \Delta_{\pi_S}\left[P, Z, \theta W\right] + \rho\left(R, H\right) = WTP_S\left[P, Z, \theta W, R, H\right] \qquad (13.2)$$

Thus, a household would be willing to pay no more than $\Delta\pi_S(\theta) + \rho$ for this service. Whittington (1998) cautions against the cavalier use and interpretation of stated preference values that are not bounded by respondents' ability to pay since disposable incomes are typically low in developing countries. By virtue of its derivation from and dependence on logging profits, the WTP measure in equation (13.2) reflects an ability to pay, not just a willingness to pay.

Using the semi-log profit function, we can specify WTP$_S$ as

$$\begin{aligned} \ln(WTP_i) &= \ln(\pi_i) + a_0 + a_h \cdot H_i + a_r \cdot R_i + \xi_i \\ &= \theta(\beta_0 + \beta_P \cdot P_i + \beta_w \cdot W_i + \varepsilon_i) + a_0 + a_h \cdot H_i + a_r \cdot R_i + \xi_i \end{aligned} \qquad (13.3)$$

This specification of the WTP function simultaneously maintains consistency with the profit function and with standard CV models (Cameron and James 1987) in that it includes a variety of demographic, behavioural, and environmental variables.

The models of logging profit and stated willingness to pay have been developed separately around two kinds of data, timber production (revealed) and CV responses (stated). However, the two models utilize different types of information to explain the same economic optimizing behavior, based on data from the same households, by using common variables. These commonalities can be exploited to build a constrained joint model with potential statistical gains from stacking the equations. In addition to the imposed theoretical consistency across the two data sources, the benefits of joint estimation are

a   reduced bias through inclusion of additional variables from RP data, balancing the hypothetical nature of SP choices,
b   efficiency through exploitation of the correlation of the two data sets,
c   efficiency for small data sets, and
d   gains in identification of the scale parameter (in discrete choice models) and any other variables that have little variation in the RP data alone.[3]

Joint estimation requires (1) restrictions on the coefficients of variables that are common to both models such that the coefficients are equal to each other and (2) compatibility of functional forms across the two models. The imposed convergence of stated and revealed preference measures can be evaluated by (a) comparing distributions of profit and stated WTP and (b) testing the equality of parameters that are common to profits and WTP functions in the system of estimated equations. Expected signs and significance of estimated parameters provide evaluation criteria for construct validity. In cases where we can only impute marginal profits, joint models of revealed profits and stated WTP data allow us to calibrate measures of non-marginal profits and evaluate convergence validity.

Survey of logger households

We implement the conceptual model by using data that were collected by researchers from Duke University and the Indonesian Ministry of Forestry in 1996 as part of a study on the economics of protected area management.[4] A socioeconomic household survey was implemented in approximately 100 households from five *desas* (villages) in the Manggarai district of Western Flores, including Carep, Golo Dukal, Pau, Tenda, and Waso, which together contain the bulk of the logging population (Moeliono 1995) (see Figure 13.1). Surveys were administered by two teams from the Universitas Nusa Cendana (West Timor) in February of 1996. The questionnaires were organized into several sections including household characteristics, logging and farming activities, nontimber forest products, and attitudes about Ruteng Park and the forest ecosystems.

On the average, a household head is 39 years old and has resided in his village for 37 years. The majority of those surveyed have some primary school level education or less (77 percent). The average family size is six. About half of our sample households have been logging and selling timber for 13 years. The best quality or Class I timber (*ajang, ngancar, wuhar, dalo, pinis, lumu, worok*)

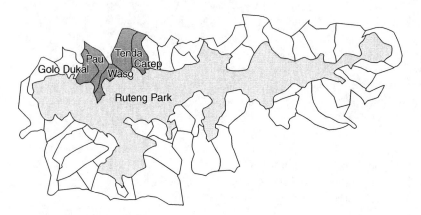

Figure 13.1 The villages surrounding Ruteng Park (study site shaded in gray).

is the most frequently logged of the four qualities or classes of timber. In addition to logging, many households collect dead wood for fuel from nearby fields and roadways.

Labor is the primary input and axes, manual hand saws, and machetes are the preferred tools for logging. Of those surveyed, 34 percent own at least one axe, 30 percent own a manual saw, and 98 percent own at least one machete. Households reported prices for various classes of timber as the price per unit of timber sold.[5] Wages in farming and logging crews are used as the cost of labor in logging. We created a capital cost for logging tools as a geometric function of the tool, the tool's age, its value when originally purchased, and the quantity of each tool (Klemperer 1995).[6] These prices are used to compute household specific forest profits as total revenue (price multiplied by quantity of forest products) less total costs (capital costs plus the product of wage rate and labor). In Table 13.1, we present the average profit measures (all monetary values shown in tables and in text are in Rupiah).

We created a wealth dummy variable to determine whether forest access and forest dependency varies across wealth groups. Accumulation of consumer goods, such as radios, appliances, motorcycles, watches, and jewelry are measures of status and well-being in Manggarai, Indonesia. Cluster analysis of the count of consumer durables identified two wealth groups: 66 percent 'poor' and 34 percent rich, or those who own at least one good. A Students t-statistic of 11.73 shows that the groups are statistically different populations. This cluster dummy was positively correlated with other wealth measures, including home quality.

The five villages lie in four watersheds. These watersheds are covered with different proportions of forests that are designated as "protected forests" by the Ministry of Forestry. The protected status of these forests does not necessarily imply that the forests do not provide forest products to all people. Instead, as argued in the previous section, accessibility (and enforcement) is probably a function of local politics and culture. We use a dummy variable to test for this difference.

Table 13.1 Descriptive statistics[1]

	Mean	Std. dev.	Min.	Max.
Ln(profit)	6.52	6.69	0	15.23
Ln(WTP)	8.89	1.73	0	11.51
Price class I	3796	856	1500	8000
Price class III	2793	698	1000	7500
Wage	2324	1058	300	7500
Primary forest cover	160	101	92	342
Secondary forest cover	169	48	54	220
Average age	38.8	10.4	19	65
Family size	5.6	1.7	1	8
Wealth indicator	0.38	0.48	0	1

Note
1 Observations=97.

Results

The results of the restricted and unrestricted models are presented in Table 13.2 and 13.3 (corresponding to the RP and SP data). The restricted model ensures that the input and output price coefficients are the same between the profit and willingness-to-pay equations. A Likelihood-ratio test of the input and output price restrictions could not reject the null of restrictions (chi-square statistic = 1.51, with 3 degrees of freedom: $p = 0.67$), meaning the restrictions should be imposed, and thereby necessitating joint estimation. Thus, we find that input and output prices affect household profits and willingness-to-pay (for forest access) in the same ways (i.e. a 1 Rupiah increase in the price of class I timber increases expected log of profits and log of willingness-to-pay by 0.0038 Rupiah).[7] In addition, joint estimation allows for survey information to be used more efficiently, as we find that when failing to impose the joint estimation framework, the unrestricted OLS model is unable to discern the statistical relationship between key regressors (e.g. input and output prices) and profit and willingness-to-pay.

A Breusch-Pagan test of cross-error correlation (in the restricted model) could not reject the null of error independence (chi-square statistic = 0.953, with 1 degree of freedom: $p = 0.32$). That is, the unexplained variation in the log of profits equation (i.e. the variation not explained by the covariates) is not correlated with the unexplained variation in the log of WTP equation. Given the tests of restrictions and cross-error correlation, the final model specification was estimated using three-stage least-squares regression with imposed price restrictions and a diagonal covariance matrix (i.e. the unrestricted model shown in Tables 13.2 and 13.3).

Each equation in the jointly-estimated model is statistical significant (profit: chi-square statistic = 38.4, $p < 0.01$; WTP: chi-square statistic = 15.2, $p = 0.06$). The independent variables explain 25 percent of the variation in the log of profits, and 13 percent of the variation in the log of willingness-to-pay. Given

Table 13.2 Statistical results of profit model (revealed preference data)

Ln(profit)	Model with restrictions			Model without restrictions		
	Coeff.	*z*	*P > |z|*	*Coeff.*	*z*	*P > |z|*
Constant	4.442	1.81	0.071	1.420	0.30	0.768
Class I	0.0004	1.87	0.061	0.0011	1.49	0.138
Class III	0.0004	1.59	0.111	0.0005	0.57	0.571
Wage	0.0003	1.45	0.148	−0.0001	−0.12	0.901
Primary forests	−0.0375	−5.78	0.000	−0.0340	−4.01	0.000
Secondary forests	0.0282	2.12	0.034	0.0307	2.21	0.029
Chi² statistic	38.43 (p<0.0001)			–		
F-statistic	–			6.37 (p<0.0001)		
R²	0.25			0.26		
N	97			97		

Table 13.3 Statistical results of contingent valuation model (stated preference data)

Ln(WTP)	Model with restrictions			Model without restrictions		
	Coeff.	z	P > |z|	Coeff.	z	P > |z|
Constant	6.943	3.21	0.001	7.212	4.19	0.000
Class I	0.0004	1.87	0.061	0.0003	1.47	0.143
Class III	0.0004	1.59	0.111	0.0004	1.45	0.148
Wage	0.0003	1.45	0.148	0.0004	1.51	0.133
Primary forest	−0.0047	−2.01	0.045	−0.0051	−2.05	0.042
Secondary forest	−0.0025	−0.63	0.527	−0.0027	−0.68	0.501
Average age	−0.026	−1.55	0.121	−0.027	−1.53	0.128
Family size	0.189	1.73	0.083	0.189	1.68	0.094
Wealth indicator	−0.560	−1.55	0.122	−0.586	−1.58	0.116
Chi^2 statistic	15.19 (p=0.06)			−		
F-statistic	−			1.71 (p=0.099)		
R^2	0.133			0.134		
N	97			97		

the small sample size of our data, we focus on those statistical relationships achieving a p-value of 0.15 or less.

Output timber class prices I (6 percent level) and III (11 percent level) are positively correlated with profits and WTP (prices of timber class II and IV were not significant and dropped for parsimony). As the market price for timber increases, profits increase, as does a household's WTP for forest access for such timber. The input wage price is also positively correlated (15 percent level) with profits and WTP, which is not expected. This may suggest that households with more business opportunities, and hence higher opportunity costs (captured by wage), tend to be more profitable than households with fewer opportunities.

Primary forest cover is negatively related to profits (1 percent level) and WTP (4 percent level). Greater access to primary forest access drives down the price received for the higher-quality class I timber because it allows for greater harvesting. The negative relationship exhibited between primary forest cover and profits and WTP is consistent with a dominant price effect (e.g. in terms of profitability, the price decline outweighs the increase in quantity harvested).

Secondary forest cover is positively related to profits (3 percent level), but not statistically related to WTP. Secondary forest cover is associated with lower-quality timber, such as the class III timber. Because lower quality timber is more abundant, the quantity effect dominates the price effect in terms of profitability.

Family size is positively correlated with WTP (8 percent level), whereas average family age (12 percent level) and the wealth indicator (12 percent level) exhibit a negative correlation with WTP. Larger family sizes provide a larger labor force, so it is not surprising these families exhibit greater willingness to pay for timber access. Older families, and those wealthier families, with access to other employment opportunities, display less desire to pay for forest access.

Based on the estimated coefficients from the WTP function, the mean annual willingness to pay is $8,753. The coefficients in Tables 13.2 and 13.3 can also be used to subtract out the household-based adjustment, and calculate a pure profit based WTP of $9,889, which is derived exclusively from the logging contributions to profit. The implied negative adjustment of –$1,136 for the typical household indicates that the negative influences outweighed the positive adjustments.

Conclusion

We have demonstrated that commonalities between revealed preference and stated preference models can be exploited to build a constrained (joint) system of equations that is more efficient than its OLS counterparts. The case of logging households in the Manggarai region of Indonesia provides a framework for understanding how various factors influence a logging household's profit-maximizing decision and their willingness-to-pay for greater forest access. Additionally, we found that joint estimation reduces bias through inclusion of additional variables from revealed preference data (i.e. household composition and structure), which balances the hypothetical nature of stated preference choices. This finding is consistent with the result in Pattanayak and Kramer (2001b), which also finds that WTP estimates from CV data are small compared to implied value of water from RP data. While in that case the authors conjectured that households might not believe that forests would consistently produce a lot of water, it was also possible that households were suspicious of the government and the park concept. The evidence presented in this chapter could reflect similar suspicion of the park's inability to appropriately manage forests and permits or to guarantee sustained logging yields.

While the case-study of logging households in the Manggarai region of Indonesia is admittedly a toy example, it illustrates potential policy value of this type of an empirical exercise. One policy implication is that a forest-access permitting program, which seeks to base permit price on those factors affecting household profitability (i.e. [input and output] prices and forest cover), will overvalue the worth of the permits. On average, such a program will overvalue the permits by 13 percent and result in too few permits being purchased. The joint model showed that other household factors, such as average family member age, average family size, and household wealth, played important roles in determining household permit value (willingness-to-pay). However, the household covariates that do not influence permit value in the same ways, and these need to be considered when setting permit price. Average family size was positively correlated with WTP, meaning older and bigger families were willing to purchase permits at prices greater than their estimated profits. Wealthier families and larger families, on the other hand, were willing to pay less than their estimated profits for a permit. The wealth and family size factors dominate the age factor, explaining why the typical adjustment was negative.

In sum, this chapter helps contribute to the knowledge gaps regarding the local economic impacts of tropical forest conservation. The use of microeconomic data from surveys of logging households in the buffer zone of Ruteng Park provides a rare example of welfare estimation using producer surplus information from a tropical forest setting. Further, we present a novel application of joint estimation of RP-SP data, and show the gains from combining some theory with data on preferences, profits, biophysical factors, and socioeconomic factors. Data combination is a useful way to reduce bias and improve welfare analysis. Concrete empirical evidence on the extent of welfare losses and potential policy mechanisms to mitigate such impacts can be valuable for design of climate change mitigation policies such as REDD.

Acknowledgments

This paper is derived from data collected by Pattanayak under a Duke University project led by Randy Kramer. We are grateful to Randy Kramer for access to the data. We would like to thank John Whitehead and participants at SOFEW (Biloxi, Mississippi) and Camp Resources (Wilmington, North Carolina) for their comments on the earlier draft.

Notes

1 Carson *et al.* (1996: 80) point out, "comparisons between contingent valuation and revealed preference estimates are generally assumed to represent tests of convergent validity rather than criterion validity." So the CV measure may come out generally lower than the revealed preference estimate, but this is not necessarily wrong—it is not assumed that the RP measure is the "true measure of the construct" (ibid.).
2 Background information on the logging in the Park region are available in Blomkvist (1995), Ministry of Forestry (1995), and Moeliono (1995).
3 Cameron (1992), and Eom and Smith (1994) are examples of studies that combine revealed and stated preference data within a common and consistent framework. Kling (1997) offers caveats and identifies cases where joint estimation may be problematic.
4 See Kramer *et al.* (1997b) for a detailed description of the project and the data collection.
5 For those households that did not specify a price per unit, the village average price is used as a reasonable proxy for the market opportunities for that timber.
6 $C=(p*r)\,((1-r)^t)$ where C is the current year equipment cost, p is the initial purchase price, r is the discount rate, and t is age of the equipment. The discount rate was set at 15 percent.
7 A Likelihood-ratio test of parameter restrictions, including those for input and output prices, as well as the primary and secondary forest cover variables, were rejected at the 1 percent level (chi-square statistic = 25.54, with 5 degrees of freedom).

References

Angelsen, A., Brockhaus, M., Kanninen, M., Sills, E., Sunderlin, W.D. and Wertz-Kanounnikoff, S. (eds.) (2009) *Realising REDD+: National strategy and policy options*, Bogor, Indonesia: CIFOR.
Blomkvist, L. (1995) *Forestry and Silviculture Specialist Report on Ruteng*, Jakarta, Indonesia: Directorate General of Forest Protection and Nature Conservation, Ministry of Forestry.

Byron, N. and Arnold, M. (1999) "What futures for the people of the tropical forests?" *World Development*, 27(5): 789–805.

Cameron, T.A. (1992) "Combining contingent valuation and travel cost data for the valuation of non market goods," *Land Economics* 68(3): 302–17.

Cameron, T.A. and James, M. (1987) "Efficient estimation methods for closed-ended contingent valuation surveys," *Review of Economics and Statistics*, 69(2): 269–75.

Carson, R., Flores, N., Martin, K., and Wright, J. (1996) "Contingent valuation and revealed preference methodologies: comparing the estimates for quasi public goods," *Land Economics*, 72(1): 80–99.

Cavendish, W. (2000) "Empirical regularities in the poverty-environment relationship of rural households: Evidence from Zimbabwe," *World Development*, 28(11): 1979–2003.

Eom, Y. and Smith, V.K. (1994) "Calibrated nonmarket valuation," mimeo, Raleigh, NC: North Carolina State University.

Freeman, A. (1993) *The Measurement of Environmental and Resource Values: Theory and Methods*, Washington, DC: Resources for the Future.

Gunatilake, H. (1998) "The role of rural development in protecting tropical rainforests: Evidence from Sri Lanka," *Journal of Environmental Management*, 53(3): 273–92.

Huang, J. and Smith, V.K. (1998) "Weak complementarity and production," *Economics Letters*, 60(3): 329–33.

Klemperer, W. (1995) *Forest Resource Economics and Finance*, New York: McGraw-Hill College Division.

Kling, C. (1997) "The gains from combining travel cost and contingent valuation data to value non-market goods," *Land Economics*, 73(3): 428–39.

Kramer, R. and Mercer, D. (1997) "Valuing a global environmental good: U.S. residents' willingness to pay to protect tropical rain forests," *Land Economics*, 73(2): 196–210.

Kramer, R., Holmes, T., and Haefele, M. (2003) "Using contingent valuation to estimate the value of forest ecosystem protection," in E. Sills and K. Abt (eds.), *Forests in a Market Economy*, Kluwer Science Series, Dordrecht: Kluwer Academic Publishers.

Kramer, R., Richter, D., Pattanayak, S., and Sharma, N. (1997a) "Ecological and economic analysis of watershed protection in eastern Madagascar," *Journal of Environmental Management*, 49(3): 277–95.

Kramer, R.A., Pattanayak, S., Sills, E., Simanjuntak, S. (1997b) *The Economics of the Siberut and Ruteng Protected Areas*, Final Report submitted to Directorate General of Forest Protection and Nature Conservancy (Indonesia), Durham, NC: Duke University.

Kremen, C., Niles, J., Dalton, M., Daily, G., Ehrlich, P., Fay, J., Grewal, D., and Guillery, R. (2000) "Economic incentives for rainforest conservation across scales," *Science*, 288(5472): 1828–32.

Laughland, A., Musser, W., Shortle, J., and Musser, L. (1996) "Construct validity of averting cost measures of environmental benefits," *Land Economics*, 72(1): 100–12.

Mäler, K., Gren, I., and Folke, C. (1994) "Multiple use of environmental resources: A household production approach to valuing natural capital," in A. Jansson, M. Hammer, C. Folke, and R. Costanza (eds.), *Investing in Natural Capital: The Ecological Economics Approach to Sustainability*. Washington, DC: Island Press.

Ministry of Forestry (1995) *Ruteng Nature Recreation Park Integrated Conservation and Management Plan, Volumes 1–3*, Directorate General of Forest Protection and Nature Conservation, Biodiversity Conservation Project in Flores and Siberut, ADB Loan No. 1187-INO (SF), Jakarta.

Moeliono, M. (1995) *Wood Use in the Manggarai*, Ruteng, Flores, Indonesia: Intercooperation.

Pattanayak, S.K. (2001) "How green are these valleys? Combining revealed and stated preference methods to account for ecosystem costs of deforestation," Working Paper 01_02, RTI International, online, available at: www.rti.org/pubs/rtipaper _01_02.pdf.

Pattanayak, S.K. (2004) "Valuing watershed services: concepts and empirics from Southeast Asia," *Agriculture, Ecosystems, and Environment*, 104(1): 171–84.

Pattanayak, S.K. and Butry, D. (2003) "Ecological services from forested ecosystems: using weak complementarity for ecosystem valuation," in E. Sills and K. Abt (eds.), *Forests in a Market Economy*, Kluwer Science Series, Dordrecht: Kluwer Academic Publishers.

Pattanayak, S.K. and Butry, D. (2005) "Complementarity of forest and farms: A spatial econometric approach to ecosystem valuation in Indonesia," *American Journal of Agricultural Economics*, 87(4): 995–1008.

Pattanayak, S.K. and Kramer, R. (2001a) "Worth of watersheds: A producer surplus approach for valuing drought control in Eastern Indonesia," *Environment and Development Economics*, 6(1): 123–45.

Pattanayak, S.K. and Kramer, R. (2001b) "Pricing ecological services: Willingness to pay for draught mitigation from watershed protection in Eastern Indonesia," *Water Resources Research*, 37(3): 771–8.

Pritchard, L., Folke, C., and Gunderson, L. (1999) "Valuation of ecosystem services in institutional context," *Ecosystems*, 3(1): 36–40.

Schwartzman, S., Moreira, A., and Nepstand, D. (2000) "Rethinking tropical forest conservation: Perils in parks," *Conservation Biology*, 14(5): 1351–7.

Shyamsundar, P. and Kramer, R. (1996) "Tropical forest protection: an empirical analysis of the costs borne by local people," *Journal of Environmental Economics and Management*, 31(2): 129–44.

Whitehead, J.C., Pattanayak, S.K., Van Houtven, G.L. and Gelso, B. (2008) "Combining revealed and stated preference data to estimate the nonmarket value of ecological services: An assessment of the state of the science," *Journal of Economic Surveys* 22(5): 872–908.

Whittington, D. (1998) "Administering contingent valuation surveys in developing countries," *World Development*, 26(1): 21–30.

World Resources Institute (WRI) (2000) "Taking stock of forest ecosystems" in *A Guide to World Resources 2000–2001: People and Ecosystems: The Fraying Web of Life*, Washington, DC: World Resources Institute.

14 Combining revealed preference and stated preference data without invoking the weak complementarity condition

Kevin J. Egan

Introduction

The valuation of public goods is routinely conducted using revealed preference data on complementary private goods. The analysis requires an untestable assumption about the relationship between the observed private good (e.g. recreation trips to a lake) and the public good of interest (e.g. water quality at the lake). The most common assumption is weak complementarity (WC; see e.g. Mäler 1974), which implies that an individual receives no utility from the public good if the resource is not visited. However, as LaFrance (1994) and Herriges *et al.* (2004) discuss, invoking WC, or any similar assumption, imposes a cardinal restriction on consumer preferences, as a utility function and a monotonic transformation of this utility function potentially generate different welfare measures, even though both will yield identical underlying ordinary demands. Since revealed preference (RP) data alone cannot distinguish between a utility function that satisfies WC and a monotonic transformation that does not, the WC restriction is also untestable (von Haefen 2007).

LaFrance (1994: 77) argues strongly throughout his paper against using WC, stating,

> the difficulty with the [weak complementarity assumption] (and its relatives) is that for the very reason that this hypothesis *permits* welfare measurement with observations on market choices, it also introduces a *cardinal* transformation of preferences. The cardinal nature of this transformation influences the size, and at times even the sign, of the welfare measures obtained.

LaFrance concludes stating, "unfortunately, using the [weak complementarity assumption] (or any of its equally speculative cousins) is a bit like making up numbers and calling them welfare measures" (1994: 83). However, Bockstael and McConnell (1993) in footnote 9, state,

> if we interpret weak complementarity as a motivation that links the private and public good, it further restricts the form that preferences, and thus the expenditure function, can take. We can never test the hypothesis of weak

complementarity; we can only judge whether this link between the public and private good is reasonable. But at the same time, this specific form of weak complementarity limits the arbitrariness of the welfare measurement.

Is the arbitrariness of welfare increased by imposing WC since it is a cardinal restriction or is it decreased because it is a reasonable restriction that has been essential to the valuation of public goods?

While LaFrance (1994) and Bockstael and McConnell (1993) are theoretical investigations, recently two papers, Herriges *et al.* (2004) and von Haefen (2007), have discussed some empirical results. Both show significant differences in welfare values when WC is imposed in seemingly innocuous different ways. However, as Herriges *et al.* suggest and von Haefen implements, using a flexible functional form may drastically reduce the difference. Therefore, yes, WC is a cardinal restriction that "arbitrarily" changes welfare values, but if one takes as given the task of valuing public goods through complementary private goods, in those situations where imposing WC is reasonable, the restriction does limit this arbitrariness. As cautioned by Herriges *et al.*, one could attempt to estimate use and nonuse values from RP data alone, but argue it may be best to assume WC in constructing welfare values.

Since WC is a cardinal and untestable restriction, with RP data alone this dispute can never be fully answered. Fortunately, Ebert (1998) offers a novel approach that combines additional stated preference data with the revealed preference data. As Ebert discusses, the heart of the problem is the lack of sufficient information to recover the complete underlying preference ordering of individuals. For example, an individual can have preferences for water quality that is completely independent of recreational trips. What is needed is additional stated preference data, the marginal willingness to pay information for the public good (e.g. an inverse demand function) where the marginal willingness to pay information is the "price" of the public good. This inverse demand function for the public good, along with the market demands, is sufficient for estimating exact welfare estimates without the WC restriction. Moreover, if WC is imposed, its restriction on preferences can now be tested. A major point is that even if the interest is only use value from a public good, SP data must be collected and combined with RP data to completely characterize preferences for the public good and the complementary private good, allowing for ordinal preferences and a proper measure of use value.

Previous papers such as Cameron (1992) and Huang *et al.* (1997) have combined revealed preference (RP) and stated preference (SP) data in estimation. The literature has argued that there are many advantages to combining RP and SP data, such as the increased precision garnered from the use of additional information to estimate the parameters. Essentially the data are viewed as complementary, with the RP data imposing the discipline of the market on the SP data, while the SP data allows for otherwise unobservable variation in the environmental quality attribute. However, most previous papers have invoked the WC condition, and therefore still impose a cardinal restriction on preferences.

Moreover, the WC condition limits the joint analysis to use values, even though with the stated preference data it is possible to provide information on both use and nonuse values.

Eom and Larson (2006) recently provided the first implementation of Ebert's (1998) suggestion. Their model combines individuals' observed recreational trips (RP data) and their responses to a dichotomous choice contingent valuation (DC-CV) question (SP data) for improved water quality. The necessary water quality variation across individuals is created by selecting the most visited site from six options in the Man Kyoung River basin. Using a semi-log specification for trip demand, and data on recreational trips in Korea, the authors integrate both the RP and SP data and test the WC restriction. They find that the total value associated with a proposed water quality improvement is composed of approximately 60 percent use value and 40 percent non-use value. Moreover, they reject an explicit test of the WC restriction.

Their analysis is a valuable first step in the implementation of Ebert's suggestion. This chapter replicates their model with a 2004 data set concerning the recreational use of eight lakes dispersed throughout Iowa and the value of water quality in these lakes. Unlike Eom and Larson, whose trip data is based upon the most frequently visited site for each individual and therefore possibly results in selection bias, the Iowa Lakes data provides a single primary site for each individual from within their region. Also, for comparison purposes, I report estimation and welfare results from the RP model alone, the SP model alone, and then the joint RP-SP model with and without WC imposed. I compare the use value collected from RP data alone (imposing WC and cardinal preferences) to theoretically correct use values resulting from a joint RP-SP model.

The remainder of this chapter is divided into four sections. The next section describes the Eom and Larson (2006) model, followed by the data section which provides an overview of the Iowa Lakes data used in my analysis. The results section discusses the estimation results from the Eom and Larson model, and finally the last section discusses conclusions and directions for future research.

Eom and Larson model

Eom and Larson (2006) employ the "integrating back" approach (von Haefen 2007) by first beginning with a semi-log specification for recreation demand and then integrating back to recover the quasi-expenditure function consistent with the semi-log specification. The quasi-expenditure function is then utilized to estimate the individual's willingness to pay (WTP) for a discrete change in quality, as discussed in a CV scenario. The key step is the constant of integration specified to depend on quality, thus leading to the possibility of a joint RP-SP model that does not impose WC, but can test it based on the non-use value parameter in the constant of integration.

In particular, Eom and Larson's specification for the recreation demand and WTP equations are given, respectively, by

$$\ln\left[x_i(p_i,q_i,m_i)\right] = \alpha + \beta p_i + \gamma q_i + \delta m_i + \eta_i, \tag{14.1}$$

and

$$WTP = \frac{1}{\delta}\ln\left[-\frac{\delta}{\beta}e^{\left(\alpha+\beta p_i+\gamma q_i^1+\delta m_i\right)} + \left(1+\frac{\delta}{\beta}e^{\left(\alpha+\beta p_i+\gamma q_i^0+\delta m_i\right)}\right)e^{\delta\psi\left(q_i^1-q_i^0\right)}\right] + \varepsilon_i, \tag{14.2}$$

where p_i denotes the travel cost, q_i denotes water quality, and m_i denotes income. The error terms (η_i, ε_i) are assumed to be drawn from a bivariate normal distribution. Derivations of equations (14.1) and (14.2) are discussed in detail in Eom and Larson.

The essential assumption in Eom and Larson concerns the manner in which quality (q) and baseline utility (u_0) enter the constant of integration. With a semilog trip demand, integrating back to derive the willingness to pay (as a compensating variation measure) for a quality change is

$$\begin{aligned}
WTP\left(q^0,q^1\right) &= \tilde{E}\left(P^0,q^0,u_0\right) - \tilde{E}\left(P^0,q^1,u_0\right) \\
&= -\frac{1}{\delta}\ln\left[-\frac{\delta}{\beta}e^{\alpha+\beta P^0+\gamma q^0} - \delta\theta\left(q^0,u_0\right)\right] \\
&\quad - \left[-\frac{1}{\delta}\ln\left(-\frac{\delta}{\beta}e^{\alpha+\beta P^0+\gamma q^1} - \delta\theta\left(q^1,u_0\right)\right)\right],
\end{aligned} \tag{14.3}$$

where $\tilde{E}(p, q, u)$ is the quasi-expenditure function from a semilog demand and $\theta(q, u)$ is the constant of integration that will not include own price but may include other prices or quality. WTP estimates for a quality change, based on only observed recreational trips (i.e. RP data), cannot estimate the functional relationship in $\theta(q, u_0)$, but rather requires an untestable assumption about this constant of integration. Since many assumptions are possible, with each changing the resulting WTP value, the assumption leads to cardinal preferences, even though the underlying trip demands is the same.

Using Ebert's insight, Eom and Larson isolate $\theta(q, u_0)$ by incorporating stated preference data along with RP data. They specify the constant of integration as

$$\theta(q,u) = e^{\delta\psi q}u, \tag{14.4}$$

and substitute this into the quasi-expenditure function. Solving for the quasi-indirect utility function, and using this to substitute for u, leads to the WTP function in equation (14.2). SP data is utilized jointly with the RP data to estimate the system of equations in (14.1) and (14.2), where it is now possible to decompose total WTP into Hicksian use and nonuse value portions. One can also impose WC and test it as a restriction of the complete preferences for recreational trips and water quality at the site. Note that this is predicated on the assumption in equation (14.4), but this is the usual functional form disclaimer.

Eom and Larson show that with the semi-log demand specification the decomposition of WTP into Hicksian use and nonuse value is

$$UV(q^0,q^1) = \frac{1}{\delta} \ln\left[-\frac{\delta}{\beta} x^1 e^{-\delta\psi(q^1-q^0)} + \left(1 + \frac{\delta}{\beta} x^0\right)\right],$$

$$NUV(q^0,q^1) = \psi(q^1 - q^0).$$

(14.5)

Eom and Larson point out that the "nonuse parameter", ψ, appears in both the Hicksian nonuse value (NUV) and use value (UV) portions, highlighting that the trip demands are not sufficient to estimate Hicksian use value. Moreover, as Bockstael and McConnell (1993) and Herriges *et al.* (2004) discuss, if one only has RP data and imposes WC to estimate Hicksian use value, there are no meaningful bounds or restrictions on the possible welfare values. The Eom and Larson approach provides a basis for empirically testing the WC assumption and its welfare implications.

In the Eom and Larson model, weak complementarity corresponds to the restriction that $\psi=0$. When WC is imposed, the Hicksian welfare functions are

$$UV(q^0,q^1) = \frac{1}{\delta} \ln\left[1 - \frac{\delta}{\beta}(x^1 - x^0)\right],$$

$$NUV(q^0,q^1) = 0.$$

(14.6)

In the next section I will discuss my data set and the data requirements to estimate a joint RP-SP model that does not impose WC. I then discuss the results from various models and test the WC restriction.

Data

The data used in this paper come from the second year of data collected as part of a four-year study begun in 2002 and aimed at understanding recreational use of Iowa Lakes and the value of water quality in those lakes. The second year survey was sent out in January, 2004 to a random sample of 8,000 Iowa residents, and inquired about their use of 131 Iowa principle recreation lakes in the previous year. Data were also collected on a dichotomous choice referendum question concerning water quality improvement on one of eight focus lakes and respondents' sociodemographic information. Respondents were provided a $10 incentive for completing the survey. From the 7,720 deliverable, there was a 68 percent response rate (with 5,281 completed surveys) and 4,809 surveys providing all of the necessary RP and SP information for the current analysis. Following Eom and Larson and empirically testing the hypothesis of weak complementarity among users, I discard the large number of nonusers (those reporting zero trips to the focus lake in their region) in the data and keep the remaining 929 households (19.3 percent of the full sample) reporting positive trips and also answering the DC-CV question.

A particular strength of this study is that the valuation survey was designed to coincide with a major data collection effort to obtain physical water quality measures by Iowa State University's Limnology Laboratory. A rich range of measures were collected including Secchi transparency, one of the most widely applied limnological parameters. Samples were taken from each lake three times throughout the year, in spring/early summer, mid-summer, and late summer/fall to cover the range of seasonal variation. In my analysis, I use the average Secchi transparency values for the 2003 season.

The surveys received by the respondent were identical in terms of the questions regarding their revealed preference data and sociodemographic characteristics. However, the stated preference portions of the survey were varied depending upon the target household's location in the state. Specifically, the state of Iowa was divided into eight zones, and all households in each zone received a description for a water quality improvement at a "focus lake" in their zone. Essentially, this can be thought of as eight separate surveys, one for each zone, that collected from each respondent their current visit levels to the focus lake (RP), the projected visit levels after the water quality improvement (SP), and their response to the referendum style dichotomous choice question (SP), "Would you vote 'yes' on a referendum to improve the water quality in [target lake] to the level described here? The proposed project would cost you $X (payable in installments over a five year period)."[1]

If a researcher's objective is to estimate the value of water quality from observing trip demands to a system of lakes (the travel cost model), a requirement is that the water quality be quantifiably measured and included as an explanatory variable in the trip demands (e.g. see Egan *et al.* 2009). The necessary extension here, for a joint RP-SP model, is that the water quality is also included in a quantifiable way in the SP data, here in the DC-CV analysis. Eom and Larson quantify their CV scenario by using the biological oxygen demand measure given in the current and proposed water quality levels. With the Iowa Lakes data, I choose to quantify the water quality by using Secchi transparency, which measures water clarity. To utilize Eom and Larson's simple one-trip demand system with quantifiable water quality variation, I pool the data pertaining to the eight focus lakes, creating water quality variation across the focus lakes, in which to test the benefits of combining RP and SP data and the potential to jointly model the use and nonuse values associated with improvements to these lakes.

Table 14.1 provides summary statistics for the sample of 929 households regarding trip, water quality, and the sociodemographic data obtained from the survey. The sample of trip-takers averaged 4.3 trips per year, varying from 1 trip per year up to 50 trips per year. Any individual taking more than 52 trips was excluded, although this only deleted eight observations.[2] The average of the current water quality measure, q_i^0, as measured by Secchi transparency, is 6.2 meters, varying from a low of 0.88 meters up to 11.5 meters. The proposed water quality improvement scenario is summarized by the increase in Secchi transparency at each of the eight focus lakes, with the improved average water quality being 10.3 meters, a 66 percent average improvement.

Table 14.1 Summary statistics: n = 929

Variable	Symbol	Description	Mean	Std. dev.	Min.	Max.
Trips	x	Number of trips to the zonal focus lake in the past year	4.29	6.00	1	50
Price	p	Travel cost of a trip	56.27	46.21	1.64	253.5
Annualized bid values	t	Bid value for the water quality improvement	33.37	16.67	10	60
CV vote	I	Response to DC-CV question (yes = 1, no = 0)	0.42	0.49	0	1
Income	m	Households' before tax income for 2003	59,005	37,459	7,500	200,000
Gender	ψ_g	= 1 if male; = 0 otherwise	0.68	0.46	0	1
Age	ψ_a	Respondent's age	51.59	15.58	15	82
School	ψ_s	= 1 if any college education; = 0 otherwise	0.71	0.45	0	1
Own boat	B	= 1 if own a boat; = 0 otherwise	0.30	0.46	0	1
Initial water quality	q_i^0	Secchi transparency (meters)	6.21	3.66	0.88	11.5
Improved water quality	q_i^1	Proposed, improved level of Secchi transparency	10.29	4.08	7	17

The average respondent is calculated to spend approximately $56 in travel cost expenditures, where the out-of-pocket component of travel cost was computed as the round-trip travel distance multiplied by $0.25 per mile and the opportunity cost of time was calculated as one-third the estimated round-trip travel time multiplied by the respondent's average wage rate. In general, the survey respondents are more likely to be male, older, have a higher income, and to be more educated than the general population. Schooling is entered as a dummy variable equaling one if the individual has attended or completed some level of post-high school education. Lastly, those surveyed were asked if they owned a boat, with 30 percent of the individuals reporting boat ownership.

Turning to the CV data, the individuals answered a dichotomous choice contingent valuation (DC-CV) question asking for a one-time payment spread over five years. It is necessary to annualize this one time payment to be consistent with the annual stream of values from the recreation demand data. A 10 percent discount rate is assumed leading to all of the one-time payments being divided by ten. The annualized bids vary from $10 to $60 and are randomly assigned to individual households, with the average bid value being $33.37 among the survey respondents. The individuals answered "yes" 42 percent of the time to the DC-CV question. Table 14.2 reports the percentage of respondents voting "yes" at each of the six bid values. As expected, the percentage responding "yes" decreases uniformly as the bid value rises. However, unfortunately the point at which 50 per cent respond "yes" is located between the lowest and second lowest bid, indicating that more precision concerning the respondent's WTP could have been gained from the inclusion of even lower bid values.

Results

The log likelihood function for the joint RP-SP model given in equations (14.1) and (14.2) is derived in Eom and Larson, and, in general, is quickly and easily estimated using the maximum likelihood routine in GAUSS.[3] I report in Table 14.3 the estimation results from four models. For comparison purposes, the first results are from the travel cost model alone (RP only), using the semi-log demand specification and a normally distributed error. The second results are from the dichotomous choice contingent valuation model alone (SP only), using a linear utility function and a normally distributed error, i.e. a bivariate probit

Table 14.2 Bid values and % yes responses at each bid value

Annualized bid values	% Yes	N
$10	55.2	165
$20	48.0	179
$30	39.2	158
$40	37.6	149
$50	34.8	161
$60	30.8	117

Table 14.3 Separate and joint estimation of revealed and stated preference data

Variable	Symbol	Model Cardinal Pref. RP only WC Imposed		Ordinal Pref. SP only		RP-SP Nonuse value		RP-SP WC Imposed	
		Coeff.	p-val.	Coeff.	p-val.	Coeff.	p-val.	Coeff.	p-val.
Parameters common to demand and WTP									
Intercept	α	0.87	0.000	-15.48	0.318	0.99	0.000	0.97	0.000
Travel cost/1,000	α	-3.83	0.000	-	-	-3.98	0.000	-3.94	0.000
WQuality	β	0.010	0.212	3.35	0.202	0.0028	0.143	0.0056	0.000
Income/1,000	δ	0.0013	0.130	-	-	0.0019	0.026	0.0019	0.021
Boat	b	0.23	0.000	1.49	0.841	0.23	0.000	0.23	0.000
WTP-only (nonuse value) parameters									
Intercept	ψ_0	-	-	-	-	0.0027	0.726	-	-
School	ψ_s	0.15	0.027	24.48	0.006	0.055	0.000	-	-
Standard errors									
Demand	σ_η	0.87	0.000	-	-	0.87	0.000	0.87	0.000
WTP	σ_ε	-	-	79.39	0.000	0.075	0.000	0.079	0.000
Correlation	ρ	-	-	-	-	0.21	0.000	0.21	0.000
Mean log-L		-6137.63		-3171.50		-1790.58		-1793.00	
Number of obs.		929		929		929		929	
χ^2 test statistic for $H_0{:}\psi=0$		-		-		-		4.84	
Critical $\chi^2_{0.05}(df)$		-		-		-		5.99 (2)	

model. The third column of results is from the joint RP-SP model which does not impose WC. The last column of results is the joint RP-SP model which does impose WC, by setting ψ to zero. The nonuse parameter ψ is allowed to vary with one individual characteristic, the school variable,

$$\psi = \left(\psi_0 + \psi_s school \right)^2 , \tag{14.7}$$

and is squared to insure the nonuse value is nonnegative.[4]

Beginning with the travel cost model, all of the parameters are of the expected sign with lower travel cost, higher income and education, higher Secchi transparency, and owning a boat, all leading to more trips to the lake. All of the parameters are statistically significant at the 5 percent level, except for income and the water quality parameter. For the probit DC-CV model, only the school variable and the standard error (i.e. the negative inverse of the coefficient on the bid value) are statistically significant at the 5 percent level. Water quality and boat ownership, while of the expected sign, are not statistically significant regressors explaining the respondent's vote on the CV referendum.[5] Generally, the joint RP-SP model produces more statistically significant parameters, including the water quality variable, γ, which now has a lower p-value of 0.14. However, the water quality intercept in the nonuse parameter ψ is not statistically significant at any reasonable level. For the joint RP-SP model that imposes WC, all of the parameters are statistically significant at the 5 percent level, now including, γ, the water quality variable.

Following Eom and Larson, I can test the hypothesis of weakly complementary preferences. However, unlike Eom and Larson's paper, I cannot reject the hypothesis of weakly complementary preferences (i.e. I cannot reject the null hypothesis that ψ equals zero) at the 5 percent level (bottom of Table 14.3). Therefore, I can use the joint RP-SP model with WC imposed to estimate theoretically correct (i.e. ordinal Hicksian) use values.

The results in Table 14.3 can be used to consider the welfare values from the joint RP-SP model for both specifications, with and without WC, as well as from the RP model alone and SP model alone. Table 14.4 provides the welfare values from these four models. From the travel cost model, the welfare measure is the additional consumer surplus from the predicted increased trips with improved water quality and therefore is a Marshallian measure. The rest of the welfare measures are Hicksian. One comparison of interest is between the consumer surplus estimate from the travel cost model alone, which requires the imposition of WC, with the proper Hicksian use value estimate from the combined RP-SP model with ordinal preferences. However, it is possible to estimate the Hicksian use value from the joint RP-SP model in two ways: from estimating the use value portion of total value when WC is not imposed, or imposing WC on the joint RP-SP model and only measuring use value. From equations (14.5) and (14.6) it is obvious the use value estimate will be different. If the interest is *only* use value, the RP-SP data was combined for the sole purpose of completing preferences to allow ordinal welfare calculations, and the researcher wants to minimize the influence of the SP data, it is possible to impose WC and measure only use value. As Eom and Larson note, the RP and SP data is used to estimate the use value, but obviously the nonuse value comes from the SP data alone. If instead the objective is to estimate total value with all of the information available and allow for the partitioning into use value and nonuse value, then the RP-SP model without imposing WC would be preferred.

Comparing first the Marshallian use value from the RP model ($33.76) to the RP-SP Hicksian use value with WC imposed ($16.97), the difference is large, with the Hicksian use value being 50 percent lower. This indicates the need for more research into the potential bias from utilizing only RP data to estimate cardinal, Marshallian use values. Although, the standard error on the RP only welfare value is high, as is true for the welfare value from the SP only model, as water quality is generally not statistically significant in these separate model estimations. However, the mean WTP estimates from the joint RP-SP models had lower standard errors, indicating more precision was gained from combining the travel cost and contingent valuation data. Next, considering the use value from the RP-SP model that does not impose WC, the mean value is smaller at $8.32, with a larger portion of the total value ($18.92) coming from nonuse value equal to a mean estimate of $10.60. However, the total value from the RP-SP model ($18.92), compares favorably with the total value from the SP only model ($15.89), with the former being 19 percent larger.

One issue with combining my RP and SP data is that the DC-CV question was asked as a one-time payment. I assumed a 10 percent discount rate to annualize this SP data and therefore divided the one-time bids by 10. Note that this annualization of the one-time CV scenario directly impacts the SP and the RP-SP model's welfare results. I also estimated the models using a 5 per cent discount rate and a 20 percent discount rate. Generally, the estimation results changed little, though with a 5 percent discount rate the SP and RP-SP annualized welfare values are cut in half, whereas with the discount rate of 20 percent, the SP and RP-SP annualized welfare values were roughly doubled. If feasible, future

Table 14.4 Annual use value, nonuse value, and total value of water quality improvements (standard errors in parentheses)

Welfare measure	Model			
	RP only WC imposed	SP only	RP-SP Nonuse value	RP-SP WC imposed
	Cardinal pref.		Ordinal pref.	
Total value	–	$15.89 (20.14)	$18.92 (8.59)	–
Use value	$33.76[1] (30.75)	–	$8.32 (6.29)	$16.97 (5.83)
Nonuse value	–	–	$10.60 (5.86)	–

Note
1 Additional consumer surplus from predicted increased trips.

nonmarket valuation surveys aiming to combine the travel cost model and the contingent valuation model can avoid the issue by asking for an annual payment. Note, the experimental and nonmarket valuation literature generally indicates that individual discount rates are large, possibly in the 20 percent range, indicating that asking for a one-time payment of $100 is equivalent to an annual payment of $20 (see, for example, Bateman and Langford, 1997; Coller and Williams, 1999; Harrison *et al.* 2002; and Zhongmin et al. 2003). Therefore, if the Iowa Lakes survey had asked for an annual payment the resulting annual welfare values would probably be higher than those reported here using a one-time payment.

Conclusions and future research

I utilized Eom and Larson's (2006) joint RP-SP model to estimate welfare values for water quality improvements at eight focus lakes spread throughout the state of Iowa. I estimated four models for comparison: RP only, SP only, and two joint RP-SP models, one with WC imposed and the other without. My results show that, for this specific example, the error from using cardinal preferences, which is always the result when a public good is valued from RP data only, is large with the proper Hicksian use value being 50 percent lower than the esti-mated Marshallian use value. This indicates the need for more research into the potential bias from utilizing only RP data to estimate use values.

An avenue for future research is the design of nonmarket valuation surveys that collect both RP and SP data that can be easily combined in a joint RP-SP model that does not impose WC. One of the main issues is that the public good, in this case, water quality, has to be quantifiable in the RP data and the SP data. Also, the Iowa Lakes data set and Eom and Larson's data set are molded to fit a simple joint RP-SP model with a single-site trip demand equation and its derived WTP function. Another avenue for future research is to consider designing non-market valuation surveys with a more complicated joint RP-SP model in mind.

Currently, the travel cost model has been used extensively to measure quality changes at one or many recreational sites, with all models requiring the cardinal WC restriction. Future work could consider how to also gather SP data for all of the recreational sites in the analysis and quantify the one or many quality changes. For example, in Egan *et al.* (2009), eight limnological water quality measures are included in the 129 lake travel cost model with multiple welfare scenarios estimated from changing the various water quality levels at various sites. To avoid the use of cardinal preferences in these large multisite travel cost models would require a huge amount of quantifiable SP data across all the lakes and water quality measures. Another extension would be a model that includes nonusers (Egan *et al.* 2010) a group that would be potentially important in dis-cerning the division between use and nonuse values.

Finally, for the welfare results, the RP only and SP only model's WTP estimates had larger standard errors than the WTP estimates from the joint RP-SP models. A possible conclusion is that this underscores the need for the joint estimation of RP and SP data to completely capture the effect of quality on preferences. As pointed out by von Haefen (2007), neoclassical economics places little structure for how quality of a resource enters preferences, and the joint estimation may better capture the price (primarily the recreation demand portion) and income (primarily the CV data) effect.

Acknowledgments

This chapter has benefited from discussions with Joseph Herriges and Catherine Kling, and helpful comments on earlier versions of this chapter were provided by Joseph Herriges.

Notes

1 The author's homepage, http://homepages.utoledo.edu/kegan2, contains a portion of the survey for one of the focus lakes, Rathbun Lake. Also, for this analysis, the contingent behavior trips are not used. However, Egan et al. (2007) develop an alternative RP-SP model approach that does include the CB trips, as well as being able to model corner solutions. An advantage of their framework is that it also incorporates non-trip-takers into the analysis. This is potentially important, given the emphasis on the division between use and nonuse values.
2 This exclusion was used to remove households living in close proximity to a given lake, who, as part of their daily activities, may report numerous visits, due to their frequent encounters with the lake.
3 The Gauss code is available from the author's homepage, http://homepages. utoledo. edu/kegan2.
4 The other available sociodemographic variables, gender, age, and household size, were considered, but were generally found not to be statistically significant, so they were dropped from the analysis.
5 I also estimated the probit DC-CV model with the travel cost variable included, but it was not a statistically significant explanatory variable (p-value of 0.81) and moreover the point estimate was of the wrong sign. Therefore, I excluded it in the final analysis.

References

Bateman, I.J. and I.H. Langford (1997) "Non-users' willingness to pay for a national park: An application and critique of the contingent valuation method," *Regional Studies*, 31(6): 571–582.

Bockstael, N.E. and K.E. McConnell (1993) "Public goods as characteristics of non-market commodities," *The Economic Journal*, 103(420): 1244–1257.

Cameron, T.A. (1992) "Combining contingent valuation and travel cost data for the valuation of nonmarket goods," *Land Economics*, 68(3): 302–317.

Coller, M. and M.B.Williams (1999) "Eliciting individual discount rates," *Experimental Economics*, 2(2): 107–127.

Ebert, U. (1998) "Evaluation of nonmarket goods: Recovering unconditional preferences," *American Journal of Agricultural Economics*, 80(2): 241–254.

Egan, K.J., J.A. Herriges, and C.L. Kling (2010) "Utilizing the Kuhn-Tucker model to combine revealed preference and stated preference data without invoking the weak complementarity condition," working paper, online, available at: www.homepages. utoledo.edu/kegan2.

Egan, K.J, J.A. Herriges, C.L. Kling, and J.A. Downing (2009) "Valuing water quality as a function of water quality measures," *American Journal of Agricultural Economics*, 91(1): 106–123.

Eom, Y. and D.M. Larson (2006) "Improving environmental valuation estimates through consistent use of revealed and stated preference information," *Journal of Environmental Economics and Management*, 52(1): 501–516.

Harrison, G.W., M.I. Lau, and M.B. Williams (2002) "Estimating individual discount rates in Denmark: A field experiment," *The American Economic Review*, 92(5): 1606–1617.

Herriges, J.A., C.L. Kling, and D.J. Phaneuf (2004) "What's the use? Welfare estimates from revealed preference models when weak complementarity does not hold," *Journal of Environmental Economics and Management*, 47(1): 55–70.

Huang, J.-C., T.C. Haab, and J.C. Whitehead (1997) "Willingness to pay for quality improvements: Should revealed and sated peference data be combined?" *Journal of Environmental Economics and Management*, 34(3): 240–55.

LaFrance, J.T. (1994) "Weak complementarity and other normative speculations," working paper in the Western Regional Research Publication, W1133, Seventh Interim Report.

Mäler, K. (1974) *Environmental Economics: A Theoretical Inquiry*, Baltimore, MD: John Hopkins University Press for Resources for the Future.

von Haefen, R. (2007) "Empirical strategies for incorporating weak complementarity into consumer demand models," *Journal of Environmental Economics and Management*, 54(1):15–31.

Zhongmin, X., C. Guodong, Z. Zhiqiang, S. Zhiyong, and J. Loomis (2003) "Applying contingent valuation in China to measure the total economic value of restoring ecosystem services in Ejina region," *Ecological Economics*, 44(2–3): 345–358.

15 Joint estimation of revealed and stated preference trip and willingness-to-pay data to estimate the benefits and impacts of an Atlantic Intracoastal Waterway dredging and maintenance program

Christopher F. Dumas, Jim Herstine and John C. Whitehead

Introduction

The River and Harbor Act of 1910 (36 Stat. 630) provided for the establishment of a continuous inland waterway along the eastern and gulf coasts of the United States (USACE 2010). Congress authorized the Atlantic Intracoastal Waterway (AIWW) in 1919 and the entire waterway was completed in 1940 (AIWA 2010). The AIWW extends 1,200 miles from Norfolk, Virginia to Key West, Florida. Some lengths consist of natural inlets, salt-water rivers, bays, and sounds; others are man-made canals. The original purpose of this sheltered passageway was to provide commercial shipping with a safer alternative to navigation in the open Atlantic Ocean. Recreational use of the AIWW by marine recreational boaters, both as a route to ocean inlets and as a final destination, has grown tremendously since construction of the AIWW. The US Army Corps of Engineers (USACE) is responsible for maintenance and operational dredging of the AIWW. The AIWW has an authorized navigable depth of 12 feet. It is currently maintained at depths ranging from six to 12 feet (USACE 2010). The average depth of the North Carolina portion of the Atlantic Intracoastal Waterway is ten feet. Federal funding for maintenance and operational dredging of the AIWW and its associated shallow draft inlets has diminished, causing numerous concerns for state and local government officials and those entities that rely on the AIWW for navigation and their livelihood.

When government pursues a coastal management policy such as dredging or beach nourishment gains and losses are distributed among consumers and firms. The economic efficiency criterion requires that the gains to the winners exceed the losses imposed on the losers. Otherwise the criterion for efficiency is not met. Benefit-cost analysis is a method used to calculate and compare monetary gains and losses (Zerbe and Bellas 2006).

Economic impacts and benefits can be defined by using the concept of demand from introductory economics. The demand curve (D_1) is the relationship between market price (P) on the vertical axis and aggregate quantity consumed by all consumers in the market (Q) on the horizontal axis (Figure 15.1). The demand curve slopes downward because (1) lower prices are required to convince a given consumer to purchase larger quantities and (2) as prices fall more consumers enter the market. If consumers purchase aggregate quantity Q_1, the rectangle below the price and to the left Q_1 measures aggregate consumer expenditure on the good (area A). "Economic impact analysis" measures the changes in jobs, wages, economic output (sales), and taxes, typically on an industry-by-industry basis, that result from a given, initial change in expenditures, such as a change in recreational boating expenditures caused by a change in dredging policy. Any economic changes beyond the initial change in expenditures are called "multiplier effects." The sum of the initial change in expenditures and any multiplier effects are defined as "total economic impacts."

Net economic benefits are different from total economic impacts. Net economic benefits are measured by the theoretical concept of "consumer surplus." Consumer surplus is a monetary measure of the net benefit that consumers gain from a transaction. It is the difference between what the consumer is willing and able to pay and the amount actually spent on the good or service. Consumer surplus is also called net willingness-to-pay (WTP) since it is willingness-to-pay net of the costs of obtaining the good. In Figure 15.1, if consumers currently purchase aggregate quantity Q_1, consumer surplus is the triangular area above the price and below the demand curve to quantity Q_1 (area B). Several economic methodologies can be used to measure consumer surplus, including revealed preference (RP) and stated preference (SP) models.

If the demand relationship changes, or "shifts," economic impacts and benefits also change. Changes in consumer income, prices of related goods,

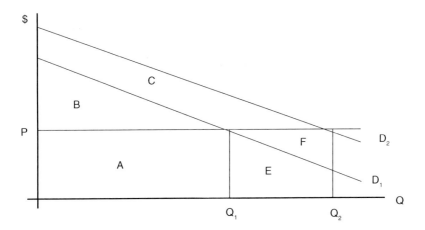

Figure 15.1 Demand, benefits and impacts.

consumer tastes or the quality of the good can cause shifts in the demand curve relationship. For example, an improvement in boating quality would increase demand for boating trips, shifting the demand curve to the right (from D_1 to D_2). When the demand curve shifts to the right the associated economic impacts and benefits increase. The change in impacts is represented by areas E+F. The change in consumer surplus is represented by area C. Similarly, if the demand curve shifts to the left, economic impacts and benefits would decrease.

Economic impact analysis provides a gross, rather than a net, measure of economic effects. For example, economic impact analysis doesn't account for the effects of substitute activities on net economic changes. If the Atlantic Intracoastal Waterway is closed, boaters would find substitute recreational activities. A portion of the expenditures that had been made on boating would likely be reallocated to other recreational activities, resulting in a smaller *net* economic effect on the regional economy than would be indicated by an economic impact analysis. Another concern with economic impact analysis is that it does not properly account for countervailing economic effects. For example, in the case of recreational boating, expenditures are positive economic impacts for the marina but negative impacts for the boater. While economic impact analysis measures the gross change in expenditure and its distribution throughout the economy, consumer surplus measures the net change in economic value. For these reasons benefit-cost analysis based on consumer surplus is the preferred analytical tool for understanding the efficiency of government programs. Economic impact analysis is appropriate for understanding the distribution of effects across different industrial sectors and interest groups (i.e. workers, owners, government) in the economy.

While marine recreational boating is an important economic activity, little economic research has been conducted to analyze boater behavior and the benefits and costs of coastal management policy related to marine boating. Lipton and Hicks (1999) use a recreation demand model and find that quality perceptions influence boat location choice. Thomas and Stratis (2002) also use a recreation demand model to assess the effects of boat speed limits designed to protect manatees. In contrast, Lipton (2004) uses the contingent valuation method to estimate marine boater willingness-to-pay for water quality improvements.

Estimation of baseline economic impacts of recreation activities is widespread (e.g. Stoll *et al.* 1988). However, there are fewer examples of studies that integrate recreation behavior and economic impact analysis in order to estimate the effects of policy changes. Loomis (1995) integrates revealed preference site selection and trip frequency models with economic impact analysis to illustrate the impacts of changes in deer hunting quality. Starbuck *et al.* (2006) integrate a stated preference trip behavior model with an economic impact model of forest recreation under different fire management policies. In this chapter we use the contingent valuation method to estimate changes in net economic benefits (i.e. changes in consumer surplus) associated with changes in dredging activities. We link stated preference trip and value data in an application of a model proposed by Whitehead (2005) in order to consider the validity of the willingness-to-pay statements. We conclude with an aggregation of benefits appropriate for benefit-cost analysis and incorporation of the stated preference data in economic impact analysis.

Survey and data

A survey instrument was designed to elicit responses from both transient and local recreational boaters along the AIWW in North Carolina about frequency of use of the AIWW, expenditures while using the AIWW and the impact that dredging or the lack of dredging of the AIWW and its associated shallow draft inlets would have on future use of the AIWW (Herstine *et al.* 2007). Survey administration began in June 2005 and concluded in late November 2005 at multiple locations from the Virginia–North Carolina border in Currituck County to the North Carolina–South Carolina border in Brunswick County. The survey administration locations in North Carolina along the AIWW included Coinjock, the Dismal Swamp Visitors' Center, Belhaven, Oriental, Beaufort, Morehead City, Atlantic Beach, Swansboro, Scott's Hill, Wrightsville Beach, Carolina Beach, and Southport. Approximately 1,400 field surveys were collected from North Carolina resident and non-resident boaters.

Willingness-to-pay is measured with the contingent valuation method (CVM). The CVM directly elicits economic values in highly structured hypothetical scenarios (Mitchell and Carson 1989). Survey respondents are presented with the following hypothetical AIWW dredging scenario:

> Federal government funds for dredging of the Atlantic Intracoastal Water-way in North Carolina (NC) are threatened. If dredging completely stops, the average depth of the NC portion of the Atlantic Intracoastal Waterway would be about 4 feet. A NC dredging and maintenance program would provide enough funding to maintain an average depth of 12 feet in the NC portion of the Atlantic Intracoastal Waterway. The dredging and mainte-nance program would be funded by a $A surcharge on your annual boating registration fee. Each registered boater with a boat longer than 16 feet using the NC portion of the Atlantic Intracoastal Waterway would be required to purchase a sticker each year to be placed alongside the registration number on the boat. Would you be willing to pay $A in additional annual boating registration fees each year for this program?

One of five dollar amounts, $A=$10, $25, $50, $75 or $100, was randomly assigned to each respondent. Respondents who answered "no" to the willingness-to-pay question were asked if they would be willing to pay $1. Respondents who answered "yes" to either question were directed to a follow-up question that asked how sure they were that they would really pay the amount if actually placed in that situation.

In order to connect hypothetical willingness-to-pay responses with behavior, boaters were asked about their boating trips under various conditions, including those presented in the hypothetical scenario. First, boaters were asked for the number of separate boat outings taken on the AIWW in North Carolina in their boat during the past 2 months. Respondents were asked the same question for the past 12 months. Then boaters were asked about the number of boat outings that they would take on the AIWW over the next twelve months under current conditions (i.e. ten foot depth) and over the next 12 months if dredging of the AIWW was increased and the average depth of the North Carolina portion was about 12 feet. Finally, boaters were asked about the number of boat outings that they would take on the AIWW over the next 12 months if dredging stopped completely and the average depth of the North Carolina portion was about four feet.

After deletion of cases with missing values we consider a sample of 902 North Carolina resident owners of boats greater than or equal to 16 feet in length. Variables considered in this analysis, their description and statistical summary are presented in Table 15.1. Survey respondents who are North Carolina residents took an average of 38 boat trips on the AIWW during the 12 months prior to the survey interview. The number of trips expected during the next 12 months with current depth, increased depth and decreased depth are 42, 46 and 23.

The cost of an AIWW boat trip is measured by the sum of money and time costs, $TC = cd + (\delta wd/mph)$, where TC is the terrestrial travel cost of an AIWW boat trip, c is the cost per mile, d is round trip distance, δ is a fraction of the wage rate, w is the wage rate and mph is miles per hour. The cost per mile is set at \$0.47 for respondents who trailer their boat and \$0.37 for all others. Round trip distance is obtained from the survey. The wage rate is household income divided by 2,000 hours. The opportunity cost of time is set at 33 percent of the wage rate. Miles per hour is set at 40 for respondents who trailer their boat and 50 for all others.

Table 15.1 Data summary[1]

Variable	Description	Mean	Std. dev.
RP-TRIPS10	Boating trips during past year	38.43	43.23
SP-TRIPS10	Expected boating trips during next year	42.33	40.81
SP-TRIPS12	Expected boating trips during next year with 12 foot depth	46.01	45.59
SP-TRIPS4	Expected boating trips during next year with 4 foot depth	23.20	32.99
INCOME	Household income (\$1000s)	85.37	25.16
INCOME2	Household income with zeros for missing income (\$1000s)	77.42	34.50
MISSINC	1 if missing income	0.09	0.29
LIKELY	1 if scenario is credible	0.70	0.46
DRAFT	Boat draft in feet	3.00	1.36
AGE	Age of boater	46.27	12.13

Note
1 Sample size=902 except for INCOME (sample size=818).

Respondents who trailer their boat to a boat launch (26 percent) are asked for the number of miles from their home to the place they usually launch their boat. Respondents who keep their boat at a marina (53 percent) are asked for the number of miles from their home to the marina. Respondents who have a private dock at their home (13 percent) and respondents who keep their boat somewhere else are assumed to travel zero miles. Mean travel cost for resident boaters is $67.

The travel cost variable is measured with error for several reasons. First, the cost of a boat trip on the AIWW is the sum of the terrestrial and aquatic cost of access to the AIWW. We have no information on the aquatic cost (i.e. the cost of the boat ride from the marina to the AIWW). Second, we have no information on the nature of the boat outing on the AIWW. The AIWW may be the destination of the outing (i.e. a single-purpose trip) or a gateway to another water body (i.e. a multipurpose trip). The calculation of travel costs for multipurpose trips is unresolved in the economics literature. For these reasons, use of a proxy for travel cost in the CVM analysis is warranted.

Recreation demand analysis requires inclusion of the price of a substitute recreation site. In our case, suppose that without dredging the NC portion of the AIWW became too shallow to navigate. North Carolina boaters might travel to the Virginia or South Carolina portions of the AIWW. We constructed substitute travel cost measures for access to Myrtle Beach using travel distance computed from the home zip code to the destination zip codes using the same travel and time cost equation as above. Travel cost to Myrtle Beach is $270 for resident boaters.

Income is typically subject to significant item non-response in household surveys. In this survey, 9 percent of residents and 12 percent of non-residents do not report their household income. For reporting households, mean household income is $85,000. In order to retain willingness-to-pay information on those boaters who do not report their income we code missing income as zero (Income2) and include a dummy variable for respondents with missing income (Missinc). The average annual household income with 9 percent of the missing income values coded as zero income is $77,000.

Almost all of the boaters are white (98 percent) and most are male (87 percent). The average age is 46, the average household size is almost three, the average number of children is less than one, 73 percent are married and the average number of years of schooling is 16. Except for age, these demographic variables are subject to significant item non-response and are not included in the analysis below.

We define "very sure" CVM respondents as those who answer seven or above on follow-up certainty scale question in order to mitigate hypothetical bias (Whitehead and Cherry 2007). Over 90 percent of resident boaters are very sure that they actually would pay the surcharge amount. After considering only those who are very sure about their willingness-to-pay, 67 percent of NC residents are willing to pay (Table 15.2). The percentage of very sure yes responses declines with the surcharge. Willingness-to-pay the surcharge amount falls from 87

Table 15.2 Willingness-to-pay data

A	Yes	Cases	% Yes
$10	164	188	87
$25	148	195	76
$50	112	176	64
$75	101	170	59
$100	81	173	47

percent to 47 percent as the amount rises from $10 to $100. Of those respondents who are not willing to pay the bid amount, 74 percent are willing to pay $1. Eighty percent are very sure about $1.

The credibility of hypothetical CVM scenarios is a necessary condition for the validity of willingness-to-pay responses. Several questions were asked of respondents in order to determine the credibility of the CVM scenarios. Boaters are asked for their perceptions of the effectiveness of the dredging program in terms of how likely they think it is that the NC portion of the AIWW would be maintained at an average depth of 12 feet. Most respondents think that it is very likely or somewhat likely. Thirty percent of resident anglers and 22 percent of non-resident anglers think that maintenance of this depth is not likely at all. We control for differences in scenario credibility in the model below.

Another measure of the credibility of the hypothetical scenarios is the change in perceived quality of the AIWW with dredging. Boaters are asked about their opinion of the navigability of the AIWW with the dredging program and an average depth of 12 feet and the current average depth of ten feet. Under current conditions, 74 percent of resident boaters think that navigability is good, very good or excellent. With a 12 foot average depth, 97 percent of residents and non-residents think that navigability would be good, very good or excellent. These differences suggest that the hypothetical scenarios lead to changes in perceptions of the quality of the AIWW.

Since the data set is collected with an on-site survey it likely suffers from avidity bias (Thomson 1991). More avid boaters are more likely to be included in our sample. We weight the regression analysis to reduce the effects of avidity bias. The sample weight is $WT = \bar{x}/x_i$ where $\bar{x}$ is sample average trips and x_i is the number of boating trips made by individual i.

Model and results

We first consider the trip change data. The non-parametric signed rank test indicates that differences in trip levels across scenario are statistically significant ($p < 0.0001$ for each comparison). However, these tests may be confounded by other variables. Holding these variables constant in the regression analysis allows for a multivariate test for differences in trip levels. The travel cost method (TCM) can be used to estimate the economic benefits of recreation trips

(Whitehead *et al.* 2000). The TCM exploits the negative relationship between distance traveled and the number of trips. The distance-trip relationship is converted to a demand relationship by converting the distance variable to a travel cost variable. With the data at hand, the difficulty of accurately measuring the full costs of an AIWW boating trip makes estimation of the economic benefit of these trips using the TCM difficult. However, the TCM is still useful in testing the validity of the trip data and conducting a multivariate test of differences in trips under different policy scenarios.

We employ four trip observations for each boater in our pseudo-panel data set. The first panel contains the revealed preference data on typical trips made during the past 12 months. The second, third and fourth panels are the stated preference trips during the next 12 months under various hypothetical scenarios. The independent variables include the travel cost to the AIWW access point (Travcost), the substitute site cost (Subcost1), income (Income2, Missinc) and boat draft (Draft). We also control for differences in the revealed preference and stated preference data with a stated preference dummy variable (SP=1 if stated preference data, 0 if revealed preference data) and interactions between the stated preference dummy variable and the travel cost variable (SPTC) and income (SPY).

We use the random effects Poisson regression model to estimate the TCM recreation demand model. The Poisson model accounts for the integer nature of the dependent variable (i.e. trips=0, 1, 2...). The random effects specification accounts for the panel data set, avoiding errors associated with assuming that each observation represents a different boater.

The TCM regression results for NC single day and multiple day boaters are in Table 15.3. The trip data are internally valid and resemble a demand curve for

Table 15.3 Random effects Poisson recreation demand model

	Single day trips		Multiple day trips	
	Coefficient	*t-ratio*	*Coefficient*	*t-ratio*
Constant	3.8785	37.90	3.5609	9.63
TRAVCOST	−0.0016	−6.79	−0.0039	−5.51
SUBCOST1	0.0012	3.98	0.0028	2.95
INCOME2	−0.0022	−2.10	−0.0028	−0.89
MISSINC	−0.1395	−1.31	−0.0940	−0.28
DRAFT	−0.0552	−2.87	−0.1018	−1.97
DEPTH4	−0.5565	−113.96	−0.9871	−103.64
DEPTH12	0.0670	10.07	0.1889	20.04
SP	0.1013	14.90	−0.0756	−4.70
SPTC	−0.0002	−5.94	0.0005	3.63
SPY	−0.0011	−16.15	0.0009	3.88
α	0.5231	18.35	0.6618	7.22
LL	−16,738	–	−3,285	–
Cases	756	–	146	–
Periods	4	–	4	–

both single-day and multiple-day trippers. In other words, the number of trips falls with an increase in travel costs and increase with an increase in the cost of the substitute. The number of trips falls and increases in income suggesting that AIWW boating traps are "inferior goods." Trips also fall with increases in boat draft.

The regression analysis indicates that differences in trip levels are significantly different. Respondents state that fewer trips would be taken with an average depth of four feet and more trips would be taken with an average depth of 12 feet. In the single day trip model, more trips are taken with stated preference data (compared to the number of trips with revealed preference data) and the boaters are less responsive to changes in travel cost and income when stating trips. Surprisingly, the stated preference results are opposite for the multiple-day trippers.

We next consider combining the trip change data with the CVM. Consider that willingness-to-pay for boating quality is a function of prices, quality and income

$$WTP = s(p, q', q, y) \tag{15.1}$$

where $s(.)$ is the variation function, q is the current quality of boat outings, q' is the degraded quality of boat outings, p is the cost of a boat outing (i.e. travel cost) and y is household income.

WTP should change with any significant change in the quality of the boating experience (e.g. ease of navigability as measured by water depth), decrease with the cost, and increase with income if boating quality is a normal good. On the other hand, if boating quality is an "inferior" good, WTP may decrease as income increases. Our CVM data suffer from two problems: (1) the potential measurement error associated with trip cost and (2) the absence of historic data on boating quality. These limitations lead to a model of WTP in which the change in boat trips that would arise from a dredging policy that changes boating quality is used as an independent variable

$$WTP = s(\Delta x(q, q'), y) \tag{15.2}$$

where $\Delta x(q,q')$ is the change in trips and WTP is expected to increase with Δx.

In order to combine the stated behavior and willingness-to-pay data in a theoretically appropriate way we estimate WTP and Δx functions jointly using a model fully described by Whitehead (2005).

$$WTP = \alpha E(\Delta x) + \beta' X_1 + e_1$$
$$\Delta x = \delta' X_1 + \lambda' X_2 + e_2 \tag{15.3}$$

The empirical WTP model is a parameterization of the theoretical model described above where α is the coefficient on the expected/predicted change in trips variable, $E(\Delta x)$, β and δ are coefficient vectors on the vector in independent variables, X_1, in the willingness-to-pay and change in trips models and λ is a coefficient vector on instrumental variables, X_2. The error terms e_1 and e_2 are normally distributed.

If the two functions in this model were estimated independently, the coefficient on the change in trips variable, α, would likely be biased since the change in trips is an endogenous variable. With endogeneity bias, the unobserved variables that affect both willingness-to-pay and the change in trips will be correlated, $r(e_1, e_2) \neq 0$, and the change in trips variable in the willingness-to-pay model will be correlated with the error term $r(\Delta x, e_1) \neq 0$.

In order to minimize endogeneity bias we estimate the change in trips as a function of all independent variables in the willingness-to-pay model and a vector of instrumental variables X_2. Instrumental variables are uncorrelated with willingness-to-pay but highly correlated with the change in trips. The predicted value from the trip change model, $E(\Delta x)$, is used as an independent variable in the willingness-to-pay model in order to avoid endogeneity bias.

In the trip change model (i.e. the second function in equation 15.3), the dependent variable Δx is specified as the difference between stated preference boating trips with a 12 foot depth and stated preference trips with a four foot depth. We estimate the trip change model with the Tobit due to the censored nature (i.e. large number of zeros) of the dependent variable (Table 15.4). Baseline boating trips, boat draft, boater age and its square are the instrumental variables. The change in trips is increasing in baseline trips, boat draft and age (at a decreasing rate). The coefficient on household income is the only other variable that is statistically significant. Households with greater income report a larger difference in trips with the change in depth. The predicted value is a change of 17 annual boating trips.

Table 15.4 Willingness-to-pay model[1]

	Tobit (Δx)		Censored probit (WTP)	
	Coefficient	t-statistic	Coefficient	t-statistic
Constant	−30.30	−4.00	24.03	1.51
A	0.01	0.36	−	−
INCOME2	0.08	3.16	0.32	1.98
MISSINC	4.46	1.40	40.85	2.02
LIKELY	1.48	1.04	30.23	3.08
SP-TRIPS10	0.35	12.97	−	−
$E(\Delta x)$ [1]	−	−	1.31	2.00
DRAFT	3.01	6.72	−	−
AGE	0.61	1.86	−	−
AGE squared	−0.01	−2.02	−	−
σ	18.74	35.18	95.67	7.52
Model χ^2	−	−	76.32 (p<0.001)	
WTP	−	−	97.21	12.74

Note
[1] Predicted from the Tobit model.

In the WTP model (i.e. the first function in equation 15.3), the probability of a yes response to the "Are you willing to pay..." survey question is equal to the probability that WTP is greater than or equal to the surcharge on the boating registration fee (i.e. the bid amount). We estimate the probability of a yes response with the censored probit model (Cameron and James 1987). Mean WTP and standard errors are constructed using the Delta Method (Cameron 1991).

The scale parameter, σ, is the negative inverse of the probit coefficient on the surcharge amount variable and is positive and statistically significant (Table 15.4). This result indicates that boaters are less likely to be willing to pay as the surcharge amount rises. The probit coefficient vector is multiplied by the scale parameter so that each coefficient can be interpreted as a marginal effect. A marginal effect is the impact on willingness-to-pay of a one unit change in the independent variable. Resident boaters who think the dredging program is "not likely at all" to be effective are willing to pay $30 less than those who think it is somewhat or very likely to be effective. Boaters are willing to pay $3.20 more for each additional $10,000 increase in household income. The income elasticity of willingness-to-pay is 0.26. Each 10 percent increase in income increases willingness-to-pay by 2.6 percent.

Boaters are willing to pay $1.31 for each additional boat outing. Considering that the average change in boat outings as average depth increases from four feet to 12 feet is 17, the value of these additional outings is about $22 of the $97 total willingness-to-pay estimate per boater. The remainder of total willingness-to-pay, $75, can be interpreted as the increased value of boat outings that are currently taken. Evaluating WTP at the mean each coefficient at the means of the independent variables, the average willingness-to-pay for the AIWW dredging programme is $97.

Economic benefits and impacts

In this section we consider the economic benefits and impacts of the dredging and maintenance policy, considering North Carolina resident and non-resident boaters. The aggregate benefits of an AIWW dredging policy is the sum of aggregate benefits to residents and non-residents of North Carolina. In February 2003, 355,453 boats were registered in NC. Of these, 144,135 were less than 16 feet. Of the 211,318 boats with length greater than or equal to 16 feet almost all, 203,953, have zip codes within the range of the zip codes of the boaters in the AIWW survey sample. We estimate that each recreational boater would be willing to pay $97 annually in the form of a surcharge on their boater registration fee to support a dredging policy that would lead to an average 12 foot depth in the North Carolina portion of the AIWW instead of a four foot depth. An estimate of the aggregate annual benefits of this policy to North Carolina residents is about $20 million.

The economic impacts of reduced AIWW navigability are determined by comparing economic activity under a baseline scenario of current navigability with economic activity under an alternative scenario of reduced navigability (four foot average depth). Economic impacts occur in two general categories: impacts resulting from changes in the number of recreational boating trips, and impacts resulting from changes in the number of boats purchased/maintained by recreational boaters (i.e. some, not all, boaters may choose to stop purchasing/maintaining vessels due to decreased navigability). In this chapter we present only the spending impacts. See Herstine *et al.* (2007) for more details.

The annual economic impacts of boater trips under baseline conditions are determined by:

1   estimating the baseline number of recreational boating trips made per year in the study region during the study time period for North Carolina resident boaters;
2   estimating the average expenditures by spending category (i.e. boat fuel, slip fees, restaurants, etc.) made per trip and the portion of expenditures spent in North Carolina;
3   multiplying the baseline trip numbers by the average expenditure numbers to generate direct impact spending estimates; and
4   using an economic input-output model to estimate the employment, wages, and taxes supported by the direct expenditures, as well as the indirect and induced effects (i.e. the multiplier effects) resulting from the direct impact spending (Miller and Blair 1985).

Indirect impacts are the impacts associated with business activities servicing and supporting the direct impacts; induced impacts are the impacts associated with additional household spending by employees and business owners who receive additional wages and profits due to the direct and indirect impacts; and total impacts are the sum of the direct, indirect, and induced impacts.

To provide a simple estimate of the impacts of changes in AIWW navigability, the revealed and stated preference travel cost demand model is used to estimate the percentage change in the average number of AIWW recreational boating trips resulting from a change in navigability conditions. The percentage changes are applied to the baseline numbers of trips to estimate changes in total trips. Changes in total trips are multiplied by average direct expenditures per trip to estimate changes in direct impact spending, and the economic impact model is used to calculate multiplier effects.

Baseline (2005) navigability conditions in the AIWW support resident recreational boater trips generating $173 million annually in economic output (sales) within North Carolina. With reduced navigability the number of AIWW recreational boating trips made by North Carolina resident boaters is estimated to fall by 37 percent (by 17 trips per boater per year, on average). The estimated state-wide annual economic impacts of reduced AIWW navigability due to reductions in the numbers of resident boater trips are losses of approximately $64 million in economic output.

Conclusions

In this chapter we estimate the recreational boater benefits and impacts of a dredging and maintenance program for the North Carolina portion of the AIWW. There are very few studies of marine recreational boater behavior and economic values for coastal management policy. We jointly estimate a revealed and stated preference trip model and find that trip changes vary in the expected direction. This model is problematic for valuation due to measurement error in travel costs. In order to measure the value of trip changes, we jointly estimate two types of stated preference data, boater trips with and without a dredging and maintenance program, and willingness-to-pay for the dredging and maintenance program in an instrumental variables model. We find that willingness-to-pay varies in the expected direction with the expected change in the number of boater trips. This result lends validity to the hypothetical willingness-to-pay statements. We use these results to estimate the aggregate economic benefits (i.e. willingness-to-pay) of the dredging and maintenance policy to be $20 million annually. The economic impacts of the policy are roughly $64 million annually. These results would be difficult to obtain with revealed preference data alone.

Acknowledgments

Funding for this study came from the North Carolina Sea Grant Program, the North Carolina Department of Environment and Natural Resources, and the North Carolina Beach, Inlet and Waterway Association.

References

AIWA (Atlantic Intracoastal Waterway Association) (2010) website, www. atlintracoastal. org, Raleigh, NC.

Cameron, T.A. (1991) Interval estimates of non-market resource values from referendum contingent valuation surveys, *Land Economics*, 67(4): 413–421.

Cameron, T.A. and James, M. (1987) Efficient estimation methods for "closed ended" contingent valuation surveys, *Review of Economics and Statistics*, 69(2): 269–276.

Herstine, J., Dumas, C., and Whitehead, J. (2007) *Economic Impacts and Economic Benefits of Recreational Boating Along the Atlantic Intracoastal Waterway (AIWW) in North Carolina*, Wilmington, NC: University of North Carolina.

Lipton, D. (2004) The Value of Improved Water Quality to Chesapeake Bay Boaters, *Marine Resource Economics*, 19(2): 265–270.

Lipton, D.W. and Hicks, R. (1999) Boat location choice: The role of boating quality and excise taxes, *Coastal Management*, 27(1): 81–89.

Loomis, J.B. (1995) Four models for determining environmental quality effects on recreational demand and regional economics, *Ecological Economics*, 12(1): 55–65.

Miller, R.E. and Blair, P.D. (1985) *Input-Output Analysis: Foundations and Extensions*, Englewood Cliffs, NJ: Prentice Hall.

Mitchell, R.C. and Carson, R.T. (1989) *Using Surveys to Value Public Goods: The Contingent Valuation Method*, Washington, DC: Resources for the Future.

Starbuck, C.M., Berrens, R.P., and McKee, M. (2006) Simulating changes in forest recreation demand and associate economic impacts due to fire and fuels management activities, *Forest Policy and Economics*, 8(1): 52–66.

Stoll, J.R., Bergstrom, J.C., and Jones, L.L. (1988) Recreational boating and its economic impact in Texas, *Leisure Sciences*, 10(1): 51–68.

Thomas, M. and Stratis, N. (2002) Compensating variation for recreational policy: A random utility approach to boating in Florida, *Marine Resource Economics*, 17(1): 23–33.

Thomson, C.J. (1991) Effects of the avidity bias on survey estimates of fishing effort and economic values, *American Fisheries Society Symposium*, 12: 356–366.

USACE (2010) *Atlantic Intracoastal Waterway General Information*, United States Army Corps of Engineers, Technical Services, Operations Branch, Norfolk District, online, available at: www.nao.usace.army.mil/Technical Services/ Operations Branch/atlantic intracoastal waterway/homepage.asp.

Whitehead, J.C. (2005) Combining willingness-to-pay and behavior data with limited information, *Resource and Energy Economics*, 27(2): 143–155.

Whitehead, J.C. and Cherry, T.L. (2007) Mitigating the hypothetical bias of willingness-to-pay: A comparison of ex-ante and ex-post approaches, *Resource and Energy Economics*, 29(4): 247–261.

Whitehead, J.C., Haab, T.C., and Huang, J.-C. (2000) Measuring recreation benefits of quality improvements with revealed and stated behavior data, *Resource and Energy Economics*, 22(4): 339–354.

Zerbe, R.O. and Bellas, A.S. (2006) *A Primer for Benefit-Cost Analysis*, Northampton, MA: Edward Elgar.

Part IV
Discrete data

16 Gauging the value of short-term site closures in a travel-cost random utility model of recreation demand with a little help from stated preference data

George R. Parsons and Stela Stefanova

Introduction

Random utility models of recreation demand are well suited for valuing closure of sites and changes in the characteristics of sites such as an improvement in water quality or increase in fish catch. In these applications the welfare effects are realized through site substitution or the choice of taking no trip on a given choice occasion. Parameter estimates from the models are used to measure the decline in utility implied by substitution along these lines and the coefficient on a trip cost variable, in turn, is used to monetize the change in utility.

The models, however, ignore the possibility of substitution across choice occasions within a given season in response to a site closure or change in site quality. For example, a closure of a beach for a weekend or two weeks may result in people delaying trips to the closed site until later in the season. In effect, these people are substituting across time instead of sites. This is a common occurrence in damage assessment cases where the short-term closure of a site may have little impact on the total visitation to the site over a season implying that people have delayed trips in response to the closure.[1]

We have designed and estimated a random utility maximization (RUM) model that accounts for substitution over time and use it to gauge the value of short-term closures. The model combines revealed and stated preference data and is applied to beach use on the Texas Gulf coast. The data were gathered by a phone survey in 2001. Respondents were asked to report information on trips to 65 beaches during the year.[2]

As part of the survey, all respondents visiting the Padre Island National Sea-shore (14 percent of the sample) were asked if they would have visited another site if Padre had been closed. If they responded yes, they were asked to report which site. If they responded no, they were asked if they would take a trip later in the season to "make up" for their lost trip to Padre. These stated preference (SP) data along with the reported trip revealed preference (RP) data are used to estimate a RUM model where a trip to Padre later in the season is treated as an alternative in the choice set. This allows us to estimate the utility for delaying a trip versus making a trip to another site and, in turn, to estimate the loss of a beach closure at Padre Island that accounts for substitution of delayed trips. Our approach does not use a dynamic choice model over a season. Instead, it offers a practical alternative; we believe a strong alternative given the limitations of our simple SP follow-up choice question. Part of our motivation for pursuing this topic was the large number of respondents who reported that they would "make up" a lost trip by visiting Padre later, leading us to wonder if conventional RUM analysis might be missing a key behavioral response to a closure and hence measuring welfare loss inaccurately.

The SP questions are shown in Figure 16.1. If a person responded "Definitely Will" or "Very Likely" or "Likely" to the follow up question we assume that they will take a make-up trip. There are drawbacks to this question format. First, instead of "closure," it uses the wording "...if you had not been able to visit..." which, in principle, could be due to reasons other than a closure. If people took a broad enough interpretation, such as being sick or the traffic being bad, there may be a great deal of latitude in our response data, and that is a reason for caution. Furthermore, even if respondents are thinking in terms of closure, the assumed reason for the closure could vary in the minds of the respondents. Oil spill? Red tide? Other? If behavioral responses are sensitive to the reason for the closure this will lead to even more latitude in the response data. Second, it does not mention how long Padre will be closed. The length of closure will affect the amount of time available during the balance of the season for a make-up trip, when during the balance of the season make-up trips would be possible, and even how many trips may be affected. We, in effect, assume a single day closure in our modeling strategy. Third, the construction of the follow-up question is

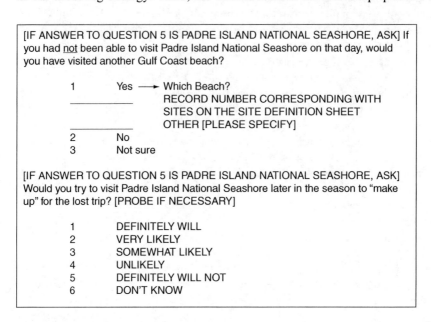

Figure 16.1 Padre Island stated preference closure questions.

such that everyone is asked if they would take a make-up trip to Padre, even if they choose another site in the first question. Only a small fraction choose both and we treated them as choosing another site only. Fourth, with any stated preference response data, what people say they will do and what they actually do can be quite different things. In the recreation demand field there is some evidence that people overstated their expected number of trips for a season when asked at the beginning of a season. We may have a similar optimistic overstatement in our make-up trip data. So, our data clearly come with some caveats, and we urge the reader to keep these in mind when interpreting or using our results.

We find that accounting for delayed trips to Padre reduces the estimated welfare loss by about 70 percent. In the next two sections we present our model and study design. Then, we turn to a short presentation of the data and the results.

A repeated discrete choice model

We use a repeated discrete-choice model to analyze our trip data. Each day of the season is treated as a separate choice occasion. On each choice occasion a person decides to take a trip to the beach or not (stage one) and, if yes, which beach to visit (stage two). We estimate the model sequentially, stage 2 first and then stage 1.[3]

Stage 1 is a simple random utility model of site choice in which an individual faces C sites.[4] Each site i is assumed to give an individual utility $U_i = \beta x_i + \beta_{tc}(y - tc_i) + \varepsilon_i$ where x_i is a vector of site characteristics at site i, y is income, tc_i is the trip cost of reaching site i, and ε_i is a random error. An individual is assumed to visit the site with the highest utility, so his or her trip utility on a given choice occasion is $V = \max\{\beta x_1 + \beta_{tc}(y - tc_1) + \varepsilon_1, \ldots, \beta x_C + \beta_{tc}(y - tc_C) + \varepsilon_C\}$. Treating site choice as the outcome of a stochastic process, an individual's expected maximum trip utility is $E(V) = E(\max\{\beta x_1 + \beta_{tc}(y - tc_1) + \varepsilon_1, \ldots, \beta x_C + \beta_{tc}(y - tc_C) + \varepsilon_C\})$.

We estimate the parameters of site utility and, in turn, the expected utility of a trip using two different models: standard (fixed parameter) logit and mixed (random parameter) logit. These models are well known and documented – see Train (2009, Chapters 3 and 6). In both models the expected maximum utility of a trip takes the familiar log-sum form $E(V) = \ln \Sigma_{i \in C} e^{\beta x_i + \beta_{tc}(y - tc_i)}$. In the mixed logit model, the log-sum is a simulated mean over the estimated distribution for the random elements in β (see Parsons and Massey 2003). The mixed logit model allows for a more general pattern of site substitution than the fixed parameter model.

Stage 2 introduces a no-trip alternative on each choice occasion which is assumed to give an individual utility $U_0 = \delta_z z + \varepsilon_0$, where z is a vector of individual characteristics believed to influence the number of trips taken in a season. In our application, z includes education, employment status, age, and so forth. Using no-trip utility and the site utilities, we model an individual's choice of taking a trip or not. An individual is assumed to choose the greater of no-trip and trip utility on each choice occasion. This outcome is referred to as a person's choice occasion utility, defined as $COU = \max\{U_0, V\}$, where V is defined above. Again, treating trip choice as the outcome of a stochastic process, an individual's expected utility on a choice occasion is $E(COU) = E\{\max(U_0, V)\}$. In our logit models $E(COU) = \ln\{e^{\delta z} + e^{\delta_{EV} E(V)}\}$, where $E(V) = \ln\Sigma_{\in C} e^{\beta x_i + \beta_{tc}(y - tc_i)}$.[5]

Now, consider a conventional analysis of site closure using revealed preference (RP) data only. Let C_2 be the set of Padre Island sites and C_1 the set of all other sites. The expected utility of a trip declines with the closure of the C_2 Padre sites from $E(V^{open}) = \ln\Sigma_{i \in \{C_1, C_2\}} e^{\beta x_i + \beta_{tc}(y - tc_i)}$ to $E(V^{cls}) = \ln\Sigma_{i \in \{C_1\}} e^{\beta x_i + \beta_{tc}(y - tc_i)}$, and the *welfare loss per choice occasion* for the closure is

$$W = \left(\ln\left(e^{\delta_{zz}} + e^{\delta_{EV} E(V^{open})} \right) - \ln\left(e^{\delta_{zz}} + e^{\delta_{EV} E(V^{cls})} \right) \right) / \beta_{tc} \qquad (16.1)$$

The expression in the numerator is the change in expected utility due to the loss of the C_2 Padre sites. The loss is monetized by dividing by the coefficient on trip cost (β_{tc}). Since the expected utility allows for no-trip and trip utility, it allows for individuals to respond to closures by visiting other sites or staying home.[6]

Incorporating delayed trips to closed sites using stated preference data

The per-choice occasion measure W in equation (16.1) relies exclusively on RP data and is the conventional way to value closures. The difficultly with this measure is that it does not allow for substitution across time periods.

Suppose a site is closed for a short time – say a week or even days. If there is little change in total visitation to the site over the season when compared to past seasons, the argument may be made that people merely delay their trips to the closed site until later in the season and that the true welfare loss may be lower than the RUM model would suggest, maybe much lower if delaying trips involves little disutility.

In an effort to capture the effect of substituting a delayed trip until later in the season as a response to a site closure in a RUM model, we designed a survey question in which we simply asked people who had visited a site on Padre Island what they would have done on this day if Padre had been closed. The stated preference responses were classified into three groups:

i   visit another site,
ii   stay home and make up for the lost trip with a trip later in the season when the site is reopened, or
iii stay home without making up the trip later.

Responses (i) and (iii) are accounted for in a conventional revealed preference analysis. Response (ii) adds the dimension of substituting a later trip.

Our analysis of closure proceeds as follows. An individual's choice set if Padre is open is $\{C_1, C_2\}$. Again, C_1 is the set of all non-Padre sites, and C_2 is the set of Padre sites. The choice set when Padre is closed when using the RP data only is C_1. The choice set when Padre is closed using the RP-SP data combined is instead $\{C_1, C_2^*\}$ where C_2^* is a delayed trip to a Padre site. In the RP only setting, the respondent is forced to visit another site or stay home. In the RP-SP setting, the respondent may also visit Padre later in the season.

To analyze the welfare implications of accounting for delayed trip substitution, let site utility for Padre site j be $U_j = \alpha_j + \beta x_j + \beta_{tc}(y - tc_j) + \varepsilon_j$ and the site utility for a delayed trip to the same site be $U_j^* = \alpha_j^* + \beta x_j + \beta_{tc}(y - tc_j) + \varepsilon_j$. These site utilities differ only by their constants, α_j and α_j^*. The parameters β and the site characteristics are the same in the two time periods. A person essentially enjoys the same trip; it is simply delayed. We assume there is some decline in utility for having to delay the trip so $\alpha_j^* < \alpha_j$ and $U_j^* < U_j$.

In the formulation accounting for delayed trips then, the expected utility of a trip declines with the closure of the C_2 Padre sites from $E(V^{open}) = \ln(\Sigma_{i \in \{C_1\}} \exp\{\beta x_i + \beta_{tc}(y - tc_i)\} + \Sigma_{i \in \{C_2\}} \exp\{\alpha_j + \beta x_j + \beta_{tc}(y - tc_j)\})$ to $E(V^{cls^*}) = \ln(\Sigma_{i \in \{C_1\}} \exp\{\beta x_i + \beta_{tc}(y - tc_i)\} + \Sigma_{j \in \{C_2\}} \exp\{\alpha_j^* + \beta x_j + \beta_{tc}(y - tc_j)\})$. The second term on the right hand side of the second expression is the expected trip utility of a delayed trip thereby allowing for delayed substitution. The *welfare loss per choice occasion* for closure then becomes

$$W^* = \left(\ln\left(e^{\delta_z z} + e^{\delta_{EV} E(V^{open})} \right) - \ln\left(e^{\delta_z z} + e^{\delta_{EV} E(V^{cls^*})} \right) \right) / \beta_{tc} \qquad (16.2)$$

This is the same form as equation (16.1) with $E(V^{cls^*})$ used in place of $E(V^{cls})$.[7]

To compare the measures of welfare empirically we first estimate a *Business-As-Usual Model* using only RP data. The results are used to estimate a business-as-usual welfare loss, W, shown in equation (16.1). Then, we estimate a new *RP-SP Model*. The results from this model give us estimates of α_j^* which, along with the business-as-usual parameter estimates, allow us to estimate a new measure of welfare loss, W^*, in equation (16.2). The difference, $W - W^*$, is an approximation of the overstatement due to ignoring delayed trip substitution.

The new *RP-SP Model* is estimated as though Padre is closed. The choices reported by Padre visitors in their SP responses are used in estimation instead of the actual choices made when Padre is open. For those who do not visit Padre when it is open, we assume their choices are unchanged in the event of the Padre closure and enter those choices accordingly in the data. We constrain all parameters in the *RP-SP Model* to be the same as in the *Business-As-Usual Model*, except for the alternative specific constants, α_j, on the Padre sites. This keeps the choice structure constant but allows us to estimate the discount assigned to delaying a trip to Padre. We divide Padre into four separate sites and allow for scale difference in the SP versus RP data. The next section discusses the data used to estimate the models.

Data

We gathered our survey data in 2001 by a phone-mail-phone survey from May through September–the peak season for beach visits. Texas residents living within 200 miles of the Gulf of Mexico were sampled by random digit dialing and recruited to participate in a series of follow-up surveys of beach use. The sample was stratified to avoid a sample dominated by residents of Houston, to assure adequate observation on trips to Padre Island, and to assure adequate participation rates in beach use. All our welfare analysis is adjusted to account for the stratification. The initial survey was conducted in May and given to the adult member of the household (> 17 years old) with the most recent birthday. English and Spanish versions of the survey were offered. Basic demographic information was gathered on each respondent in the initial phone survey. The follow-up surveys were confined to reporting beach trips. About 60 percent of the respondents stayed on through all of the follow-up surveys.

Those who agreed to participate in the follow-up survey received a mail packet that included a map of the coast, a list of 65 beaches, a calendar to help record trips from May through September, and a decorative magnet of the state of Texas for posting the calendar. Individuals were then contacted monthly by phone to report trips in the previous month. The calls were made monthly to reduce the difficulty of recall. Respondents reported 2692 trips over the five-month period to the 65 beaches.[8]

Of the 884 respondents who completed the survey, 14 percent had made at least one trip to the Padre Island National Seashore. If they reported having made a trip to Padre, they were asked what they would have done if Padre had been closed. These responses formed our SP data. Table 16.1 shows the breakdown for each category of response – 19 percent chose to visit another site in the same time period, 5 percent chose to stay at home and not make-up the trip later, and 76 percent chose to make up the trip later.

The second part of our data set covers the characteristics of the sites. We collected data on all of the public beaches on the Texas Gulf coast including information on facilities, amenities, services, and physical characteristics. The beaches included bay side and gulf beaches and were defined using the *2002 Texas Beach and Bay Access Guide* and a two-week field trip to the coast. The delineation of beaches was intended to be as the public generally perceived the boundaries.

The beach characteristic data came from several sources: interviews with beach managers at the city, county, and state levels; the *Access Guide* mentioned above; other independent travel guides; field trips to each of the beaches; and on-line maps of the area. The variables used for site characteristics in our model are presented in Table 16.2 along with descriptive statistics.

Table 16.1 Stated preference responses for adjustment to Padre Island closure

Option	% of SP responses (adjusted for stratification)
Visit another beach now	19
Visit Padre later	76
Stay home	5

Table 16.2 Site characteristics for 65 beaches in choice set

Beach characteristics		Number of beaches	Mean or % of beaches
Beach length (miles)		–	5.35
Yes/No dichotomous variables:			
Gulf access	Beach is located on the Gulf	48	74
State park	Beach is part of a state park	4	6
Remote	Must leave major road to visit beach	22	34
Vehicle-free	Vehicles disallowed on beach	26	40
Manual clean	Beach is routinely manually cleaned	33	51
Machine clean	Beach is routinely machined cleaned	36	55
Restroom	Restrooms located at beach	37	57
Lifeguards	Lifeguards at beach	17	26
Concession	Concession located at beach	15	23
No fishing	Not listed as a fishing area in *2002 Texas Beach and Bay Access Guide*	3	5
No swimming	Not listed as a swimming area in *2002 Texas Beach and Bay Access Guide*	6	9
Red tide history	Beach has a recent history of red tide according to local beach managers	12	18
Advisory/closure history	Beach has a recent history of closures and/or advisories according to local beach managers	11	17

Travel cost was calculated at 36.5 cents per mile plus any fee paid to use a beach. Time cost is valued at one-third of household income divided by 2000 as a proxy for a person's wage. Distances and times to beaches were calculated using *PC Miler*. Average trip cost of reaching a chosen site was $56. The average cost to all sites was $182. Accounting for stratification, about 30 percent of all trips were less than 30 miles one-way. About 50 percent were less than 50 miles, and 80 percent were less than 100 miles. It is also interesting to note that only 4 percent of all trips were taken to the beach closest to a person's home and only about 36 percent were taken to one of the five closest beaches. All beaches within 300 miles of an individual's home were included in the choice set.

Table 16.3 shows the individual characteristics used in the second stage model. We have no strong priors on how these will predict visitation, but have included characteristics that have typically been used in past analyses–age, education, work status, ownership of recreational equipment, and so forth. Finally, Table 16.4 is a frequency distribution of trips to four Padre Island sites used in our closure analysis.

Coefficient and welfare estimates

The results for our *Business-As-Usual Model*, which uses only RP data, are shown in Table 16.5 for the standard and mixed logit models. In the mixed model we allow *Vehicle Free Access* and seven geographic variables (*Gulf*

Table 16.3 Individual characteristics for 884 people

Variable	Mean or % of sample (adjusted for stratification)
Age	41 years
Yes/No dichotomous variables:	
Work fulltime	62
Children under 17	49
High school	32
College	24
Graduate school	10
Retired	9
Spanish	9
Female	60
Own fishing equipment	49
Own pool	24
Own coastal property	7

Table 16.4 Frequency distribution of trips to Padre Island sites

Option	% of Padre trips (adjusted for stratification)
Padre 1: North Beach	64
Padre 2: Malaquite Beach	14
Padre 3: South Beach	19
Padre 4: Shell Beaches/Mansfield Cut	3

Access, Remote, and *five Region Constants*) to have random coefficients. These represented the lines along which we felt there would be important shared unobserved characteristics. In all cases we assume that the parameters are normally distributed. The model was estimated using 100 Halton draws.

The results work more or less as expected. The coefficient on trip cost is negative and significant.[9] All else constant, people prefer a beach closer to home. Variables that predict a higher probability of visiting a site with significance, all else constant, include *Gulf Access, Vehicle Free, Beach Length*, and *Manual* and

Table 16.5 Business-as-usual model: parameter estimates for site utility

Variable	Logit	Mixed logit	
		Fixed coefficients	
Trip cost	$-0.02\ (-22.08)^1$	$-0.03\ (-17.95)$	
Beach length	0.27 (8.66)	0.27 (8.53)	
State park	0.20 (0.75)	0.25 (0.95)	
Manual clean	0.78 (6.01)	0.77 (5.87)	
Machine clean	0.80 (7.13)	0.89 (7.06)	
Restroom	-0. 06 (-0.50)	-0.05 (-0.44)	
Lifeguards	-0.04 (-0.40)	-0.03 (-0.11)	
Concessions	-0.01 (-0.10)	-0.04 (-0.37)	
No fishing	-0.26 (-2.21)	-0.28 (-2.31)	
No swimming	-0.98 (-4.38)	-0.99 (-4.20)	
Red tide history	-1.95 (-5.86)	-1.84 (-5.39)	
Advisory/closure history	-0.63 (-2.99)	-0.61 (-2.85)	
Constant for Padre 1	2.80 (12.49)	3.04 (11.64)	
Constant for Padre 2	-0.27 (-0.86)	0.04 (0.12)	
Constant for Padre 3	1.80 (6.38)	2.11 (6.75)	
Constant for Padre 4	0.06 (0.12)	0.50 (0.94)	
		Random Coefficients	
		Mean	*Std. dev.*
Gulf access	0.53 (3.77)	0.58 (4.06)	0.003 (0.004)
Vehicle-fFree	0.99 (10.27)	1.01 (9.92)	0.002 (0.004)
Remote	0.15 (1.49)	-0.02 (-0.14)	0.98 (2.56)
Region 1	0 (Fixed)	0 (Fixed)	0.002 (0.002)
Region 2	0.97 (3.42)	1.02 (3.45)	0.02 (0.04)
Region 3	2.15 (4.73)	2.13 (4.48)	0.004 (0.015)
Region 4	0.82 (2.18)	0.83 (2.05)	0.03 (0.05)
Region 5	1.24 (3.69)	1.30 (3.53)	1.45 (5.02)
Region 6	-0.14 (-0.36)	-0.39(-0.79)	1.76 (3.78)
Log likelihood	-3926	-3912	
Number of people	561	561	
Number of choices	2692	2692	

Note
1 t-statistics in parentheses.

Machine Cleaning. Variables that predict a lower probability with significance include *No Fishing, No Swimming, Red Tide History,* and *Advisory/Closures History.* Variables having little significance in predicting site choice include *Remote, Restroom, Lifeguard, Concessions,* and *State Park.* The regions run from north to south with *Region 1* being the northernmost. *Region 6,* located in the south near Brownsville, is the excluded region. The regions with the largest coefficients are 2, 3, and 5. These are beach areas near Galveston, Freeport, and Corpus Christi. These are near the largest population centers and are popular beaches. Padre Island is located in *Region 5.* The standard deviation estimates in the mixed logit model are largest, relative to their means, for *Remote, Region 5,* and *Region 6.* This suggests that substitution among sites within these geographic areas is strongest, at least in a stochastic sense.

If there were any surprises, it was that the man-made characteristics like *Restroom, Lifeguard,* and *Concessions* seemed to play a small role in site choice. It was also somewhat surprising that *Vehicle Free Access* was positive, large, significant, and had a small estimated standard deviation in the mixed logit. We had expected a large standard error signaling large substitution (or perhaps population heterogeneity) among these sites.

The parameter estimates for no-trip utility in the *Business-as-Usual Model* in the standard and mixed logit form are shown in Table 16.6. The coefficients imply that trips increase, all else constant, with education, having children in the household, being younger, and speaking Spanish. Also, men are more likely to take trips than women. And finally, the coefficient on expected trip utility (also reported in Table 16.6 alongside the no-trip parameters) is positive and significant in both regressions as expected.

Table 16.6 Business-as-usual model: parameter estimates for no-trip utility

Variable	With logit site choice	With mixed logit site choice
Intercept	8.36 (29.20)[1]	7.69 (27.87)
Log(Age)	−0.27 (4.01)	−0.27 (3.94)
Female	0.21 (5.07)	0.20 (4.97)
Work fulltime	0.00 (0.09)	0.01 (0.19)
Spanish	−0.47 (6.98)	−0.48 (7.07)
Retired	0.06 (0.74)	0.06 (0.75)
Children under 17	−0.18 (4.18)	−0.17 (4.10)
Graduate school	−0.12 (1.61)	−0.11 (1.49)
College	−0.30 (6.15)	−0.29 (6.06)
High school	0.21 (4.23)	0.22 (4.09)
Own coastal property	−0.00 (0.02)	−0.00 (0.04)
Own fishing equipment	−0.17 (4.26)	−0.17 (4.10)
Own pool	0.03 (0.55)	0.03 (0.63)
Coefficient on expected trip utility (δ_{EV})	0.74 (28.73)	0.62 (28.88)
Log likelihood	11983.86	11999.62

Note
1 t-statistics in parentheses.

The parameter estimates from Tables 16.5 and 16.6 provide the information we need to calculate W – our business-as-usual welfare loss. Using equation (16.1), the value for the closure of all four beaches on the Padre Island National Seashore is $0.054 per choice occasion in the standard logit model and $0.038 per choice occasion in the mixed logit model.[10] The lower values in the mixed logit reflect that model's ability to account better for substitution across sites. This is driven by the large standard error on *Region 5*, which suggests that other sites in the Corpus Christi area are good substitutes for the Padre sites.

Now let's turn to our estimates of the *RP-SP Model*. These are needed to calculate the new welfare measure W^* which accounts for delayed trip substitution. The *RP-SP Model* is estimated assuming that the Padre Island National Seashore is closed. All the RP choices for the Padre Island visitors are replaced with their SP choices. For respondents who did not visit Padre Island when it was open, we assume their choices are unchanged. We constrained the parameters on all of the site characteristics to be the same with and without closure, but allowed the Padre Island constants to change. This keeps the behavioral model constant and allows us to isolate the effect of a delayed trip to Padre Island.

Table 16.7 Revealed and stated preference model: parameter estimates on site utility[2]

Variable	Logit	Mixed logit	
		Fixed coefficients	
Constant for Padre 1	2.46 (17.23)[1]	–2.66 (–17.65)	
Constant for Padre 2	–0.89 (–2.74)	–0.62 (–1.88)	
Constant for Padre 3	1.67 (7.61)	1.95 (8.65)	
Constant for Padre 4	–1.38 (–1.46)	–0.97 (–1.03)	
		Random coefficients	
		Mean	*Std. dev.*
Gulf Access	n/a	–	0.06 (0.10)
Vehicle Free	n/a	–	0.01 (0.02)
Remote	n/a	–	0.96 (5.08)
Region 1	n/a	–	0.01 (0.007)
Region 2	n/a	–	0.03 (0.04)
Region 3	n/a	–	0.002 (0.01)
Region 4	n/a	–	0.01 (0.02)
Region 5	n/a	–	1.52 (8.31)
Region 6	n/a	–	1.59 (3.59)
Log likelihood	–3906	–3893	
Number of people	561	561	
Number of choices	2692	2692	

Notes
1 Estimates for all coefficients except the alternative specific constants for Padre sites and all random coefficients are constrained to equal the estimates in the RP model shown in Table 16.5.
2 t-statistics in parentheses.

The *RP-SP Model* results are shown in Table 16.7 and include only the coefficients that vary from the *Business-As-Usual Model*. Following Brownstone *et al.* (2000) we estimated a scaling parameter on the SP choices relative to the RP choices using a normal mixing distribution for a dummy variable on the SP choices with zero mean. We found no significant scale difference in the data sets. We also estimated separate standard deviations on all the parameters with mixing distributions expecting somewhat larger variability in *RP-SP Model*. As shown, the coefficients estimates are reasonably close in the two models. This may be due to the similarity of the SP and RP choices and limited number of observations affected. As expected, the coefficients on the Padre Island constants fall in the *RP-SP Model* relative to the *Business-As-Usual Model*. This captures the decline in utility that comes with having to delay a trip. The per choice occasion value for a closure of all Padre sites, W^*, is \$0.016 in the logit model and \$0.011 in the mixed logit model. These are about 30 percent of the value estimated when delayed trips are not taken into account, so the implication of ignoring delayed trip substitution, if the SP data are believed, is not trivial. The standard and mixed logit differences from the *Business-As-Usual Model* are about the same. These results are, of course, driven by the larger number of respondents reporting that they would make-up their lost trip with a trip later in the season.

Conclusions

Applications of the Travel Cost RUM Model to value short-term site closures sometimes leads to controversy over the handling of substitution between time periods in the same season. In cases where there is a short-term closure of a site (closes and opens within the same season) but the number of the trips to the site over the entire season shows little change compared with past seasons, the argument is sometimes made that people are merely substituting future trips for lost current trips. Since the conventional RUM Model does not account for substitution across time periods and indeed forces substitution to another site or staying home, the argument is sometimes made that it may lead to an overstatement of loss because the model disallows what may be the best substitute for many individuals—delaying a trip to the closed site.

We explored this potential overstatement in a model of beach use in Texas with an SP question posed to all respondents who had visited the Padre Island National Seashore—14 percent of our sample. The question simply asked visitors what they would have done if Padre had been closed. The responses allowed for staying home, visiting another site, or taking a trip later in the season to Padre to "make-up" for the lost Padre trip. About 75 percent of the respondents chose to make-up the trip later, suggesting the potential for a significant overstatement if ignored. We found that estimated losses were about 70 percent lower when delayed trips were incorporated in the model.

The implication, if the SP data are believed, is that the conventional estimates of loss using RUM models of recreation demand may consistently lead to overstatement. In our application it is rather large. The results would no doubt vary across different resources and settings. In general, the greater the likelihood of substitution to other sites or staying home, the more reliable the conventional RUM analysis. Also, the longer the period of closure, the less likely there will be substitution within the same season.

As noted earlier, our analysis is somewhat speculative. There is considerable room for improvement in our SP question, need for validation with actual trip data before and after a closure, and a desire for validation with an explicit dynamic model. At this stage, we hesitate to draw strong conclusions. Nevertheless, our findings suggest that further inquiry may be in order.

Acknowledgments

Funding for this study came from the National Oceanic and Atmospheric Administration's Coastal Response Research Center at the University of New Hampshire and the National Park Service. We thank Chris Leggett, Kevin Boyle, and Ami Kang for help on data construction, model development, and ideas throughout the project. The data were collected originally by Industrial Economics, Inc. under contract with the National Park Service.

Notes

1 If people delay trips across seasons, the argument may be extended further. We would expect the replacement value of trips delayed that long would be substantially diminished.
2 For another application using these data, see Parsons *et al.* (2009).
3 Morey *et al.* (1993) introduced the repeated discrete-choice model to recreation demand.
4 For some examples of the random utility model applied to beach recreation see Lew and Larson (2008), Whitehead *et al.* (2010), Murray *et al.* (2001), and Parsons and Massey (2003).
5 This formulation nests the model by trip and no-trip and introduces δ_{EV} as a coefficient on the log-sum (or inclusive value) for trip.
6 See Hanemann (1999) or Haab and McConnell (2002) or for more on welfare analysis in the context of RUM models of recreation demand.
7 The Padre constants α_j are subsumed in the parameter vector β in the previous section.
8 We collapse six Padre Island sites into four, leaving 63 sites in our final analysis.
9 In estimation y drops out of $\beta_{tc}(y-tc)$ and β_{tc} is estimated as a negative coefficient on tc.
10 Per choice occasion values are averaged over all respondents – non-participants and participants visiting any site.

References

Brownstone, D., D.S. Bunch, and K. Train (2000) Joint mixed logit models of stated and revealed preferences for alternative fuel vehicles, *Transportation Research Record B*, 34(5): 315–38.

Haab, T.C. and K.E. McConnell (2002) *Valuing Environmental and Natural Resources: The Econometrics of Non-Market Valuation*, Northampton, ME/Cheltenham: Edward Elgar.

Hanemann, W.M. (1999) Welfare analysis with discrete choice models, in C.L. Kling and J.A. Herriges (eds.), *Valuing Recreation and the Environment: Revealed Preference Methods in Theory and Practice*, Chapter 2, Cheltenham: Edward Elgar.

Lew, D.K. and D.M. Larson (2008) Valuing a beach day with a repeated nested logit model of participation, site choice, and stochastic time value, *Marine Resource Economics*, 23(3): 233–52.

Morey, E., R.D. Rowe, and M. Watson (1993) A repeated nested-logit model of Atlantic salmon fishing, *American Journal of Agricultural Economics*, 75(3): 578–92.

Murray, C., B. Sohngen, and L. Pendelton (2001) Valuing water quality advisories and beach amenities in the Great Lakes, *Water Resources Research*, 37(10): 2583–90.

Parsons, G.R. and D.M. Massey (2003) "A Random Utility Model of Beach Recreation" Chapter 12 in *The New Economics of Recreation Demand* (eds. N. Hanley, W.D. Shaw, and R.E. Wright) Edward Elgar Publishing: Northampton, MA & Cheltenham UK.

Parsons, G.R., A. Kang, C. Leggett, and K. Boyle (2009) Valuing beach closures on the Padre Island National Seashore, *Marine Resource Economics*, 24(3): 213–35.

Train, K. (2009) *Discrete Choice Methods with Simulation*, second edition, Cambridge: Cambridge University Press.

Whitehead, J.C., D. Phaneuf, C.F. Dumas, J. Herstine, J. Hill, and B. Buerger (2010) Convergent validity of revealed and stated preference behavior with quality change: A comparison of multiple and single site demands, *Environmental and Resource Economics*, 45(1): 91–112.

17 Modeling behavioral response to changes in reservoir operations in the Tennessee Valley region

Paul M. Jakus, John C. Bergstrom, Marty Phillips, and Kelly Maloney

Introduction

In 1933, the United States Congress created the Tennessee Valley Authority (TVA) to help bring economic development and quality-of-life improvements to people living in the Tennessee River watershed. The TVA was one of the hallmarks of President Franklin D. Roosevelt's "New Deal" program responding to the US "Great Depression." From its inception, the primary goals of TVA have been providing flood control within the valley, assuring a navigable channel on the Tennessee River, and the provision of electric power (TVA 2010). A fourth goal, regional economic development, was added in later years.

Over the past 75 years, electricity from TVA power plants has played a key role in the economic development of the TVA service region composed of parts of seven states: Alabama, Georgia, Kentucky, Mississippi, North Carolina, Tennessee and Virginia. TVA generates electricity through hydroelectric dams, coal-fired power plants, nuclear plants and some "green power" (e.g. wind, solar) sites. Hydroelectric plants currently account for about 10 percent of total TVA electricity generation. TVA operates an interconnected system of 49 dams and reservoirs, of which 35 projects are important for the generation of hydropower.

During the previous two decades, especially the 1990s, recreational use of TVA reservoirs increased dramatically. This recreational use comes not only from those who live adjacent to the reservoirs but also from visitors who live much farther away. Increased recreational use of TVA reservoirs can sometimes compete with other reservoir benefits. For example, many recreation users desire high reservoir water levels to support recreational activities such as boating, water skiing and swimming. However, if the TVA were to reduce reservoir water releases during the summer to support higher lake levels, there may be a loss of public power generation and navigation benefits. Thus, an important management policy issue facing the TVA is balancing the multiple objectives and benefits of TVA reservoirs including growing recreational use and continued power generation, navigation and flood control needs.

To facilitate reservoir management, the TVA initiated a comprehensive reservoir operations study (ROS) in 2001. The ROS examined the environmental, social and economic impacts of reservoir management alternatives. The results of the ROS were published in 2004 in the form of a final ROS programmatic environmental impact statement (TVA 2004). One of the objectives of the ROS was to assess the effects of fluctuating reservoir water levels associated with different management alternatives on recreation visitation and economic impacts.

The effects of fluctuating reservoir water levels on recreation visitation were examined using a combined travel cost and trip response model. Standard travel cost models are classified as revealed preference (RP) nonmarket valuation approaches. Revealed preference approaches are so called because individuals reveal their preferences or demand for a nonmarket good or service through actual behavior (for a discussion of the travel cost model as revealed preference method, see Parsons 2003). For example, individuals reveal their demand for recreation trips to reservoirs at different water levels through the actual number of trips they make to reservoirs at fluctuating water levels.

A trip response model is a type of intended or contingent behavior model (Bergstrom *et al.* 2004; Betz *et al.* 2003; Loomis 1993; Teasley *et al.* 1994). Intended or contingent behavior models are classified as stated preference (SP) nonmarket valuation approaches. Stated preference approaches are so called because individuals state their preferences or demand for nonmarket goods and services directly through survey questions. For example, in a survey, individuals may state how many recreational trips they would take to a reservoir at different water levels.

The combined RP-SP recreation demand model estimated in this study presents a behavioral response model that combines actual behavior under current reservoir operating guidelines and intended behavior contingent on future reservoir conditions under proposed management alternatives. Water levels at different times during the recreation season are treated as quality shifters, which are then used to predict changes in recreation behavior for any of the potential management alternatives. We supplement our RP data with SP data because a revealed preference model based on a single year of observed recreation could not include a meaningful measure of policy-relevant water levels: at any given site the actual water level is what it is as determined by current management and environmental factors (e.g. rainfall patterns).

Management alternatives proposed by the TVA result in different water elevations at a given site, so a model must be able to include responses to higher or lower water levels at a site. One modeling option is to treat observed changes in actual trip behavior with changes in actual water levels as "natural experiment" data and estimate a RP recreation demand model showing the relationship between changes in actual trips and water levels. However, even if one could introduce site level variation by using multiple years of RP data, the water levels of many of the proposed management alternatives would be outside the levels experienced in the past, thus introducing the problem of "out-of-sample" prediction.

Another complicating factor in the design of our modeling strategy was that TVA had developed 65 different management scenarios at the time the survey was to be implemented, and the model had to accommodate any and all of these alternatives. Combining RP and SP data allowed us to incorporate more variation in water levels within and across reservoirs in our study than would have been available using the "natural experiment" revealed preference data alone. The end result was a flexible, empirical recreation demand model capable of handling many "what if" scenarios related to fluctuating water levels. This flexible model helped to meet one of the primary policy needs and purposes of the ROS is study which was to assess changes in recreation visitation to TVA projects with changes in water level management.

Literature review

Before discussing the survey methodology and empirical RP-SP recreation demand model results, we provide a brief review of the small but growing literature addressing how recreational use responds to changing water management regimes. Cordell and Bergstrom (1993) were among the first to examine recreational response to changing water levels. These authors used contingent behavior data to estimate the welfare effects of maintaining full summer pools on four reservoir projects in northern Georgia and western North Carolina. The studies did not examine how visitation would affect recreation at other nearby projects, but instead focused on changes in welfare at the four reservoirs under study.

Eiswerth *et al.* (2000) focused on the effect of water levels at a single lake in northern Nevada. Walker Lake had few nearby recreational alternatives, so a single-site Poisson model used RP and SP data to estimate changes in recreation. The SP scenarios linked the "end-of-year" 20-foot increase (or 20-foot decrease) in water levels to changes in total annual visitation, with the authors concluding that each one foot drop in elevation results in a loss of 0.1 trips per person per year.

Cameron *et al.* (1996) looked at the effect of reservoir management scenarios at nine federal water projects in the Pacific Northwest under the administration of federal agencies in the Columbia River Basin. This study is especially relevant because the management of reservoirs and dams, and the distribution of hydropower, is managed somewhat similarly to that of the Tennessee and Cumberland River Basins. Further, Cameron *et al.* (1996) introduced a seasonal element into the model, noting that the timing of water levels was critical in recreational trip-making decisions. Finally, this study used a combination of RP and SP data to gauge recreation response to different patterns of water management. The recreation demand for each project was modeled individually, with substitution effects among water projects incorporated by including cross-price and "cross-water" terms in each demand equation. The authors find that much of the effect of water management occurs at a selection stage (the decision to recreate at a particular water body). If a person decides to visit a particular project, changes in water management do not greatly affect overall visitation at that project. The statistical performance of the cross-price and "cross-water" effects in the nine demand equations was described by the authors as "mixed."

Jakus *et al.* (2000) incorporate substitution effects differently from Cameron *et al.* (1996), and these authors are the only ones who rely exclusively upon RP data to gauge the effect of changing water levels. This study used a Random Utility Model (RUM) to link recreational use at 12 TVA projects located in east Tennessee to water levels. The data set was derived from four separate surveys conducted between 1994 and 1998, and was based on recreational visits by anglers to any of the 12 projects over a six-month period between March 1 and August 31 of each year. The authors were fortunate in that over the four-year period of data collection, the east Tennessee region experienced one year with relatively low water levels, another year with relatively high water levels, and two somewhat "normal" years. Taking advantage of this natural variation (e.g. "natural experiment" data), the authors conclude that reservoir anglers take more visits when water levels are higher in late summer. Holding lakes at "full-pool" through the end of August would increase annual visits by about 0.3 trips per person.

Data collection

Survey activities

The empirical RP-SP recreation demand model is based on intercept data collected from May 2002 through October 2002. As of 2002, TVA's reservoir management policy had been in place for over a decade and called for reservoirs to reach full summer pool levels by June 1. Restricted draw downs (i.e. water releases following prescribed guidelines) were permitted for June and July, with unrestricted draw downs beginning on August 1, allowing TVA to produce hydropower that can be sold at high, late summer prices. It was the unrestricted drawdown after August 1 that had proved most controversial for recreationists, as it sometimes resulted in very low water levels by the Labor Day holiday (the first week of September) and worsened through the remainder of the fall season. For this reason it was decided that the survey would focus on reservoir water levels in the months of August, September and October.

In consultation with TVA officials, nine projects were selected for survey activities to gather RP and SP data. These reservoirs were selected on the basis of standard TVA classifications: whether the project was (a) managed as tributary storage, mainstem storage or run-of-river project, (b) whether the project was located in an urban, rural or remote location, and (c) whether recreational activity at the project was considered high, medium or low. Six sites (Blue Ridge, Cherokee, Douglas, Hiwassee, Norris and South Holston) are drawn down from 20 to 50 feet each year. Another project (Chatuge) is usually drawn down only ten feet, while the remaining two sites (Kentucky and Pickwick) have gradual and minimal (four feet) drawdowns.

Respondents were intercepted at public access points and commercial establishments. Respondents in our sample took an average of 12 trips during the season. Just over 25 percent of respondents were female, and just under 25 percent had a college degree. With an average age of 45 years old, some 46 percent were anglers and almost 29 percent used a boat on their most recent trip. Just over 10 percent said they spent their most recent trip in a tailwater section of the TVA project (i.e. below the dam as opposed to on the reservoir). The self-administered survey asked respondents about the number of trips in August, September and October in a typical year under current management conditions for both the site at which they had been intercepted and for another site that they visited most frequently. Respondents were also asked how the number of reservoir visits to these sites would change under alternative reservoir management scenarios. Thus, our data collection methodology assured that respondents were not restricted to choosing only TVA projects as substitute sites. Alternatives cited by respondents were often located outside of TVA's watershed region and included numerous sites operated by the Army Corps of Engineers in Tennessee, Georgia, Mississippi and Alabama, as well as a host of smaller projects.

Stated preference data and measured water levels

Two stated preference scenarios were used (Figure 17.1). The first scenario, administered to about half of the respondents, asked how trips during the time period would change if minimum summer pool levels were maintained through the Labor Day weekend, where minimum pool level referenced the August 1 water level. Respondents were free to choose an increase in trips, a decrease in trips or no change in trips. The second scenario, administered to the remaining half of the sample, asked how trips during this time period would change if minimum summer pool levels were maintained through October 1. Again, respondents could indicate an increase, decrease or no change in trips.

The SP questions were written quite generally so as to accommodate intended recreation trips made under any of the 65 potential reservoir management scenarios. Each reservoir has had a fill/drawdown "guide curve" in place for over a decade, so it could be safely assumed that most users were familiar with the pattern of summer drawdowns. By referencing the "minimum" summer pool levels, the TVA guide curves for each project could be used as the baseline against which to compare the water levels of any alternative management scenario. The target water levels of the future management scenarios could be above or below those of the current management policy, and could be well outside the experience of those who regularly visit the reservoirs.

Water levels under the stated preference scenarios were measured as deviations from the elevation given by the current guide curve on Labor Day and October 1 at each site. Under baseline conditions that govern the RP data, these measured deviations are zero for both dates because pool elevations would remain the same in the future as it has since the 1991 Reservoir Improvement Plan. The two alternative management scenarios outlined in the survey, full pool through Labor Day or full pool through October 1, assume that unrestricted drawdowns will not begin until Labor Day or October 1. For the empirical model, the two SP scenarios were quantified by measuring the deviation from

8.   In an average year, approximately how many trips of 1 or more consecutive days do you make to the reservoir/river for recreational purposes? If you are a permanent or seasonal resident, a trip = one day. (*Fill in the blank for each month; if you do not visit this reservoir/river in a specific month, write 0.*)

# trips	# trips	# trips
_____ January	_____ May	_____ September
_____ February	_____ June	_____ October
_____ March	_____ July	_____ November
_____ April	_____ August	_____ December

Typically, the water level at this reservoir (or the reservoir feeding the river) is lowered at a more rapid rate starting August 1. Suppose the water level at this reservoir and at nearby reservoirs were kept at or above minimum summer levels until LABOR DAY.

12.   If the water level at this reservoir/river remained at or above minimum summer level until LABOR DAY, would you make more, fewer or the same amount of trips to THIS reservoir in August, September, and October? (*Check one box AND fill out the number of additional or fewer trips.*)

☐ More   ⟶   How many more trips would you make?
        _____ Aug.   _____ Sept.   _____ Oct.

☐ Fewer   ⟶   How many more trips would you make?
        _____ Aug.   _____ Sept.   _____ Oct.

☐ Same

13.   Do you usually visit any other reservoirs/rivers in August, September, or October?
    ☐ Yes
    ☐ No   SKIP TO QUESTION 16

14.   What OTHER reservoir/river do you visit the most in August, September, or October and how many trips do you usually make to this other reservoir/river?

    Other reservoir/river: _____

    City and State: _____

    How many trips each year? _____ Aug. _____ Sept. _____ Oct.

15.   If the water level at the reservoir/river you are visiting TODAY remained at or above minimum summer level until LABOR DAY, would you make more, fewer or the same amount of trips to the reservoir listed in Question 14 in August, September, and October? (*Check one box.*)

☐ More   ⟶   How many more trips would you make?
        _____ Aug.   _____ Sept.   _____ Oct.

☐ Fewer   ⟶   How many more trips would you make?
        _____ Aug.   _____ Sept.   _____ Oct.

☐ Same

Figure 17.1 Contingent behavior questions (Labor Day scenario).

the "traditional" August 1 elevation, defined as the median pool elevation on August 1 for the 1991–2001 time period. The Labor Day SP scenario was designed so that the Labor Day elevation would be equal to the traditional August 1 elevation, after which drawdowns would follow the current pattern. The October 1 elevation would then be a simple four week temporal translation of the 1991–2001 median drawdown pattern.

For example, the typical August 1 elevation on Cherokee Lake for the 1991–2001 time period under current management was 1062 feet, on Labor Day it was 1049 feet, and on October 1 it was 1043 feet. Under the Labor Day altern-ative management scenario it is assumed that the August 1 elevation will be maintained though Labor Day, resulting in a deviation from the current manage-ment scenario of 13 feet (1062 feet minus 1049 feet). Assuming the post-Labor Day drawdown follows the typical pattern, the simple four-week shift implies the October 1 deviation would also be 13 feet. Under the October 1 alternative management scenario, the August 1 elevation would be maintained through October 1. This means that the Labor Day deviation from the current manage-ment scenario would be 13 feet, whereas the October 1 deviation would be 19 feet (i.e. 19 feet higher than the typical October 1 elevation). Similar calculations were completed for all reservoirs; some scenarios called for lower elevation than the current operating guide, which resulted in negative deviations. With the exception of Barkley Lake, which is linked to Kentucky Lake via a canal, all non-TVA reservoirs were assumed to maintain current operating practices such that deviations from traditional water levels were zero.

Econometric modeling

The general empirical model relates trip-making behavior to characteristics of the various TVA and non-TVA Reservoirs and the regions in which Reservoirs are located, which may fall within or outside the TVA power service area (201 counties covering 80,000 square miles). A two-stage modeling approach was used. In the first stage, site and region characteristics were used to model the probability that any given reservoir is visited on any one choice occasion. The information from this model was aggregated into an index of the "utility" associ-ated with reservoir and tailwater recreation. The index was then used in the second stage of the model, relating the utility index and individual character-istics to explain the total number of trips taken to all reservoirs and tailwaters during the three-month period of interest, whether the reservoir is administered by TVA or not.

Site/region choice model

A version of the repeated nested logit model was used to estimate the probability that a site was visited on any given site choice occasion, where the recreationist chooses the site/region combination that yields the most satisfaction from recreation depending on the available site and region characteristics. The model can be thought of as having two parts: the first part models the "region" choice whereas the second part models the "site" choice, conditional on having chosen a region. Figure 17.2 provides a conceptual overview of the first stage nested site choice model, showing a three-region, seven-site choice model. Region 1 has three sites, region 2 has two sites and region 3 has two sites.

A standard assumption for such models is that site choices are distributed according to the generalized extreme value distribution (Morey 1999). Looking solely at the "bottom" site-choice portion of Figure 17.2, this assumption yields the standard conditional site choice probabilities,

$$\pi_{j \mid k} = \frac{\exp(\beta X_j)}{\displaystyle\sum_{i=1}^{J} \beta X_i} \tag{17.1}$$

where the $\pi_{j\mid k}$ is the probability of having chosen site j conditional on having chosen region k, exp(.) references the exponential operator, X_j is a vector of site attributes, β is a vector of parameters to be estimated, and J is the number of sites in region k. The vector X_j includes site characteristics such as distance from the respondent's home, the number of boat ramps and campgrounds at any given site, and deviations from pool elevations on particular dates (Labor Day and October 1). One of the site attributes, namely distance to the site from the respondent's home, varies across people so that the site choice probabilities vary across respondents even if all other site attributes are identical across people.

For example, assume that Region 1 has three sites, Lakes A, B and C. For any given parameter vector β and characteristics vector X_i, the denominator represents the sum of the site characteristics index across all sites. The numerator includes the characteristics index of only one site, such that the equation is clearly less than one. Let $j=1$, such that the numerator is an index of Lake A

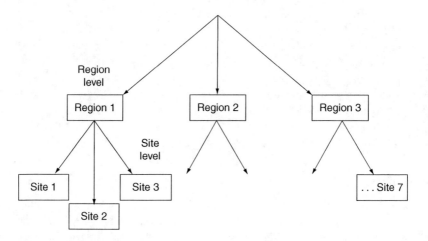

Figure 17.2 First-stage nested logit site/region choice model.

characteristics, whereas the denominator sums the index of all sites in the region. The ratio of the numerator to the denominator can then be interpreted as a probability that A will be visited on any given choice occasion, conditional on the decision to visit Region 1. Similar conditional probabilities can be calculated for other sites in the region. Given the denominator, the sum of the three conditional probabilities is assured to be one.

One may summarize the information within any given region through its "inclusive value". The inclusive value can be thought of as an index of utility or satisfaction, where higher levels of the index indicate greater levels of satisfaction. The inclusive value for all J sites within any region k can be calculated as

$$IV_k = \ln[\sum_{i=1}^{J} \exp(\beta X_i)] \tag{17.2}$$

The inclusive value for each region is then passed to the "upper" portion of the model, the region choice level. Similar to the lower-level site-choice level, one may estimate the probabilities associated with the choice of any given region, such that the probability of choosing region k is given by,

$$\pi_k = \frac{\exp(\gamma Z_k)}{\sum_{i=1}^{K} \exp(\gamma Z_i)} \tag{17.3}$$

where π_k is the probability of choosing region k, Z_k is a vector of attributes of region k and γ is a vector of parameters to be estimated. Regional characteristics included in Z_k include measures of precipitation, temperature, the percentage of the region covered by water and the inclusive value IV_k arising from the site choice model for all sites in region k.

Total trips model

The second portion of the empirical model estimates the total number of trips taken during the three-month time period. The connection to the site choice model is also made through an inclusive value index, where the index is calculated at the "regional" level. That is, the inclusive value passed to the total trips model is given by,

$$IV = \ln[\sum_{k=1}^{K} \exp(\gamma Z_k)] \tag{17.4}$$

where the summation is over all sites k. Note that because the vector Z_k includes the inclusive value for all sites in region k, all the information associated with the site choice is passed to the total trips model. Also, this inclusive value includes the effect of distance to sites that varies across people, so that an inclusive value is calculated for each person. In addition to the utility index associated with recreation, the total trips model will also measure the effect of other attributes of the respondent as these attributes affect overall recreation. The general model for total trips is then,

$$Trips = \exp(\alpha + \delta IV + \omega C_n) \tag{17.5}$$

where IV is the inclusive value arising from the site/region choice model as calculated for person n and C_n is a vector of characteristics of the individual n. The total trips model in equation (17.5) is presented in the standard parameterization for the Poisson distribution, a distribution that accounts for the discrete, non-negative nature of the trips data. A complete version of this linked site-choice aggregate trips model may be found in Hausman *et al.* (1995). Parsons *et al.* (1999) show that this model is theoretically equivalent to the repeated discrete choice model advocated by Morey (1999).

Model implementation

The empirical RP-SP recreation demand model is based on respondents who have satisfied a number of criteria. First, respondents must have indicated a willingness to take a trip to a reservoir or associated tailwater during the months of August, September or October under either baseline or the alternative SP management scenario. This does *not* mean that the person must have made a trip under current reservoir management conditions during any of these three months. In fact, surveying was also conducted in May, June and July. Respondents interviewed in these months could (and did) report zero trips in August, September and October under current reservoir operations, yet reported a positive number of trips (or zero trips) during these three months under the alternative reservoir management scenarios described in the survey. A respondent must have reported at least one trip under either current *or* alternative scenarios because the site/region choice model cannot be estimated for those who make no choice (i.e. do not make a trip) under any reservoir management conditions. Similar to both Cameron *et al.* (1996) and Jakus *et al.* (2000), the modeling approach allows for substitution among sites as water levels change, and also allows for the overall number of trips to change (i.e. people opt out of reservoir recreation).

Second, the respondent must have indicated that recreation at the reservoir or tailwater was the primary reason for the trip. Finally, the respondent must have provided complete information for all questions providing the information necessary for the modeling effort (e.g. providing a home zip code such that distance to the reservoir could be calculated) and satisfied a number of "common sense" rules (e.g. one cannot make more than 92 trips during the 92 day [three month] time period).

Over 100 reservoirs, lakes and rivers were identified as primary or substitute recreation areas for the sites at which survey data were collected. Some of the sites either (a) could not be identified or (b) were mentioned by too few people to be included in the model. Analysis of the data and consultation with TVA's lead recreation specialist indicated that a 39-site, nine-region model was adequate to model recreation both inside and outside the TVA region (Table 17.1). Regions included TVA's seven power service areas (Tri-Cities, Knoxville, Chattanooga, Alabama, Nashville, Western and Mississippi) as well as two other regions, the North Carolina non-Power Service Area, and the north Georgia region. The North Carolina non-PSA region includes a portion of the TVA watershed, but is a region to which TVA supplies no electrical power. The northern Georgia region includes counties that TVA excludes from its Chattanooga region. This region was defined solely for purposes of this research because it includes important substitute sites outside of TVA's watershed or power regions. It should be noted that some of the 39 sites represent a combination of a number of nearby water projects (e.g. the Bear River and Cedar Creek projects in Northern Alabama).

All data, unless noted below, come from the intercept survey or information provided by TVA personnel or documents. At the site choice level, site attributes include distance from a respondent's origin zip code area, the number of boat

Table 17.1 Region/site nests

Region	Sites	Region	Sites
Tri-Cities		*Nashville*	
	Boone		Barkley
	South Holston		Dale Hollow
	Watauga		Old Hickory
Knoxville			Percy Priest
	Cherokee		East side of Kentucky Lake
	Douglas	*Western*	
	Fort Loudon		Beech/Cedar/Pin Oak
	Melton Hill		Mississippi River
	Norris		Reelfoot
	Tellico		West side of Kentucky Lake
Chattanooga		*Mississippi*	
	Burton/Rabun		Bay Springs
	Carters		Enid/Sardis
	Chatuge	*North Carolina (non-PSA)*	
	Chickamauga		Fontana
	Hiwassee		Santeelah/Nantahala
	Nottely	*North Georgia*	
	Blue Ridge		Allatoona
	Ocoee		Savannah COE Lakes
	Watts Bar		Sidney Lanier
Alabama			
	Bear/Cedar Creek		
	Guntersville		
	Wheeler		
	Wilson		
	Pickwick		

ramps and campgrounds, the location and type of reservoir. Travel distance was calculated from the centroid of the origin zip code to the dam location using the USDA Economic Research Service product ZIPFIP, where a destination point for combined sites was selected on the basis of the road network in the area of the combined site. Boat ramps and campgrounds were calculated using the state-level Gazetteers as published by DeLorme, Inc., Yarmouth, Maine. The location and type of reservoir (urban, rural or remote; mainstem storage, tributary storage or run-of-river) was determined from TVA documents. Non-TVA water projects were classified based on similarity to TVA water projects. Regional climate characteristics were collected from AccuWeather.com for major cities within each region. Regional areas covered by water were collected from county-level Gazetteer files maintained by the U.S. Bureau of Census. Table 17.2 shows the sample statistics for regional data used in our model.

Empirical results

The model is based on a sample size of 2507. The number of observations is roughly double the number of respondents providing complete information. The majority of the sample reported at least one trip under baseline conditions and at least one trip under alternative conditions, so that the observation appears twice in the data set. A small portion of the sample reported making a trip under baseline conditions but no trips under alternative conditions (or vice versa); an observation of this type appears only once.

Table 17.3 shows the model parameters for the two-stage RP-SP recreation demand model. The top portion shows the nested logit site/region-choice model, whereas the bottom portion shows the Poisson total trips model. Nearly all parameters are of the expected sign and are statistically significant. Exceptions include *Campgrounds* and *Mean August Precipitation* in the site/region-choice portion of the model (unexpected signs) and *Angler* in the Total Trips model (statistically insignificant).

The two parameters of interest are the deviations in Labor Day and October 1 water elevations. Both signs are positive and statistically significant, indicating that, in general, higher water elevations increase the probability that a site will be visited. The absolute values of the two parameters suggest that a larger response is elicited for the higher elevations through Labor Day than for the higher elevations through October 1. This is makes good sense for two reasons. First, higher water levels through Labor Day also imply higher water levels through October 1 because the unrestricted drawdown begins at a later date. Second, one might expect that higher water levels are more important prior to Labor Day due to factors not in the model such as the school year for those with children, as well as the traditional Labor Day end to the summer. Overall, the models are each statistically significant. The chi-square values reported for each of the first-stage and second-stage models test the hypothesis that all parameters in the model are jointly equal to zero. The values reported in Table 17.3 show that each hypothesis is soundly rejected.

Table 17.2 Regional data

Region (number of sites)	August temperature (mean degrees F)	August precipitation (mean inches)	Area covered by water (%)	Boat ramps (mean)	Campgrounds (mean)	Labor Day water deviation (mean feet)[1]	October 1 water deviation (mean feet)[1]
Tri-Cities (3)	72.8	3.00	1.24	13.0	1.0	4.7	9.0
Knoxville (6)	76.9	2.89	3.34	29.0	2.2	3.3	7.8
Chattanooga (9)	78.5	3.59	2.39	15.1	4.1	2.6	4.9
Alabama(5)	78.6	3.32	3.88	18.6	2.6	0.6	0.9
Nashville (5)	78.0	3.28	1.78	44.2	9.2	0.6	0.6
Western (4)	78.8	2.88	2.82	27.7	5.0	0.8	0.8
Mississippi (2)	79.6	2.67	1.34	18.5	8.0	0.0	0.0
NC Non-PSA (2)	71.8	4.30	0.85	4.0	3.0	10.5	17.0
North GA/SC (3)	78.1	4.14	2.34	58.0	12.3	0.0	0.0

Note
1 As measured using the stated preference scenarios of Figure 17.3.

Table 17.3 Revealed and stated preference recreation demand model (2507 observations)

Two-Level Nested Site Choice Model
39 Sites, 9 Regions

Site Choice Stage	beta	p-value
Distance	−6.14866	<0.01
Ramps*UseBoat	0.12781	<0.01
Campgrounds	−0.07744	<0.01
Tributary	1.94403	<0.01
Mainstem	2.73044	<0.01
Urban	−2.40403	<0.01
Deviation from median Labor Day Water Elevation	0.07870	<0.01
Deviation from median October 1 Water Elevation	0.00865	<0.01
Region choice	*beta*	*p-value*
Mean August temperature	0.20664	<0.01
Mean August precipitation	0.59385	<0.01
% of regional area in water	0.73696	<0.01
Inclusive value from site choice	0.95518	<0.01
Chi-square (all beta=0)	658,921	–
Second stage – Trips Model		
Poisson (Negative Binomial)	*beta*	*p-value*
Intercept	0.75945	<0.01
Inc. val. from nested logit	0.07850	<0.01
Angler	0.02491	<0.64
Boater	−0.15675	<0.01
Tailwater user	0.21985	<0.01
Tailwater angler	−0.31382	<0.01
Female	−0.10045	<0.05
College	−0.10417	<0.05
Age	0.00546	<0.01
Overdispersion parameter	0.89307	<0.01
Chi-Square (all beta=0)	494.36	–

Evaluating alternative water management scenarios

The empirical model was used to evaluate the percentage change in total trips under a variety of water management alternatives. The positive sign on the water elevation variables suggests that, all else equal, regions with reservoirs that have higher elevations relative to the baseline will gain recreation trips, whereas regions with reservoirs that have lower water elevations will lose recreation trips.

By the end of the data collection period, TVA had narrowed its management alternatives from 65 to seven. The seven alternatives are summarized in Table 17.4. In addition to the impacts on recreation, TVA also evaluated each alternative in detail for impacts on navigation, flood control, power generation and economic development, as well as the effects on air resources, climate, water quality, water supply, groundwater resources, aquatic resources, wetlands,

Table 17.4 The seven "final" reservoir operations alternatives

Alternative name	Description
Reservoir recreation A	Increase reservoir recreational opportunities while maintaining a degree of power system reliability
Reservoir recreation B	Increase reservoir recreation opportunities
Summer hydropower	Increase the production of hydropower during the peak summer demand period
Equalized summer/winter flood risk	Seasonally equalize flood risk by adjusting summer and winter elevations
Commercial navigation	Increase the reliability and reduce the cost of commercial navigation on the Tennessee River
Tailwater recreation	Increase tailwater recreational opportunities
Tailwater habitat	Improve conditions in tailwater aquatic habitats

aquatic plants, terrestrial ecology, invasive species, mosquito control, threatened and endangered species, ecologically significant sites, land use erosion, conversion of farmland, cultural resources, visual resources and dam safety.

We evaluated all seven alternatives with regard to the impact on reservoir and tailwater recreation. For illustrative purposes we focus on reservoir recreation for a subset of these alternatives, namely, "Reservoir recreation B," "Summer hydropower," and an eighth alternative, a "Blended alternative" of the seven final candidates (the "Blend" was eventually chosen as the preferred management alternative). The Reservoir recreation B alternative attempts to maximize reservoir recreation benefits and satisfies other TVA obligations (such as maintaining a navigable channel) at only minimal levels. As such, reservoir water levels are held high for much longer periods. At Cherokee Lake, the Labor Day elevation would be approximately 1071 feet, some 22 feet higher than the water level under current conditions (1049 feet). The October 1 elevation would be about 1066 feet, or 23 feet above the current management target (1043 feet).

The "Summer hydropower" alternative was designed to maximize the value of hydropower generation by drawing down tributary and mainstem storage projects more aggressively during the months of August and September. For Cherokee Lake this would mean a Labor Day elevation 2 feet lower than the management policy in effect at the time of the study (1047 feet rather than 1049 feet), and an additional foot lower than the October 1 elevation (1042 feet instead of 1043 feet). The alternative eventually selected, the so-called "Blended" alternative, was designed after a thorough review of the effects of the original seven final alternatives. Under this alternative, most TVA reservoirs storage projects were drained more slowly relative to the guideline in place at the time of the survey. Cherokee Lake would have a Labor Day elevation of about 1061 feet and an October 1 elevation of about 1054 (some 12 feet and 11 feet higher, respectively, on Labor Day and October 1). Figure 17.3 illustrates the guide curve for Cherokee Lake under the preferred Blended alternative relative to the median baseline elevation in effect for the previous 11 years.

The percentage change in trips is calculated relative to a baseline level of trips. The baseline is calculated by evaluating each observation in the sample at the baseline value for each variable. Thus, the utility index (inclusive value) from the site/region-choice model is based on the calculated distance to each site within a region from the origin zip code for each person, as well as other site and region characteristics. The baseline inclusive value is then used in the total trips model, in combination with individual characteristics, to estimate total baseline trips. Recreationists' responses to changing reservoir management scenarios were estimated by substituting alternative specific values for water level deviations, calculating the new site/region inclusive value, and then estimating the new number of trips. Differences between "new" and baseline trips were converted to percentage form. In addition, region level differences were determined by allocating, for both baseline and "new" total trips, the appropriate region choice probabilities.

Predicted baseline and "new" trips were calculated for 1138 observations reporting at least one trip to a reservoir under either baseline or new conditions. This structure allows for alternative water levels to move people to or from "zero trips." That is, we capture those people who take zero trips under current conditions, but a positive number under alternative conditions, or vice versa. Table 17.5 shows the predicted changes in trips, by region, for reservoir users under the three alternatives.

The results in Table 17.5 show that under the Reservoir Recreation B alternative, a 4.5 percent increase in total trips to reservoirs would occur. However, the increase in trips would not be distributed uniformly across TVA and non-TVA regions. The largest increases in reservoir recreation would occur in

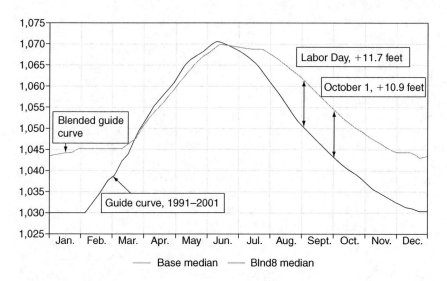

Figure 17.3 Measuring water elevation levels, blended alternative: Cherokee Lake.

Table 17.5 Change in reservoir use under three alternatives (%)

	Reservoir recreation B	Summer hydropower	Preferred "blended" alternative
All regions	4.50	–1.76	2.08
Tri-Cities	–2.40	6.83	1.28
Knoxville	14.93	–6.52	6.51
Chattanooga	6.79	–5.29	2.10
Alabama	1.63	–2.01	2.34
Nashville	1.73	0.01	–2.22
Western	–2.41	2.93	–3.15
Mississippi	–5.71	6.06	–5.89
North Carolina, non PSA	40.67	–3.63	20.71
North Georgia	–20.20	12.08	–8.97

regions with higher water elevations (the tributary regions of Knoxville, Chattanooga and North Carolina non-PSA), although the Tri-cities region would see a drop-off in visitation. Despite maintaining higher elevations than under baseline conditions, the Tri-cities region loses visitation because of substitution effects (more people stay in the Knoxville region under the alternative than under baseline conditions). Areas with no increase in water elevations (western, Mississippi and north Georgia) would experience fewer recreational visits, again due to substitution effects.

Under the "Summer hydropower" alternative, the reservoirs in the Knoxville, Chattanooga and North Carolina non-PSA regions are aggressively drained to produce hydropower. Drawdown on the two most popular of the three upstream Tri-cities reservoirs is delayed a bit under this alternative, allowing this region to benefit as people move substitute recreation to this region during the month of August. The substitution effects also benefit regions with reservoirs that do not have large drawdowns (i.e. those with more "run-of-river"projects) or have projects operated by entities other than TVA (e.g. the north Georgia region is home to many US Army Corps of Engineers projects).

Finally, the Blended alternative maintains the same or higher elevations on all TVA projects in the model. As such, regions composed exclusively of TVA projects, such as the Tri-cities and Knoxville regions, gain visitation, whereas regions that have many projects operated by other entities (e.g. north Georgia) lose visitation due to regional substitution. The estimate of 2–3 percent increase in trips under the Labor Day scenario compares well with the estimate by Jakus *et al.* (2000) in which higher water levels on east Tennessee reservoirs through August 31 were estimated to result in a 3.5 percent increase in trips by anglers.

Summary and conclusions

In this study, revealed preference (RP) and stated preference (SP) data were combined in a RP-SP recreation demand model to estimate the relationships between the quantity of recreation trips made to Tennessee Valley Authority (TVA) reservoirs and site characteristics focusing on reservoir water levels. The model proved to be an effective tool for assessing how recreational behavior and trips are likely to change with fluctuating water levels under different reservoir management alternatives. This information was used by the TVA along with other analyses of the environmental, social and economic impacts of reservoir management alternatives to develop a "preferred alternative" which was eventually approved by the TVA Board of Directors to guide future TVA reservoir operations. The "preferred alternative" blends and balances water allocation to support recreation during the summer months (June 1 through Labor Day) while releasing enough water from reservoirs to meet required "minimum flows" needed to support downstream benefits. Thus, this is a case where we can track how preference data for environmental evaluation was actually used in the policy-decision process and what outcomes resulted.

The use of the model in this application was especially effective because during the survey design and data collection phase of this project, the TVA had not yet identified the specific reservoir management alternatives to be evaluated. Thus, we needed to estimate a flexible preference model linking recreation trip behavior (e.g. quantity of recreation trips taken to a reservoir) with general site characteristics including reservoir water levels. The combined RP-SP recreation demand model we estimated is a tool well-suited to this task. Armed with the estimated model, we were able to conduct *ex post* policy analysis for the TVA needed to complete the final environmental impact statement. This *ex post* policy analysis consisted of the TVA engineers and planners providing us with data on how proposed reservoir management alternatives were projected to affect reservoir water levels. We then used this information and our estimated RP-SP recreation demand model to project changes in quantity of recreation trips under different management alternatives.

In our experience working with natural resource and environmental agencies, it is often the case that agencies do not have crisply defined a priori management policies or alternatives. In these cases they look toward economists to provide flexible environmental preference assessment tools which can be applied in *ex post* "what if" policy analysis. In studies of natural resource and environmental preferences, a major reason why policy makers and managers are often unable to identify specific policy options or management alternatives prior to data collection and model estimation is the high degree of inherent uncertainty. How the natural environment will respond to policy and management changes, and what policy and management change may be feasible given budget and political realities, may simply not be known in advance of data collection and model estimation.

As natural resource and environmental problems become even more complex and subject to even more uncertainty (e.g. think about problems and issues related to global climate which may take decades or centuries to play out), the need for flexible, environmental preference tools is likely to increase. This need probably cannot be met through "natural experiment" and revealed preference approaches alone since some environmental changes and human responses to these changes have yet to happen and be observed (again, think about global climate change). A major advantage of stated preference approaches is that environmental changes that have not yet happened can be posed in a survey and we can observe people's stated responses to these changes. Although RP and SP models can be estimated alone, combining RP and SP data into a single model may provide a more robust and useful tool for *ex post* policy analysis as demonstrated in this chapter. Thus, we encourage further research and development of these combined models with applications to the many and varied natural resource and environmental problems and challenges facing us today and in the future.

References

Bergstrom, J.C., J.H. Dorfman and J.B. Loomis (2004) Estuary management and recreational fishing benefits, *Coastal Management*, 32(4): 417–432.

Betz C.J., J.C. Bergstrom and J.M. Bowker (2003) A contingent trip model for estimating rail-trail demand, *Journal of Environmental Planning and Management*, 46(1): 79–96.

Cameron, T.A., W.D. Shaw, S.E. Ragland, J.M. Callaway and S. Keefe (1996) Using actual and contingent behavior data with differing levels of time aggregation to model recreation demand, *Journal of Agricultural and Resource Economics*, 21(1): 130–149.

Cordell, H.K. and J.C. Bergstrom (1993) Comparison of recreation use values among alternative reservoir water level management scenarios, *Water Resources Research*, 29(2): 247–258.

Eiswerth, M.E., J. Englin, E. Fadali and W.D. Shaw (2000) The value of water levels in water-based recreation: A pooled revealed preference/contingent behavior model, *Water Resources Research*, 36(4): 1079–1086.

Hausman, J.A., G.K. Leonard and D. McFadden (1995) A utility-consistent, combined discrete choice and count model: Assessing recreational losses due to natural resource damage, *Journal of Public Economics*, 56(1): 1–30.

Jakus, P.M., P. Dowell and M.N. Murray (2000) The effect of fluctuating water levels on reservoir fishing, *Journal of Agricultural and Resource Economics*, 25(2): 520–532.

Loomis, J. B. (1993) An investigation into the reliability of intended visitation behavior, *Environmental and Resource Economics*, 3(2): 25–33.

Morey, E.R. (1999) Two RUMs uncloaked: Nested-logit models of site-choice and nested-logit models of participation and site choice, in J.A. Herriges and C.L. Kling (eds.), *Valuing Recreation and the Environment*, Chapter 3, Northampton, MA: Edward Elgar.

Parsons, G.R. (2003) The travel cost method, in P.A. Champ, K.J. Boyle and T.C. Brown (eds.), *A Primer on Nonmarket Valuation*, Chapter 9, Dordrecht: Kluwer Academic Publishers.

Parsons, G.R., P.M. Jakus and T. Thomasi (1999) A comparison of welfare estimates from four models for linking seasonal recreational trips to multinomial logit models of site choice, *Journal of Environmental Economics and Management*, 38(2): 143–157.

Teasley, R.J., J.C. Bergstrom and H.K. Cordell (1994) Estimating revenue-capture potential associated with public area recreation, *Journal of Agricultural and Resource Economics*, 19(1): 89–101.

TVA (Tennessee Valley Authority) (2004) *Programmatic Environmental Impact State-ment: Tennessee Valley Authority Reservoir Operations Study*, Knoxville, TN, online, available at: www.tva.gov/environment/reports/ros_eis/ros_rod.pdf [accessed May 20, 2010].

TVA (Tennessee Valley Authority) (2010) *Valley Facts: A Guide to the Tennessee Valley Authority*, Chattanooga, TN, online, available at: www.tva.gov/foia/ foia_guide.htm [accessed May 20, 2010].

18 Estimating the nonmarket value of green technologies using partial data enrichment techniques

Brett R. Gelso

Introduction

Many cities throughout the United States currently face important water management issues. Among the most prominent of these issues is the control of storm water runoff from urban and nearby agricultural areas, which potentially contaminates water bodies and contributes to the risk of property damage from flooding. As an alternative to managing water flow with traditional technologies, civil engineers and urban planners are becoming increasingly interested in "green technologies." Examples of these technologies, those that will both prevent flooding and mediate contamination before runoff enters water bodies, are planting trees in strategic locations and constructing wetlands. Green technologies may better be viewed as restoring natural water control methods, since urban growth replaces vegetation with unnatural impervious surfaces such as buildings and pavement.

Recent literature has suggested that there needs to be a greater empirical basis to estimate the benefits from scenery, wildlife, and the social values associated with urban trees. Gelso (2002) developed a cost-minimization model that chose the optimal combination of traditional facilities, urban trees, and restored wetlands, where the non-water benefits of green technologies are taken explicitly into account. Based on likely parameter values for the city of Topeka, numerical simulations of this model suggested that green technologies may be a cost-effective way to manage urban runoff. Yet, the results were sensitive to unquantified external benefits.

Although revealed preference hedonic methods may be used to estimate how much a resident will pay for scenery provided from residential trees, some research, such as Earnhart (2001), has suggested that a combination of revealed and stated preference methods will more accurately account for the amenity benefits from urban trees in residential neighborhoods.

As noted repeatedly in this book, combining revealed preference (RP) and stated preference (SP) methods may ameliorate respective weaknesses of each data source, while taking advantage of respective strengths. Such "combined" models often impose the restriction that all model parameters are independent of the data source—i.e. that RP and SP data are generated from the same set of preferences. However, Swait *et al.* (1994) suggested that the hypothesis of parameter equality is not supported in many applications, perhaps due to the known sources of bias inherent in these types of data. In such cases, Louviere *et al.* (2000) investigated "partial data enrichment," when combining RP and SP data, where only certain model parameters are restricted to be equal across data sources and others are data-specific. Combined models offer many attractive economic and econometric properties. By adding stated preference data to observed data, variables may be orthogonal by design, non-use values are included, statistical efficiency may be improved, and stated preference data is at least partially based on observed data. In the current chapter, we develop a combined choice experiment (stated preference), recreational site choice (revealed preference) model to estimate the benefit of green technologies. In the process, we test and correct for scale differences between RP and SP data. Further, we test for structural differences in preference functions between RP and SP data sources and use partial data enrichment techniques to allow for flexibility in the modeling of behavioral functions derived from different data sources.

Theory of the combined methods

To understand the context for our combined choice experiment/site choice model, consider a model of consumer choice based on Louviere *et al.* (2000). Using the well-established Random Utility Model (RUM), we define our utility specifications for the RP and SP data

$$U_i^{RP} = \alpha_i^{RP} + \beta^{RP} X_i^{RP} + \omega Z_i + \varepsilon_i^{RP}, \forall i \in C^{RP} \tag{18.1}$$

$$U_i^{SP} = \alpha_i^{SP} + \beta^{SP} X_i^{SP} + \delta W_i + \varepsilon_i^{SP}, \forall i \in C^{SP} \tag{18.2}$$

where, i is an alternative in choice sets C^{RP} or C^{SP}, α's are alternative specific constants (ASCs), X_i^{RP} and X_i^{SP} are attributes common to both C^{RP} or C^{SP}, Z_i and W_i are unique to C^{RP} or C^{SP}, respectively, and the Greek letters are utility parameters. The deterministic part of utility is a linear function of observable attributes for each data set, but the utility specifications do not need to be identical across data sets. Notice also that the random portion of utility (ε_i^{RP} and ε_i^{SP}) is allowed to differ.

Assuming IID type I extreme value (EV1) error distribution for the RP and SP decision models, with associated scale parameters λ^{RP} and λ^{SP}, the probability person i will pick alternative j with $J = 1, \ldots, n$ alternatives in the choice set of RP or SP data are represented by the multinomial logistic (MNL) probabilities:

$$P_i^{RP} = \frac{\exp\left[\lambda^{RP}\left(\alpha_i^{RP} + \beta^{RP} X_i^{RP} + \omega Z_i\right)\right]}{\sum_{j \in C^{RP}} \exp\left[\lambda^{RP}\left(\alpha_j^{RP} + \beta^{RP} X_j^{RP} + \omega Z_j\right)\right]}, \forall i \in C^{RP} \tag{18.3}$$

$$P_i^{SP} = \frac{\exp\left[\lambda^{SP}\left(\alpha_i^{SP} + \beta^{SP} X_i^{SP} + \omega Z_i\right)\right]}{\sum_{j \in C^{SP}} \exp\left[\lambda^{SP}\left(\alpha_j^{SP} + \beta^{SP} X_j^{SP} + \omega Z_j\right)\right]}, \forall i \in C^{SP} \tag{18.4}$$

Foreshadowing our discussion of the importance of controlling for scale differences between RP and SP data, note that in equations (18.3) and (18.4) that the scale factor is a multiplicand of the utility parameters. In conventional estimation methods, the scale factor is confounded within the utility parameters. The estimated coefficients are actually estimates of $\lambda^{RP}\beta^{RP}$ and $\lambda^{SP}\beta^{RP}$. Hence, if the error variance is not identical across equations, but the preference parameters across data types are identical, the parameter estimates are not identical due to the scale factor.

Scaling parameters are crucial in properly combining the RP and SP choice models. In conventional estimation methods for the MNL model, the scale factor cannot be estimated independently from the slope parameters of the utility function. The estimated parameters in any MNL model are confounded with the scale factor such that $E(\beta) = \lambda\beta$. According to Louviere *et al.* (2000: 142), the scale factor of the EV1 distribution is inversely proportional to its variance, such that $\text{var}(\varepsilon) = \dfrac{\pi^2}{6\lambda^2}$. Thus, for an individual data set where the error variance is assumed to be constant, the parameter identification problem is usually resolved by normalizing the error variance such that $\lambda = 0$ (and, hence, $\text{var}(\varepsilon) = \pi^2/6$). However, this assumption is purely arbitrary.

Fixing λ at any constant value is inappropriate when comparing parameter estimates from different data sets that may have different error variances. If we expect that the variability of agents' choices differs across SP and RP data then the scale factor should be allowed to differ across data sources. If the estimated parameters from these data sets differ, one cannot infer whether the cause is differences in utility coefficients or different scale factors.

To illustrate this point, suppose that conventional methods were used to estimate (18.3) and (18.4) separately, generating slope coefficient vectors $\hat{\beta}^{RP}$ and $\hat{\beta}^{SP}$ respectively. Since the scale factor cannot be independently recovered from these estimations, they are confounded with the true slope coefficients, such that $E(\hat{\beta}^{RP}) = \lambda^{RP}\beta^{RP}$ and $E(\hat{\beta}^{SP}) = \lambda^{SP}\beta^{SP}$. Even if the deterministic part of the utility functions are the same (i.e. $\beta^{RP} = \beta^{SP} = \beta$), we should still *expect* different parameter estimates if $\lambda^{RP} \neq \lambda^{SP}$. However, the relationship between the parameter estimates can be characterized in this case, which is the basis for testing preference equality. If $\beta^{RP} = \beta^{SP} = \beta$ then $E(\hat{\beta}^{SP}) = \lambda^{SP}\beta$ and $E(\hat{\beta}^{RP}) = \lambda^{RP}\beta$. These conditions imply that $\dfrac{E(\hat{\beta}^{SP})}{E(\hat{\beta}^{RP})} = \dfrac{\lambda^{SP}}{\lambda^{RP}}$, or rearranging, $E(\hat{\beta}^{SP}) = \dfrac{\lambda^{SP}}{\lambda^{SP}} E(\hat{\beta}^{SP})$.

Clearly, similar error variances results in $\hat{\beta}$ closer between data sources (i.e. similar scales imply comparable data sets). If parameter equality does exist between data sets, then a plot of RP parameters against the SP parameters yields a cloud of points passing through the origin with a slope of $\lambda^{SP}/\lambda^{RP}$. To the extent the cloud of points is too dispersed or points lay in quadrants II and IV of the Cartesian graph, the likelihood of preference equality is greatly reduced.

Swait and Louviere (1993) show that only after testing and correcting for different variances in the two data types can one test for whether they originate from the same set of preferences. As Greene (1998: 587) describes,

If the variances are, indeed, the same, then a ratio of any two of them equals 1.0. This provides the basis for a test of equality. When they are not equal, setting the variance in one data set equal to 1.0 and estimating the variance in the other will provide the appropriate scaling parameter needed to validate pooling the two data sets.

This simple scaling procedure has emerged as a required step to test for preference equality in studies that seek to combine RP and SP data.

Data and survey

Data for this analysis is from interviews of 216 random patrons at 16 parks in Topeka, Kansas. Survey questions were designed to identify amenity value of environmental services by identifying the respondent's travel costs and stated choice among Topeka parks.

Since the purpose of this analysis is to combine RP and SP data to value green technologies, the survey instrument used standard on-site choice/travel cost questions to identify observed recreational behavior to Topeka parks, and a complementary choice experiment to elicit hypothetical travel decisions under varying amenity scenarios. To allow for site substitution, we collect information on visits to the observed park choice as well as information on the other parks the respondent chooses to visit. We determine the agent's opportunity cost of leisure time through standard calculations in Fugitt and Wilcox (1999).

In estimation, a large number of possible sites in a choice set render standard models difficult to estimate. Parsons and Kealy (1992) show that relatively small choice sets for each person can be constructed by including the chosen alternative(s) and as few as three randomly drawn rejected alternatives. Our study adopts this approach. In particular, each respondent's choice set contains the parks actually visited plus three additional randomly selected parks.

For eliciting preferences over currently non-existent amenities, we use a hypothetical choice experiment (CE) to mirror the observed travel decision of the respondent. After collecting information on their actual recreation choices, respondents are asked to make hypothetical choices among three parks that vary in five park attributes including the existence of a playground, water feature and garden, athletic field, or high or low tree density. Each respondent faces a choice set of three parks with 2^5 combinations of park amenities. This procedure is repeated three times per person. We use an Orthogonal Main Effects design to reduce the dimensionality of the choice experiment.

Figure 18.1 illustrates the CE experimental design for this analysis. In this example, the respondent is faced with four amenities including a playground, a garden, an athletic field, and a high level of tree density. Water Feature is not explicitly included since the attribute level of this amenity is at its lower level (i.e. = 0).

As mentioned earlier in this analysis, the benefit of stated preference data is that it may be designed to have several desirable statistical qualities such as low

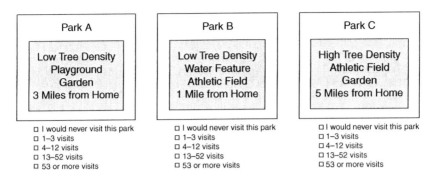

Figure 18.1 Example of intensity of preferences and conjoint experiment.

collinearity and standard errors. Conversely, observed data for environmental explanatory variables are often highly related and therefore collinear. As such, if preference equality exists, the stated preference data may be combined with the observed data to result in parameter estimates that are statistically efficient. Indeed, statistical efficiency is a desirable quality to researchers, as it provides more stable and efficient parameter estimates.

Yet another desirable quality of our conjoint data is the inclusion of intensity of preferences for parks to mirror the observed travel resource allocation. While prior studies have combined travel cost and conjoint data, our study uniquely combines intensity of preferences in both observed and hypothetical choice of Topeka parks.

Econometric analysis

The variables included in the RP and SP models are listed and defined in Table 18.1. In order to identify the demand for park amenities, dummy variables are used for high or low tree density, as well as existence of a water feature, garden, athletic field, and playground. Price is interacted with demographic features of respondents, since price is the only feature that varies among individuals (Earnhart 2001: 19). In instances where there is no universal choice set, Earnhart (2001) also suggested interacting price with socioeconomic characteristics, since socioeconomic characteristics do not change across choice sets per survey respondent. Typically, individual characteristics can enter the choice models with universal choice sets as part of the alternative specific constant (ASC).

All models were estimated by maximum likelihood using LIMDEP Econometric Software Version 7.0. Results for the multinomial logit for the separate and combined models are presented in Table 18.2. We first compare the coefficient estimates of the separate RP and SP choice models. Several coefficients are similar in sign and magnitude, while many coefficients are quite dissimilar in sign and magnitude. The parameters WATER FEATURE, GARDEN,

Table 18.1 Summary statistics and variable descriptions[1]

Variable	Description	Stated	Revealed	Combined
I. Park amenities:				
Athletic field	if present (=1), otherwise (=0)	0.484	0.966	0.580
		(0.499)	(0.182)	(0.493)
Water feature	if present (=1), otherwise (=0)	0.459	0.648	0.497
		(0.499)	(0.478)	(0.500)
Tree density	high (=1), low (=0)	0.496	0.393	0.476
		(0.500)	(0.489)	(0.500)
Garden	if present (=1), otherwise (=0)	0.538	0.637	0.558
		(0.498)	(0.482)	(0.497)
Playground	if present (=1), otherwise (=0)	0.493	0.989	0.592
		(0.500)	(0.106)	(0.491)
II. Demographic characteristics				
Education	years of education	15.131	15.381	15.181
		(2.66)	(2.620)	(2.658)
Sex	gender (1=Male)	0.406	0.358	0.396
		(0.491)	(0.481)	(0.489)
Adults	number of adults	1.920	1.897	1.915
		(0.627)	(0.706)	(0.644)
Children	number of children	1.320	1.225	1.301
		(1.215)	(1.064)	(1.186)
Urban	residential location (1 = Urban)	0.783	0.805	0.787
		(0.412)	(0.396)	(0.409)
Income	dollars of income per annum	51285.71	52681.30	51564.41
		(33785.11)	(33052.56)	(33632.23)
Age	years of age	30.360	30.616	30.411
		(10.059)	(9.310)	(9.911)

III. *Price of resource site and observed park attributes*

Price	price of travel plus opportunity cost of leisure time	8.98 (6.37)	17.26 (16.506)	10.64 (9.89)

IV. *Characteristics Unique to Observed Parks*

Center	presence of community center	—	0.293 (0.456)	0.058 (0.235)
Gage	very large park	—	0.344 (0.475)	0.0686 (0.252)
Small Park	small park	—	0.003 (0.061)	0.0007 (0.027)
Size	size of park in acres	—	202.236 (268.126)	40.385 (144.408)
No. of observations		1050	262	1312

Note
1 Standard deviations are in parentheses.

Table 18.2 Multinomial logit regression results[1,2]

Variable	Stated	Revealed	Combined	Partially combined
I. Park amenities:				
Athletic field	0.422***	—	0.722***	0.212_{SP}***
	(0.018)	(0.059)	(0.008)	(0.008)
Water feature	0.374***	0.0924*	0.603***	0.184_{SP}***
	(0.018)	(0.055)	(0.033)	(0.008)
Tree density	0.176***	−0.345***	0.328***	0.079_{SP}***
	(0.195)	(0.066)	(0.036)	(0.009)
Garden	0.224***	0.055	0.225***	0.111_{SP}***
	(0.018)	(0.080)	(0.037)	(0.009)
Playground	0.550***	3.750***	1.412***	0.271_{SP}***
	(0.017)	(0.305)	(0.040)	(0.008)
II. Price and demographic characteristics interacted with price:				
Price	−0.009	−0.096***	−0.076***	-0.112_{C}***
	(0.050)	(0.022)	(0.02)	(0.013)
Education	−0.022***	0.009***	0.007***	0.010_{RP}***
	(0.003)	(0.001)	(0.001)	(0.0005)
Sex	0.028**	−0.074***	−0.065***	-0.065_{RP}***
	(0.015)	(0.006)	(0.006)	(0.005)
Adults	0.105***	−0.0004	0.007**	0.043_{SP}***
	(0.011)	(0.004)	(0.006)	(0.004)
Children	−0.0003	0.021***	0.017***	0.015_{RP}***
	(0.005)	(0.002)	(0.004)	(0.002)
Urban	−0.004	−0.065***	−0.059***	-0.037_{C}***
	(0.017)	(0.008)	(0.002)	(0.005)
Income	−0.01E-05	−0.581E-06***	−0.556E-06***	$-0.511E\text{-}06_{C}$***
	(0.02 E-05)	(0.830E-07)	(0.824E-07)	(0.642E-07)
Age	−0.08E-02	0.002***	0.001***	0.0007_{C}***
	(0.07E-02)	(0.0003)	(0.0003)	(0.0002)

III. Characteristics unique to observed parks

Size	—	0.0003***	0.0002***	0.0009$_{RP}$***
		(0.614E-04)	(0.572E-04)	(0.523E-04)
Center	—	-0.351***	0.258***	-0.038$_{RP}$
		(0.051)	(0.041)	(0.301)
Gage	—	0.840***	0.093**	0.896$_{RP}$***
		(0.075)	(0.047)	(0.029)
Small park	—	-1.913***	-1.582***	-1.723$_{RP}$***
		(0.074)	(0.071)	(0.069)
Number of observations	350	167	517	517
Beginning LL	-23345.51	-21150.48	-67841.51	-67841.51
Ending LL	-22117.14	-13615.72	-36427.52	-36286.66
McFadden's ρ^2	0.05262	0.35625	0.46305	0.46513
Estimated scale factor λ			0.40	2.00
Test statistic for data pooling:			1389.32	43.15
$2[(L^{RP}+L^{SP}]-L^{Joint}]\sim\chi\beta_1^2$			Accept=No	Accept=No

Note
1 *90% statistical significance, **95% statistical significance, ***99% statistical significance.
2 Standard errors are in parentheses.

PLAYGROUND, URBAN, INCOME, and PRICE have the same sign in both models. However, the coefficients for TREE DENSITY, EDUCATION, SEX, ADULTS, CHILDREN, and AGE yielded opposite signs. Also, even though PLAYGROUND is the same sign in RP and SP results, the magnitude of the coefficient is much larger in the RP model than the SP model. Given that there was very little statistical variation in the RP data for PLAYGROUND, it is hypothesized that this lack of variation resulted in a sign reversal. In terms of data enrichment, this data suggests that some, but not all utility parameters are comparable between revealed and stated preference models.

Results for the combined SP and RP model are presented in Table 18.2. All coefficient estimates are significant at the 0.01 level. The pseudo r-square indicates a very high goodness of fit for the model. Perhaps the most interesting interpretation of model results is the estimated value of the scale factor of 0.40, indicating that the error variance in the RP data is about 16 percent of that of the SP data *if* preference equality exists. In other words, if preference equality exists, then the parameter estimates must be rescaled for direct comparison. Using a standard likelihood ratio test, we reject the null hypothesis of parameter equality between the RP and SP models. However, this parameter inequality could be caused by differences in preference parameters, differences in scale, or both.

To test the hypothesis of preference parameter equality between RP and SP parameters, we use the visual test first used by Swait and Louviere (1993). In order to test for preference equality, we are testing $\lambda^{RP}\beta^{RP} = \lambda^{SP}\beta^{SP}$. Rearranging this expression, we may obtain the expression $\beta^{RP} = \lambda^{SP}/\lambda^{RP}(\beta^{SP})$, where the slope of this function is $\lambda^{SP}/\lambda^{RP}$. Using the estimated coefficients for RP and SP data from Table 18.1, the RP coefficients are plotted against the SP coefficients. According to Louviere *et al.* (2000: 235), estimates in quadrants I and III along the line through the origin with the slope $= \lambda^{SP}/\lambda^{RP}$ is preliminary evidence of preference equality across respective utility sets. However, since relaxing the IID/EV1 assumption results in parameter estimates that are a multiplicand of the scale factor such that $\lambda^{RP}\beta^{RP} = \lambda^{SP}\beta^{SP}$, the plot only contains information regarding the equality of utility parameters and entirely ignores error variance.

Figure 18.2 illustrates the visual test for preference equality across RP and SP preference data. While the parameters PRICE, INCOME, URBAN, WATER FEATURE, GARDEN, and TREE DENSITY are in quadrants I and III, as would be expected if preferences were equal across data sources, the coefficients for TREE DENSITY, EDUCATION, SEX, ADULTS, CHILDREN, and AGE are not in expected regions. Also, PLAYGROUND exists far outside the cloud of points in quadrants I and III. Louviere *et al.* (2000) indicates that this plot pattern suggests preference parameter inequality across data sources. However, it may be the useful to pursue "partial data enrichment" such that only particular parameters reflect the same utility preferences in RP and SP preference data.

Louviere *et al.* (2000) suggest that removing certain parameters from the combined model may result in acceptance of the hypothesis of data enrichment. If coefficients in the visual test are in quadrants II and IV, or are far away from the cloud of points generated by other parameters, the authors recommended removing such

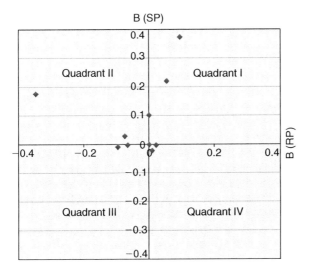

Figure 18.2 Visual test for the preference equality of estimated coefficients.

parameters from the joint model. Louviere *et al.* (2000) suggested that the process of choosing which variables to include in the partially enriched model depends on the experience of the researcher and economic theory. The authors also indicate that few studies have addressed which variables to include in partially enriched models, and that this is a subject that needs to be addressed in future research.

In our partially enriched model, we combine explanatory variables with the same sign and magnitude, but deleted variables in quadrants II and IV with unexpected signs and magnitudes. The RP travel cost data behaved much better than the SP data. In most cases, coefficient estimates were the expected sign and were consistent with economic theory. Hence, the variables EDUCATION, SEX, and CHILDREN were included in the RP portion of the combined model. Also, the travel cost data is thought to have popular playgrounds. It is thought that the coefficient is overstated in the RP data. In our partially combined model the utility coefficients for URBAN, INCOME, AGE, and PRICE were combined since separate models suggested these parameters were the same in sign as well as magnitude. Results for the partially combined model are presented in the fourth column of Table 18.2. Even in the case of partial enrichment the hypothesis of data enrichment is rejected at the 1 percent level of significance, suggesting the utility functions in the empirical model are quite dissimilar.

Welfare analysis

The Compensating Variation (CV) of income is estimated for the Green Technologies at Topeka parks. Table 18.3 presents the welfare effects for the separate and combined models. The CV for the MNL model of choice is defined as:

Table 18.3 Per trip welfare calculations ($)

Natural feature	Stated	Revealed	Combined	Partially combined
Water feature	21.57	0.59	4.55	0.94
Tree density	9.46	−2.53	2.56	0.42

$$CV = \frac{-1}{\mu}\left[\ln \sum_{i=1}^{n} e^{V_i^0} - \ln \sum_{i=1}^{n} e^{V_i^1}\right] \tag{18.5}$$

where μ is the marginal utility of income, the price coefficient from the esti-mated regression. Equation 18.5 can be interpreted as how much an individual is willing to pay for a higher level of environmental quality, which is represented as the difference in the initial condition V_I^0 and the new condition V_I^1.

In general, reasonable welfare estimates were obtained from the RUM. However, the SP data produced an unexpected large CV for both WATER FEATURE and TREE DENSITY. Such overstatement of willingness-to-pay in SP surveys is consistent with prior research, since respondents are not bound by a budget constraint and may overstate or understate true preferences. The sign reversal for TREE DENSITY (i.e. $CV < 0$) in the RP model indicates that indi-viduals obtained disutility of income from the presence of high TREE DENSITY. However, this type of problem commonly occurs in RP data due to lack of variation in data (Louviere *et al.* 2000). Such results illustrate the useful-ness of the combined models. Even though we fail to reject the hypothesis of data enrichment in the combined and partially combined models, results suggest that welfare calculations are more reasonable compared to separate SP and RP models.

Conclusions

In this study, our primary benefit from the pooled models is thought to be the improvement of statistical efficiency and robustness of regression results. Fur-thermore, economic theory tells us that the RP data should have the same under-lying utility sets as the SP data (Cameron 1992). However, examining the results of our data may suggest that the connection between economic theory and empirical studies is tenuous at best.

Due to the numerous forms of bias, it is clearly challenging to combine RP and SP data for environmental goods. The rejection of data enrichment in this chapter may serve to highlight the obvious demands of data combination and joint estimation. From economic theory it is understood that RP and SP have an identical underlying set of utility preferences. However, in practice, the nexus between economic theory and applied analysis is indeed less transparent.

References

Cameron, T. (1992) "Combining contingent valuation and travel cost data for the valuation of nonmarket goods," *Land Economics*. 68(3): 302–17.

Earnhart, D. (2001) "Combining revealed and stated preference methods to value environmental amenities at residential locations," *Land Economics*, 77(1): 12–29.

Fugitt, D. and S. Wilcox (1999) *Cost-Benefit Analysis for Public Sector Decision Makers*, London: Quorium Books.

Gelso, B. (2002) *Combining Revealed and Stated Preference Data to Estimate the Nonmarket Value of Green Technologies*, doctoral thesis, Manhattan, KS: Kansas State University Department of Agricultural Economics.

Greene, W. (1998) *Limdep User's Manual: Version 7.0.*, Plainview, NY: Econometric Software, Inc.

Louviere, J.J., D.A. Hensher, and J. Swait (2000) *Stated Choice Methods*, New York: Cambridge University Press.

Parsons, G. and M. Kealy (1992) "Randomly drawn opportunity sets in a random utility model of lake recreation," *Land Economics*, 68(1): 93–106.

Swait, J. and J. Louviere (1993) "The role of scale parameter estimation in the estimation and comparison of multinomial logit models," *Journal of Marketing Research*, 30: 304–314.

Swait, J., J. Louviere, and M. Williams (1994) "A sequential approach to exploiting the combined strengths of SP and RP data: Application to freight shipper choice," *Transportation*, 21(2): 135–52.

Part V
Benefit transfer

19 Are benefit transfers using a joint revealed and stated preference model more accurate than revealed and stated preference data alone?

Juan Marcos González-Sepúlveda and
John B. Loomis

Introduction

Benefit transfer refers to the application of existing information and knowledge to new contexts. It is the adaptation of economic information derived from a prior "study site" with certain resource and policy conditions and applied to a "policy site" where no data is available. Economists often lack the information for the policy site because of budget constraints, time limitations or low expected resource impacts. In this scenario, and in the need to evaluate the effect that a particular action may have, benefit transfers become a second best approach to consider economic effects that would otherwise not be accounted for (Rosenberger and Loomis 2001).

There are two broad types of transfers: value transfers and function transfers. In the first one a single benefit estimate is transferred to the policy site. This measure could be a single point estimate from a similar study site. In recreation, these single values are most often obtained from travel cost models (TCM) and/ or contingent valuation methods (CVM). On the other hand, a function transfer is to derive a benefit or demand function from the study site to be used to predict benefits and/or site visitation by inserting the particular characteristics of the policy site into the estimated function.

Single value estimates and visitation estimates for benefit transfers are commonly obtained from different sources. Even when these estimates are obtained from the same data source, they are often not derived consistently in a unified utility theoretic framework. We address this shortcoming by using a consistent joint estimation procedure that makes use of all the information available for the estimation of single values by combining CVM and TCM. The joint estimation procedure permits consistent transfer to predict both recreation demand and seasonal/annual benefits for a policy site. This is of particular interest when the policy site is newly available to the public at which neither past use nor per-trip benefit is known.

Joint estimation

Joint estimation of TCM and CVM has become increasingly common in recent years. Many attempts have been made to complement the information provided by these two valuation methods and deal with the shortcomings that each one has as well as expanding the values that they were meant to capture (Cameron 1992; Adamowicz *et al.* 1994; Englin and Cameron 1996; McConnell *et al.* 1999; Azevedo *et al.* 2003; Eom and Larson 2006).

We combine the two valuation methods updating the work by Cameron (1992) who estimates a joint set of parameters by assuming a quadratic utility function that is dependent on two goods, a numeraire good and trips to a site. As in Cameron, we use data gathered from a dichotomous choice contingent behavior question that is answered affirmatively if the difference between the utility obtained from the proposed scenario is larger than the alternative. The change between the scenarios in this application is strictly linked to an increase in the cost per visit at the current number of trips or avoiding the increase entirely by reducing the number of trips taken. A semi-log specification typical of count data models is used as the demand for trips.

Since the trip demand function obtained through the TCM is the result of an optimization problem that relates back to the individual's utility function, we can convert the utility differential, typically estimated through the CVM, into an indirect utility differential by substituting the travel cost function for trip demand into the utility functions. The challenge however, is that the researcher has to make sure that the utility function and the trip demand function are theoretically connected. In Cameron's case, she chooses a somewhat arbitrary utility function and derives the appropriate specification for trip demand. However, this process results in an uncommon, although consistent, trip demand function rarely used by economists. This paper approaches the same issue in a slightly different, yet meaningful, manner. Since most current TCM studies make use of count data models for the estimation of the trip demand function, we start from a traditional semi-logarithmic trip demand function. We then work back to a consistent utility function that we can use to determine the utility differentials for the CVM estimation process. This ensures that we can estimate a demand function that is consistent with the underlying preferences stated through a dichotomous choice question and with the count data nature of trip demand.

Generating a joint model framework has important consequences. As suggested by Azevedo *et al.* (2003), a joint model allows us to take advantage of each data type's strength without imposing preconceived notions regarding the superiority of one type of data over the other. In addition, combining a travel cost and a dichotomous choice model in a single framework disciplined by a common utility framework ensures that we have a single welfare measure for the site of interest. This is of particular interest when we find apparent significant differences across the models and the results have policy implications.

Another important gain from combining the two valuation methods has to do with efficiency. The additional information, otherwise incorporated through a panel setup of the data, is expected to considerably reduce the variability of parameter estimates. This reduction stems from the idea that we now incorporate information on the intensive or "horizontal" margin of the demand for trips and the extensive or "vertical" margin of participation with an increase in the price.

In other words, we use the horizontal distance from the origin to the observed number of trips given a fixed price and the extent to which users will remain users as we increase the price they face.

To test for the gains in efficiency in the transfer of non-market values and demand functions we estimate a separate regression for each model and a joint estimation with the consistent parameter restrictions. We then estimate the same models for a policy site in the vicinity of the study sites. The policy site is visited by the same population and offer services more or less equal to the study sites. After obtaining the estimates for the policy site we use a convolutions method proposed by Poe *et al.* (2005) to empirically evaluate any statistical difference between the values estimated by our separate and joint models in the study site and the ones obtained from the policy site. We specifically compare the WTP values, expected trip demand and seasonal benefits with the mean characteristic levels of the policy sites. Calculating and comparing confidence intervals will allow us to evaluate any improvement in efficiency as well as the accuracy of the estimates of WTP for the policy site obtained from the study site.

In the next sections we present the derivation of this consistent estimation process and the implied parameter restrictions across the models. After that, we present an empirical application of the model and the results obtained from it. Finally, we present some conclusions about the effectiveness of the joint estimation for benefit transfer.

Deriving the utility framework

We start by explaining the theoretical underpinnings of the optimization process that relates the two data sources we use here. Economic theory establishes that individuals have a set of preferences that can be represented with a utility function. This utility function depends on the consumption of different goods and services given their relative prices and available income. In the simple scenario we explore, this utility function U is simply dependent upon the consumption of two goods, a numeraire labeled z and trips to the site of interest q while conditioned on the associated prices (p_z, p_q) and income (Y).

$$U = f\left(z, q \mid p_z, p_q, Y\right) \tag{19.1}$$

Individuals maximize this function by choosing a level of z and q while satisfying that the amount paid for both goods does not exceed their available income.

From this optimization process one can derive the optimal level of (Marshallian) trips demanded, given the full prices and income faced. In the case of the count data models this solution has a semi-logarithmic form:

$$q(M, G, Y) = \exp\left(\alpha + \beta M + \gamma G + \delta Y\right) \tag{19.2}$$

where M is the full price or marginal cost per visit, G represents a set of site characteristics, Y is full income and q is the number of trips to the sites of interest.

292 J.M. González-Sepúlveda and J.B. Loomis

An alternative way to solve the same optimization problem is to fix the utility level and determine the consumption that would reach that fixed level while minimizing the associated expenses. In this setup we obtain an expenditure function which is related to the Marshallian demand function through Shephard's Lemma. Such a relationship allows us to get from the count data Marshallian demand function expressed above to the appropriate expenditure function and, from there, to the consistent indirect and regular utility functions.

Now, looking at our particular application, it is important to mention that the information is assumed to be obtained from the CVM question whether a visitor would have taken the last trip to a site if the marginal price of that visit were increased. This means that: (1) the surveyed individuals must have at least one trip to the site of interest, (2) we do not alter any of the site characteristics for the dichotomous choice question and (3) only the marginal price of the last visit is affected by the hypothetical scenario. This defines the way the utility differential is believed to motivate the CVM responses. Although the next paragraphs make use of this particular information to derive consistent utility difference and trip demand function, we show that this is only a special case that can be extended to all hypothetical changes in price with an associated loss of access or trips taken.

In the context of our particular application, visitors would only say yes if:

$$\Delta U = \max_{q} U\left(Y - M\left(q-1\right) - \left(M + B\right), q\right) - \max_{q} U\left(Y - M\left(q-1\right), \left(q-1\right)\right) > 0$$

(19.3)

where B is the bid increase to marginal cost (tc per visit).

ΔU is the change in the level of utility experienced by visitors. The first term on the right-hand-side of (19.3) is the maximum of utility obtained from consuming optimal q (trips) and the numeraire good given Y, M and B. The price of each of the first $q-1$ trips is M and the price for the current trip is raised to $M+B$. The price of the numeraire is normalized to one so that the consumption of the numeraire is $(Y-M(q-1)-(M+B))$. The second term is the maximum utility from consuming optimal q and the numeraire good given that the price of each trip is M.

The expression (19.3) can be simplified as follows.

$$\Delta U = \max_{q} U\left(Y - Mq + M - M - B, q\right) - \max_{q} U\left(Y - M\left(q-1\right), \left(q-1\right)\right) > 0$$

$$= \max_{q} U\left(Y - Mq - B, q\right) - \max_{q} U\left(Y - M\left(q-1\right), \left(q-1\right)\right) > 0$$

(19.4)

or

$$\Delta V = V\left(Y - B, M, G\right) - V\left(Y, M, G\right) > 0$$

(19.5)

Note that while we restrict $q \geq 1$, this is consistent with the CVM question suggested above, hence, the second term becomes $U(Y-M(q-1), (q-1)) = U(Y-0, 0)$

in the case where q is assumed the lowest possible value. Recall that the dichotomous choice question presented to visitors refers to an *ex post* increase of the price for the current visit.

Economists use count data models to estimate seasonal trip demand functions for recreation purposes because they exhibit desirable properties that match the form of trip demand. These models, typically the Poisson and Negative Binomial models, assume a semi-log function for the mean parameter and make use of travel costs to obtain the needed variation in price. As shown in Eom and Larson (2006), the semi-log demand function that is typically used in the TCM, $q(M, G, Y) = \exp(\alpha + \beta M + \gamma G + \delta Y)$, corresponds to a quasi-expenditure function of the form:

$$\tilde{E}(M, G, c(U)) = \frac{-1}{\delta} \ln\left[\frac{-\delta}{\beta} e^{(\alpha + \beta M + \gamma G)} - \delta c(U)\right] \tag{19.6}$$

where $c(U)$ is a constant of integration. Unlike Eom and Larson, we assume weak complementarity of the site attributes (no non-use value) and set this constant of integration as a utility index $U.$[1] Hence, the associated quasi-indirect utility function can be shown to be:

$$\tilde{V}(M, G, Y) = -\frac{1}{\delta} e^{-\delta Y} - \frac{1}{\beta} e^{(\alpha + \beta M + \gamma G)} \tag{19.7}$$

and the corresponding direct utility function has the following form:

$$U(M, G, Y) = e^{-\delta Y}\left[\frac{-(\beta + \delta q)}{\delta\beta}\right] \tag{19.8}$$

The optimal level of trips chosen, defined as q^*, is estimated through the TCM as $q(M, G, Y) = \exp(\alpha + \beta M + \gamma G + \delta Y)$. As shown in Gonzalez-Sepulveda (2008), the consistent representation of utility difference at q^* is:

$$\Delta\tilde{V} = e^{-\delta Y}\left(e^{\delta B}\xi - \eta\right) \tag{19.9}$$

where $\xi = \left[\dfrac{-(\beta + \delta q^*)}{\delta\beta}\right]$ and $\eta = \left[\dfrac{-(\beta + \delta(q^* - 1))}{\delta\beta}\right]$. Now we have a consistent

definition of the utility function and the demand function used in count data models.

Thus our application is simply a special case of a broader problem where we constrain visitors to lose only their last trip if they do not pay the general increase in the cost of the trip (B). Our results can be easily applied to other dichotomous choice scenarios including the one presented by Cameron (1992) with an update to the count data TCM.

The analytical results in this section will be used to determine the parameter constraints required to consistently and jointly estimate a count data TCM and a dichotomous choice model that follow the scenarios presented above. The next section discusses the statistical considerations in order to jointly estimate the parameters in the utility differential and trip demand functions.

Joint estimation

To jointly estimate TCM and CVM parameters, we employ and modify the joint probability function presented in González-Sepúlveda *et al.* (2008). It combines a negative binomial distribution for the TCM and a probit model for the CVM. The joint distribution is derived by taking advantage of the fact that a joint density can be written as the product of a conditional and a marginal density function. This requires one of the two equations in the model to be conditioned on the other. The requirement is satisfied by the setup we present here where the assumed utility difference is conditional on the number of trips, which is determined by our trip demand function. In Gonzalez-Sepulveda *et al.*, a negative binomial model, corrected for on-site sampling, is used. Minor modification of their model is needed for our case of uncorrected parameter restrictions.[2] From the original form of the joint density function presented in González-Sepúlveda *et al.*, we derive the uncorrected equivalent of the joint distribution function

$$L_i = \left[(\pi_i)^{y_{cvm,i}} (1-\pi)^{1-y_{cvm}} \right] \times \left(\frac{\Gamma(\theta+q_i)}{\Gamma(\theta)\Gamma(q_i+1)} \right) \left(\frac{\theta}{(\lambda_i+\theta)} \right)^{\theta} \left(\frac{\lambda_i}{(\lambda_i+\theta)} \right)^{q_i} \quad (19.10)$$

where $\pi_i = \Phi\left[\left(\frac{\Delta U}{\sigma} + \rho Z_i \right) \middle/ (1-\rho^2)^{0.5} \right]$, $\lambda_i = \exp(\alpha + \beta M + \gamma G + \delta Y)$, $\theta = \frac{\theta_0}{\lambda_i}$,

$Z_i = \left(y_{tcm,i} \quad E(y_{tcm,i}) \right) \middle/ \left(Var(y_{tcm,i}) \right)^{0.5}$, and $E(y_{tcm,i}) = \lambda_i + \theta_0$.

The parameter ρ is the correlation parameter between the two models, σ is the standard error of our probit estimation, and $\Phi(\cdot)$ is the cumulative standard normal distribution function.

Combining data from the CVM and the TCM, coupled with appropriate preference consistency restrictions, the price parameter estimated for the joint model is expected to be more efficient than that same coefficient obtained from separate estimation of the behavioral functions. We would also expect that the point estimates of the WTP from the joint model will make use of the additional information and will have a tighter confidence interval.

To test whether this gain in efficiency translates into an improvement in the process of transferring benefits to a policy site, we examine three measures that are commonly presented in the benefit transfer literature: point estimates of WTP, expected level of visitor use and seasonal benefits. These measures can be derived from individual CVM and TCM, or the proposed complete combinational approach (the joint model). The results from the complete combinatorial approach can be compared to those from the convolutions method proposed by Poe *et al.* (2005). Convolution is a mathematical operator that takes two functions and produces a third one that represents the amount of overlap between the two original ones. With the complete combinatorial approach we determine the level of statistical difference between the measures of interest without requiring any normality assumption.

Data

Data for this study was collected at the El Yunque National Forest in Puerto Rico. Surveys were administered during the summers of 2005–2006 as part of a comprehensive study on the impact of site characteristics on social and physical conditions in and around the forest streams.

In-person interviews were conducted at nine recreation sites along the Mameyes and Espíritu Santo rivers in 2005 and the Fajardo River in 2006. Information collected include visitor's demographics, site characteristics (fixed and variable), trip information and a contingent valuation question: "Taking into consideration that there are other rivers as well as beaches nearby where you could go visit, if the cost of this visit to this river was $\_\_\_\_$ more than what you have already spent, would you still have come today?"

For the purpose of our benefit transfer exercise, we will call Mameyes and Espíritu Santo rivers the study site and the Fajardo River the policy site. Hence, the unique advantage is that we have original data at the policy site to evaluate the quality of benefit transfer based on different valuation models (CVM, TCM and the joint model).

Over 900 observations were obtained and coded, but only 463 observations from the study sites and 272 from the policy site were used in this analysis to avoid multiple destination bias. We further omitted visitors who took more than 100 trips, because these subjects appear to be quite different from the rest of the subjects surveyed. The omission of outliers is not uncommon, as pointed out by Englin and Shonkwiler (1995) where they limited their Negative Binomial model estimation to visitors with fewer than 12 trips. Eliminating visitors with more than 100 trips resulted in a reduction of six and two observations in the study and policy sites, respectively.

Our monetary price variable is gasoline costs and we control for travel time using a separate variable. This specification helps us avoid the arbitrary use of a particular fraction of the wage rate as the opportunity cost of time, however, it also requires us to consider two separate budgets. Since the optimization process now responds to two constraints (money and time), our resulting trip demand should depend on both. However, we do not have information on the visitors' available time in our dataset. Without differentiated levels of time budgets we can only assume a single one for our entire sample. Under this assumption, the information contained in this time budget variable is folded into the intercept term of the demand equation, leaving the price parameter unchanged.

Table 19.1 presents the descriptive statistics of variables at the policy and study sites. The bid amount each visitor was asked to pay in the CVM question was randomly selected from a set of price increases that ranged from $1 to $200 per trip. The site characteristics included were mean annual discharge, median pebble size and waterfall (a dummy that specifies whether there is a waterfall around the recreation area of interest).

Results

Table 19.2 shows the estimation results of different models and the impact they have on the variable of interest, WTP for the site. Estimation of individual CVM and TCM for the policy site, and individual and joint estimation for the study site are presented. As expected, the price coefficients for all specification and estimation methods are negative (although not significant) for the policy site TCM. Note that the separate CVM model for the study site uses a linear utility function, not the one corresponding to a semi-log demand function previously derived for joint estimation. Also, the set of parameters from the joint model includes a parameter rho. Rho is the correlation parameter that accounts for any relationship of *unobservables* between the TCM and CVM models. The statistical insignificance of rho suggests that in the fully specified models, there is less unexplained variation to be accounted for in the joint estimation. It can also be the result of underlying differences in visitor behavior in the quantity of trips decision of the TCM and the direct valuation of a trip decision in the CVM.

Comparing the WTP estimates per day trip at the study and policy sites, the joint model at the study site provides a mean benefit estimate that is $15 higher than the CVM predicted WTP and $33 higher than the TCM predicted WTP at the policy site. The estimated per trip WTP based on the individual TCM at the study site is about half of that from the CVM, and is about 37 percent smaller than the estimated WTP from the individual TCM at the policy site. The real gain from estimating TCM and CVM jointly seems to come from a significant reduction in the standard errors of the estimated price coefficient in the joint model. This should not be too surprising given that in joint estimation we consistently add two sources of information on price variation.

The reduction of standard errors in the joint model gives tighter confidence intervals of the surplus measures. This is shown in Table 19.3 where we present the lower and upper bounds of the 90 percent confidence interval of the mean WTP for each model at either policy or study site. In the table we also repeat the mean value and report the span (or difference) between the upper and lower bounds for each model.

It is seen in Table 19.3 that the 90 percent confidence interval of the joint estimate at the study site is much narrower than the individual TCM counterpart and that it still overlaps with the estimated benefit intervals of the policy site. The notable narrower confidence interval for the benefit estimate is due to efficiency gain in joint estimation. For policy analysis, improving precision in the valuation of alternative policy schemes is always desirable. Table 19.3 also

Table 19.1 Summary statistics of explanatory variables

Variable	Fajardo River (policy site)			Mameyes & Espiritu Santo Rivers (study site)		
	Obs.	*Mean*	*Std. dev.*	*Obs.*	*Mean*	*Std. dev.*
Gas cost	272	6.78	7.48	463	2.90	2.91
Travel time	272	39.36	26.41	463	64.31	64.06
Income	272	21553.30	18866.64	463	27606.45	23384.67
Mean annual discharge	272	2.89	0.040	463	0.84	0.58
Median pebble size	272	73.24	12.13	463	461.38	566.14
Waterfalls	272	0.20	0.40	463	0.49	0.50

Table 19.2 Estimated models based on policy and study site data[1,2]

Variable	Policy site data		Study site data		Joint
	CVM[3]	TCM	CVM[3]	TCM	
Gas cost (TCM) and Bid (CVM)	-0.0096*** (0.002)	-0.0132 (0.010)	-0.0042*** (0.001)	-0.0210* (0.011)	-0.0092*** (0.001)
Travel time	–	-0.0115*** (0.003)	–	-0.0032*** (0.001)	-0.0033*** (0.001)
Income	1.76E-05 (4.32E-05)	-3.26E-05 (0.0001)	-7.00E-06 (1.10E-05)	-7.00E-06 (1.80E-05)	-4.84E-06 (1.68E-05)
Mean annual discharge	-2.0124 (3.006)	0.0220 (3.356)	0.0398 (0.051)	-0.1062 (0.066)	-0.1018 (0.087)
Median pebble size	-0.0022 (0.007)	-0.0229*** (0.008)	-2.60E-05 (0.000)	0.0001* (0.000)	0.0001 (0.000)
Waterfall	0.0069 (0.254)	-0.3655 (0.345)	0.0847 (0.054)	-0.1449* (0.079)	-0.1531* (0.084)
Constant	6.8300 (8.893)	4.1485 (10.001)	0.4052*** (0.064)	1.4763*** (0.223)	1.4444*** (0.115)
Over dispersion	–	1.1048*** (0.095)	–	1.2973*** (0.115)	1.3023*** (0.154)
Rho		–		–	-0.0221 (0.046)
Log likelihood	-157.658	-798.6406	-250.7271	-943.5436	-1185.5425
WTP	$93.29	$75.71	$107.33	$47.72	$108.75

Notes
1 Significant beyond 90% confidence level, ** significant beyond 95% confidence level, *** significant beyond 99% confidence level.
2 Standard errors are in parentheses.
3 CVM results are obtained by estimating a typical linear utility differential, not the one derived in the text that is consistent with a semi-log trip demand equation.

Table 19.3 Confidence intervals of willingness to pay for a day trip[1]

	Lower bound	Mean	Upper bound	Difference
Policy site				
CVM	$74.80	$93.29	$108.90	$34.10
TCM	$(288.76)	$75.71	$398.70	$687.46
Study site				
CVM data	$95.98	$107.33	$122.15	$26.17
TCM individual	$22.24	$47.72	$201.47	$179.23
Joint model	$96.73	$108.75	$125.24	$28.51

Note
1 The means are calculated using $1/\beta_{tc}$ for the TCM and $\beta_0/abs(\beta_{bid})$ for CVM where β_0 is a grand constant term (that it includes all non-bid coefficients multiplied by the respective mean value of the variables). The bounds give the 90% confidence intervals. The confidence intervals for the CVM WTPs are derived using the Krinsky-Robb method.

reports WTP intervals from the CVM models for both the policy and study sites. In both cases, variation around the CVM estimates of WTP is much smaller than those based on the TCM estimation. The WTP estimate from the joint model is closer to those from CVM than TCM, suggesting that CVM contributes more in the joint estimation. In this study the estimated WTPs are similar between the linearly specified CVM and the more complex joint model. We may conclude that our WTP estimates from the CVM are not sensitive to the functional form assumptions for the individual utility function.

Table 19.4 presents the predicted number of trips to the policy site using both the actual data from the policy site and the functional transfers from the study site. The actual average number of trips taken to the policy site is reported at the bottom of the table for comparison. The predicted number of trips for the policy site via functional transfer is computed using the parameter estimates from the individual and joint models of the study site and the values of the variables at the policy site. It is seen that using the joint estimates in the benefit transfer to predict visitation to the policy site does not offer much gain in accuracy.

Table 19.4 Predicted number of trips to the policy site[1]

Expected number of trips	Lower bound	Mean	Upper bound
Transferred based on study site data			
TCM individual	2.73	3.38	7.35
TCM joint	2.37	3.60	7.39
Based on policy site data			
TCM individual	0.98	4.49	29.58
Actual average number of trips	–	6.84	–

Note
1 The bounds give the 90% confidence intervals.

The predicted number of trips for the policy site has to be paired with the per trip WTP estimate to derive the *seasonal or annual* benefits. The proposed joint estimation procedure provides both the predicted use level and the estimated per trip WTP based on an unified utility theoretic framework. Table 19.5 reports the mean seasonal benefits for the policy site that are derived from different models with either the policy site data or functional transfers based on the study site. As expected, the joint model provides the tightest interval around the seasonal benefits, since the variation of the WTP estimates is the smallest in the joint model. We also find that both estimates (from the individual and joint model) transferred based on the study site are not statistically different from that of the policy site.

Conclusions

This chapter updates prior estimation methods when combining travel cost and dichotomous choice contingent valuation data. Following Cameron (1992), we look at the appropriate parameter restrictions that would make both models consistent with a common underlying utility function. Instead of choosing an arbitrary utility function and solving for a consistent demand equation, we start with the most common estimation model for the TCM and work our way back to a consistent utility differential expression. Although our particular CVM question dealt with changes in the marginal cost of the last trip taken, we present a utility differential setup that can be generalized to all types of price changes and a corresponding limit to the number of trips available to users.

Our results support the idea that imposing a consistent utility structure and jointly estimating TCM and CVM generate greater accuracy in point estimates of benefit per day trip and seasonal benefits, compared to those derived from individual TCM. The simulated confidence intervals and the convolutions operator results show that we cannot reject the hypothesis that the point estimate from the individual model is not statistically different from the one obtained at the policy site. This result stems mainly from the inefficiency of the parameter estimates as compared to the parameter estimates of the joint model.

Table 19.5 Estimated seasonal benefits of visitors to the policy site[1] ($)

Seasonal benefit sat policy site	Lower bound	Mean	Upper bound
Transferred based on study site data			
TCM individual	65.90	161.12	892.46
TCM joint	272.45	391.58	730.01
Based on policy site data			
TCM individual	(419.40)	340.05	1,556.03

Note
1 The bounds give the 90% confidence intervals.

As for the estimation of visitor use, we find that little is gained from the combination of the valuation models due to the little information that is added to the intensive margin of use with the joint estimation. Despite this, when combining use predictions and point estimates of trip values, we find that the joint estimation brings the mean transferred seasonal benefit values much closer to the one estimated with the policy site data.

There is a sizeable improvement in estimating benefits per trip at the policy site using the joint model as compared to the individual TCM. However, given the small gain of the joint model estimate of benefits per trip relative to the individual CVM model's estimate for our data, one question is whether it is worth using the proposed joint model for benefit transfer purposes. Based on the joint model's more accurate estimate of the policy site's mean seasonal benefits, the ultimate goal of benefit transfer, we recommend the joint model. We also argue that the joint model is preferred to the individual TCM model based on the tighter confidence intervals around the seasonal benefit estimates from the joint model.

From the standpoint of methodological advancement, the proposed joint model has several important contributions and improvements to the benefit transfer literature. We obtain more accurate point estimates for benefit transfer purposes, we are able to predict visitor use using all available information in a utility theoretic consistent manner and we considerably improve the efficiency of both per day and seasonal benefit estimates.

Notes

1 Assuming non-use values would complicate the form of the expenditure function because it requires that $c(\underline{U})$ is also a function of site characteristics. This will imply that non-users can also receive benefits from site characteristics even when they do not visit the site. Since we do not consider any quality changes, there is little gain in relaxing our assumption of weak complementarity.
2 For the on-site corrected model, see González-Sepúlveda *et al.* (2008).

References

Adamowicz W., J. Louviere and M. Williams (1994) "Combining revealed and stated preference methods for valuing environmental amenities," *Journal of Environmental Economics and Management*, 26: 271–292.

Azevedo, C.D., J.A. Herriges and C.L. Kling (2003) "Combining revealed and stated preferences: Consistency tests and their interpretations," *American Journal of Agricultural Economics*, 85: 525–537.

Cameron, T.A. (1992) "Combining contingent valuation and travel cost data for valuation of nonmarket goods," *Land Economics*, 68: 302–317.

Englin, J. and T.A. Cameron (1996) "Augmenting travel cost models with contingent behavior data: Poisson regression analyses with individual panel data." *Environmental and Resource Economics*, 7: 133–147.

Englin, J. and J.S. Shonkwiler (1995) "Estimating social welfare using count data models: An application to long-run recreation demand under conditions of endogenous stratification and truncation," *Review of Economics and Statistics*, 77: 104–112.

Eom, Y.-S., and D. Larson (2006) "Improving environmental valuation estimates through consistent use of revealed and stated preference information," *Journal of Environmental and Economic Management*, 52: 501–516.

González-Sepúlveda, J.M. (2008) "Challenges and solutions in combining TCM and CVM data to value recreation," in *A Utility Consistent Joint Estimation of Count Data and Dichotomous Choice Models*, dissertation, Colorado State University, Fort Collins, CO.

González-Sepúlveda, J.M., J. Loomis and A. González-Cabán (2008) "A joint estimation method to combine dichotomous choice CVM models with count data TCM models corrected for truncation and endogenous stratification," *Journal of Agricultural and Applied Economics*, 49: 681–697.

McConnell, K., Q. Weninger and I.E. Strand (1999) "Joint estimation of contingent valuation and truncated recreational demands," in J.A. Herriges and C.L. Kling (eds.), *Valuing Recreation and the Environment: Revealed Preference Methods in Theory and Practice*, Edward Elgar Publishing Limited, Cheltenham.

Poe, G., K. Giraud and J. Loomis (2005) "Computational methods for measuring the difference of empirical distributions," *American Journal of Agricultural Economics*, 87: 353–365.

Rosenberger S.R. and J.B. Loomis (2001) "Benefit transfer of outdoor recreation use values," RMRS-GTR-72, Rocky Mountain Research Station, USDA Forest Service, Fort Collins, CO, online, available at: www.treesearch.fs.fed.us/pubs/ 4578.

20 Benefits transfer of a third kind

An examination of structural benefits transfer

George Van Houtven, Subhrendu K. Pattanayak, Sumeet Patil, and Brooks Depro

Introduction

The policy community frequently uses benefits transfer methods because they offer a practical and low cost way to provide benefit estimates for benefit-cost analyses, natural resource damage assessments, and other natural resource policy and management analyses. These methods take and adapt results from existing primary valuation studies and apply them to assess the benefits of selected policy changes.

For the most part, benefits transfer approaches fall into two categories – "unit value" transfers or "value function" transfers – where the key distinction between the two approaches is the degree to which differences between the study and policy contexts are formally accounted for in the transfer. In unit value transfers, a single value or range of values, such as the value per recreation day or per unit change in water quality, is usually transferred with little or no adjustment for differences between the two settings. With benefit, or value, function transfers, information from existing studies is used to identify a functional relationship between the value of interest and the factors that may influence the magnitude of the value (e.g. using meta-regression analysis). This functional relationship allows the analyst to account for differences between the two settings and adapt the transfer estimates accordingly.

One of the main limitations of these traditional approaches is that they do not always make full and best use of existing evidence from stated preference and revealed preference studies. To the extent that they do use evidence from both revealed preference and stated preference studies, they typically combine them in an ad hoc manner. That is, they do not explicitly impose consistency with the economic theory that is assumed to underlie the value estimates drawn from different nonmarket valuation techniques.

To address these limitations, a third kind of benefits transfer – "structural benefits transfer" (or "preference calibration") – has been proposed in which the transfer methodology is directly tied to utility theory via the preference structure (Smith *et al.* 2002; Bergstrom and Taylor 2006). Structural benefits transfer is in essence a form of benefit function transfer; where the functional form is specifically derived from an assumed utility function. Although this third approach has the potential to improve and strengthen benefits transfers, it has thus far only been applied and evaluated in a limited number of examples.

The purpose of this paper is to further examine and evaluate structural benefits transfer as an alternative transfer method, by extending existing applications in two main directions. First, using a single set of benefit estimates from the nonmarket valuation literature, we apply the preference calibration approach using several different utility function specifications, and we compare their implications for predicting benefits. Through these applications we show that the calibration approach can be generalized, in that a distinct set of preference parameters can be calibrated for each alternative specification. We also show that the calibration framework provides a number of opportunities for comparing the internal consistency and plausibility of the different assumed preference structures. For a given set of benefit estimates reported in the literature, these checks allow us to evaluate which specifications are most suitable for representing the conditions that produced the estimates.

Second, whereas existing applications have focused on use-related values for environmental improvements, we explicitly include nonuse values in the preference specifications. This addition is particularly important for combining evidence from revealed and stated preference methods. Although value estimates from the two methods may be derived with the same underlying preference structure, only stated preference estimates – in this case, value estimated drawn from a contingent valuation study – will shed light on the nonuse component of this structure.

This chapter begins in the next section by providing a background discussion of the structural benefits transfer approach. The third section then introduces and describes the preference specifications that will be applied, and subsequent section discusses how estimates from different nonmarket valuation methods can be directly linked to these preference specifications. Following that, we present a case study application focusing on water quality changes using the five preference specifications. The results and implications of these applications are then discussed in the final section along with suggested directions for future research.

Background

The main concept underlying preference calibration is that, if one is willing to make explicit assumptions about the functional form of utility with respect to a nonmarket commodity (e.g. environmental quality or health), then information from existing empirical valuation studies can in principle be used to estimate the parameters of the function. When both the utility function parameters and available benefit estimates are few in number, it is possible to calibrate the parameter values such that they produce benefit measures that match the observed empirical estimates. This is the approach used in this paper. As the number of available benefit estimates increases, structural meta-analysis techniques can instead be used to statistically estimate the parameter values (Smith and Pattanayak 2002; Bergstrom and Taylor 2006).

Structural benefits transfer recognizes that the selected preference specification has direct implications for both the functional form and the parameters of the corresponding welfare functions (i.e. willingness to pay (WTP), quasi-expenditure, or variation functions, as described for example by McConnell (1990) and Whitehead (1995)). Therefore, it defines a benefits transfer function with (1) a functional form that is directly derived from the preference specification and (2) parameters that are calibrated from existing empirical estimates.

The preference calibration logic was initially presented and illustrated in studies focusing on water quality changes using a utility specification with a modified constant elasticity of substitution (CES) form (described in more detail below). Using this simple form, which did not specifically include nonuse values, Smith *et al.* (2000) combined travel cost estimates from Englin *et al.* (1997) and contingent valuation (CV) estimates from Carson and Mitchell (1993) to calibrate preferences. Smith *et al.* (2002) expanded this approach by including hedonic property value estimates from Boyle *et al.* (1999), recalibrating the preference parameters, and generating illustrative benefit estimates with the calibrated function. More recently, the general approach has been extended to the area of health valuation related to both morbidity and mortality (Van Houtven *et al.* 2004; Smith *et al.* 2006) and visibility benefits (Smith and Pattanayak, 2002).

In all of these cases, the process for developing a structural benefits transfer function generally involves the following steps:

1 Specify a "representative" individual's preference function.
2 Define explicitly the relationships between the available benefits measures and the specified preference function.
3 Derive the structural benefit function that is implied by the assumed preference structure.
4 Adapt the available information from existing benefit studies to assure cross-study compatibility.
5 Calibrate or estimate preference function parameters that are as consistent as possible with the observed benefit measures.
6 Insert the calibrated or estimated parameters into the structural benefit function.

In the following sections we apply these steps to develop and compare structural benefit transfer functions based on five different preference specifications. For each specification, we illustrate the preference calibration process using the same set of existing revealed and stated preference estimates for water quality changes.

Specifying preferences

To characterize the preferences of a representative individual with respect to changes in water quality, we specify five alternative indirect utility (V) functions, which we refer to as

1   modified constant elasticity of substitution (CES);
2   linear trip demand;
3   semi-log demand;
4   log-linear demand; and
5   Stone-Geary specifications.

Using these alternative specifications allows us to explore the sensitivity of benefits transfer predictions (for changes in water quality) with respect to the assumed functional form of utility.

As shown below, each indirect utility function is specified in terms of income (Y), round-trip travel cost (P), and water quality level (Q).

- Modified CES:

$$V_A = \left(\phi_A Q^{\psi_A}\right) + \left((P - Q^{\gamma_A})^{-\alpha_A} Y^{\delta_A}\right)^{\beta_A} \tag{20.1}$$

- Linear Demand:

$$V_B = \phi_B Q^{\psi_B} + \left[Y + \frac{1}{\delta_B}\left(\alpha_B - \beta_B P + \gamma_B Q - \frac{\beta_B}{\delta_B}\right)\right] \cdot \exp\left[\frac{\delta_B}{\beta_B}\left(\gamma_B Q - \beta_B P\right)\right] \tag{20.2}$$

- Semi-log Demand:

$$V_C = \phi_C Q^{\psi_C} + \frac{Y^{(1-\delta_C)}}{(1-\delta_C)} + \left(\frac{1}{\beta_C}\right) \cdot \exp\left(-\beta_C P + \alpha_C + \gamma_C Q\right) \tag{20.3}$$

- Log-linear Demand:

$$V_D = \phi_D Q^{\psi_D} + \frac{Y^{(1-\delta_D)}}{(1-\delta_D)} - (1-\beta_D)^{-1} e^{\alpha_D} Q^{\gamma_D} P^{(1-\beta_D)} \tag{20.4}$$

- Stone-Geary:

$$V_E = \phi_E Q^{\psi_E} + Q^{\gamma_E} \cdot \ln\left(\frac{Q^{\gamma_E}}{-\beta_E P}\right) + \left(1 + Q^{\gamma_E}\right) \cdot \ln\left(\frac{Y^{\delta_E} - \alpha_E - \beta_E P}{1 + Q^{\gamma_E}}\right) \tag{20.5}$$

Equation (20.1) is similar to the modified CES indirect utility function used in previous preference calibration analyses (Smith *et al.* 2002, 2000). Equations (20.2), (20.3), and (20.4) are derived respectively from linear, semi-log, and log-linear trip demand specifications, and equation (20.5) is based on a Stone-Geary utility function (see for example, Larson, 1991 and Herriges *et al.* 2004).[1] To capture nonuse values, each specification includes an additively separable subcomponent (of the form ϕQ^{ψ}), which is independent of P and Y. These nonuse values will not be manifested in value estimates based on revealed preference methods, but they are likely to be included in estimates from stated preference studies.

All five preference specifications include six parameters. For each specification, we represent the vector of parameters as θ_j, such that, for example, $\theta_A = (\alpha_A, \beta_A, \gamma_A, \delta_A, \phi_A, \psi_A)$ is the parameter vector for the modified CES preferences. These are the parameters to be calibrated.

Linking benefit measures to the preference function

In this paper, we calibrate these preference parameters for each specification by combining results from a travel cost and a contingent valuation analysis. The travel cost analysis provides estimates of recreation demand (i.e., number of water based recreation trips per year [X]) and changes in Marshallian consumer surplus (ΔMCS) resulting from changes in water quality. The CV method provides estimates of Hicksian compensating surplus (WTP) for changes in water quality.

Tables 20.1 and 20.2 report algebraic expressions for X, ΔMCS, and WTP, which are directly derived from the preference functions listed in equations (20.1) to (20.5). The demand functions are derived by applying Roy's Identity to the indirect utility functions, and the ΔMCS functions are derived by changing the level of water quality (from Q_0 to Q_1) in these demand equations. The WTP functions are derived by solving for the compensating surplus that equalizes indirect utility for different levels of Q. Each expression is a function of the exogenous variables Y, P and Q, and each one also includes parameters from its corresponding preference specification.

Once their parameters vectors are calibrated, the expressions in Tables 20.1 and 20.2 can be interpreted and used as structural benefits transfer functions. Most importantly, the WTP expressions in Table 20.2 can be used to predict WTP for water quality changes at a policy site of interest, as defined by the average income, travel cost, and water quality conditions at that site. In the following section, we demonstrate how the calibrated parameters can be used in this way to predict WTP for different assumed values of Q_0, Q_1, Y and P. We also use these predictions to compare and evaluate results based on the five different preference specifications.

Preference calibration application

The first objective of this preference calibration application is therefore to identify values for the preference parameters that replicate as closely as possible the observed empirical estimates of X, WTP, ΔMCS (based on conditions defined by Y, P, and Q). We can then insert these calibrated parameter values in the WTP equations shown in Table 20.2 and use these equations as structural benefits transfer functions.

The two empirical studies used in this application were conducted in the early 1980s as part of a larger research project for EPA.[2] Both studies focused on measuring water quality benefits for households living in the vicinity of the Monongahela River in southwestern Pennsylvania. The two studies also used

Table 20.1 Algebraic expressions for trip demand and change in Marshallian consumer surplus

Preference specification	Trip demand $X=X(p, Q, Y; \theta)$[1]	Change in Marshallian Consumer Surplus (ΔMCS) $\Delta MCS = M(p, Q_0, Q_1, Y; \theta)$
Modified CES:	$X_1 = \dfrac{\alpha_A}{\delta_A} \cdot \dfrac{Y}{\left(P - Q_1^{\gamma A}\right)}$	$\Delta MCS = \dfrac{\alpha_A}{\delta_A} \cdot Y \cdot \left[\ln\left(P - Q_0^{\gamma A}\right) - \ln\left(P - Q_1^{\gamma A}\right) \right]$
Linear demand:	$X_1 = \alpha_B - \beta_B P + \delta_B Y + \gamma_B Q_1$	$\Delta MCS = \dfrac{\left(X_1^2 - X_0^2\right)}{2\beta_B}$
Semi-log demand:	$X_1 = \exp(\alpha_C - \beta_C P + \delta_C \ln(Y) + \gamma C Q_1)$	$\Delta MCS = \dfrac{\left(X_1 - X_0\right)}{\beta_C}$
Log-linear demand:	$X_1 = e^{\alpha D} Q_i^{\gamma D} P^{-\beta D} Y^{\delta D}$	$\Delta MCS = \dfrac{\left(X_1 - X_0\right) \cdot P}{\left(\beta_D - 1\right)}$
Stone-Geary:	$X_i = \left(\dfrac{Q_i^{\gamma E}}{1+Q_i^{\gamma E}} \right) \cdot \left\| \dfrac{Y^{\delta E} - \alpha_E}{P \cdot \left(\delta_E Y^{\delta E-1}\right)} \right\| + \dfrac{\beta_E}{\left(1+Q_i^{\gamma E}\right) \cdot \left(\delta Y^{\delta E-1}\right)}$	$MCS_i = \left\{ \left(\dfrac{Q_i^{\gamma E}}{1+Q_i^{\gamma E}} \right) \cdot \left\| \dfrac{Y^{\delta E} - \alpha_E}{\delta_E Y^{\delta E-1}} \right\| \cdot \left[\ln\left[Q_i^{\gamma E} \left(\dfrac{Y^{\delta E} - \alpha_E}{-\beta_E} \right) \right] - \ln(P) - 1 \right] \right\}$ $- \dfrac{\beta_E P}{\left(1+Q_i^{\gamma E}\right) \cdot \left(\delta_E Y^{\delta E-1}\right)}$ $\Delta MCS = MCS_1 - MCS_0$

Note
1 The corresponding inverse demand functions can be specified by solving for P: $P = X^{-1}(X, Q, Y, \theta)$.

Table 20.2 Algebraic expressions for Hicksian willingness to pay

Preference specification	Hicksian WTP $WTP = W(P, Q_0, Q_1, Y; \theta)$
Modified CES:	$WTP = Y - \left[\dfrac{\left(\varphi_A Q_0^{\psi_A} \right) - \left(\varphi_A Q_1^{\psi_A} \right) + \left((P - Q_0^{\gamma_A})^{-\alpha_A} Y^{\delta_A} \right)^{\beta_A} \left[(P - Q_1^{\gamma_A}) \right]^{\frac{-\alpha_A}{\delta_A}}}{} \right]^{\frac{1}{\beta_A \cdot \delta_A}}$
Linear demand:	$WTP = \dfrac{1}{\delta_B} \left[\left(X_1 - \dfrac{\beta_B}{\delta_B} \right) - \left(X_0 - \dfrac{\beta_B}{\delta_B} \right) \cdot \exp\left(\dfrac{\delta_B \gamma_B}{\beta_B} (Q_0 - Q_1) \right) \right] + \phi_B \left(Q_1^{\psi_B} - Q_0^{\psi_B} \right) \cdot \exp\left(\dfrac{\delta_B}{\beta_B} (\beta_B P - \gamma_B Q_1) \right)$
Semi-log demand:	$WTP = Y - \left\{ Y^{-\delta_C} \cdot \left[Y - \dfrac{(X_1 - X_0)}{\beta_C / (1 - \delta_C)} - \varphi_C \left(Q_1^{\psi_C} - Q_0^{\psi_C} \right) \cdot (1 - \delta_C) \right] \right\}^{\frac{1}{(1 - \delta_C)}}$
Log-linear demand:	$WTP = Y - \left\{ Y^{-\delta_D} \cdot \left[Y - \dfrac{(X_1 - X_0) \cdot P}{(\beta_D - 1)/(1 - \delta_D)} - \varphi_D \left(Q_1^{\psi_D} - Q_0^{\psi_D} \right) \cdot (1 - \delta_D) \right] \right\}^{\frac{1}{(1 - \delta_D)}}$
Stone-Geary:	$WTP = Y - \alpha_E - \beta_E P - (1 + Q^{\gamma_E})^{*}$
	$\exp\left(\dfrac{\varphi_E \left(Q_0^{\psi_E} - Q_1^{\psi_E} \right)}{1 + Q_1^{\gamma_E}} + \left(\dfrac{Q_0^{\gamma_E}}{1 + Q_1^{\gamma_E}} \right) \cdot \ln\left(\dfrac{Q_0^{\gamma_E}}{-\beta_E P} \right) - \left(\dfrac{Q_1^{\gamma_E}}{1 + Q_1^{\gamma_E}} \right) \cdot \ln\left(\dfrac{Q_1^{\gamma_E}}{-\beta_E P} \right) + \left(\dfrac{1 + Q_0^{\gamma_E}}{1 + Q_1^{\gamma_E}} \right) \cdot \ln\left(\dfrac{Y - \alpha_E - \beta_E P}{1 + Q_0^{\gamma_E}} \right) \right)$

data from the same 1981 survey of residents living within the Monongahela River Valley. This survey was based on a stratified sample of 393 households from the five-county area surrounding the Pennsylvania portion of the Monongahela River, including the Pittsburgh metropolitan area. Administration of the survey resulted in 301 completed interviews.

The first study used data from the survey to estimate a recreation demand travel cost model (Smith *et al.* 1983). This study identified 13 recreation sites along the Pennsylvania portion of the river and 69 respondents who had visited at least one of these sites. The total number of user-site combinations, each of which represented a single observation, was 94. Smith *et al.* applied a generalized travel cost model to estimate trip demand functions for each site. They then used these demand functions to estimate the increase in consumer surplus per household per season that would result from increasing water quality levels from boatable conditions to fishable conditions and from boatable to swimmable conditions.

The second study was based on responses to a contingent valuation scenario that was presented as part of the survey (Desvousges *et al.* 1987). At the time of the survey, the overall water quality levels in the Pennsylvania section of the Monongahela were assumed to be characterized by boatable conditions. Respondents were asked to value three water quality changes: (1) raising levels from boatable to fishable conditions, (2) raising levels from fishable to swimmable condition and (3) avoiding a decrease from boatable to nonboatable conditions. The survey used different elicitation methods (iterative bidding, open-ended, and payment card) for different subsamples. For this analysis, we use the open-ended responses, which were collected from 51 respondents, including both users and nonusers of the Monongahela river sites.

Defining consistent measures across the studies

To define a continuous unit of measure for Q that is consistent across the two studies, we use the same Resources for the Future (RFF) water quality ladder/ scale (Vaughan 1986) that was presented to respondents in the contingent valuation survey to describe water quality changes. According to this one-to-ten point scale, nonboatable, boatable, fishable, and swimmable water quality levels are assigned values of 0.5, 2.5, 5.1, and 7, respectively.

The summary statistics and benefit estimates used in the calibration applications are summarized in Table 20.3. The travel cost study provides estimates of the average baseline number of trips (X = 7.22), average income, and average travel cost for the sample of 94 recreators. All dollar values from these studies have been converted to 2005 dollars using the consumer price index (CPI). The baseline demand for trips is assumed to be evaluated at a water quality level that is "consistent with supporting boating (the current [1977] recreational use of the river)" (Smith *et al.* 1983: 434) ($Q_0 = 2.5$). The travel cost study also provides ΔMCS estimates for two water quality improvements—one to fishable quality ($Q_1 = 5.1$) and the other to swimmable quality ($Q_1 = 7$).

Table 20.3 Summary estimates and data from water quality valuation studies[1]

	Travel cost study (Smith et al. 1983)		Contingent valuation study (Desvousges et al. 1987)		
	(1)	(2)	(3)	(4)	(5)
Mean household income[2] (Y)	$46,398	$46,398	$41,977	$41,977	$41,977
Mean travel cost[2] (p)	$18	$18	n.r[3]	n.r	n.r
Mean number of trips (X$_0$)	7.22	7.22	n.r	2.41	n.r
Initial WQ (Q$_0$)	2.5	2.5	0.5	2.5	5.1
Improved WQ (Q$_1$)	5.1	7.0	2.5	5.1	7.0
Mean change in MCS[2] (ΔMCS)	$14.57	$30.58	–	–	–
Mean willingness to pay[2] (WTP)	–	–	$52.64	$37.81	$26.64

Notes
1 The values in italics define the six conditions used to calibrate the six preference parameters.
2 In 2005 dollars.
3 n.r. = not reported.

The contingent valuation study also provides estimates of average income and baseline trips for its sample of respondents. Average income is 10 percent lower than for the travel cost study sample, and average baseline trips is 67 percent lower, primarily because two-thirds of the CV sample are nonusers. Average travel costs (P) are not reported for the CV sample; however, they can be derived by inverting the trip demand functions in Table 20.3 and expressing P as a function of Y, X, Q and the preference parameters. The WTP estimates for the three water quality changes range from \$26.64 (improving water quality from $Q_0 = 5.1$ to $Q_1 = 7$) to \$52.64 (avoiding a decrease from $Q_1 = 2.5$ to $Q_0 = 0.5$).

Calibrating parameters

To calibrate parameters for each specification, we define six conditions representing the percent difference between observed values for X, ΔMCS, and WTP (numbers in bold italics in Table 20.3) and their predicted values using the equations in Tables 20.1 and 20.2. From the first column of travel cost results in Table 20.3 we define:

$$7.22 - X(18, 2.5, 46,4398; \boldsymbol{\theta}) = \varepsilon_1 * 7.22 \qquad (20.6)$$

$$14.57 - \Delta MCS\,(18, 2.5, 5.1, 46,398; \boldsymbol{\theta}) = \varepsilon_2 * 14.57 \qquad (20.7)$$

From the second column of travel cost results we define:

$$30.58 - \Delta MCS\,(18, 2.5, 7.0, 46,398; \boldsymbol{\theta}) = \varepsilon_3 * 30.58 \qquad (20.8)$$

From the three columns of CV results we define:

$$52.64 - WTP(P, 0.5, 2.5, 41,977; \boldsymbol{\theta}) = \varepsilon_4 * 52.64 \qquad (20.9)$$

$$37.81 - WTP(P, 2.5, 5.1, 41,977; \boldsymbol{\theta}) = \varepsilon_5 * 37.81 \qquad (20.10)$$

$$26.64 - WTP(P, 5.1, 7.0, 41,977; \boldsymbol{\theta}) = \varepsilon_6 * 26.64 \qquad (20.11)$$

where P is derived from the inverse demand function $X^{-1}(2.4\ 2.5, 41,977; \boldsymbol{\theta})$ (see footnote to Table 20.1) at baseline conditions for the CV sample and ε_i represents the percent difference between observed and predicted values for each of the six equations (i = 1 ... 6).

Ideally, we would identify solutions for the parameter vector $\boldsymbol{\theta}$ that would make each of the six equations exactly equal to zero. However, due to the nonlinearities in this system, no exact solution could be found for any of the five preference specifications. As an alternative, we solved for values of the parameter vector $\boldsymbol{\theta}$ that minimize the sum of squared differences (SSD, with differences expressed in percentage terms) between observed and predicted values in equations (20.6) to (20.11) – i.e. minimize $\Sigma_i(\varepsilon_i)^2$.

The calibrated parameter results are reported in Table 20.4 for each specification. Overall, the linear demand specification provides the closest fit, with an SSD=0.000143, followed by the semi-log demand specification (SSD=0.008). The interpretation of the parameters is often different across preference specifications; however, all indirect utility specifications include an additively separable subcomponent of the form ϕQ^{ψ} representing nonuse values. As expected, these parameters are always found to have positive values, implying that water quality has a positive effect on nonuse related utility. In all but one specification (log-linear), the calibrated value for ψ is less than one, implying a declining marginal effect of water quality on nonuse values. Also, in all specifications the γ parameter determines the marginal effect of water quality on the use-related component of indirect utility. Its calibrated value is consistently positive across specifications. Similarly, the δ parameter determines the marginal effect of income on utility, and its calibrated value is also consistently positive.

In the linear, semi-log and log-linear demand models, the β, δ, and γ parameters can also be interpreted as representing the marginal effects of travel cost, income and water quality on trip demand. When the calibrated value for β has a positive sign, as it does in the three specifications, it implies a negative effect of P on trip demand, which is consistent with expectations. The log-linear demand model implies an almost unit elastic trip demand with respect to P, and the linear demand implies that each dollar decrease in round trip costs increase the annual number of trips by almost five. Similarly, the positive calibrated values for the δ parameter imply that trips are a normal good, with an income elasticity between 0.45 and 0.68 in the semi-log and log-linear models.

Predicting values with the calibrated parameters

The main purpose of developing calibrated functions for WTP is to use them as structural benefit functions, i.e. to predict benefit estimates that are tailored to the water quality, income and travel cost conditions at a policy site of interest. In this application, we can also use these predictions to further evaluate the calibrated parameters and the different preference specifications. We do this by inserting the calibrated parameters back into the equations in Tables 20.1 and 20.2, and predicting X, ΔMCS and WTP for selected combinations of individual characteristics (Y and P) and changes in water quality (Q_0 and Q_1). The predictions, which are shown in Table 20.4, provide important additional internal validity checks on the calibrated parameters. For each preference specification, the six numbers shown in italics are the predicted values associated with equations (20.6) to (20.11). Since these are the equations that were used to calibrate the parameters, the predicted values all match closely with the corresponding values in Table 20.3. The other values reported in Table 20.4 include

1 predicted average travel cost for the CV sample,
2 predicted trips for the two samples under different water quality conditions,
3 predicted ΔMCS values for the CV sample, and
4 predicted WTP values for the travel cost sample.

Table 20.4 Calibrated parameters and predicted values for six preference specifications

Calibrated Preference Parameters				Travel cost study		Contingent valuation study		
				(1)	(2)	(3)	(4)	(5)
				Predicted values				
MODIFIED CES								
α_A = 0.001640	δ_A = 0.680081		P	—	—	$44.35	$44.35	$44.35
β_A = 0.105856	ϕ_A = 0.000197		X_0	7.12	7.12	2.31	2.41	2.53
γ_A = 0.901721	ψ_A = 0.501745		X_1	8.20	9.16	2.41	2.53	2.62
SSE = 0.029351			ΔMCS	$15.73	$28.16	$4.13	$5.09	$3.70
			WTP	$55.58	$90.80	$50.92	$41.41	$24.51
LINEAR DEMAND								
α_B = 50.06902	δ_B = 0.000842		P	—	—	$18.22	$18.22	$18.22
β_B = 4.910293	ϕ_B = 134.65826		X_0	7.22	7.22	—	2.41	9.12
γ_B = 2.582500	ψ_B = 0.229865		X_1	13.93	18.84	2.41	9.12	14.03
SSE = 0.000143			ΔMCS	$14.46	$30.84	$0.59	$7.88	$11.57
			WTP	$44.44	$75.74	$52.73	$37.87	$26.53
SEMI-LOG DEMAND								
α_C = 0.759377	δ_C = 0.686323		P	—	—	$20.76	$20.76	$20.76
β_C = 0.371970	ϕ_C = 0.044946		X_0	7.19	7.19	1.57	2.41	4.19
γ_C = 0.213500	ψ_C = 0.428440		X_1	12.52	18.79	2.41	4.19	6.29
SSE = 0.008004			ΔMCS	$14.34	$31.18	$2.25	$4.80	$5.64
			WTP	$52.24	$89.98	$51.60	$40.19	$25.18
LOG-LINEAR DEMAND								
α_D = 0.000103	δ_D = 0.453201		P	—	—	$51.54	$51.54	$51.54
β_D = 1.000979	ϕ_D = 0.0465354		X_0	7.219	7.219	2.406	2.407	2.407
γ_D = 0.000177	ψ_D = 1.1985167		X_1	7.220	7.220	2.407	2.407	2.407
SSE = 0.069741			ΔMCS	$16.78	$24.23	$36.15	$16.02	$7.11
			WTP	$41.31	$68.47	$50.98	$39.46	$25.96
STONE-GEARY								
α_E = 0.000414	δ_D = 0.94819		P	—	—	$16.43	$16.43	$16.43
β_E = −1,527.578	ϕ_E = 0.003731		X_0	7.18	7.18	—	2.41	43.73
γ_E = 0.042245	ψ_E = 0.19086		X_1	48.79	67.25	2.41	43.73	62.07
SSE = 0.008398			ΔMCS	$15.26	$29.37	$0.03	$11.47	$11.73
			WTP	$46.29	$75.20	$52.00	$39.61	$25.41

In the linear and log-linear demand models, the predicted average travel cost for the CV sample is respectively 1 percent and 15 percent higher than for the travel cost sample, and in the Stone-Geary model it is 9 percent lower. In contrast, the modified CES and log-linear models predict average travels costs for the CV sample that are more than double. Two opposing effects make it difficult to form strong priors about the expected sign and magnitude of these differences. On the one hand, the predicted average travel cost for the CV sample should be higher than for the travel cost sample because the former includes nonusers who are expected on average to live farther from the water resource. On the other hand, the CV sample's average income is 10 percent lower, which implies a lower opportunity cost for travel. Nevertheless, the Stone-Geary results, with 9 percent lower travel costs for the CV sample, do not seem plausible.

Compared to the linear, semi-log and Stone-Geary models, the modified CES and log-linear models also predict that trip demand is much less sensitive to water quality changes. The log-linear model shows virtually no changes in trips even for large changes in water quality, whereas the linear and semi-log models predict that trips for the travel cost (user) sample would more than double (from 7.22 to almost 19 trips per year) if water quality increased from boatable to swimmable. On the other end of the spectrum, the Stone-Geary specification predicts an almost tenfold increase in trips. The lack of sensitivity of the log-linear model to water quality changes and oversensitivity of the Stone-Geary model cast doubt on the validity of these calibrated preferences for benefits transfer.

For similar water quality changes, all models predict lower ΔMCS for the CV sample, and higher WTP for the travel cost sample. These differences occur because the average income for the CV sample is lower and because all of the models predict higher travel costs and fewer trips for the CV sample. Again, the smallest differences come from log-linear model.

The values reported in Table 20.4 are fundamentally "in-sample" predictions, because they are based on observed conditions in the two source studies. In Figures 20.1 through 20.3, we use a broader set of conditions to evaluate the calibrated models as transfer functions for "out-of-sample" WTP predictions. For these figures, we selectively vary water quality changes, income and travel cost, and we compare WTP predictions across the preference specifications.

Figure 20.1 shows how predicted WTP for a 1 unit change in water quality (on a ten-point scale) varies with respect to baseline water quality (Q_0). Income is held constant at $45,000 and travel cost at $18 for all predictions. In each case, WTP is highest when starting from the lowest baseline level ($Q_0 = 1$), and it decreases as long as Q_0 is less than five (below fishable). Above the fishable level, however, predicted WTP for a unit change is U-shaped for all specifications, except the log-linear and Stone-Geary models which predict monotonically declining WTP. None of these WTP predictions are implausible, but the semi-log model is distinctly more convex than the other models.

Figure 20.2 shows predicted WTP for a change in water quality from fishable ($Q_0 = 5.1$) to swimmable ($Q_1 = 7$) conditions when average annual household income is varied between $30,000 and $70,000 and average travel cost is held

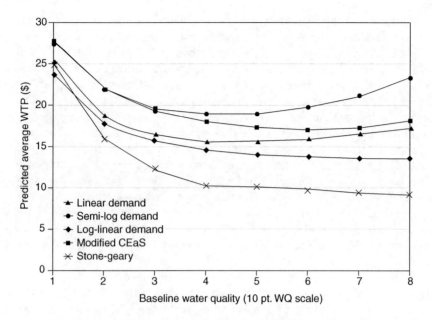

Figure 20.1 Predicted willingness to pay for a unit change in water quality: sensitivity to baseline water quality.

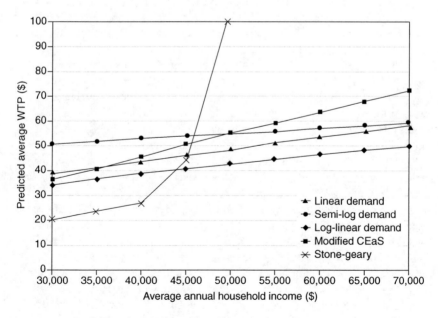

Figure 20.2 Predicted willingness to pay for a boatable-to-fishable water quality change: sensitivity to income.

constant at $18 per round trip. Figure 20.3 shows predicted WTP when average travel cost is varied between $16 and $20 and average household income is held constant at $45,000. As expected, all specifications predict increasing WTP with respect to income and decreasing WTP with respect to travel costs. The log-linear demand model is least sensitive to both types of variation. In particular, it shows almost no sensitivity to changes in travel cost, which again casts doubt on the validity of this specification for representing preferences for water quality changes. Again, on the other end of the spectrum, the Stone-Geary model exhibits extreme sensitivity to both income and travel cost changes.[3] In contrast, the linear demand model predicts roughly unit elasticity of WTP with respect to income variation and declining WTP (from $56 to $30) when travel cost increases by 25 percent from $16 to $20. The WTP predictions from the semi-log demand are only slightly less sensitive to income and travel cost changes than the linear demand model. The modified CES shows similar sensitivity to income, but is relatively insensitive to travel cost changes.

Discussion and conclusions

This paper demonstrates how the preference calibration method for developing structural benefits transfer functions can be generalized to several alternative preference specifications and can be expanded to include nonuse values. In addition to using a modified CES utility specification, similar to the one used in

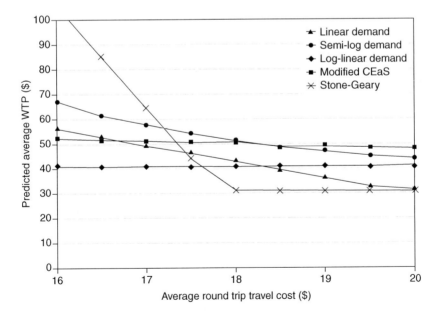

Figure 20.3 Predicted willingness to pay for a boatable-to-fishable water quality change: sensitivity to travel cost.

previous applications, we calibrated preference parameters using four other specifications. In each case, we combined summary data and estimates from a travel cost study with estimates from a contingent valuation study. Both of these source studies estimate nonmarket values for specific improvements in river water quality, and they also provide information on average use levels (trips), travel costs and incomes for their respective samples.

For each preference specification, we calibrated six preference parameters. These parameters have somewhat different interpretations and roles in the respective specifications; however, their calibrated values all have plausible signs. For example, the parameters ϕ, ψ and γ are all directly related to the marginal utility of water quality improvements, and as expected they are all calibrated with positive signs.

To more thoroughly evaluate the parameter estimates and their implications for benefits transfer, we apply them to the Hicksian WTP functions derived from each specification. In effect, this gives us a calibrated benefits transfer function for each specification, which we use to predict average WTP for selected combinations of water quality levels and changes, income and travel costs. This process mimics how the functions would be used to estimate benefits for selected policy conditions and changes.

The results show that the structural benefits transfer estimates can be very sensitive to the selection of preference specification. However, they also highlight the strengths and limitations of different specifications, by providing plausibility checks on the range of predicted outcomes.

The linear demand model provides the most consistently plausible results, with (1) positive WTP between $15 and $25 for each unit increment in water quality, (2) close to unit elasticity of WTP with respect to income variation and (3) declining WTP with respect to travel cost. The semi-log demand and modified CES specifications also produce sensible estimates of WTP; however, the semi-log demand model produces WTP estimates that are notably more convex with respect to baseline water quality than other specifications, and the modified CES estimates are relatively insensitive to differences in travel cost. In contrast, the Stone-Geary model produces the least reliable results. In particular, the WTP estimates are implausibly sensitive to both income and travel cost differences. The results from the log-linear model are also somewhat suspect for opposite reasons–they show virtually no sensitivity to travel cost differences and very low sensitivity to income changes.

In addition to providing structural WTP functions, the preference calibration results can also be used to specify functions for predicting trip demand (or travel costs) and Marshallian consumer surplus. These predictions are not only relevant for policy analysis (as measures of behavioral changes and use values), but they also provide secondary checks on the plausibility of the calibrated results. These secondary predictions (reported in Table 20.4) confirm the findings from the WTP functions–that the linear demand, semi-log demand, and modified CES specifications generate more plausible estimates than the log-linear and, in particular, the Stone-Geary specifications.

It is important to note that these results should not be interpreted as a *general* assessment of the five different preference specifications for use in preference calibration and benefits transfer. Rather, the observed advantages and limitations of the different preferences are specific to the context in which they have been applied in this paper. The more salient point is that preference calibration provides a framework for evaluating which preference structures are best suited to representing underlying conditions in the context of interest.

A main advantage of structural benefits transfer is that it imposes a degree of internal validity on the benefits transfer process, by requiring consistency with preferences and economic theory. It allows one to fully utilize available information (e.g. results from both revealed and stated preference studies) to develop benefits transfer functions that are internally consistent with different preference specifications. We expect that this advantage will also result in more accurate benefit estimates, at least compared to more traditional benefits transfer approaches that either do not make use of estimates from multiple valuation methods or that do so in an ad hoc manner. However, more research is required to determine whether the advantages of structural benefits transfer extend to convergent validity. The existing empirical research evaluating the convergent validity of traditional benefits transfer approaches, where "out of sample" benefits transfer estimates are compared to benefit estimates using original valuation results, has yielded at best mixed results (Shrestha and Loomis 2003; Downing and Ozuna 1996; Kirchhoff *et al.* 1997). It remains to be seen whether structural benefits transfer can improve on these results.

An inherent feature of the preference calibration approach described in this paper is that it is most applicable when there are a limited number of available benefit estimates from different nonmarket valuation studies. In this case we use two ΔMCS estimates from a travel cost study and three WTP estimates from a CV study. However, when a large number of such estimates are available (e.g. values related to mortality risks) the logic of preference calibration can in principle be extended to statistical estimation and meta-regression analysis. This concept of "structural meta-analysis," as introduced by Smith and Pattanayak (2002) and discussed in more detail in Smith *et al.* (2006) and Bergstrom and Taylor (2006), presents a number of empirical challenges, but it continues to be a potentially fruitful area for future research.

Notes

1 To match the number of parameters used in the other functional forms, an additional parameter, δ, is added to the income term in the Stone-Geary model.
2 These are admittedly older studies than one would ideally want to use for a current benefits transfer application; however, they provide a convenient set of data for this more illustrative application and examination of the preference calibration logic. For both an overview and detailed summary of this larger research project, see Smith and Desvousges (1986).
3 Below $45,000 income and above $18 travel cost, which are close to the values where the model was calibrated, the Stone-Geary model predicts zero trips. As a result, the Stone-Geary curves "flatten out" in these regions and only reflect nonuse values.

References

Bergstrom, J.C. and L.O. Taylor (2006) "Using meta-analysis for benefits transfer: Theory and practice," *Ecological Economics*, 60(2): 351–360.

Boyle, K.J., P.J. Poor and L.O. Taylor (1999) "Estimating the demand for protecting freshwater lakes from eutrophication," *American Journal of Agricultural Economics*, 81(5): 1118–1122.

Carson, R.T. and R. Cameron Mitchell (1993) "The value of clean water: The public's willingness to pay for boatable, fishable, swimmable quality water," *Water Resources Research*, 29(7): 2445–2454.

Desvousges, W.H., V.K. Smith and A. Fisher (1987) "Option price estimates for water quality improvements: A contingent valuation study for the Monongahela River." *Journal of Environmental Economics and Management*, 14(3): 248–267.

Downing, M. and T. Ozuna Jr. (1996) "Testing the reliability of the benefit function transfer approach," *Journal of Environmental Economics and Management* 30(3): 316–322.

Englin, J., D. Lambert and W.D. Shaw (1997) "A structural equations approach to modeling consumptive recreation demand," *Journal of Environmental Economics and Management*, 33(1): 31–43.

Herriges, J.A., C.L. Kling and D.J. Phaneuf (2004) "What's the use? Welfare estimates from revealed preference models when weak complementarity does not hold," *Journal of Environmental Economics and Management*, 47(1): 55–70.

Kirchhoff, S., B. Colby and J. LaFrance (1997) "Evaluating the performance of benefit transfer: An empirical inquiry," *Journal of Environmental Economics and Management*, 33(1): 75–93.

Larson, D.M. (1991) "Recovering weakly complementary preferences," *Journal of Environmental Economics and Management*, 21(2): 97–108.

McConnell, K.E. (1990) "Models for referendum data: The structure of discrete choice models for contingent valuation," *Journal of Environmental Economics and Management*, 18(1): 19–34.

Shrestha, R.K. and J.B. Loomis (2003) "Meta-analytic benefit transfer of outdoor recreation economic values: Testing out-of-sample convergent validity," *Environmental and Resource Economics*, 25(1): 79–100.

Smith, V.K. and W.H. Desvousges (1986) *Measuring Water Quality Benefits*, Boston, MA: Kluwer-Nijhoff.

Smith, V.K. and S.K. Pattanayak (2002) "Is meta-analysis a Noah's ark for non-market valuation?" *Environmental and Resource Economics*, 22(1): 271–296.

Smith, V.K., W.H. Desvousges and M.P. McGivney (1983) "Estimating water quality benefits: An economic analysis," *Southern Economic Journal*, 50(2): 422–437.

Smith, V.K., G.L. Van Houtven, S.K. Pattanayak and T.H. Bingham (2000) "Improving the practice of benefit transfer: A preference calibration approach," prepared for the US Environmental Protection Agency, Office of Water, February, online, available at: http://water.epa.gov/lawsregs/lawsguidance/cwa/316b/upload/2000_ 04_17_economics_benefits.pdf.

Smith, V.K., G.L. Van Houtven and S.K. Pattanayak (2002) "Benefit transfer via preference calibration: 'Prudential algebra' for policy," *Land Economics*, 78(1): 132–152.

Smith, V.K., S.K. Pattanayak and G.L. Van Houtven (2006) "Structural benefit transfer: An example using VSL estimates," *Ecological Economics*, 60(2): 361–371.

Van Houtven, G.L., S.K. Pattanayak and V.K. Smith (2004) *Benefit Transfer Functions for Avoided Morbidity: A Preference Calibration Approach*, National Center for Environmental Economics, Working Paper #04–04, online, available at: http://yosemite.epa.gov/ee/epa/eed.nsf/WPNumber/2004-04/$File/2004-04.PDF.

Vaughan, W.J. (1986) *The Water Quality Ladder*, included as Appendix B in R.C. Mitchell and R.T. Carson (eds.), *The Use of Contingent Valuation Data for Benefit/Cost Analysis in Water Pollution Control*, CR-810224–02, prepared for US Environmental Protection Agency, Office of Policy, Planning, and Evaluation, Washington, DC, online, available at: http://yosemite.epa.gov/ee/epa/eerm.nsf/ vwFUS/2B37DFD67 EE8870A8525644D0053BE87.

Whitehead, J.C. (1995) "Differentiating use and non-use values with the properties of the variation function," *Applied Economics Letters*, 2(10): 388–390.

21 Conclusions and future research

John C. Whitehead, Timothy C. Haab, and Ju-Chin Huang

One of the major contributions of environmental economists to economic knowledge is the estimation of the benefits and costs of environmental policy. If you want an estimate of the environmental cost of the BP oil spill to Gulf of Mexico anglers or an environmentalist far from the blowout, an environmental economist can give you a hard, cold monetary answer. This often leads to disagreements with those on the right and left of the environmental spectrum and, even, other economists.

Not surprisingly, business people don't like so much attention paid to the benefits of environmental policy because it might cost them money. So, they tend to hire non-environmental economists, who are already queasy about "nonmarket valuation" methods, to discredit the methods of environmental economists (e.g. the "contingent valuation debate"). Measuring the benefits of environmental policy is also often questioned by environmentalists who either say it is immoral or crass to put dollar values on intangible benefits or that these benefits are infinitely valued. One response is that people through their behavior put finite values on the environment every day. Environmental economists simply report this behavior.

To some economists certain methods of nonmarket valuation may seem like pseudo-science since we consider behavior that is generally outside the market (where there are no obvious demand or supply curves). For example, we might consider the importance of the response of recreation travel to environmental quality or trust willingness-to-pay statements about environmental quality to infer benefits about environment policy.

Within this broader context, this book demonstrates, in a number of ways, that the nonmarket valuation methods of environmental economists are of great use in the debates and analysis of environmental policy. The combination of revealed preference (RP) and stated preference (SP) data can exploit the advantages of each data source while mitigating the problems associated with their weaknesses.

The gaps in this book suggest several directions for future research. In this chapter we briefly summarize four of these: econometric advances, new study designs, new types of data combination and new applications. While there has been some headway made in each of areas, significant growth is needed.

When using discrete RP and SP data the mixed (i.e. random parameter) logit and finite mixture (i.e. latent class) models provide opportunities to incorporate panel data. However, efforts at controlling for different scale effects have not made way into the environmental valuation literature. Researchers should strive to provide comparisons between the conditional logit model and the mixed logit model to determine the conditions when the more restrictive conditional logit model is problematic. Research using choice experiment surveys has found that there is a limit to the number of scenarios that respondents can assimilate before they tire of the survey task. Research is needed to determine the tradeoff between the increased variance (or bias) of additional observations and efficiency of additional observations.

One of the purported advantages of SP data is the ability to forecast beyond the range of historical experience. Only a few studies consider the relative ability of RP, SP and RP-SP studies to forecast future behavior. More out-of-sample tests of predictive validity are also needed to better understand the implications of combined RP-SP methods. Intertemporal RP data, with multiple observations from different time periods, offer vast opportunities for explaining and predicting demand. A potentially promising approach would be to combine static SP panel with time series RP panel data. Long-term panel data sets are needed that allow the collection of RP and SP data with time for respondents to experience and react to gradual and rapid environmental change.

Mitigation of hypothetical bias in the contingent valuation method has proceeded with joint estimation with data collected from laboratory experiments or with survey design advances such as cheap talk and certainty ratings. Hypothetical bias in the contingent valuation method may also be mitigated by joint estimation. The key to collection of these data is an experimental design in which the money represented by hypothetical willingness-to-pay statements can actually be collected in a natural field experiment. Ready opportunities exist with voluntary donations, fishing and hunting license purchase, participation in green energy programs and referendum voting.

New combinations of RP and SP data are worth pursuing. Thus far, mixed data models have primarily focused on the joint estimation of frequency RP behavioral data and SP willingness-to-pay data. Future research should pursue joint estimation of frequency data RP-SP behavioral models and willingness-to-pay models. RP-RP and SP-SP joint estimation is likely to generate convergent validity tests and econometric efficiencies. Risk perceptions, environmental attitudes and other types of value data are used by noneconomists. These are typically included as explanatory variables in behavior or willingness-to-pay models but their joint estimation could improve economic valuation.

Relative to consumer applications, only a few studies have combined data to assess the decisions of firms. Further application of these methods to business firms facing new production choices can be used to assess the extent to which new technologies can be expected to lead to environmental quality improvement. Most of the existing RP-SP research has been conducted in developed countries.

Applications in which the natural resources play a much more critical role in the lives of households as producers could present valuable insights.

Another omission in the joint estimation literature is the averting behavior method for health valuation. The value of risk reductions has been independently estimated with the averting behavior method. When combined with the magnitude of risk avoided the value of statistical life can be estimated and joint estimation may lead to improvements in the controversial estimation of the value of statistical life.

Finally, we must admit that data combination and joint estimation is not a remedy for all environmental preference data limitations. It is simply an underused (in our opinion) tool for understanding the values placed on the environment. A better understanding of environmental values should be a common goal amongst all members of society. We look forward to the pursuit of a better understanding of environmental values with further application of the methods presented in this book and along avenues suggested in this chapter.

Index

Page numbers in *italics* denote tables, those in **bold** denote figures.

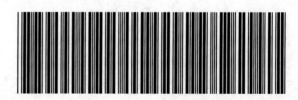